Understanding Administrative Law in the Common Law World

Understanding Administrative Law in the Common Law World

PAUL DALY

OXFORD
UNIVERSITY PRESS

OXFORD
UNIVERSITY PRESS

Great Clarendon Street, Oxford, OX2 6DP,
United Kingdom

Oxford University Press is a department of the University of Oxford.
It furthers the University's objective of excellence in research, scholarship,
and education by publishing worldwide. Oxford is a registered trade mark of
Oxford University Press in the UK and in certain other countries

First Edition published in 2021

Impression: 4

Published in the United States of America by Oxford University Press
198 Madison Avenue, New York, NY 10016, United States of America

British Library Cataloguing in Publication Data

Data available

Library of Congress Control Number: 2021933936

ISBN 978–0–19–289691–9

DOI: 10.1093/oso/9780192896919.001.0001

Printed and bound by
CPI Group (UK) Ltd, Croydon, CR0 4YY

For Marie-France, Liam, Lorna and Luke

Preface

Why write a book like this one? There are three reasons.

First, I want to make the subject understandable to those who work with it—students, practising lawyers, legal academics, administrative decision-makers, legislators and judges—and comprehensible to those outsiders who wish to know more. Demonstrating that there is an intelligible structure to what might look at first glance like a random collection of discrete rules and standards gathering like barnacles on the hull of a shipwreck will help people to grasp administrative law.

Second, theoretical work is useful in rationalising the rapid development of administrative law since the latter half of the 20th century.[1] In a sense, tort and contract have a one-hundred year headstart on administrative law. Those areas of law were liberated from the constraints of the writ system in the late 1800s, a full century before the so-called 'prerogative writs'—the predecessors of today's 'application for judicial review'—were abolished or tamed. Administrative lawyers have some catching up to do. Indeed, administrative lawyers have been accused of creating a subject which has the 'core' of a 'seedless grape'.[2] Think of this book as an attempt to answer the 'seedless' gripe.

In another sense, though, administrative law existed long before the procedural reforms of the mid-20th century. Just as the contemporary law of tort and contract can be traced back to writs used many centuries ago, administrative law has been with us at least since the 16th and 17th centuries, when the courts began to use the prerogative writs to control administrative decision-makers. Long ago, common law courts used concepts of legality, rationality and procedural fairness which are familiar to the contemporary reader.[3] The point is that the abolition of a system of writs, where substantive law can only be found 'in the interstices of procedure',[4]

[1] See the 'private law envy' of Adam Perry, 'Plan B: A Theory of Judicial Review' (2017) *Social Science Research Network*:

> In private law, I see an abundance of doctrinally-oriented theory. I don't mean theories of this or that doctrine (of course there are those, too). I mean theories of whole areas of law: tort law, contract law, and the law of unjust enrichment. I'm thinking of promissory theories of contract law, corrective justice-based theories of tort law, and the like. I'm not saying these theories succeed. For all I know, they don't. It's the ambition that impresses me, because in administrative law, things could hardly be more different.

[2] Ernest Gellhorn and Glen Robinson, 'Perspectives on Administrative Law' (1975) 75 *Columbia Law Review* 771, 779–780.

[3] Paul Craig, 'English Administrative Law History: Perception and Reality' in Michael Ramsden and Swati Jhaveri eds, *Indigenizing Administrative Law* (Cambridge University Press, Cambridge, 2021).

[4] Henry Maine, *Dissertations on Early Law and Custom* (John Murray, London, 1883), 389. Maine was writing about legal systems in general, but the point is so elegantly put as to justify taking it slightly out of context.

makes it easier to conceptualise a body of substantive law, such as 'tort', 'contract' or 'administrative law'. I aim in this book to enhance the understanding of administrative law as it has been rationalised in recent decades.

Third, I quite like the core features of contemporary administrative law. I think common law courts have done good work in recent decades, requiring administrative decision-makers to live up to relatively high standards of justification, transparency and intelligibility. But the courts have no obvious warrant for imposing such requirements, which in turn creates the risk of a backlash from those concerned about judicial overreach, about the courts exercising too much power over the other branches of government. So far, administrative law has not caused concerned citizens to man the barricades. But that could change. And mounting a defence of the legitimacy of the work judges have done in recent decades seems valuable to me, as someone who appreciates these judicial efforts. At the time of going to press, the United Kingdom had embarked on an exercise designed—in the view of some—to rein in judicial review of administrative action.[5] This book was not conceived of as a defence of contemporary administrative law against those sceptical of judicial power, but my analysis is certainly relevant to the United Kingdom's reform project. If I am right that today's law of judicial review of administrative action rests on morally desirable foundations, the case for reform is not as strong as some might like it to be.[6]

* * *

This book is about judicial review, that is, the principles that determine *how* courts are to exercise their reviewing function and *what* sorts of decisions are subject to judicial review. I use the terms 'administrative law' and 'judicial review of administrative action' interchangeably throughout, solely for the purposes of readability (and, to simplify matters, I will refer invariably to the 'applicant' for judicial review). This hardly exhausts the broad field of administrative law, which also includes such important topics as the structure of the state and the content of administrative justice. I do not address these in this book. In many ways, these other topics are *more important* than judicial review of administrative action, because for most people their first point of contact with the administrative state—the immigration

[5] Ministry of Justice, *Terms of Reference for the Independent Review of Administrative Law* (31 July 2020) <https://www.gov.uk/government/news/government-launches-independent-panel-to-look-at-judicial-review>. For concerns about the motivations underlying the creation of the Review, see Mark Elliott, 'The Judicial Review Review I: The Reform Agenda and its Potential Scope', *Public Law for Everyone*, 3 August 2020, <https://publiclawforeveryone.com/2020/08/03/the-judicial-review-review-i-the-reform-agenda-and-its-potential-scope/>. My own view is more sanguine: Paul Daly, 'The Inexorable Rise of Judicial Review', *Prospect Magazine*, 28 September 2020, <https://www.prospectmagazine.co.uk/politics/the-inexorable-rise-of-judicial-review-supreme-court-law-constitution>.

[6] See e.g. Richard Ekins, 'It's Time to Rein in the Supreme Court', *Spectator Magazine*, 3 August 2020, <https://www.spectator.co.uk/article/it-s-time-to-rein-in-the-supreme-court>. Such debates about the judicial role are not new and, in the United Kingdom at least, cross ideological lines: see e.g. Richard Rawlings, 'Review, Revenge and Retreat' (2005) 68 *Modern Law Review* 378.

officer, the government employee at the service counter, the tax collector—is also their last. Most administrative decisions are never judicially reviewed. Making sure that those front-line decisions which escape judicial oversight are lawful, rational and fair is, accordingly, an important task.

To some extent, judicial decisions about the core features of administrative law do have an impact on public administration. Measuring this impact is difficult but it is reasonable to assume that administrative decision-makers, from front-line officials stamping application forms and inspecting shipping consignments to agency chiefs formulating general policy guidelines, try to act in accordance with the principles generated by judicial decisions. It is also reasonable to suggest that understanding administrative law in terms of values will assist administrative decision-makers: where the doctrinal detail is contained within an intelligible structure it should, all things considered, be easier to understand. But I do not want to overstate these points. I recognise that for public administration to meet the needs of the society it serves, judicial review of administrative action is certainly not enough on its own. My motivation in writing this book is to improve our understanding of judicial review of administrative action, not to improve public administration (though this may be a welcome side-effect). Judicial review of administrative action is now a substantial part of the workload of common law courts. Better, then, to have intelligible administrative law.

***

I am indebted to the friends and colleagues who read and commented on drafts of various chapters: John Allison, Janina Boughey, Peter Cane, Marie-France Fortin, Grant Huscroft, Graham Mayeda, David Mullan, John Murphy and Greg Weeks. In their capacity as editors of the edited collections arising from the first two Public Law Conferences, Mark Elliott and Jason Varuhas made incisive comments on work which provided the foundation for this book. Others provided venues in which I could present components of this book: the *ATLAS* consortium, the Canadian Institute of Advanced Legal Studies, the Centre for Public Law at the University of Cambridge, the Centre de recherche en droit public at the Université de Montréal, the Faculty of Law at the University of Ottawa and the Public Law Conference. Work on this book spanned three academic institutions (the Université de Montréal, the University of Cambridge and the University of Ottawa), where Olivier Dulude, Sarah Richert, Lesley Dingle and Kseniya Kudischeva provided invaluable support, and was financed in part by a grant from the *Fonds de recherche du Québéc—société et culture*.

Contents

Table of Cases

1
A Values-based Approach

As I explained in the Preface, this book has three goals. This chapter introduces the means by which these goals will be achieved.

The *primary goal* is to enhance *understanding* of administrative law by developing a fresh framework which students, practitioners, legal academics and scholars from other fields can quickly and easily grasp. This is no small undertaking. The contemporary law of judicial review of administrative action has developed incrementally over the centuries, with a period of particularly rapid growth triggered by a series of procedural reforms in the mid-20th century.

I describe this background in this chapter, setting the stage for the introduction of my framework. These procedural reforms led to the generation by judges of a set of general principles of administrative law—of, broadly speaking, legality, rationality and procedural fairness. In this book, I propose a further synthesis of the decided cases, placing them in a framework composed of four values: individual self-realisation, good administration, electoral legitimacy and decisional autonomy. Sometimes these values operate in a complementary fashion to give shape to administrative law, sometimes judges must strike a balance between them. By reference to these values, the reader will be better able to comprehend the principles relating to institutional structures, procedural fairness, substantive review, remedies, restrictions on remedies and the scope of judicial review—in other words, the whole of the contemporary law of judicial review of administrative action.

My approach is pluralist, in the following sense. I do not offer a 'monist' theory of administrative law which attempts to trace legal principles to a meta-concept, meta-principle or meta-value.[1] There are those who maintain that judicial review is all (or mostly) about 'jurisdiction' or the 'public interest' and others who analyse areas of administrative law through a monist lens, such as 'dignitarian' or 'instrumental' perspectives on procedural fairness. I eschew any search for a grand global theory. Rather, I argue, the subject is best understood by reference to a plurality of values, not one master-value.

This book is aimed at readers interested in or knowledgeable about judicial review of administrative action in a selection of leading jurisdictions of the common law world: Australia, Canada, England and Wales, Ireland and New Zealand. The

[1] Joanna Bell, *The Anatomy of Administrative Law* (Hart, Oxford, 2020), chapter 7.

Understanding Administrative Law in the Common Law World. Paul Daly, Oxford University Press. © Paul Daly 2021.
DOI: 10.1093/oso/9780192896919.003.0001

administrative law of other countries is modelled on the administrative law of these jurisdictions and so readers from elsewhere in the common law world will find much of value in the pages which follow. My focus, moreover, is on the core features of judicial review of administrative action, those which are common to multiple jurisdictions. Thus my fresh framework for administrative law covers a broad swathe of the common law world.

A *second goal* is to *guide* the development of administrative law. This is the subject of Chapter 8 but it will be briefly discussed in this chapter too. That the values operate in a complementary fashion or permit the striking of a balance between them indicates not only that they provide a framework for *understanding* the law but also for *guiding* the future development of the law. Put another way, the values describe what the law *is* and also suggest what the law *ought to be* (or ought to become).

A *third goal* is to *justify* contemporary administrative law. The interpretive approach I follow risks collapsing the is/ought distinction, drawing lessons about what the law *ought* to be from what the law *is*. This distinction is valuable: it prevents chroniclers of legal principles from injecting their own preferences about what the law *ought to be* into their analysis of what the law *is*. But this distinction should not be overemphasised either. Any attempt to hunt and gather legal principles into a coherent structure has to be guided to some extent by the preferences of the hunter-gatherer. Accordingly, I also defend my fresh framework in normative terms, explaining why it is morally desirable.

In this chapter, I first provide some background. I then introduce the four values of individual self-realisation, good administration, electoral legitimacy and decisional autonomy, explaining also how they sometimes shape the law in a complementary fashion but that judges sometimes strike a balance between them. Next, I discuss my interpretive approach before moving to explain the comparative terrain to which my framework extends. Lastly, in the concluding parts of this chapter, I outline the interpretation of administrative law advanced in this book and provide an overview of the material which will be covered.

1.1 Background

1.1.1 Historical Development and Procedural Reform

Judicial review of administrative action is a creature of the common law, 'a judicial invention to secure that decisions are made by the executive or by a public body according to law even if the decision does not otherwise involve an actionable wrong'.[2] The so-called 'prerogative writs' of certiorari, mandamus, prohibition, quo

[2] *Mercury Energy Ltd v Electricity Corporation of New Zealand* [1994] 1 WLR 521, 526 per Lord Templeman.

warranto and habeas corpus were developed first to control inferior courts and were gradually extended to administrative bodies more generally. Much occurred in the 17th century, 'that great constitutional watershed of our institutions, [which] gave form to the institution of judicial review as it gave form to so much else in our polity'.[3] As Lord Parker CJ once explained, 'the exact limits' of the prerogative writs 'have never been and ought not to be specifically defined' but rather 'have varied from time to time, being extended to meet changing conditions'.[4]

However, in view of the pitfalls for the unwary created by technicalities and, to a lesser extent, the risk that historical restrictions on the writs might impede their extension to some forms of administrative decision-making,[5] as well as the emergence of the declaration as an effective remedy for administrative unlawfulness, procedural changes followed in many parts of the common law world.[6] The goal of procedural reform was 'to substitute for [the prerogative writs] a single simplified procedure for obtaining all forms of relief',[7] accomplished sometimes by rules of court (as in England and Wales, with the development of a new 'Order 53'[8]) and sometimes by legislation (as in New Zealand and Australia[9] and the Canadian provinces[10]).

Historically, the scope of the prerogative writs was co-extensive with the scope of judicial review. Which bodies were reviewable, and what types of error might be put in issue before the superior courts of record, depended on the scope of the prerogative writs.[11] This depended in turn on a tripartite classification of

[3] Louis Jaffe and Edith Henderson, 'Judicial Review and the Rule of Law: Historical Origins' (1956) 72 *Law Quarterly Review* 345, 347.

[4] *R v Criminal Injuries Compensation Board, ex parte Lain* [1967] 2 QB 864, 882 (in relation to certiorari specifically, but his comments are generally applicable). See also Law Commission of Canada, *Working Paper 25: Independent Administrative Agencies*, 1980, 20; SA de Smith, 'The Prerogative Writs' (1951) 11 *Cambridge Law Journal* 40, 48.

[5] See generally SA de Smith, 'The Prerogative Writs' (1951) 11 *Cambridge Law Journal* 40. As John Griffith and Harry Street commented: 'The remedies, for no practical reason are plural; some of them cannot be used if another remedy is available; the lines between them are imprecise and shifting [and] the judges employ vague concepts (which they do not define) in marking the boundaries of each remedy': *Principles of Administrative Law* (Sir Isaac Pitman & Sons, London, 1966), 236. Compare David Mullan, 'Reform of Administrative Law Remedies: Method or Madness?' [1975] *Federal Law Review* 340, 342, suggesting that the 'deficiencies' of the prerogative writs 'have probably been exaggerated'.

[6] See variously, JC McRuer, *Report of the Royal Commission: Inquiry into Civil Rights* (Queen's Printer, Toronto, 1968) (Ontario); Fourth Report of the Public and Administrative Law Reform Committee, *Administrative Tribunals: Constitution, Procedure and Appeals* (Wellington, Government Printer, 1971) (New Zealand); RJ Ellicott, FJ Mahoney and LJ McAuley, *Prerogative Writ Procedures: Report of Committee of Review* (Parliamentary Paper No 56, 1973) (Australia); The Law Commission, *Report on Remedies in Administrative Law* (Law Com No 73, 1976) (England and Wales).

[7] *R v Inland Revenue Commissioners, ex parte National Federation of Self-Employed and Small Businesses Ltd* [1982] AC 617, 638 per Lord Diplock.

[8] SI 1955/1977. A statutory footing was later created in the Senior Courts Act 1981.

[9] Judicature Amendment Act 1972 and Administrative Decisions (Judicial Review) Act 1977 (Cth) respectively.

[10] John Evans, 'Judicial Review in Ontario—Recent Developments in the Remedies—Some Problems of Pouring Old Wine into New Bottles' (1977) 55 *Canadian Bar Review* 148.

[11] See especially SA de Smith, 'Wrongs and Remedies in Administrative Law' (1952) 15 *Modern Law Review* 189, 206.

administrative decisions into rigid, formal categories—'administrative' and 'legislative' decisions taken free from judicial oversight and 'judicial' decisions subject to the full rigours of natural justice and (such as it was) superior court scrutiny. But this set of distinctions did not survive the 20th century and 'the modern view, now received doctrine, is that the classification of powers is not a sound criterion for the operation of precise rules of law'.[12]

Judicial cremation of the tripartite classification was followed by legislative and regulatory burial of the prerogative writs.[13] Once one appreciates the general background against which the wave of procedural reform washed over the common law world, one also comes to appreciate that the effect was to decouple judicial review remedies from the scope of the prerogative writs, allowing a reviewing court to 'grant any order or orders it considers appropriate' in the circumstances of a given case.[14] As Lord Roskill explained:

> ... the changes thereby effected ... were and were intended to be far-reaching. They were designed to stop the technical procedural arguments which had too often arisen and thus marred the true administration of justice, whether a particular applicant had pursued his claim for relief correctly, whether he should have sought mandamus rather than certiorari, or certiorari rather than mandamus, whether an injunction or prohibition, or prohibition rather than an injunction or whether relief by way of declaration should have been sought rather than relief by way of prerogative order. All these, and the like technical niceties, were to be things of the past. All relevant relief could be claimed under the general head of 'judicial review,' and the form of judicial review sought or granted (if at all) was to be entirely flexible according to the needs of the particular case.[15]

This decoupling had more dramatic effects. Just as the bonfire of the writ system in the late 19th century had the effect of allowing 'tort' and 'contract' to rise from the ashes of 'trespass' and 'assumpsit', the demise of the prerogative writs meant that administrative law could no longer be organised around them. This is not to suggest that 'tort', 'contract' or 'administrative law' owe their very existence to procedural reforms. After all, the first edition of Professor de Smith's seminal treatise, *Judicial Review of Administrative Action*, which drew common themes from the judicial decisions gathered around the prerogative writs, was published in 1959, well before the writs' demise. Many of the significant features of contemporary

[12] *R v Toohey, ex parte Northern Land Council* (1981) 151 CLR 170, 225 per Mason J.

[13] Cf the Administrative Decisions (Judicial Review) Act 1977 (Cth), s 3(1) which defines 'decision' for the purposes of the Act as a 'decision of an administrative character'.

[14] Philip Joseph, *Constitutional and Administrative Law of New Zealand* 4th edn (Thomson Reuters, Auckland, 2014), 1147.

[15] *R v Inland Revenue Commissioners, ex parte National Federation of Self-Employed and Small Businesses Ltd* (n 7) 657 .

administrative law emerged on the landscape before the procedural reforms. And that judicial review of administrative action in Australia is still organised to some extent around the prerogative writs entrenched in the Australian Constitution has not prevented courts in that jurisdiction from developing general principles of administrative law.[16] Nonetheless, with the procedural reforms eliminating or reducing the importance of the prerogative writs, thereby increasing demands for 'internal coherence' of this area of legal doctrine,[17] it has become much more natural to speak of 'administrative law' or 'judicial review of administrative action' rather than of 'the law of the prerogative writs'.[18]

In recent decades, administrative law has blossomed as a result of judicial creativity. In the early 20th century, administrative action could be reviewed only in a narrow set of cases, where officials exercising statutory authority had determined, by a judicial process, the rights of an individual.[19] In the 1960s, a leading judge was able to comment that common lawyers 'do not have a developed system of administrative law'.[20] Yet by the mid-1980s, the law had been 'virtually transformed':[21] it was safe to say that any governmental decision affecting the rights, interests, property, privileges or liberties of any person was reviewable by the courts to ensure the legality and rationality of the decision and the fairness of the decision-making process.[22]

Since then, the common law of judicial review of administrative action has developed still further in the jurisdictions studied in this book: Australia, Canada, England and Wales, Ireland and New Zealand. In England and Wales, for example, factual findings of officials may be reviewed;[23] officials can be bound to promises made by them to individuals;[24] and in many situations, individuals are entitled

[16] Section 75(v) provides that the High Court of Australia has 'original jurisdiction' in matters 'in which a writ of Mandamus or prohibition or an injunction is sought against an officer of the Commonwealth'.

[17] Tarunabh Khaitan and Sandy Steel, 'Theorising Areas of Law', *Social Science Research Network* (4 October, 2019), 7.

[18] Traces remain, however, especially in those jurisdictions which have retained the prerogative remedies, albeit that the old technicalities tend no longer to stand in the way of a remedy being granted where an unlawful decision has been identified: see e.g. *Ainsworth v Criminal Justice Commission* (1992) 175 CLR 564, 580–581. See also the wise, cautionary words of Professor David Williams:

> [Administrative law] cases range over many thousands of statutory provisions: this militates against any effective doctrine of *stare decisis* and explains why administrative law is primarily a subject of *obiter dicta*, with hallowed passages, such as the *Wednesbury* rule or the *Carltona* principle, offering judges convenient shorthand principles in the application of the *ultra vires* rule.

'Statute Law and Administrative Law' [1984] *Statute Law Review* 157, 160.

[19] *R v Electricity Commissioners, ex parte London Electricity Joint Committee Co* [1924] 1 KB 171, 204–205; *R v Legislative Committee of the Church Assembly, ex parte Haynes-Smith* [1928] 1 KB 411, 415.

[20] *Ridge v Baldwin* [1964] AC 40, 72 per Lord Reid.

[21] *Council of Civil Service Unions v Minister for the Civil Service* [1985] AC 374, 407 per Lord Diplock.

[22] Lord Woolf of Barnes, 'Droit Public—English Style' [1995] *Public Law* 57.

[23] *E v Secretary of State for the Home Department* [2004] EWCA Civ 49; [2004] QB 1044. See also *KV (Sri Lanka) v Secretary of State for the Home Department* [2019] UKSC 10.

[24] *R v North and East Devon Health Authority, ex parte Coughlan* [1999] EWCA Civ 1871; [2001] QB 213.

to reasons for adverse decisions.[25] There has been 'a dramatic and indeed radical change in the scope of judicial review'.[26] Where once administrative decision-makers could gaily err within jurisdiction[27] (especially when sheltered by a privative clause), now they must accord significant participatory rights to individuals whose legal position may be modified by their decisions,[28] which in turn are subject to searching review for the robustness of the legal analysis,[29] the evidentiary basis of the underlying findings[30] and the reasons given (sometimes as a matter of legal obligation[31]) in support of the conclusions.[32] Even in jurisdictions that have a doctrine of 'deference', judicial review is more intense than the word 'deference', with 'its overtones of cringing abstention to superior status',[33] suggests. In Canada, for example, although administrative decision-makers are permitted now to choose between competing possible interpretations of statutory terms, their choice is subject to judicial oversight.[34]

Administrative law's breadth *and* depth have increased: these intrusive grounds of review are available against a wide variety of actors performing governmental functions. For the tentacles of administrative law embrace not only officials acting under express statutory authorisation but, sometimes, private bodies performing public functions.[35]

The constraints courts impose on administrative decision-makers can usefully be grouped under the headings of legality, rationality and procedural fairness.[36] Many of these constraints are not justified by reference to statutory language but have been woven out of whole cloth by judges. It is true that 'legality' generally means that administrative decision-makers must direct themselves correctly in law and can thus be said to be tethered to statute: in assessing the 'legality' of administrative action, judges can certainly claim simply to be enforcing the express will

[25] *Dover District Council v CPRE Kent* [2017] UKSC 79; [2018] 1 WLR 108.

[26] *Council of Civil Service Unions v Minister for Civil Service* (n 21) per Lord Roskill.

[27] *R v Nat Bell Liquors* [1922] 2 AC 128. See also *R (Martin) v Mahoney* [1910] 2 IR 695 (on which see generally Kevin Costello, '*R (Martin) v Mahoney*: The History of a Classical Certiorari Authority' (2006) 27 *Journal of Legal History* 267). See further DM Gordon, 'The Relation of Fact to Jurisdiction' (1929) 45 *Law Quarterly Review* 459; 'The Observance of Law as a Condition of Jurisdiction' (1931) 47 *Law Quarterly Review* 386 and 557.

[28] See e.g. *Re Pergamon Press Ltd* [1971] Ch 405; *Dellway Investments v National Asset Management Agency* [2011] IESC 4; [2011] 4 IR 1.

[29] See e.g. *Anisminic v Foreign Compensation Commission* [1969] 2 AC 167.

[30] See e.g. *Bugdaycay v Home Secretary* [1987] AC 514; Paul Craig, 'Judicial Review and Anxious Scrutiny: Foundations, Evolution and Application' [2015] *Public Law* 60.

[31] See e.g. *Baker v Canada (Minister for Citizenship and Immigration)* [1999] 2 SCR 817.

[32] See e.g. *Re JR55* [2016] UKSC 22 [30].

[33] *R (Lord Carlile of Berriew QC) v Home Secretary* [2014] UKSC 60; [2015] AC 945 [22] per Lord Sumption. Compare Gary Lawson and Guy I Seidman, *Deference: The Legal Concept and the Legal Practice* (Oxford University Press, Oxford, 2020), 116–117.

[34] *McLean v British Columbia (Securities Commission)* 2013 SCC 67; [2013] 3 SCR 895; *Canada (Citizenship and Immigration) v Vavilov* 2019 SCC 65.

[35] Dawn Oliver, *Common Values and the Public-Private Divide* (Butterworths, London, 1999).

[36] See e.g. *Council of Civil Service Unions v Minister for Civil Service* (n 21); *Canada (Attorney General) v TeleZone Inc.* 2010 SCC 62; [2010] 3 SCR 585.

of the legislature. Yet even here, matters are not always so clear; in England judicial review of factual error comes under the rubric of legality,[37] but one would scour the statute book in vain for legislation that permits judges to intervene because an administrative decision-maker erred badly on factual matters.[38] Rationality and procedural fairness have developed almost entirely autonomously of the operation of any statute.[39] The idea that a decision can be quashed because it is one no reasonable decision-maker would have made cannot be traced to statutory language, a point that applies *a fortiori* to the possible introduction of proportionality as a new common law ground of review of administrative action;[40] and one of the most fascinating features of contemporary Australian administrative law is the extent to which rationality review has expanded in spite of legislative efforts to restrict it.[41] As for fairness, it is surely sufficient to recall the famous language from *Cooper v Wandsworth Board of Works* to the effect that where matters of procedure are concerned 'the common law will supply the omission of the legislature'.[42]

Individual parts of this judicial construction project have been carefully scrutinised. Review of factual error,[43] close control of errors of law[44] and

[37] *E v Secretary of State for the Home Department* (n 23). Contrast the position in Canada, where review of factual error now falls under the rubric of reasonableness: *Blanchard v Control Data Canada Ltd* [1984] 2 SCR 476; *Quebec (Commission des droits de la personne et des droits de la jeunesse) v Bombardier Inc (Bombardier Aerospace Training Center)* 2015 SCC 39; [2015] 2 SCR 789; *Vavilov* (n 34).

[38] Indeed, for a more traditionalist position, see *Richardson v Mahon* [2013] IEHC 118.

[39] *Knight v Indian Head School, Division No 19* [1990] 1 SCR 653, 668.

[40] See e.g. *Pham v Secretary of State for the Home Department* [2015] UKSC 19; [2015] WLR 1591. For a collection of essays debating this point, see [2010] NZLR 265 *et seq*. Obviously, in many areas of law proportionality has been taken to be constitutionally mandated.

[41] See especially *Minister for Immigration & Multicultural Affairs; ex parte Applicant* S20/2002 (2003) 198 ALR 59 and the discussion in Mark Aronson, 'The Growth of Substantive Review: The Changes, their Causes and their Consequences' and on England, Carol Harlow and Richard Rawlings, '"Striking Back" and "Clamping Down": An Alternative Perspective on Judicial Review' in Bell et al. eds, *Public Law Adjudication in Common Law Systems: Process and Substance* (Hart, Oxford, 2016).

[42] (1863) 14 CB (NS) 180. In *Kioa v West* (1985) 62 ALR 321, 367, Brennan J attempted to tie the duty of procedural fairness to legislative intent: 'There is no right to be accorded natural justice which exists independently of statute and which, in the event of a contravention, can be invoked to invalidate executive action taken in due exercise of a statutory power.' This is unrealistic. See e.g. *Annetts v McCann* (1990) 170 CLR 596, 598; *Plaintiff M61/2010E v Commonwealth of* [2010] HCA 41, 352. Compare the recognition by Jacobs J, in a previous decision of the High Court of Australia 'that the search for legislative intention can be described as somewhat artificial. What the courts do in the absence of express legislative intention is to ensure that power, whether it be judicial or quasi-judicial or executive, be exercised fairly, weighing the interests of the individual and the interests of society as a whole' (*Salemi v MacKellar (No 2)* (1977) 14 ALR 1, 44. See also *Saeed v Minister for Immigration and Citizenship* [2010] HCA 23; (2010) 241 CLR 252, 258–259).

[43] See e.g. Paul Craig, 'Judicial Review, Appeal and Factual Error' [2004] *Public Law* 788; Paul Daly, 'Judicial Review of Factual Error in Ireland' (2008) 30 *Dublin University Law Journal* 187; Christopher Forsyth and Emma Dring, 'The Final Frontier: The Emergence of Material Error of Fact as a Ground for Judicial Review' in Forsyth et al eds, *Effective Judicial Review: A Cornerstone of Good Governance* (Oxford University Press, Oxford, 2010), 245; Paul Daly, 'Facticity: Judicial Review of Factual Error in Comparative Perspective' in Cane et al eds, *The Oxford Handbook of Comparative Administrative Law* (Oxford University Press, Oxford, 2021).

[44] Compare BC Gould, '*Anisminic* and Jurisdictional Error' [1970] *Public Law* 358 with Paul Daly, 'Deference on Questions of Law' (2011) 74 *Modern Law Review* 694.

discretionary powers,[45] enforcement of substantive legitimate expectations[46] and an ever-wider right to reasons[47] have, for instance, attracted sustained academic attention, as has the extension of judicial review to non-statutory bodies.[48] However, the whole has come in for less scrutiny.[49] This may simply reflect a belief that these developments make sense on their own terms, or that they can only be studied in isolation because they are products of a common-law system in which the law moves forward (or back) only incrementally,[50] in response to different concerns and social values at different times.[51] My primary goal in this book is to set out a framework for understanding the contemporary law of judicial review of administrative action, as created by common law judges (with subsidiary aims of guiding judges in making further changes in the future and of evaluating the justifiability of judicial creativity in administrative law).

1.1.2 Contemporary Debates

There is some controversy about the baseline against which the changes I have described should be measured. As Professor Paul Craig has demonstrated in ground-breaking historical work, many of the familiar features of contemporary administrative law have counterparts which are several centuries old.[52] These seem to have been forgotten during the 'long sleep' of administrative law, that late 19th and early 20th century period in which judges more narrowly confined the breadth and depth of judicial review of administrative action,[53] before being uncovered

[45] See e.g. Janina Boughey, *Human Rights: The Newest Despotism? Human Rights and Administrative Law in Australia and Canada* (Hart, Oxford, 2017).

[46] See generally Matthew Groves and Greg Weeks, *Legitimate Expectations in the Common Law World* (Hart, Oxford, 2017).

[47] See e.g. Mark Elliott, 'Has the Common Law Duty to Give Reasons Come of Age Yet?' [2011] *Public Law* 56; Kendrick Lo, 'When Efficiency Calls: Rethinking the Obligation to Provide Reasons for Administrative Decisions' (2018) 43 *Queen's Law Journal* 325.

[48] Neil Duxbury, 'The Outer Limits of English Judicial Review' [2017] *Public Law* 235; Mark Elliott, 'Judicial Review's Scope, Foundations and Purposes: Joining the Dots' (2012) *New Zealand Law Review* 75; Dawn Oliver, 'Is the Ultra Vires Rule the Basis of Judicial Review?' [1987] *Public Law* 543.

[49] Cf Thomas Poole, 'The Reformation of English Administrative Law' (2009) 68 *Cambridge Law Journal* 142; TRS Allan, *Constitutional Justice: A Liberal Theory of the Rule of Law* (Oxford University Press, Oxford, 2001); Adrian Vermeule, *Judging Under Uncertainty: An Institutional Theory of Legal Interpretation* (Harvard University Press, Cambridge, 2006); and David Dyzenhaus, 'Form and Substance in the Rule of Law: A Democratic Justification for Judicial Review?' in Christopher Forsyth ed, *Judicial Review and the Constitution* (Hart, Oxford, 2000).

[50] See e.g. Stephen Waddams, *Dimensions of Private Law: Categories and Concepts in Anglo-American Legal Reasoning* (Cambridge University Press, Cambridge, 2003).

[51] See e.g. Paul Craig, *UK, EU and Global Administrative Law: Foundations and Challenges* (Cambridge University Press, Cambridge, 2015).

[52] See e.g. Paul Craig, 'Proportionality and Judicial Review: A UK Perspective' in Stephan Vogenauer and Stephen Weatherill eds, *General Principles of Law: European and Comparative Perspectives* (Hart, Oxford, 2017).

[53] Robert Stevens, *The English Judges* (Hart, Oxford, 2005), 19.

more recently. Judges have sometimes openly engaged in law-office archaeology,[54] sometimes developed modern versions of fossils of whose existence they are unaware. Whether the baseline is provided by administrative law prior to or after its period of somnolesence, however, there have undoubtedly been significant changes to its breadth and depth. Demonstrating that today's administrative law has historical antecedents is an important means of rebutting the claims of those who believe that the modern administrative state is a constitutional aberration; it also casts doubt on claims that 20th-century procedural reforms led to the creation of a novel body of 'administrative law'.[55] Recent research serves the important function of putting contemporary audiences on notice that the core features of today's administrative law may have a strong historical basis.[56] Nevertheless, core features of contemporary law call for justification in their own right: for example, that proportionality review existed in some form in the 17th century cannot provide a conclusive response to the critic who argues that proportionality review exercised by today's judges violates contemporary democratic norms by investing the judiciary with too much power relative to the political branches of government.

Given that the absence of any statutory warrant for judicial development of general principles of administrative law is obvious enough (the 'legality' grounds of review partly excepted), debate has focused on how best to square this judicial creativity with the orthodox view of parliamentary sovereignty. Two camps emerged, one flying the 'common law' banner which depicted the judges as (largely) autonomous in developing grounds of review,[57] one waving the 'modified *ultra vires*' banner, whose members insist that Parliament must be taken to intend to legislate consistently with the rule of law, as ultimately enforced by the courts.[58] Both sides largely agreed, however, that the development of the law of judicial review was for the judges (as amply demonstrated by the historical record), permissible as long as some 'reasoned justification' could be provided.[59] They disagreed only about how to accommodate judicial creativity as a matter of constitutional theory. This debate only seeks to square the legitimacy of judicial development of administrative law with orthodox (and, let it be said, very English[60]) notions of parliamentary sovereignty, an important exercise but one which does not provide a justification for

[54] See e.g. Lord Denning in *R v Northumberland Compensation Appeal Tribunal, ex parte Shaw* [1952] 1 KB 338, excavating error of law on the face of the record from a shallow grave.

[55] My claim is much more modest: the procedural reforms made it easier to conceive of 'administrative law' as a body of general principles distinct from the prerogative writs which judges developed to control inferior courts and, later, public administration.

[56] See generally Paul Craig, 'English Administrative Law History: Perception and Reality' in Michael Ramsden and Swati Jhaveri eds, *Judicial Review Across the Common Law World: Origins and Adaptations* (Cambridge University Press, Cambridge, 2021).

[57] See e.g. Paul Craig, 'Ultra Vires and the Foundations of Judicial Review' (1998) 57 *Cambridge Law Journal* 63.

[58] See e.g. Mark Elliott, *The Constitutional Foundations of Judicial Review* (Hart, Oxford, 2001).

[59] Craig (n 57) 89.

[60] See Gerard Hogan, David Gwynn Morgan and Paul Daly, *Administrative Law in Ireland*, 5th edn (Roundhall, Dublin, 2019) [10–31]:

judicial creativity in general and which would not represent an adequate response to complaints that judicial development of administrative law has, on the whole, gone too far.

Curiously, there has been little or no dissent from a third camp whose members might be thought to have an interest in debating the appropriate limits of judicial power to develop new grounds to review an ever-wider variety of administrative action. So-called 'political constitutionalists' tend to look askance at judicial control of public administration, preferring government to be held to account politically. Political accountability is said to be preferable for normative reasons,[61] and because it coheres better with Westminster-style democracy.[62] Political constitutionalists are particularly sceptical of judicial enforcement of fundamental rights, on the basis that rights questions are best left to the ordinary democratic process.[63] Yet these theorists have left well enough alone as far as judicial review of administrative action is concerned.[64] Faced with judicial development of increasingly intrusive grounds of review, available against an increasingly broad swathe of statutory and non-statutory bodies—causing a marked shift from a preference for political accountability towards a preference for legal accountability[65]—commentators have been surprisingly quiet.

In general, the academic commentary on the increased breadth and depth of judicial review has been positive. First, Harlow and Rawlings' treatment of legitimate expectations is a useful example, because these authors are at least sceptical about the displacement of political accountability by legal accountability. Discussing the seminal *Coughlan* case,[66] in which a public body wished to renege upon the promise of a 'home for life' which it had made to residents of a care facility, the authors criticise the more expansive elements of the Court of Appeal's decision but indicate that they would have been nonetheless content had the Court of Appeal treated the promise as merely one factor among many others to be considered by

> [T]he Irish observer may feel like the superior neighbour with a fancy car in the garage, who looks over the fence to find his neighbours admiring their car because it does not require a starting handle. To put it in simple terms, much of the difficulty which has engaged the attention of the great contemporary British legal thinkers stems from the need to fit the modern motor of individual rights into a chassis devised for a by-gone century. The reason is that the unequivocal status of the Constitution as a higher law makes it clear that the values which it establishes possess an incontestable status such that statute law must bow before them and there is no need for any sophistry to justify this result. This may explain why there has been little or no mention of the *ultra vires* debate in Irish judgments or writing.

61 See e.g. Richard Bellamy, *Political Constitutionalism* (Cambridge University Press, Cambridge, 2007).

62 See e.g. Adam Tomkins, *Our Republican Constitution* (Oxford University Press, Oxford, 2005).

63 See e.g. Jeremy Waldron, *Law and Disagreement* (Clarendon Press, Oxford, 1999).

64 Jeremy Waldron, 'The Core of the Case against Judicial Review' (2006) 115 *Yale Law Journal* 1346, 1353–1354.

65 See e.g. Mark Elliott and Robert Thomas, *Public Law*, 3rd edn (Oxford University Press, Oxford, 2017).

66 *R v North and East Devon Health Authority, ex parte Coughlan* (n 24).

the public body in the husbandry of its resources.[67] But even treating a promise unsupported by statute as a relevant factor is to place a constraint on administrative discretion which the legislature did not expressly endorse. Second, in discussing the possibility of judicial review of the reasonableness and proportionality of administrative action, a prominent political constitutionalist could only bring himself to say 'we need a judicial review that is appropriately responsive to, and respectful of . . . other constitutional goods and accords them due weight' and that a 'balanced mix' is required.[68] In other words, even those most likely to claim that the invention of judicially enforceable constraints of rationality and fairness are illegitimate power grabs have been—so far—reluctant to do so.[69]

It is nonetheless easy to perceive how the judges might be vulnerable to accusations of overstepping the appropriate bounds of the judicial role.[70] The sweeping changes to judicial review of administrative action have been so far-reaching as to invite an evaluation of the whole of the current body of administrative law, not just the individual parts, to determine whether 'an open-ended lawmaking power' has been conferred 'on unelected judges'.[71] Moreover, those who are generally content with the current state of judicial review of administrative action should be on their guard. Already there have been important political reactions against the expanding powers of the courts[72] and academic talk of legitimacy crises[73] will doubtless increase public awareness of the extent to which, on the whole, courts control an ever-wider swathe of public administration and to a much greater extent than they did in the past. Although differences of detail remain, the trend to more intensive judicial review over a wider range of administrative decision-making is one common to Australia, Canada, England and Wales, Ireland and New Zealand.[74] The creation, as this book was going to press, of an Independent Review of Administrative Law by the United Kingdom government underscores this trend; the Reviewers were asked to 'bear in mind how the legitimate interest in the citizen being able to

[67] Carol Harlow and Richard Rawlings, *Law and Administration*, 3rd edn (Cambridge University Press, Cambridge, 2009), 232.

[68] Adam Tomkins, 'What's Left of the Political Constitution?' (2013) 14 *German Law Journal* 2275, 2287.

[69] See generally Paul Craig, 'Political Constitutionalism and Judicial Review' in Forsyth et al eds, *Effective Judicial Review: A Cornerstone of Good Governance* (Oxford University Press, Oxford, 2010).

[70] See also Thomas Poole, 'Legitimacy, Rights and Judicial Review' (2005) 25 *Oxford Journal of Legal Studies* 697.

[71] Jeffrey Jowell, 'Of *Vires* and Vacuums: the Constitutional Context of Judicial Review' [1999] *Public Law* 448, 449.

[72] See e.g. on Australia, Aronson (n 41) and on England, Harlow and Rawlings (n 41).

[73] Jason Varuhas, *Judicial Capture of Political Accountability* (Policy Exchange, London, 2016), 50–51; Richard Ekins, 'A Legitimacy Crisis in Judicial Review', *ConservativeHome* (8 June 2016).

[74] See e.g. Paul Daly, 'Substantive Review in the Common Law World: *AAA v Minister for Justice* in Comparative Perspective' (2019) 1 *Irish Supreme Court Review* 105; Dyson Heydon, *Enclaves and Exclaves: Limits and Exceptions to the Doctrine of Judicial Review* (Policy Exchange, London, 2018).

challenge the lawfulness of executive action through the courts can be *properly balanced with the role of the executive to govern effectively under the law*'.[75] A subsidiary—but important—aim of this book is to use the framework created for understanding administrative law to defend the contemporary law of judicial review of administrative action against accusations of illegitimacy.

1.1.3 Administrative Law Today

Setting out the background in terms both of the development of administrative law and academic thinking illuminates the questions I will address in this book. First, and most importantly, there are evidently questions about how one should *understand* the contemporary law of judicial review of administrative action, as it has emerged since the procedural reforms of the 1970s and 1980s. Does it have an intelligible structure, or are the judges simply doing their best on a case-by-case basis to operationalise legality, rationality and fairness?[76] Second, what are the considerations that might *guide* the decision in an individual case and/or the further development of administrative law principles?[77] Third, can the current law of judicial review of administrative action be *justified*: is it acceptable and defensible, normatively speaking?[78]

Perhaps because of the need, once the procedural reforms had decoupled the substance of judicial review of administrative action from its procedures, it began to be said, especially since the English courts began to reformulate administrative law in the latter half of the 20th century,[79] that the purpose of judicial review is to combat 'abuse of power'[80] or to control government by law: through judicial review judges seek to prevent public officers from using their powers in legally inappropriate ways.[81] However, the term 'abuse of power' itself 'is not a distinct legal criterion'[82] as it 'goes no distance to tell you, case by case, what is lawful and what is not'; rather, '[l]egal principle lies between the overarching rubric of abuse of power

[75] Ministry of Justice, *Terms of Reference for the Independent Review of Administrative Law* (31 July 2020), 1 <https://www.gov.uk/government/news/government-launches-independent-panel-to-look-at-judicial-review>. Emphasis added.

[76] See Chapters 2 to 7.

[77] See Chapter 8.

[78] See Chapter 9.

[79] Jason Varuhas, 'The Public Interest Conception of Public Law: Its Procedural Origins and Substantive Implications' in Bell et al eds, *Public Law Adjudication in Common Law Systems: Process and Substance* (Hart, Oxford, 2016).

[80] See e.g. *In re Preston* [1985] 1 AC 835, 851 (Lord Scarman), 864 (Lord Templeman); *R v North and East Devon Health Authority, ex parte Coughlan* (n 24) [71]. For an early usage, see Sir Alfred Denning, *Freedom under the Law* (Stevens & Sons, London, 1949), 99–126.

[81] For the sake of convenience, in what follows I will generally refer to abuse of power.

[82] *R (Gallaher Group Ltd) v Competition and Markets Authority* [2018] UKSC 25; [2019] AC 96 [41] per Lord Carnwath.

and the concrete imperatives of a rule-book'.[83] Abuse of power is an abstract concept that needs to be operationalised.[84] Similarly, although in general common lawyers would accept that contemporary judicial review is concerned with legality, rationality and procedural fairness,[85] the 'application' of these heads of review 'is largely dependent on the specific context under review';[86] they must somehow be translated into 'hard clear law'.[87] *Understanding* how this has been done is the primary aim of this book, with the questions of *guidance* and *justification* taken up in Chapters 8 and 9.

Variants of the argument that there is 'too much flabbiness and too little toughness about many aspects of our public law' are recurrent and pose an important challenge to administrative lawyers.[88] One response is to more or less accept the criticism and celebrate the pragmatism of the common law tradition.[89] But many administrative lawyers do not accept the criticism and so approach the subject in search of some sort of meta-concept, meta-principle or meta-value that holds the entire enterprise together: 'abuse of power', 'jurisdiction', 'the public interest' or 'the rule of law'. Although I do not accept the argument that administrative law is intellectually flabby, I am sceptical that a field that has expanded so rapidly—in all directions—in recent years can be unified by one meta-principle.[90] To my ear it sounds much more plausible to say that administrative law is best understood as balancing several values, not privileging one above all others. It also sounds, as I will argue in Chapter 9, much more normatively attractive.

[83] *R (Nadarajah) v Secretary of State for the Home Department* [2005] EWCA Civ 1363 [67] per Laws LJ.

[84] See e.g. Matthew Groves, 'The Surrogacy Principle and Motherhood Statements in Administrative Law' in Linda Pearson, Carol Harlow and Michael Taggart eds, *Administrative Law in a Changing State: Essays in Honour of Mark Aronson* (Hart, Oxford, 2008).

[85] *Council of Civil Service Unions v Minister for Civil Service* (n 21); *Canada (Attorney General) v TeleZone Inc* (n 36).

[86] TRS Allan, 'Doctrine and Theory in Administrative Law: An Elusive Quest for the Limits of Jurisdiction' [2003] *Public Law* 429, 431.

[87] *R v Department of Education and Employment, ex parte Begbie* [1999] EWCA Civ 2100; [2000] 1 WLR 1115 [77] per Laws LJ. See generally Paul Daly, 'The Language of Administrative Law' (2016) 94 *Canadian Bar Review* 519.

[88] David Hughes Parry, 'The Place of Constitutional Law and International Law in Legal Education' (1950) 28 *Canadian Bar Review* 189, 193. Note, though, that Parry's proposed remedy was for more University-level study of the subject.

[89] See e.g. *Miller v Secretary of State for Exiting the European Union* [2017] UKSC 5; [2018] AC 61 [40].

[90] Again, this is not to suggest that recent developments should be understood as historical aberrations, as there is a strong case to be made that in developing contemporary controls on administrative action judges are acting much as they have done since the Middle Ages: Paul Craig, 'English Foundations of US Administrative Law: Four Central Errors', Oxford Legal Studies Research Paper No 3/2017.

1.2 Four Values

I argue that four values derived from the decided cases—which I call *individual self-realisation*, *good administration*, *electoral legitimacy* and *decisional autonomy*—can be understood to structure the core features of the contemporary common law of judicial review of administrative action.[91] Here, I offer an overview of the values and their most prominent manifestations in case law, setting out themes to be elaborated upon later in this book.[92]

1.2.1 Individual Self-realisation: Protecting Individual Interests

Common law courts protect, through the judicial review jurisdiction, individual interests which are important because they contribute to individual self-realisation, that is to individuals' ability to plan their affairs whilst being treated with respect by administrative decision-makers.

The term 'important' calls 'for no narrow or rigid interpretation'.[93] It is intended to capture the sheer extent of judicial willingness to treat individual interests in benefits distributed by the state and individuals' ability to participate in regulated activities as deserving of the protection of the courts.[94] Importance is broadly construed to include 'the rights, interests, property, privileges, or liberties of any

[91] In earlier work I labelled these the rule of law, good administration, democracy and separation of powers, hoping that familiar terms would draw in the reader. See Paul Daly, 'Administrative Law: A Values-based Approach' in Bell et al eds, *Public Law Adjudication in the Common Law World: Process and Substance* (Hart, Oxford, 2016); 'A Pluralist Account of Deference and Legitimate Expectations' in Groves and Weeks (n 46); and 'Administrative Law: Characteristics, Legitimacy, Unity' in Mark Elliott, Jason Varuhas and Shona Wilson-Stark eds, *The Unity of Public Law? Doctrinal, Theoretical and Comparative Perspectives* (Hart, Oxford, 2018). Although I emphasised that my conceptions of the values were defined by reference to their manifestations (as I perceived them) in decided cases, it has become clear to me that these labels carry significant conceptual baggage (see e.g. Alistair Mills, 'Review: *Legitimate Expectations in the Common Law World*' (2018) 134 *Law Quarterly Review* 334, 335) and, in different jurisdictions, wear distinctive constitutional garb (see e.g. Rosalind Dixon, 'Functionalism and Australian Constitutional Values' in Rosalind Dixon ed, *Australian Constitutional Values* (Hart, Oxford, 2018), 24). As such, they risked becoming a barrier to communication between author and reader. Only good administration has survived, because I use it in an entirely conventional sense: see e.g. *R v Monopolies and Mergers Commission, ex parte Argyll Group* [1986] 2 All ER 257, 266. For the others, I have developed bespoke labels designed to capture the content of the considerations I have drawn from the decided cases.

[92] For similar resort to values, see e.g. Oliver (n 35); Sarah Nason, *Reconstructing Judicial Review* (Hart, Oxford, 2016). Professor Oliver developed a set of values which, she argued, were shared by public and private law and, accordingly, cast doubt on the appropriateness of the distinction between public and private law. Dr Nason derived her values from an empirical assessment of first-instance decisions in administrative law cases, whereas (as I will explain later) my focus is on appellate-level statements of general principle and, given this divergence of purpose, my set of values is inevitably different.

[93] *Ansett Transport Industries Ltd v Minister for Aviation* (1987) 72 ALR 469, 496 per Lockhart J.

[94] See e.g. Charles Reich, 'The New Property' (1964) 73 *Yale Law Journal* 733.

person',[95] with reference to interests 'understood as relating to personal liberty, status, preservation of livelihood and reputation, as well as to proprietary rights and interests'.[96] Exercises of power 'must respect the integrity and the dignity of individuals who are subject to that power'.[97] What matters is the effect on an individual of a given administrative decision.

Where once judicial review of administrative action did not extend to mere 'privileges', today it encompasses any modification of an individual's legal position with the potential to impact their interests, whether it be the granting or withholding of public housing, a restriction on entry into a regulated profession, deportation to a foreign country or a preliminary investigation into professional misconduct. One significant implication is that judges have held that individuals are entitled to procedural protections—the right to notice and comment—prior to decisions adverse to their interests. Another is that administrative decisions that have significant effects on individuals, such as decisions interfering with the right to liberty or freedom of expression, are subject to an extremely stringent standard of justification. There is, further, a presumption that unlawful administrative action will be remedied by a court order issued against the responsible official, though this may not be appropriate if the effect would be to interfere with the interests of third parties. Finally, interference with individual interests might justify the extension of the judicial review jurisdiction to some private bodies.

Such interests are typically protected indirectly—by judicial imposition of restrictions on how, say, benefits may be distributed or parole decisions taken—and sometimes directly—by judges taking individual self-realisation into account in shaping the principles of administrative law, for instance by allowing individuals to choose to waive restrictions which would otherwise be imposed on administrative decision-makers.[98] I do not make much of the direct/indirect distinction, as the same underlying concern is present on both sides of the divide: respect for individual self-realisation. For the most part, the relevant individual interests are held by those who seek to initiate an application for judicial review but, as mentioned, the interests of third parties will occasionally be pertinent.

[95] *Martineau v Matsqui Institution Disciplinary Board (No 2)* [1980] 1 SCR 602, 623 per Dickson J, dissenting. See e.g. *Schmidt v Secretary of State for the Home Department* [1969] 2 Ch 149 (immigration); *Daganayasi v Minister of Immigration* [1980] 2 NZLR 130 (immigration); *Chief Constable of the North Wales Police v Evans* [1982] 1 WLR 1155 (probationary police officer); *Mahon v Air New-Zealand Ltd* [1984] AC 808, 820 (public inquiry influencing one's 'career or reputation'); *Irvine v Canada (Restrictive Trade Practices Commission)* [1987] 1 SCR 181 (regulatory investigation); *Annetts v McCann* (n 42) (coroner inquiry); *Ramsever v Mahon* [2005] IESC 82; [2006] 1 IR 216 (coroner inquiry).

[96] *Kioa v West* (n 42) 345 per Mason J. Note though that Mason J considered the statutory provisions 'relating to the issue of entry permits and the status of a person as a prohibited immigrant' to be 'of critical importance' (344).

[97] *ABT17 v Minister for Immigration* [2020] HCA 34 [107] per Gordon J.

[98] See e.g. TRS Allan, *The Sovereignty of Law: Freedom, Constitution and Common Law* (Oxford University Press, Oxford, 2013), 89.

1.2.2 Good Administration: Avoid Compromising Effective and Efficient Public Administration

Courts are naturally limited in their ability to promote the effective and efficient attainment by public bodies of their statutory goals.[99] What is manifest in the decided cases is that courts seek, in formulating the law of judicial review of administrative action, to do no harm, to avoid compromising effective and efficient public administration.

My definitions of 'effective' and 'efficient' are thin: effective decision-making relates to the ability of an administrative decision-maker to pursue its objectives; and efficient decision-making relates to making decisions in a cost-effective manner. On my thin definitions, effectiveness does not depend on whether an administrative decision-maker subscribes to a particular normative approach to its interactions with individuals, drawn from public policy theory[100] or scholarship on administrative justice;[101] and efficiency is not to be measured, as an economist might measure it, by reference to Pareto superiority or wealth maximisation.[102] In this, I am confident that I use the term 'good administration' more or less as courts do when they use it (as they often do).

A particularly prominent manifestation of judicial concern for good administration is the flexible approach taken by courts to the content of procedural fairness, which is carefully calibrated so as not to impose overly onerous obligations on administrative decision-makers. Similarly, the courts recognise that there are limits to the principle that administrative decision-making should be impartial; the impartiality expected of a court cannot realistically be imposed on non-judicial bodies without compromising effective and efficient public administration. Where a particular remedy would cause administrative inconvenience, courts will, moreover, be reluctant to grant it. Courts can, however, hold administrative decision-makers to their published policies unless there are objectively good reasons for departing from or revising the policies; the reasonable assumption here is that consistent decision-making is more likely, in the long run, to lead to effective and efficient public administration. In a similar vein, where judicial review is sought of private bodies, courts are more comfortable intervening where they are asked to hold a private body to a policy the body itself has formulated.

[99] As Hayne J observed, '[i]t is not the province of the courts to say whether particular administrative practices are prudent or efficient ...': *Minister for Immigration and Multicultural Affairs v Bhardwaj* [2002] HCA 11; (2002) 209 CLR 597, 645.

[100] See e.g. Christopher Hood, 'A Public Management for All Seasons' (1991) 69 *Public Administration* 3.

[101] See e.g. Michael Adler ed, *Administrative Justice in Context* (Hart, Oxford, 2010).

[102] See generally Richard Posner, *The Economics of Justice* (Harvard University Press, Harvard, 1981).

1.2.3 Electoral Legitimacy: Respecting the Roles of Elected Representatives

In the Westminster tradition common to the jurisdictions studied in this book, laws are made by elected politicians,[103] some of whom, moreover, hold ministerial roles,[104] in which capacity they sometimes discharge administrative decision-making functions. The same is true of municipal bye-laws, made by those who have run an electoral gauntlet, who in turn (like their national counterparts) regularly adjudicate on individual issues of local government law.[105]

As such, courts give effect to constitutionally valid statutory provisions, as they represent the considered choices of a parliamentary majority (or a municipal majority), which explains, for instance, the rule that procedural fairness must yield to a clear expression of legislative intent to exclude or modify common law principles. Courts also privilege institutional and procedural decision-making mechanisms which are likely to enhance the accuracy with which administrative decision-makers implement the considered choices of elected representatives. The extent of any deference to administrative decision-makers' determinations of law turns, also, on the intention of the legislature to accord an interpretive role to non-judicial bodies. Where ministers exercise discretionary powers, the procedural protections for individuals are generally attenuated, and the scope of the considerations that a minister may lawfully take into account will typically be broader. Moreover, an elected representative who exercises adjudicative functions is subject to a relaxed standard of impartiality, so as not to 'chill' their expression of views in public to the detriment of open debate and discussion.

Again, my definition of electoral legitimacy is thin: I make no grand claims about the meaning of 'democracy', and I should not be understood as denying that decision-making processes which privilege participation by citizens, directly or indirectly through the medium of interest groups, can be as democratic as (or, indeed, more democratic than) Westminster-style legislation. On any understanding of democracy and certainly any understanding of the Westminster tradition, those who have been elected to public office and who exercise associated authority can claim an electoral mandate. When I use the term 'electoral legitimacy', I do so to refer to this electoral mandate.

[103] With, sometimes, input from unelected members of a legislative chamber and/or an elected or unelected Head of State.

[104] Typically, constitutional law (as in Ireland: see Article 28.7) and constitutional convention (as in the United Kingdom: *The Cabinet Manual: A Guide to Laws, Conventions and Rules on the Operation of Government* (October 2011), 22) provides that ministers must be members of the legislature.

[105] See also David Gwynn Morgan, 'Cinderella Must Go to the Ball: The Significance and Accountability of State Agencies' in Eoin Carolan and Oran Doyle eds, *The Irish Constitution: Governance and Values* (Thomson Roundhall, Dublin, 2008), 195, 217: 'Even if one takes the view that the strict party system has rendered ministerial responsibility ... a fairy story, this does not affect the fact that each minister knows that he or she has to face a showdown with the electorate every four or five years.'

1.2.4 Decisional Autonomy: Maintaining Distinct Roles for Courts and Administrative Decision-makers

Judicial review of administrative action, in the common law tradition, is conducted by the ordinary courts, presided over by generalist judges, not by the specialist administrative courts common in civilian systems.[106] The role of the common law judge is to assess the lawfulness, not the merits, of the administrative decision under review; they may condemn a decision as unlawful but not second-guess it:

> The court does not ask itself the question, 'Is this decision right or wrong?' Far less does the judge ask himself whether he would himself have arrived at the decision in question ... The only question for the judge is whether the decision taken by the body under review was one which it was legally permitted to take in the way that it did.[107]

Both the court and the administrative decision-maker thus retain a zone of decisional autonomy, with lawfulness for the courts and the merits for administrative decision-makers. Similarly, private bodies are generally not subject to judicial review but are instead given a space in which their members can flourish free of the constraints of administrative law. At issue here, fundamentally, are 'supervision and checks and balances',[108] the powerful idea that 'foxes should not guard henhouses'.[109] One might term this a 'separation of powers' or a 'separation of functions', but these terms come with unhelpful conceptual and constitutional baggage and are thus liable to cause confusion,[110] whereas 'decisional autonomy' accurately captures the phenomena observable in the decided cases.

Whilst the creation of 'spheres' of legitimate and illegitimate judicial activity has (rightly) been condemned as having retarded the development of contemporary administrative law,[111] and it is accordingly important to recognise that there are for the most part no areas of 'policy' that should be marked off from judicial

[106] See generally John Henry Merryman, *The Civil Law Tradition*, 2nd edn (Stanford University Press, Stanford, 1985), chapter 18.

[107] *R v Somerset County Council, ex parte Fewings* [1995] 1 All ER 513, 515 per Laws J. As JA Jolowicz pithily puts it: 'The administrator's right of decision must be and is preserved': *On Civil Procedure* (Cambridge University Press, Cambridge, 2000), 322.

[108] Eoin Carolan, 'Separation of Powers and Administrative Governance' in Eoin Carolan and Oran Doyle eds, *The Irish Constitution: Governance and Values* (Thomson Roundhall, Dublin, 2008), 213, 226.

[109] Cass Sunstein, *After the Rights Revolution: Re-conceiving the Regulatory State* (Harvard University Press, Cambridge, Mass, 1990), 143.

[110] For discussion, see Eoin Carolan, *The New Separation of Powers* (Oxford University Press, Oxford, 2009).

[111] Murray Hunt, 'Sovereignty's Blight: Why Contemporary Public Law Needs a Concept of "Due Deference"' in Nicholas Bamforth and Peter Leyland eds, *Public Law in a Multi-Layered Constitution* (Hart, Oxford, 2003).

oversight,[112] the courts have long recognised, through the merits/lawfulness distinction, that some decisional autonomy for administrative decision-makers and private bodies should be preserved. Equally, courts have been anxious to ensure that there are no inappropriate incursions into their decisional autonomy, and thus their ability to ensure the legality, rationality and procedural propriety of governmental action.

Put another way, there is *a* (rather than *the*) separation of powers. The distinction is subtle but important: *the* separation of powers implies to the legal mind the Montesquian distinction between legislative, executive and judicial branches, whereas *a* separation of powers implies only some separation of functions between different bodies. The difference is between assuming that some functions are magically 'legislative', 'executive' or 'judicial' in nature and should be assigned accordingly and understanding simply that distinct parts of the governmental apparatus should exercise distinct functions.

***

As intimated earlier, I offer here only a sketch of the values, to be fully illuminated by the detailed analysis contained in subsequent chapters. The argument will be that the four values can be understood as having structured the principles that judges apply and the decisions that judges reach.[113] Moreover, even this sketch makes clear that the considerations have the potential to be a source of 'reasoned justification' for judicial review principles and decisions,[114] guiding the development of administrative law in the future and justifying the contemporary law of judicial review of administrative action:

Individual self-realisation ensures that individuals are treated with concern and respect by governmental decision-makers and are permitted to flourish;

Good administration facilitates governmental decision-makers' achievement of their objectives and thus allows them to serve their citizens;

Electoral legitimacy empowers representatives who have been chosen by voters; and

Decisional autonomy preserves distinct areas in which different decision-makers can do what they do best.

[112] Paul Daly, *A Theory of Deference in Administrative Law: Basis, Application and Scope* (Cambridge University Press, Cambridge, 2012), chapter 7.

[113] Daly (n 91). See also Michael Taggart, 'The Province of Administrative Law Determined?' in Michael Taggart ed, *The Province of Administrative Law* (Hart, Oxford, 1997); Chief Justice James Allsop, 'Values in Public Law' (2017) 91 *Australian Law Journal* 118, 130.

[114] Craig (n 57).

Taken together, these values provide a solid normative basis for contemporary administrative law in liberal democratic states which are designed to serve individuals within their territories.[115]

In that regard, using the term 'values' flags for the reader that individual self-realisation, good administration, electoral legitimacy and decisional autonomy have normative implications; they are not neutral. Indeed, one of my goals is to defend the legitimacy of contemporary administrative law. As such, describing them as values has the benefit of putting the reader on notice that issues of legitimacy will be addressed in this book.

1.2.5 Structure: Complementarity and Balance

It should already be clear that a balance must on occasion be struck between the values. Procedural fairness is an area of creative tension, for example. If the protection of individual interests were pushed to the extreme, the implication would be that any governmental decision-making mechanism should afford full trial-type procedures to anyone liable to be affected. This, however, would render effective and efficient public administration virtually impossible. Instead, the courts can be understood as having sought to strike a balance between two competing considerations: individual interests on the one hand, effective and efficient public administration on the other. Notably, the balance struck here also ensures that the courts and administrative decision-makers retain a degree of decisional autonomy: trial-type procedures are not the gold standard against which administrative decision-making processes are to be measured. Rather, administrative decision-makers are given the freedom to adapt their processes to the particular context in which they operate.

This last point indicates that the values can function—and they often do—in a complementary fashion. Consider the right to reasons for administrative decisions. The general rule that there is no general duty at common law to give reasons can be understood as a manifestation of the importance attached to effective and efficient public administration, inasmuch as imposing a duty to give reasons in all cases has the potential to gum up the works of public administration. Yet this general rule is subject to exceptions which can be understood in terms of the other values: where the legislature has afforded a right of appeal, reasons must be given, for otherwise the intention of the elected representatives making laws in the legislature would be set at naught; where a decision is of great importance to an individual—where liberty is at stake, for instance—reasons will be required to be given; and where reasons are necessary to ensure that the decision-maker has acted lawfully—that is,

[115] See generally Nick Barber, *Principles of Constitutionalism* (Oxford University Press, Oxford, 2018).

to ensure that the court can fulfil its distinct function of reviewing the lawfulness of the impugned decision—then they will also be required. Again, however, this is only a sketch: throughout this book, I will demonstrate how judges can be understood to have used the values in a complementary way, or to have struck a balance between them in situations of potential conflict. This complementarity and balance, I will argue, provides contemporary administrative law with an intelligible structure.

I will demonstrate in Chapters 2 to 7 that the values of individual self-realisation, good administration, electoral legitimacy and decisional autonomy permeate contemporary administrative law and, moreover, that judges can be understood to have deployed them in a *complementary* way.[116] There is ample evidence, moreover, that judges can *balance* these four values where they would potentially come into conflict.[117]

In some areas, not all of the values will be present. Whilst each of the values appears at some point and plays a prominent role in each of the chapters, they do not necessarily appear under every sub-heading within each chapter. As far as procedural fairness is concerned, for instance, the value of decisional autonomy can be understood to play a role in the general structure of the contemporary duty of fairness, in that administrative decision-making processes are not to be modelled on the trial-type procedures of the courts. As to individual procedural rights, however, such as the right to notice or to legal representation, the value does not feature.[118]

This leads to a related point, that the degree of structure provided by the values I have outlined is somewhat limited. These values do not provide a mathematical equation which one could apply to different areas of judicial review of administrative action in order to deduce what the law is or ought to be. Sometimes, as mentioned, one or more of the values will be absent from a particular area, because it is clear that it has no traction there. Nonetheless, it is clear that across the very large domain of contemporary judicial review of administrative action in Australia, Canada, England and Wales, Ireland and New Zealand, these values can be understood to have influenced the structure of the law time and again. They do not provide a unified field theory of the subject but they enhance and advance understanding of its core features.

In turn, this leads to a final point. It has been argued by some authors that administrative law can be understood by reference to one single meta-concept[119]—such

116 See the detailed list in Chapter 9.3.

117 See, again, the detailed list in Chapter 9.3.

118 Cf Chapter 3.3.5, 'Rules of Evidence'.

119 John Murphy describes as 'reductionist theories' those 'presenting an account of tort law centred upon a single norm, principle or other organising feature which putatively underpins and renders intelligible the disparate array of tort actions'. 'The Heterogeneity of Tort Law' (2019) 39 *Oxford Journal of Legal Studies* 455, 456.

as the *ultra vires* doctrine or 'jurisdiction',[120] institutional theory,[121] the rule of law[122] or the notion of public interest[123]—or that individual areas of judicial review of administrative action can be similarly understood: legitimate expectation is all about 'trust',[124] fettering of discretion all about 'fairness'[125] and procedural fairness, depending on one's perspective, all about 'instrumental' or 'dignitarian' concerns.[126] This book represents a vigorous disagreement with such 'monist' visions.[127] My view is that a plurality of values can be understood to have influenced the structure of contemporary administrative law as a whole and of particular areas of the law of judicial review of administrative action. Accordingly, I am extremely sceptical that the subject and or its component parts can be reduced to one single meta-concept.[128] Indeed, I believe that the *best* understanding of the contemporary law of judicial review of administrative action is that it reflects a pluralist approach, in that judges use several values in a complementary fashion and strike a balance between the values in situations of potential conflict.

1.3 Interpreting Administrative Law

In developing the thesis that the values of individual self-realisation, good administration, electoral legitimacy and decisional autonomy can be understood as influencing the structure of contemporary administrative law, I conduct, for the most part, an interpretive inquiry, motivated less by 'a desire to *explain*' than by a desire 'to *understand*'.[129] There are 'historical, prescriptive, and descriptive elements'[130] to the analysis, but this book is designed to provide an *interpretation* of contemporary administrative law. My interpretation has implications for future development of the law but it is not designed to explain historical developments; these are taken as given, as facts to be interpreted and placed in an intelligible structure.

[120] See e.g. Elliott (n 58) (though in fairness to Professor Elliott, he does not suggest that the features of the law of judicial review can be *derived* from the concept of 'jurisdiction', rather that the concept of 'jurisdiction' is fundamental to the legitimacy of the law of judicial review).

[121] See e.g. Vermeule (n 49).

[122] See e.g. Allan (n 49).

[123] See e.g. Varuhas (n 79).

[124] Paul Reynolds, 'Legitimate Expectations and the Protection of Trust in Public Officials' [2011] *Public Law* 330.

[125] Adam Perry, 'The Flexibility Rule in Administrative Law' (2017) 76 *Cambridge Law Journal* 375.

[126] See the overview in Matthew Groves and Greg Weeks, 'The Legitimacy of Expectations About Fairness: Can Process and Substance be Untangled?' in Bell et al eds, *Public Law Adjudication in Common Law Systems: Process and Substance* (Hart, Oxford, 2016).

[127] Bell (n 1) chapter 7.

[128] At the same time, I have no difficulty in accepting that different sets of values might achieve similar goals to those I set out to achieve in this book. Cf Nason (n 92).

[129] Geoffrey Samuel, *An Introduction to Comparative Law Theory and Method* (Hart, Oxford, 2014), 87.

[130] Stephen Smith, *Contract Theory* (Oxford University Press, Oxford, 2004), 5.

Following an interpretive approach means I look at the subject of judicial review of administrative action 'from the inside, trying to make sense of lawyers' reasons and arguments as they are actually presented and defended'.[131] Rather than starting from the constitutional basis of judicial review and working backwards to practice, I start by identifying the values revealed by the practice of administrative law and then work forwards to analyse how they can be understood as having influenced the law.

It is not necessarily the case that judges have been relying upon such considerations explicitly: 'What an interpreter is trying to understand—to interpret—is the law, not what motivated the judges who made the law.'[132] The goal is to reveal 'an *intelligible order* in the law, so far as such an order exists'.[133] How individual lawyers might *explain* a given decision may well provide the basis for a study from a different methodological perspective, but is, strictly speaking, irrelevant to an interpretive inquiry, which is interested in the 'public institution of the law', not the 'inner minds of legal actors'.[134] It may be true, for instance, that the so-called '*Carltona* exception' 'arose out of practical necessity',[135] in a time of increasing burdens on ministerial decision-making, but I am not interested in *Carltona* as a historical artefact. My interest is, rather, in understanding how it fits with the rest of contemporary administrative law—in particular, whether the values which can be understood to structure the *Carltona* exception are the same values whose influence can be understood to be present in other areas of judicial review of administrative action. This is not a 'matter of making explicit what is already known clearly; it is a matter of *making sense* of law, as much as of finding the sense which is already there'.[136] The interpretivist 'does not try to interpret the judges' actual intentions, but to determine what their intentions *should* have been'.[137] On an interpretive approach the claim is that the judges have, like Molière's bourgeois gentleman, been adjudicating in terms of these values all along, without necessarily knowing it.

This is familiar territory for common lawyers. The common law, it has been said, is 'chaos with a full index',[138] having developed in fits and starts, the heavy hand of the legislator or magic of the constituent assembly largely absent from the development by judges of legal principles. Seeking common themes, principles or values in the decided cases, with a view to demonstrating that the law can be understood as having an intelligible structure is a response to the disorderly nature

[131] Allan (n 98).
[132] Smith (n 130) 6.
[133] Ibid, 5. Emphasis original.
[134] Ibid, 14.
[135] *Devanney v District judge Shields* [1998] 1 ILRM 81, 92 per McCracken J.
[136] Neil McCormick, *Legal Reasoning and Legal Theory*, rev edn (Clarendon, Oxford, 2003), 234.
[137] Allan Beever and Charles Rickett, 'Interpretive Legal Theory and the Academic Lawyer' (2005) 68 *Modern Law Review* 320, 324. Emphasis added.
[138] Sir Thomas Holland, cited by Gerald Postema, 'Introduction: Search for an Explanatory Theory of Torts' in Gerald Postema ed, *Philosophy and the Law of Torts* (Cambridge, Cambridge University Press, 2001), 1, 1.

of the common law and a well-established mode of inquiry.[139] There is nothing 'distinctively Canadian' about my approach.[140] Certainly the law of judicial review of administrative action has 'evolved',[141] which—given that this is a field of human, not biological or divine, endeavour—suggests some sort of intelligent design; and that jurists may properly 'shape the development … '[142] of the subject. This holds out the prospect that there is a coherent set of values which can be understood as structuring contemporary administrative law.

It has been said that an interpretive inquiry is unavoidably influenced by what the interpreter thinks the law *should* represent and that some slippage between what the law 'is' and what the law 'ought to be' is therefore inevitable.[143] But sensible interpretivists are alive to the risk that what proves to be in the materials will depend on who is looking and why[144] and accept that an interpretive theorist seeks to portray the law 'in the better light, all things considered'.[145] On my approach, judges' intentions *should* have been to use the values of individual self-realisation, good administration, electoral legitimacy and decisional autonomy in administrative law cases in a complementary way, striking a balance between them in situations of potential conflict if necessary: judges *should* have regard to the values; judges *should* use them in a complementary way and judges *should* strike a balance between the values in situations of potential conflict. This is implicit in the analysis in Chapters 2 to 7 and made explicit in Chapters 8 and 9.

My argument over the course of this book is, accordingly, that administrative law 'is' a product of the values I have identified *and* that administrative law 'ought' to be a product of these values. This does not imply, however, that I think contemporary administrative law is the only legitimate body of administrative law. Rather, I consider it to be *a* legitimate body of administrative law, with legitimacy conferred by the use of these four values;[146] my argument is that today's law of judicial review of

139 See e.g. *Gillick v West Norfolk and Wisbech Health Authority* [1986] AC 112, 183 per Lord Scarman:

> The mark of the great judge from Coke through Mansfield to our day has been the capacity and the will to search out principle, to discard the detail appropriate (perhaps) to earlier times, and to apply principle in such a way as to satisfy the needs of their own time

140 Cheryl Saunders, 'Common Law Public Law: Comparative Reflections' in Bell et al eds, *Public Law Adjudication in Common Law Systems: Process and Substance* (Hart, Oxford, 2016), 353, 361. Though Professor Saunders is quite right to observe that the values (as I had then described them) are viewed quite differently in Australia (see n 82), I note in passing that the *Irish* Ombudsman wrote of a 'values-based approach' to public administration in his 2000 Annual Report, though this was explicitly tied to a 'human rights approach to service provision' (13–14).

141 *Council of Civil Service Unions v Minister for Civil Service* (n 21) 414 per Lord Roskill.

142 Ibid, 417 per Lord Roskill.

143 Paul Craig, 'Theory and Values in Public Law: A Response' in Paul Craig and Richard Rawlings eds, *Law and Administration in Europe: Essays for Carol Harlow* (Oxford University Press, Oxford, 2003), 23, 24.

144 Peter Cane, 'Theory and Values in Public Law' in Paul Craig and Richard Rawlings eds, *Law and Administration in Europe: Essays for Carol Harlow* (Oxford University Press, Oxford, 2003), 3, 11 (describing 'Dworkinian interpretivism'). Emphasis added.

145 Ronald Dworkin, *Law's Empire* (Belknap Press, Cambridge Mass, 1986), 53.

146 See similarly Jeffrey A Pojanowski, 'Neoclassical Administrative Law' (2020) 133 *Harvard Law Review* 852, 883 describing the author's interpretive work as a project which 'pulls together disparate

administrative action rests on 'recognizably moral foundations'—provided by the interaction of individual self-realisation, good administration, electoral legitimacy and decisional autonomy—not that these are necessarily the 'best possible moral foundations'.[147]

My preference for an interpretive approach to judicial review of administrative action is not intended to denigrate other ways of studying the subject. I have learned a great deal from empirical,[148] doctrinal,[149] analytical,[150] historical,[151] institutional,[152] interdisciplinary,[153] philosophical,[154] comparative[155] and normative[156] approaches to administrative law (albeit that these approaches have not typically been applied, as mine will be, to *all* of the core features of contemporary administrative law). In the social sciences, the notion that there are multiple schemes of intelligibility is widely accepted, each scheme 'giving only partial access to reality' and not involving the elaboration of 'some grand global theory'.[157] There is no right or wrong way to study administrative law, for lawyers are not mathematicians or engineers with theorems to use and hypotheses there to be disproved: 'We can only evaluate [legal theorists'] positions according to such factors as the coherence of their arguments and the consensus they receive amongst the law community.'[158] With methodologies in public law, 'the proof of the pudding must be in the eating, and people's tastes in food vary'.[159] I intend to provide a meal capable of satisfying a

strands of the jurisprudence, identifies their underlying commitments, and offers an argument for why that way of understanding administrative law is the best way forward' and also noting, first, that the author's is not 'the only way' to understand the current law and, second, that the author's is not necessarily 'the best of all possible regimes as a matter of ideal legal and political theory'.

[147] Smith (n 130) 24. These are what Smith has subsequently described as 'intermediate moral principles' or justifications: 'Intermediate and Comprehensive Justifications for Legal Rules' in Simone Degeling, Michael Crawford and Nicholas Tiverios eds, *Justifying Private Rights* (Hart, Oxford, 2020). See further Khaitan and Steel (n 17), explaining that an interpretive theorist cannot be fully detached from the area of law they are trying to interpret. On my approach, the four values offer 'some objective threshold of value' (16) for the interpretation I develop.

[148] See e.g. Nason (n 92).

[149] See e.g. Jason Varuhas, 'Taxonomy and Public Law' in Mark Elliott, Jason Varuhas and Shona Wilson-Stark eds, *The Unity of Public Law? Doctrinal, Theoretical and Comparative Perspectives* (Hart, Oxford, 2018).

[150] See e.g. Bell (n 1).

[151] See e.g. Craig (n 51).

[152] See e.g. Peter Cane, *Controlling Administrative Power: An Historical Comparison* (Cambridge University Press, Cambridge, 2016).

[153] See e.g. Paul Craig, *Public Law and Democracy in the United Kingdom and the United States of America* (Clarendon, Oxford, 1990).

[154] See e.g. Matthew Lewans, *Administrative Law and Judicial Deference* (Hart, Oxford, 2016).

[155] See e.g. Hilary Biehler, *Judicial Review of Administrative Action: A Comparative Analysis*, 3rd edn. (Roundhall, Dublin, 2013); Boughey (n 45).

[156] See e.g. Allan (n 49).

[157] Samuel (n 129).

[158] Ibid, 167. See also John Baker, *The Law's Two Bodies* (Oxford University Press, Oxford, 2001), 4: '[T]he profession of the law often seems to a lawyer more like an art of perception than an exercise in deduction.'

[159] Cane (n 152). Indeed, 'there will always remain ... in legal science generally ... an area where only sound judgment, common sense or even intuition can be of any help. For when it comes to evaluation,

diverse range of palettes. In particular, the recipe provided by the four values I have outlined achieves three things:

First, it can enhance *understanding* of the core features of contemporary administrative law (a task to which most of this book is devoted);
Second, it can *guide* the development of administrative law generally and in individual cases; and
Third, it can *justify* the balance judges have struck between protecting individual interests, efficient and effective public administration, the influence of elected representatives on administrative decision-making and the need to maintain separate roles for distinct entities.[160]

1.4 Comparative Administrative Law

Administrative law has been 'relatively neglected by the boom in comparison' across private and public law in recent decades.[161] Such neglect is not especially surprising. Comparative lawyers can be extremely ambitious, if not messianic.[162] Take Zweigert and Kötz, who claimed that only comparative law can pave the way for a true legal science. For them, comparative law 'permits us to catch sight, through the differences in detail, of the grand similarities and so to deepen our belief in the existence of a unitary sense of justice'.[163] For their part, Mauro Bussani and Ugo Mattei described their common core project as 'part of building a common European legal culture'.[164] Such lofty objectives might dissuade those who would consider engaging in comparative administrative law analysis. For public lawyers have long appreciated that those 'rules which organise constitutional, legislative, administrative or judicial institutions ... are the ones most resistant to transplantation'.[165] The institutions of public law 'arise not only from deliberate design

to determining which of the various solutions is the best, the only ultimate criterion is often the practical evidence and the immediate sense of appropriateness.' Konrad Zweigert and Hein Kötz, *An Introduction to Comparative Law*, trans Tony Weir, 3rd edn (Oxford University Press, Oxford, 1998), 33.

160 See also Randy Barnett, 'The Richness of Contract Theory' (1999) 97 *Michigan Law Review* 1413, 1419.

161 Janina Boughey, 'Administrative Law: the Next Frontier for Comparative Law' (2013) 62 *International and Comparative Law Quarterly* 55, 56.

162 Cf Mathias Siems, 'Malicious Legal Transplants' (2018) 38 *Legal Studies* 103.

163 Zweigert and Kötz (n 159) 3. They go on to say: 'The *political* aim behind such unification is to reduce or eliminate, so far as desirable and possible, the discrepancies between the national legal systems by inducing them to adopt common principles of law.' Ibid, 24.

164 Mauro Busani and Ugo Mattei, 'The Common Core Approach to European Private Law' (1997) 3 *Columbia Journal of European Law* 339, 341.

165 Otto Kahn-Freud, 'On Uses and Misuses of Comparative Law' (1974) 37 *Modern Law Review* 1, 17. See also Michael Taggart, 'Globalisation and Administrative Law' in Grant Huscroft and Michael Taggart eds, *Inside and Outside Canadian Administrative Law: Essays in Honour of David Mullan* (University of Toronto Press, Toronto, 2006), 259, 274.

(typically from the national legislator or national legal professions) but from both history and underlying social problems, such as religious or linguistic diversity'.[166] Arguably, then, comparative analysis in the field of public law 'assumes a shared understanding of political, social and economic functions of the state that cannot be taken for granted'.[167]

Nonetheless, 'the common law tradition involving in particular England, Ireland, Canada, Australia, New Zealand ... has been an active forum of debate' because there is 'a significant commonality in traditions and approaches': they bear a 'sufficient family resemblance' to justify comparative study.[168] These jurisdictions have a 'filial relationship'[169] as part of the common law tradition of controlling administrative action through supervision by the ordinary courts. These jurisdictions are part of a shared constitutional tradition, inherited from the Westminster system of government.[170] Indeed, 'a New Zealand lawyer [say] not perceiving their own law as a form of common law is virtually one-eyed'.[171] Moreover, these jurisdictions have faced a common problem since the end of the 1970s. With the abolition of the prerogative writs, it has become necessary—in Australia, Canada, England and Wales, Ireland and New Zealand—to replace the old structure with a new framework. My concern in this book is therefore a classically comparative concern, with those 'rules which perform the same function and address the same real problem ...' in similarly situated jurisdictions.[172]

1.5 Pluralist Administrative Law

My primary claim is that the four values I have identified can be understood as providing an intelligible structure for the core features of administrative law in the

[166] John Bell, 'Public Law in Europe: Caught between the National, the Sub-National and the European?' in Mark Van Hoecke ed, *Epistemology and Methodology of Comparative Law* (Hart, Oxford, 2004), 259, 265.

[167] Mathias Siems, *Comparative Law*, 2nd edn (Cambridge University Press, Cambridge, 2018), 34.

[168] John Bell, 'Comparative Administrative Law' in Mathias Reimann and Reinhard Zimmermann eds, *The Oxford Handbook of Comparative Law* (Oxford University Press, Oxford, 2006), 1259, 1266. Professor Bell also emphasises constitutional values (including the rule of law and fundamental rights) and standards of good administration as appropriate grounds for comparative administrative law inquiry: *ibid*, 1271–1274.

[169] Samuel (n 129). See also Alan Watson, *Legal Transplants* (Scottish Academic Press, Edinburgh, 1974), 21, noting how 'legal transplants—the moving of a rule or a system of law from one country to another, or from one people to another—have been common since the earliest recorded history'.

[170] Han-Ru Zhou, 'A Contextual Defense of "Comparative Constitutional Law"' (2014) 12 *International Journal of Constitutional Law* 1034, 1037, arguing that 'between the common-law-based systems of the Commonwealth countries, the judicial use of comparative constitutional law is rooted in legal history and tradition and can be coherently explained by the nature and structure of the common law and the various constitutions based on the "Westminster model"'. The Westminster tradition is a fertile source of comparative analysis in fields related to law. See e.g. RAW Rhodes, John Wanna, and Patrick Weller, *Comparing Westminster* (Oxford University Press, Oxford, 2009).

[171] Jaako Husa, *A New Introduction to Comparative Law* (Hart, Oxford, 2015), 69.

[172] Zweigert and Kötz (n 159) 10.

Commonwealth jurisdictions I have identified. By 'core' I mean those rules found in leading cases and textbooks relating to *institutional structures*, *procedural fairness*, judicial scrutiny of the *substance* of administrative decisions, *remedies* judges may issue, *restrictions on remedies* and the *scope* of judicial review of administrative action, which any administrative lawyer anywhere in the Commonwealth would instinctively recognise as central to judicial review of administrative action.

In a book like this one—not an encyclopaedia—it is not possible to comment on every single aspect of the law of judicial review of administrative action. Textbooks and manuals used by practitioners run to many thousands of pages, covering a multitude of principles derived from legislation, delegated legislation, soft law instruments and decided cases. Demonstrating that my interpretive framework assists in understanding every single aspect of administrative law would be the task of at least several volumes, if not a lifetime. Determining which features of administrative law are core features requires a series of judgement calls on my part—these judgement calls are based on instinct honed by experience, not by logic or any other falsifiable means. The 'parameters' of the core are determined 'by the consensus of those familiar with the law'.[173] To put the point in concrete terms: where I refer to cases, it is on the assumption that the case could safely be cited to a judge in Australia, Canada, England and Wales, Ireland or New Zealand.

I do not mean, however, to diminish national differences: 'To have a theory which covers *all* legal systems, in *all* societies, over *all* time periods is to make a claim that would seem hard to justify (especially on the relatively modest grounding of scholarship and practice that most of us theorists bring to the task).'[174] In comparative law, 'profound unification is still a utopia'.[175] It would be quite wrong for me 'to look only for similarities and overlook differences or look only for differences and overlook similarities'.[176] Indeed, 'in their explorations on foreign territory comparatists may come upon natives lying in wait with spears'.[177] Sure enough, an Australian barrister could not parachute into an English or Canadian courtroom and adequately conduct proceedings; similarly, a lawyer from Calgary teleported to Canberra would have significant difficulties, not just because the accents and intonations are different but because the minutiae of the law and the procedures of the courts are different. Equally, however, 'it would be wrong to think that comparative enquiries which aim at unification or harmonization cannot accept difference'.[178] My goal is

173 Smith (n 130) 9.

174 Brian Bix, 'The Promise and Problems of Universal, General Theories of Contract Law' (2017) 30 *Ratio Juris* 391, 392.

175 Husa (n 171).

176 E Örücü, *The Enigma of Comparative Law: Variations on a Theme for the Twenty-First Century* (Martinus Nijhoiff, Leiden, 2004), 213.

177 Mathias Siems, *Comparative Law*, 2nd edn (Cambridge University Press, Cambridge, 2018), 22, citing Ernest Rabel, as cited in Zweigert and Kötz (n 159), 36.

178 Gerhard Dannemann, 'Comparative Law: Study of Similarities or Differences?' in Mathias Reimann and Reinhard Zimmermann eds, *The Oxford Handbook of Comparative Law* (Oxford University Press, Oxford, 2006), 383, 402.

not to provide an exhaustive account of every doctrinal twist and turn administrative law has taken throughout the Commonwealth, still less to provide an overview of legal rules unique to individual legal systems (such as Ireland's non-delegation doctrine or the duty to consult Indigenous peoples required of Canadian administrative decision-makers as a matter of domestic constitutional law). Rather, the argument advanced in this book is that there is an intelligible structure which can help law students, lawyers, judges and those from other disciplines to understand the core features of judicial review of administrative action, about which there is a remarkable degree of agreement across the common law world; that is not to say there is consensus—and where there is none I acknowledge it to be the case—but that on the features discussed in this book national differences are not especially profound. Even a sceptic of universal theories must admit that 'theorizing can be of great practical value, in making the law more coherent, applying the law to new issues, and explaining law to students and to the general public'.[179]

Indeed, it would be naïve to claim that these values *alone* are responsible for the structure of contemporary administrative law. A common law judge 'is not a knight-errant, roaming at will in pursuit of his own ideal of beauty or of goodness'.[180] In the common law tradition, judicial creativity is constrained by respect for precedent and the role of the legislature, and limited mostly to incremental change based primarily on legal principle;[181] though judges in some jurisdictions will feel freer to roam than their counterparts elsewhere.[182] In addition, different jurisdictions might have different *constitutional rules*; to take a well-known example, Australian judges are constitutionally prohibited from exercising non-judicial power, something that imposes limits on the doctrinal rules that courts can develop in the area of judicial review of administrative action.[183] Similarly, the law in a particular jurisdiction might have developed by way of *precedent and tradition* so as to rule out a particular innovation; in Australia and Canada, for example, judges have repeatedly—and strongly—insisted that substantive enforcement of legitimate expectations by courts cannot be countenanced, which greatly reduces the scope for creative judicial innovation in this area in those jurisdictions.[184] Finally, *analytical arguments* might be made, perhaps on the basis of incoherence in the application of concepts (e.g. jurisdictional error) or perhaps on the basis of

[179] Bix, 'The Promise and Problems of Universal, General Theories of Contract Law' (n174), 400.

[180] Benjamin Cardozo, *The Nature of the Judicial Process* (Yale University Press, New Haven, 1921), 141.

[181] See e.g. *Watkins v Olafson* [1989] 2 SCR 750; *Woolwich Building Society v Commissioners of Inland Revenue* (1992) 65 Tax Cases 265.

[182] See generally Paul Daly ed, *Apex Courts and the Common Law* (University of Toronto Press, Toronto, 2019).

[183] *Huddart, Parker & Co Pty Ltd v Moorhead* (1908) 8 CLR 330; *Shell Co of Australia Ltd v Federal Commissioner of Taxation* [1931] AC 275; *R v Kirby; ex parte Boilermakers' Society of Australia* (1956) 94 CLR 254.

[184] *Reference Re Canada Assistance Plan (BC)* [1991] 2 SCR 525; *Minister for Immigration and Border Protection v WZARH* [2015] HCA 40; (2015) 256 CLR 326.

consistency with other areas of domestic law (e.g. if there is no reliance requirement for, say, estoppel, it is inconsistent to have one for legitimate expectations). These will have greater or lesser force depending on the historical development of the law in a particular jurisdiction. In general, the *lower* the level of abstraction, the *greater* the weight these other considerations will have. As to the core features of judicial review of administrative action, the intelligible structure provided by individual self-realisation, good administration, electoral legitimacy and decisional autonomy can be clearly perceived; but as one delves into the minutiae of national legal systems, they will tend to fade from view, albeit that even here they might be useful in guiding the development of the law.[185]

A final word is appropriate about the meaning I ascribe to 'administrative law' and 'judicial review of administrative action'. I will refer to them as a body of 'principles', generally eschewing the terms 'doctrine' and 'rules'. This is not because I have a critical disposition which makes me doubt whether judicial review of administrative action can truly be regarded as 'law'. Like others I fear that insufficient attention to fine doctrinal details will cause us 'to drown in the rough seas of personal preference and individual ideological and idiosyncratic views'.[186] Mine is in many respects a doctrinal book, working the decided cases into a structure for ease of exposition and understanding. What I want to avoid is any implication that administrative law is a series of levers and pulleys that manufactures predictable products. Principle is a broad term designed to evoke something lying between the all-or-nothing character of rules on the one hand and the case-by-case nature of standards on the other.

1.6 Overview

In the following chapters, I address the discrete topics of institutional structures (Chapter 2), procedural fairness (Chapter 3), substantive review (Chapter 4), remedies (Chapter 5), restrictions on remedies (Chapter 6) and scope of review (Chapter 7), demonstrating how the law in these areas is permeated by administrative law values. A word of explanation as to the division is necessary. By 'institutional structures', I mean the law relating to the institutional arrangements for administrative decision-making, or in other words, the legal principles used to determine which structures for administrative decision-making are permissible and which are not. For instance, pursuant to the no-bias principle, decisions must be

[185] See e.g. Paul Daly, 'Reasons and Reasonableness in Administrative Law: *Delta Air Lines Inc. v Lukacs*' (2018) 31 *Canadian Journal of Administrative Law & Practice* 209, discussed further in Chapter 4.3.3.

[186] David Stratas, '"It All Depends on the Circumstances": The Decline of Doctrine on the Grounds and Intensity of Review' in Mark Elliott, Jason Varuhas and Shona Wilson-Stark eds, *The Unity of Public Law? Doctrinal, Theoretical and Comparative Perspectives* (Hart, Oxford, 2018), 219, 226.

taken by decision-makers who do not have inappropriate prior knowledge of the individual concerned; this has an effect on how administrative decision-making may be structured. Under the 'institutional structures' heading I have also grouped the law relating to retention of discretion: a decision-maker must not delegate their powers, or fetter them, and so on. In Chapter 3 I move to consider 'procedural fairness', by which I mean the law relating to the procedures that decision-makers must follow in order to reach lawful decisions. The concern of Chapter 4 is 'substantive review'. Under this heading, I group judicial scrutiny of jurisdictional errors—factual and legal in nature—judicial review for abuse of discretion and relevancy and propriety. Remedies is the subject of Chapter 5, the law relating to the manner in which judges provide redress for breaches of the principles of institutional structures, procedural fairness or substantive review, with restrictions on remedies—such as the exhaustion principle and privative clauses—covered in Chapter 6. Then, in Chapter 7, I outline the law on the scope of judicial review of administrative action: the extent to which private bodies are subject to judicial oversight when exercising public functions; and whether judicial review extends to the exercise of private law powers (such as entering contracts) by public bodies.

This, then, is my *fresh framework* for contemporary administrative law: four values holding together legal principles across the vast field of judicial review of administrative action. The framework being constructed of the core features of the subject, its geographical scope extends to Australia, Canada, England and Wales, Ireland and New Zealand.

In Chapter 8, I address how judges should respond to situations of potential conflict between the values. I argue that judges ought to reconcile the values. I also demonstrate the feasibility of this approach by particular reference to the contested area of legitimate expectation.[187] In Chapter 9, I assess my approach against a set of criteria—fit, transparency, coherence and morality. The application of the last of these also allows me to argue that the modern law of judicial review of administrative action is morally desirable, because judicial solicitude for individual self-realisation, good administration, electoral legitimacy and decisional autonomy facilitates the flourishing of individuals, of public administration and of the liberal-democratic system.

[187] Daly, 'A Pluralist Account of Deference and Legitimate Expectations' (n 91).

2
Institutional Structures

In this chapter, I am concerned with the structure of administrative decision-making institutions. Two general aspects of this important topic are particularly relevant to the law of judicial review of administrative action. First, the no-bias principle ensures that decision-making is impartial, by preventing decision-makers from acting where their personal interests, conduct or history could conceivably raise a concern about their ability to make a dispassionate decision on the merits. Second, the principle that a decision-maker must retain their discretion prevents decision-makers from delegating their powers (subject to an exception in the case of government ministers) and limits the scope for the development of policies about how discretionary powers will be exercised in the future. These principles can be understood as being structured by the values of individual self-realisation, good administration, electoral legitimacy and decisional autonomy.

One preliminary comment is in order: there are very few rules, properly so called, in this area. Once one excludes the rule—operative in some jurisdictions only—that a decision-maker with a personal interest in a matter is automatically disqualified from adjudicating on the matter, the law of institutional structures is entirely context-sensitive. The contextual reasonable apprehension of bias standard applies to attempts to disqualify a decision-maker on the basis of lack of impartiality. Whether a decision-maker has fettered their discretion depends upon a contextual analysis of the statutory discretionary power at issue. Occasionally the case law and commentary refers to the 'rule' against bias, or the no-fettering 'rule'. To avoid confusion, however, I will refer to them as 'principles'.

As to the no-bias principle, a brief introductory remark, from a historical perspective, is appropriate. Previously, the no-bias principle was one of the two rules of natural justice. These were *nemo iudex in sua causa* (no one shall be a judge in their own cause) and *audi alteram partem* (hear both sides). Contemporary understandings of the latter rule will be addressed in detail in Chapter 3, under the label of procedural fairness. They have, however, a shared history, which it is convenient to note at this stage. When the prerogative writ of certiorari was used to control judicial decision-making, the courts originally required strict compliance by decision-makers with the rules of natural justice. Administrative decision-makers whose decisions were subject to the writ of certiorari had to respect the same standards of natural justice as courts. Gradually and incrementally, over a period of many years, the courts extended the scope of the prerogative writs to cover a broad range of administrative decision-making. One consequence was that

Understanding Administrative Law in the Common Law World. Paul Daly, Oxford University Press. © Paul Daly 2021.
DOI: 10.1093/oso/9780192896919.003.0002

it became entirely unrealistic to require all decision-makers to respect the rules of natural justice to the letter—to so require would be to bring the machinery of the administrative state to a grinding halt. Instead, the courts began to relax the rules of natural justice, taking an avowedly context-sensitive approach to their application, whereby the exigencies of natural justice would vary from case to case.[1] The discussion of the no-bias principle in this chapter and procedural fairness in Chapter 3 will reveal how the contemporary contextual approach operates and how it can be understood in light of the four values of individual self-realisation, good administration, electoral legitimacy and decisional autonomy.

2.1 The Structure of the No-Bias Principle

Impartial, unbiased decision-making is a basic requirement of contemporary administrative law. Different jurisdictions formulate the test for impartiality differently, but the 'semantic differences'[2] should not obscure the general principle that where a decision-maker's participation in a decision would give rise to a reasonable apprehension of bias, they must recuse themselves unless the party or parties concerned waive their right to object. Such is the importance of impartiality to the legal system that the test operates in cases where bias might merely be perceived: 'it is not merely of some importance but is of fundamental importance that justice should not only be done, but should manifestly and undoubtedly be seen to be done.'[3] The concern here is with apprehended bias, rather than actual bias; it involves an objective inquiry into all relevant contextual information, not a subjective inquiry into the state of mind of the decision-maker.[4] Moreover, the context-sensitive manner in which the no-bias principle is now applied to administrative decision-making means that the precise semantic formulation of the test is of relatively minor importance.

The basic structure of the no-bias principle can be understood in terms of the four values of individual self-realisation, good administration, electoral legitimacy and decisional autonomy. To begin with, the no-bias principle does not operate as strictly in respect of administrative decision-making as it does in respect of judicial decision-making, a reflection of the distinct roles of the courts and administrative

[1] The definitive treatment remains David Mullan, 'Fairness: The New Natural Justice' (1975) 25 *University of Toronto Law Journal* 281.

[2] *Saxmere Co Ltd v Wool Board Disestablishment Co Ltd* [2009] NZSC 72; [2010] 1 NZLR 35 [3] per Blanchard J.

[3] *R v Sussex Justices, ex parte McCarthy* [1924] 1 KB 256, 259 per Lord Hewart CJ. In the foundational case on direct interests in litigation, *Dimes v Proprietors of Grand Junction Canal* (1852) 3 HL Cas 759, it was the 'appearance of labouring under' a personal interest that grounded a finding of a reasonable apprehension of bias against the judge.

[4] See e.g. *Michael Wilson & Partners Ltd v Nicholls* (2011) 244 CLR 427, 437–438 per Gummow ACJ and Hayne, Crennan and Bell JJ.

decision-makers: 'What is to be expected of a judge in judicial proceedings or a decision-maker in quasi-judicial proceedings will often be different from what is expected of a person making a purely administrative decision.'[5] Despite the judicial origins of the no-bias principle, 'the courts have been tactful in not clumsily treating administrative processes as lesser forms of a judicial trial'.[6] In general, the 'content' of the no-bias principle is 'flexible, varying with the factual and legal circumstances of the case ... at its most demanding when applied to the judiciary, and at its least demanding when applied to informal, low-level administrative bodies'.[7]

Nonetheless, the no-bias principle remains important, in part as a device to serve the 'overriding public interest that there should be confidence in the integrity of the administration of justice',[8] which applies also to 'the integrity and fairness of those officials and statutory committees who are the repositories of executive discretion'.[9] This can be understood as serving the interests of effective and efficient public administration, in that biased decision-making is likely to corrode public trust in government over time. Similarly, one might suggest that biased decision-making is more likely to be inaccurate. As biased decision-makers might well favour their personal interests over the accurate implementation of the statutory scheme, the no-bias principle can be understood as operating so as to ensure respect for the decisions of elected representatives, who have laid down in legislation the 'authoritative standards by which the cases should be decided'.[10] Both good administration and electoral legitimacy can thus be understood to support the no-bias principle.

Concern for individual self-realisation can also be understood to support the no-bias principle. Lord Hope of Craighead noted in *R v Bow Street Magistrates, ex parte Pinochet (No. 2)* that the applicant was '*entitled* to the judgment of an impartial and independent tribunal' on the question at issue.[11] In their comprehensive review of the cases on bias, an extremely strong bench of the Court of Appeal of England and Wales emphasised at the outset the personal interest of individuals in impartial decision-making, describing it as 'fundamental': allowing 'any judicial decision to be influenced by partiality or prejudice deprives the litigant of the important right' to a fair hearing by an impartial tribunal,[12] thereby failing to treat them with respect. The Court was concerned here with

[5] *Hot Holdings Pty Ltd v Creasy* [2002] HCA 51; (2002) 210 CLR 438 [70] per McHugh J.

[6] Denis Galligan, *Due Process and Fair Procedures: A Study of Administrative Procedures* (Clarendon, Oxford, 1996), 444.

[7] Philip Joseph, *Constitutional and Administrative Law in New Zealand* 4th edn (Thomson Reuters, Wellington, 2014), 1076.

[8] *R v Gough* [1993] AC 646, 659. See similarly *Gillies v Secretary of State for Work and Pensions* [2006] UKHL 2; [2006] 1 WLR 781 [23].

[9] *Meadowvale Stud Farm Ltd v Stratford County Council* [1979] 1 NZLR 342, 348 per Mahon J.

[10] Galligan (n 6) 441.

[11] [2000] 1 AC 119, 143. Emphasis added.

[12] *Locabail (UK) Ltd v Bayfield Properties Ltd* [1999] EWCA Civ 3004; [2000] IRLR 96, at pp 98–99. See e.g. *Auckland Casino Ltd v Casino Control Authority* [1995] 1 NZLR 142; *Orange Ltd v Director of Telecommunications (No. 2)* [2000] 4 IR 159.

bias in the context of judicial decision-making but the basic point holds for administrative decision-makers too.[13] To permit an administrative decision-maker to favour their own interests over those of an applicant for a licence, a recipient of a benefit or a subject of a disciplinary complaint has the potential to undermine the protection of those interests which support individuals' ability to plan their affairs.

2.1.1 Waiver

That violations of the no-bias principle may be waived[14] serves to emphasise the importance of individual choice in the operation of the no-bias principle. From the availability of waiver one might conclude that unbiased decision-making is first and foremost a concern of the individual subject to the jurisdiction of the administrative decision-maker: 'denying a person a fair hearing is a wrong that is personal to that person.'[15] Waivers may not be made lightly, however, as one would expect given the force the values of good administration and electoral legitimacy can be understood to exert in the context of the no-bias principle. As has been said, 'the entitlement to a manifestly impartial and independent judicial and like decision is not one that belongs only to the parties to the proceeding. It also belongs to citizens.'[16] Accordingly, a waiver must be 'clear and unequivocal' and 'made with full knowledge of all the facts relevant to the decision whether to waive or not',[17] which can be understood as striking a balance between the protection of individual interests and the demands of effective and efficient public administration and accurate decision-making.

[13] This might be thought to be an example of rules applicable to courts of law applying with equal force to administrative decision-makers, which might in turn be thought to undermine any suggestion that they play distinct roles. This would be to overstate the point. Philip Joseph, 'The Bias Rules in Administrative Law Reconsidered' [2005] *New Zealand Law Journal* 110, distinguishes 'presumptive' from 'apparent' bias, the former arising where a direct interest is involved and leading to automatic disqualification, the latter (requiring a context-sensitive analysis) in all other cases. The most that can be said is that the rules relating to 'presumptive' bias are identical in some jurisdictions as between judges and administrative decision-makers. The rules relating to 'apparent' bias clearly are not. Moreover, it would be perfectly possible to abolish 'presumptive' bias as a distinct category, with 'apparent' bias instead applicable in all cases. See e.g. *Ebner v Official Trustee in Bankruptcy* [2000] HCA 63; (2000) 176 ALR 643; *Saxmere Co Ltd v Wool Board Disestablishment Co Ltd* (n 1) [42] per McGrath J. If so, then a context-sensitive approach to the no-bias principle as applied to direct interests could lead to different results in cases involving judges as distinct from cases involving administrative decision-makers.

[14] See e.g. *Wakefield Local Board of Health v West Riding and Grimsby Rly Co* (1865) 1 QB 84; *R v Nailsworth Licensing Justices, ex parte Bird* [1953] 1 WLR 1046; *Muir v Franklin Licensing Committee* [1954] NZLR 152; *Corrigan v Irish Land Commission* [1977] IR 317; *Auckland Casino Ltd v Casino Control Authority* (n 12); *MH6 v Mental Health Review Board* [2009] VSCA 184; (2009) 25 VR 382.

[15] *R (Hill) v Institute of Chartered Accountants in England and Wales* [2013] EWCA Civ 555; [2014] 1 WLR 86 [46] per Beatson LJ.

[16] *Smits v Roach* [2006] HCA 36; (2006) 227 CLR 423, 465 per Kirby J.

[17] *Locabail (UK) Ltd v Bayfield Properties Ltd* (n 12) 100.

2.1.2 *De Minimis* Exception

Not all situations in which an administrative decision-maker has an interest in the outcome of a particular decision will require recusal. Some courts have hewed to an automatic disqualification rule: where a decision-maker has a direct interest in a matter, they are automatically disqualified.[18] However, the harsh effects of this rule have been tempered by the development of a *de minimis* exception pursuant to which interests 'incapable' of having any effect on the decision do not disqualify the decision-maker,[19] as in *Dublin and County Broadcasting Ltd v Independent Radio and Television Commission*, where residual legal rights in shares of which a member of the Commission had divested himself were too remote to justify a finding of bias.[20] Similarly, in a Canadian case involving the power of a regulator of the legal profession to recoup the costs of disciplinary proceedings from a disciplined lawyer, the potential financial interest that members of the disciplinary tribunal would have (in, for instance, a potential reduction in their annual membership fees) was far too remote to exert any influence on the tribunal members' decision.[21] In Canada, there is no automatic disqualification rule,[22] but the difference in practice between the automatic disqualification rule and the application of the reasonable apprehension of bias standard to direct interests is likely to be minimal, as it would be 'odd ... if the two doctrines rendered different results'.[23] A *de minimis* exception can readily be understood in terms of administrative law values, as remote interests are extremely unlikely to cause decision-makers to favour their interests over those of individuals, to compromise the accuracy of decision-making or to undermine the efficient and effective accomplishment of the decision-maker's objectives.

2.1.3 Elected Officials

In situations involving elected officials, the threshold for bias changes to make it more difficult to demonstrate a breach of the no-bias principle. The elevated threshold can be understood, primarily, as justifiable given the electoral legitimacy

[18] Joseph (n 13).

[19] *Locabail (UK) Ltd v Bayfield Properties Ltd* (n 12) 99.

[20] Unreported, (Irish) High Court, 12 May 1989.

[21] *Pearlman v Manitoba Law Society* [1991] 2 SCR 869. See also *R (Project Management Institute) v Minister for the Cabinet Office* [2016] EWCA Civ 21; [2016] 1 WLR 1737 (albeit a case of an indirect interest). See similarly the amusing case of *Gammie v Turner* 2013 ONSC 4563, where a businessman's membership of an organisation distributing government largesse for a public festival did not cause a conflict of interest under legislation. Compare *Meadowvale Stud Farm Ltd v Stratford County Council* (n 9) where members were disqualified because of the pecuniary interests they enjoyed as shareholders in a company.

[22] *Old St Boniface Residents' Association v Winnipeg (City)* [1990] 3 SCR 1170, 1196.

[23] *R (Kaur) v Institute of Legal Executives Appeal Tribunal* [2011] EWCA Civ 1168 [44] per Rix LJ.

of the officials involved (and those who chose to empower them by statute). Where the legislature has confided a discretionary power in a minister, '[i]t would be naïve to suppose that Parliament can have meant Ministers to refrain from forming and expressing, even strongly, views' that they hold about questions submitted to them.[24] Municipal politicians, similarly, are not required to 'cast aside views on ... policy they will have formed when seeking election or when acting as councillors'.[25] Accordingly, an applicant must demonstrate that an elected official had a 'closed mind' in order to justify judicial intervention,[26] which will only be possible in cases where the official was 'so committed to a conclusion already formed as to be incapable of alteration, whatever evidence or arguments may be presented'.[27] A striking example of what it takes to meet this high threshold is *Isitt v Quill*, where a majority of the licensing committee who decided not to renew liquor licences in the committee's district were publicly pledged prohibitionists.[28] Where elected officials are concerned, 'keeping an open mind does not mean an empty mind',[29] allowing them a relatively large margin of appreciation consistent with their electoral mandate and role in democratic governance.

Effective and efficient public administration can be understood to provide further justification for the different threshold for bias in respect of elected officials. For electing or appointing representatives to regulatory bodies may make those bodies more able to achieve their objectives: 'No doubt many boards will operate more effectively with representation from all segments of society who are interested in the operations of the Board.'[30] This is not to sacrifice the interests of individuals

[24] *CREEDNZ Inc v Governor General* [1981] 1 NZLR 172, 179 per Cooke P. See also *R v Amber Valley District Council, ex parte Jackson* [1985] 1 WLR 298; *Mulcreevy v Minister for the Environment* [2004] 1 ILRM 419, 437.

[25] *R (Lewis) v Persimmon Homes* [2008] EWCA Civ 746; [2008] LGR 781, 802 per Pill LJ. See similarly ibid, 809 per Rix LJ: 'there can be no pretence that such democratically accountable decision-makers are intended to be independent and impartial just as if they were judges or quasi-judges. They will have political allegiances, and their politics will involve policies, and these will be known'; *Old St Boniface Residents' Association v Winnipeg (City)* (n 22) 1192 per Sopinka J: 'I must assume that the Legislature was aware that in this capacity the members of Council will have fought an election in which the matter upon which they are called upon to decide may have been debated and on which the would-be councillors may have taken a stand some pro and some con. Indeed, the election of a particular councillor may have depended on the position taken.'

[26] See e.g. *Condron v National Assembly for Wales* [2006] EWCA Civ 1573; [2007] LGR 87, 102–103. In Canada, conduct prior to an adjudicative hearing is subject to the 'closed mind' standard but conduct during the hearing is subject to the ordinary standard for reasonable apprehension of bias. See *Newfoundland Telephone Co v Newfoundland (Board of Commissioners of Public Utilities)* [1992] 1 SCR 623.

[27] *Minister for Immigration and Multicultural Affairs v Jia Legeng* [2001] HCA 17; (2001) 205 CLR 507, 532 per Gleeson CJ and Gummow J. See also *Franklin v Minister of Town and Country Planning* [1948] AC 87, 102–103; *McGovern v Ku-ring-gai Council* [2008] NSWCA 209; (2008) 72 NSWLR 504, 508; *Back Country Helicopters Ltd v Minister of Conservation* [2013] NZHC 982; [2013] NZAR 1474, 1507.

[28] (1893) 11 NZLR 224. See similarly *Beaverford v Thorhild (County No 7)* 2013 ABCA 6.

[29] *R v Secretary of State for the Environment, ex parte Brent London Borough Council* [1982] QB 593, 643 per Ackner LJ.

[30] *Newfoundland Telephone Co v Newfoundland (Board of Commissioners of Public Utilities)* (n 26) 635.

on the altar of electoral legitimacy and good administration: the no-bias rule still applies to protect individual self-realisation, just with less force than usual, in order to take account of concerns for electoral legitimacy and good administration. The different threshold can be understood to reflect the striking of a balance between the values.

2.1.4 Principle of Necessity

Decision-making that would raise a reasonable apprehension of bias may sometimes be permissible.[31] Where a decision-maker would otherwise be unable to render a decision, the principle of necessity will permit them to act notwithstanding their bias. This principle can be understood to sound in respect for the role of elected representatives. Were the decision-maker identified by the legislature unable to act by reason of bias, the power vested in them would be nugatory, which would frustrate the intention of those law-makers who adopted the statutory provisions in issue.[32]

2.2 Determinations as to whether Conduct Leads to Bias

The four values can be understood not only to influence the structure of the no-bias principle but also to influence why and when particular conduct on the part of an administrative decision-maker will lead to a finding that they ought to have recused themselves. Although '[t]his is a corner of the law in which the context, and the particular circumstances, are of supreme importance',[33] which makes generalisation hazardous,[34] the influence of the four values can nonetheless be felt in determining whether there is a reasonable apprehension of bias.

Some preliminary analytical observations are appropriate. Often, the test for bias is expressed in terms of the view a 'reasonable observer' would take of the relevant facts. But the suggestion that the so-called 'reasonable observer' might actually be a real person is a source of intractable difficulty in this area.[35] This

[31] See e.g. *O'Neill v Beaumont Hospital Board* [1990] 1 ILRM 419; *Laws v Australian Broadcasting Tribunal* (1990) 170 CLR 70; *Day v Saunders* [2015] NSWCA 324; (2015) 90 NSWLR 764.

[32] *Meerabux v Attorney General of Belize* [2005] UKPC 12; [2005] 2 AC 513 [28]. But this principle has been described as 'ancient and now limited', on the basis that it will typically be possible to make alternative arrangements for the making of a decision: *O'Callaghan v Mahon* [2007] IESC 17; [2008] 2 IR 514, 641 per Hardiman J.

[33] *Man O'War Station Ltd v Auckland City Council (No 1)* [2002] UKPC 28; [2002] 3 NZLR 577 [11].

[34] See e.g. *Lower Hutt City Council v Bank* [1974] 1 NZLR 545, 549 per McCarthy P: 'the extent to which this fundamental principle [against bias] applies must be governed by the relevant circumstances, including, especially, the statutory provisions relating to the function.'

[35] Abimbola A Olowofoyeku, 'Bias and the Informed Observer: A Call for a Return to *Gough*' (2009) 68 *Cambridge Law Journal* 388, 393–396.

'reasonable observer' is purely a judicial construct; indeed, in attributing various degrees of knowledge to the hypothetical observer, a judge may simply be 'holding up a mirror to himself'.[36] Although it is more accurate to say that 'the court in cases such as these personifies the reasonable man'[37], any reference to the 'fictional postulate'[38] of the hypothetical reasonable person 'encourages the conflation of "descriptive" attributes of the person with the normative standard of behaviour'.[39] A court faced with an allegation of biased decision-making does not ask: 'Would the hypothetical reasonable person think the decision-maker was not impartial?' Rather, the question is: *Should* the decision-maker recuse themselves? Or, as the High Court of Australia would have it, '[t]here must be an articulation of the logical connection between the matter and the feared deviation from the course of deciding the case on its merits'.[40] The relevant question is the judge's considered view of the decision-maker's ability to conduct a fair proceeding. As Gageler J put it in an Australian case in which a prosecutor had also participated in the adjudication of proceedings she had earlier been involved in:

> [A] person who has been the adversary of another person in the same or related proceedings can ordinarily be expected to have developed in that role a frame of mind which is incompatible with the exercise of that degree of neutrality required dispassionately to weigh legal, factual and policy considerations relevant to the making of a decision which *has the potential adversely to affect interests of that other person*.[41]

Thus, 'personifying the reasonable man',[42] the reviewing court determines whether a decision-maker *ought* to have recused themselves. The inquiry in bias cases is always 'highly fact-specific',[43] the 'result of composed and considered appraisal of the

[36] Lord Rodger, 'Bias and Conflicts of Interest: Challenges for Today's Decision-Makers', 24th Sultan Azlan Shaw Lecture. See similarly *British American Tobacco Australia Services Ltd v Laurie* [2011] HCA 2; (2011) 242 CLR 382, 406 per French CJ: 'interposition of the fair-minded person could never disguise the reality that it is the assessment of the court dealing with a claim of apparent bias that determines the claim'.

[37] *R v Gough* (n 8) per Lord Goff.

[38] *Smits v Roach* (n 16) 457 per Kirby J.

[39] Mayo Moran, *Rethinking the Reasonable Person: An Egalitarian Reconstruction of the Objective Standard* (Oxford University Press, Oxford, 2003), 9. See similarly Simon Atrill, 'Who is the "Fair-Minded and Informed Observer"? Bias after *Magill*' (2003) 62 *Cambridge Law Journal* 679. See also *Hot Holdings Pty Ltd v Creasy* (n 5) [48] per Gaudron, Gummow and Hayne JJ, warning that it would 'be wrong to place too much emphasis on metaphorical references ...', to a decision being 'infected' or 'tainted' by bias.

[40] *Ebner v Official Trustee in Bankruptcy* [2000] HCA 63; (2000) 205 CLR 337, 345, approved in *Saxmere Co Ltd v Wool Board Disestablishment Co Ltd* (n 1). See also *CNY17 v Minister for Immigration and Border Protection* [2019] HCA 50 [21], [69]. For a not dissimilar formulation, see *R (Royal Brompton and Harefield NHS Foundation Trust) v Joint Committee of Primary Care Trusts* [2012] EWCA Civ 472 [125] per Arden LJ.

[41] *Isbester v Knox City Council* [2015] HCA 20; (2015) 255 CLR 135, 157. Emphasis added.

[42] *Locabail (UK) Ltd v Bayfield Properties Ltd* (n 12) 101.

[43] *Wewaykum Indian Band v Canada* 2003 SCC 45; [2003] 2 SCR 259 [77].

relevant facts',[44] taking account of the whole context.[45] 'There are no shortcuts',[46] because '[t]hese are not easy cases'[47] and they require 'rigorous' analysis.[48] Prejudicial comments before or during a decision-making process,[49] prior involvement in the decision-making process,[50] intermingling of investigative and adjudicative functions,[51] a prior relationship with a party,[52] pre-judgement of the issues[53] or overly vigorous prosecution[54] can in principle make a decision-maker's position untenable.[55] This can be a case-specific or general inquiry.[56]

There are two difficulties peculiar to administrative law with which judges have had to grapple in bias cases. The first relates to prior knowledge administrative decision-makers will have of their area of regulation (and perhaps of individual regulatees); the second relates to statutory authorisation of decision-making structures that would ordinarily create a reasonable apprehension of bias.

2.2.1 Prior Knowledge

Prior relationships will almost inevitably develop in contemporary administrative decision-making structures, because 'it is more than likely that the same decision-makers will have repeated dealings with a given party on a number of occasions and for a variety of reasons'.[57] Overlapping functions are also

[44] *Re Purcell's Application* [2008] NICA 11 [22] per Kerr LCJ.

[45] *Imperial Oil Ltd v Quebec (Minister of the Environment)* 2003 SCC 58; [2003] 2 SCR 624 [31] per LeBel J.

[46] *Wewaykum Indian Band v Canada* (n 43) [77].

[47] *Belize Bank Ltd v Attorney General of Belize* [2011] UKPC 36 [72] per Lord Dyson.

[48] *Muir v Commissioner of Inland Revenue* [2007] NZCA 334; [2007] 3 NZLR 495 [62] per Hammond J.

[49] See e.g. *Turner v Allison* [1971] NZLR 833; *Newfoundland Telephone Co v Newfoundland (Board of Commissioners of Public Utilities)* (n 26); *Minister for Immigration and Multicultural Affairs v Jia Legeng* [2001] HCA 17; (2001) 205 CLR 507; *Porter v Magill* [2001] UKHL 67; [2002] 2 AC 537; *O'Driscoll v Law Society* [2007] IEHC 352.

[50] See e.g. *R v Gaisford* [1892] 1 QBD 381; *Cooper v Wilson* [1937] 2 KB 309; *R v Pwllheli Justices, ex parte Soane* [1948] 2 All ER 815; *Stollery v Greyhound Racing Control Board* (1973) 128 CLR 509; *Heneghan v Western Regional Fisheries Board* [1986] ILRM 225.

[51] See e.g. *Frome United Breweries Co Ltd v Bath Justices* [1926] AC 586; *Stephen v College of Physicians and Surgeons (Sask)* (1989) 61 DLR (4th) 496; *Isbester v Knox City Council* (n 41).

[52] See e.g. *Leeson v General Council of Medical Education and Registration* [1889] 43 Ch D 366; *Metropolitan Properties (FGC) Ltd v Lannon* [1969] 1 QB 577; *Murdoch v New Zealand Milk Board* [1982] 2 NZLR 108; *Wewaykum Indian Band v Canada* (n 43); *R (Kaur) v Institute of Legal Executives Appeal Tribunal* (n 23).

[53] See e.g. *English v Bay of Islands Licensing Committee* [1921] NZLR 127; *R v Nailsworth Licensing Justices, ex parte Bird* (n 14); *Beaverford v Thorhild (County No. 7)* (n 28).

[54] See e.g. *College of Physicians & Surgeons (Ontario) v Casullo* [1977] 2 SCR 2; *Re Refugee Review Tribunal, ex parte H* [2001] HCA 28; (2001) 179 ALR 425.

[55] The 'in principle' qualification is important: in many of the cases listed, the court held that the rule against bias had not been breached.

[56] See e.g. *2747-3174 Québec Inc v Quebec (Régie des permis d'alcool)* [1996] 3 SCR 919.

[57] *Brosseau v Alberta Securities Commission* [1989] 1 SCR 301, 313. See also *Ó Ceallaigh v An Bord Altranais* [2009] IEHC 470.

inevitable, as the rise of the modern administrative state has 'deranged our three-branch legal theories'.[58] Financial regulators, for instance, 'are involved in overseeing the filing of prospectuses, regulating the trade in securities, registering persons and companies who trade in securities, carrying out investigations and enforcing the [statutory] provisions'.[59] Members of administrative decision-making bodies will often have gained expertise through their work in a particular field, possibly due to having exercised multiple functions: 'the individuals concerned will often be particularly suited to adjudicate on the matter precisely because of the experience and wisdom on the topic which they have accumulated in those other roles'.[60]

In such circumstances, some degree of pre-judgement of relevant issues or prior involvement in some aspects of matters giving rise to dispute is only to be expected,[61] as the decision-maker, which is 'expected to build up "expertise"', 'will bring to the task' at hand 'a great deal of information and ideas which have been accumulated or formed in the course of deciding other applications'.[62] And it may be entirely natural—indeed, a necessary component of a decision-maker's statutory role—for members of regulatory bodies to make public comments, to stimulate debate, that might indicate how they intend to develop the bodies' policies in the future. As the High Court of Australia noted, in relation to a body responsible for matters relating to equal pay:

> It is not necessarily out of place, and indeed it might be expected that a member of the Commission from time to time in the course of discharging his duties should express more or less tentative views as to the desirability of change in some principle of wage fixation. The very nature of the office of a member of the Commission requires that he should apply his mind constantly to general questions of arbitral policy and consider the lines along which the processes of conciliation and arbitration for the prevention and settlement of industrial disputes ought to move.[63]

[58] *Federal Trade Commission v Ruberoid Co* 343 US 470, 487 (1952) per Jackson J. See generally Eoin Carolan, *The New Separation of Powers* (Oxford University Press, Oxford, 2009).

[59] *Brosseau v Alberta Securities Commission* (n 57).

[60] *R v Secretary of State for the Home Department, ex parte Al-Hasan* [2005] UKHL 13; [2005] 1 WLR 688, 692 per Lord Rodger of Earlsferry. See e.g. *Devonport Borough Council v Local Government Commission* [1989] 2 NZLR 203; *Francis v Canada (Immigration and Citizenship)* 2012 FC 1141 [37].

[61] See e.g. *Timmins v Gomerly* [1999] EWCA Civ 3004 [85]; *Pring v Wanganui District Council* [1999] NZCA 173 [11] per Blanchard J; *Riverside Casino Ltd v Moxon* [2001] 2 NZLR 78, 100 per Gault J; *Muin v Refugee Review Tribunal* [2002] HCA 30; (2002) 190 ALR 601, 661 per Hayne J.

[62] *Minister for Immigration and Multicultural Affairs v Jia Legeng* [2001] HCA 17; (2001) 205 CLR 507, 562–563 per Hayne J

[63] *R v Commonwealth Conciliation and Arbitration Commission, ex parte Angliss Group* (1969) 122 CLR 546, 553. But this does not necessarily license opinionated commentary on controversial topics. See e.g. *MZWCL v Minister for Immigration and Multicultural and Indigenous Affairs* [2006] FCA 635.

Perfect impartiality—with administrative decision-makers walled off from the outside world altogether—would in fact be inimical to effective and efficient public administration and accurate decision-making. In this regard, moreover, an administrative decision-maker is unlike a court, a point relating to the distinct roles played by distinct bodies, which can be understood in terms of the decisional autonomy of administrative decision-makers. Accordingly, good administration, electoral legitimacy and decisional autonomy can be understood to be important considerations in this area.

Just such considerations were live issues in *Gillies v Secretary of State for Work and Pensions*.[64] Here, a doctor who provided independent expert evidence in benefits cases also sat as a member of a disability allowance appeal tribunal. Her adjudicative work often required her to resolve conflicts of evidence between claimants and doctors who performed similar work to her. The House of Lords held that this did not give rise to a reasonable apprehension of bias. In *both* her roles, as an independent expert *and* as an adjudicator, the doctor was 'called upon to exercise an independent professional judgment, drawing upon her medical knowledge and her experience' and the advantage of her professional experience was that she 'would be just as well placed to spot weaknesses in these reports as to spot their strengths'.[65] Indeed, '[t]o have such expertise available on the tribunal can only be an advantage to it'.[66] As Lord Hope explained, her experience 'was an asset which was available, through her, for the other tribunal members to draw upon when they were considering the whole of the evidence'.[67] Considerations of accurate decision-making and effective and efficient public administration can be understood as having influenced the analysis here, with the distinctiveness of administrative (as opposed to judicial) decision-making also of significance.

Individual self-realisation can also have traction in this area. Consider the contrasting result reached in *R v Secretary of State for the Home Department, ex parte Al-Hasan*.[68] At issue here was an order to squat search almost 200 prisoners in a high security prison. Squat searches are highly invasive forms of strip search which require subjects to squat so as to expose their anus and genitals (and, so the thinking goes, any contraband hidden there). The decision to order the search was taken on the basis of positive indications given by sniffer dogs. When the modalities of the implementation were discussed with the prison Governor, who ordered the search and signed off on the modalities, the Deputy Governor was present. Subsequently, prisoners who refused to submit to the squat search were subject to disciplinary proceedings. These disciplinary proceedings were heard by none other than the same Deputy Governor.

64 [2006] UKHL 2; [2006] 1 WLR 781.
65 Ibid, [20] per Lord Hope.
66 Ibid, [40] per Lady Hale.
67 Ibid, [21].
68 (n 60)

According to the House of Lords, the Deputy Governor was disqualified by reason of his prior involvement, for in Lord Brown's words, 'by the very fact of his presence when the search order was confirmed', he 'gave it his tacit assent and endorsement'.[69] Notably, these searches involved direct interference with privacy interests and the consequence of refusing to obey the order could have been further detention,[70] and these individual interests can be understood as having weighed heavily in the balance.

But their Lordships recognised that prior involvement in a disciplinary process could never be an absolute bar to playing an adjudicative role. In prisons, effective and efficient operation of disciplinary processes requires prior knowledge of the prison environment in general and the circumstances leading up to contested events in particular:

> [I]t was clearly necessary that sensitive security information was not disclosed to the prisoners in the course of the adjudications and, to guard against that risk, any governor trying these charges would necessarily have had to be given in advance of the hearing precisely the same sort of background information about the search as [the Deputy Governor] already had.[71]

Effective and accurate decision-making would not, however, have been compromised by a finding of bias in this case, as another governor could have been brought in—from another prison if necessary—to adjudicate the dispute.[72] As Lady Hale put it, 'it must have been practicable for someone who had not been so closely associated with giving the order to have conducted the adjudications based upon it'.[73]

One way of understanding the result in *Al-Hasan* is that the individual interests of the prisoners ultimately outweighed considerations of effectiveness and efficiency, especially as a workable alternative mode of decision—untainted by prior involvement—was available. In *Gillies*, by contrast, such weighty considerations sounding in individual self-realisation were quite absent.

2.2.2 Statutory Authorisation

On occasion, conduct that would ordinarily give rise to a perception of partiality will be authorised by statute, expressly or by necessary implication:[74]

[69] Ibid, [39].

[70] Though, on the facts, only one of the prisoners was given additional detention; the other had some privileges revoked.

[71] *R v Secretary of State for the Home Department, ex parte Al-Hasan* (n 60).

[72] Ibid, 41.

[73] Ibid, 16.

[74] See generally *Rich v Christchurch Girls' High School Board of Governors (No 1)* [1974] 1 NZLR 1.

> Administrative tribunals are created for a variety of reasons and to respond to a variety of needs. In establishing such tribunals, the legislator is free to choose the structure of the administrative body. The legislator will determine, among other things, its composition and the particular degrees of formality required in its operation. In some cases, the legislator will determine that it is desirable, in achieving the ends of the statute, to allow for an overlap of functions which in normal judicial proceedings would be kept separate. In assessing the activities of administrative tribunals, the courts must be sensitive to the nature of the body created by the legislator. If a certain degree of overlapping of functions is authorized by statute, then, to the extent that it is authorized, it will not generally be subject to the doctrine of 'reasonable apprehension of bias' *per se*.[75]

If so, it is natural for courts mindful of the desirability of respecting the decisions of a democratically legitimate parliamentary majority to give effect to legislative choice and permit the conduct complained of.[76] Where the legislature has provided for an administrative mechanism to determine rights and liabilities, the indirect interests that, say, members of a self-regulated profession might have in disciplinary matters, cannot justify judicial intervention to quash a decision on the ground of bias:[77] 'the rules of natural justice cannot be invoked to frustrate the intended operation of a statute which sets up a tribunal and requires it to perform the statutory functions entrusted to it.'[78]

These considerations were very much to the fore in *Belize Bank Ltd v Attorney General of Belize*.[79] Here, the new Prime Minister of Belize had been very critical of how his predecessor and the Bank had handled financial aid received from Venezuela. At one point he said his administration would 'continue to pursue justice on behalf of the Belizean people and will leave no stones unturned to bring to account those who have robbed the people of this country'. An investigation led the banking regulator to issue a directive requiring the payment to the government of some of the monies received. When the Bank appealed, the Prime Minister, who was also the Minister of Finance, acting through a delegate, named two members of the appeal board. Their impartiality was unsuccessfully challenged by the Bank. The advice of the Privy Council was that the Prime Minister's involvement in the

75 *Brosseau v Alberta Securities Commission* (n 57) 310 per L'Heureux-Dubé J. The same applies to independence, inasmuch as it is recognised as a legal principle distinct from the principle of impartiality. See especially *Ocean Port Hotel Ltd v British Columbia (General Manager, Liquor Control and Licensing Branch)* 2001 SCC 52; [2001] 2 SCR 781.

76 See e.g. *Jeffs v New Zealand Dairy Production Marketing Board* [1967] 1 AC 551; *Canadian Union of Public Employees v Ontario (Minister of Labour)* 2003 SCC 29; [2003] 1 SCR 539 [117]; *Imperial Oil Ltd v Quebec (Minister of the Environment)* (n 45) [33].

77 See e.g. *Pearlman v Manitoba Law Society* (n 21).

78 *Laws v Australian Broadcasting Tribunal* (n 31) 89 per Mason CJ and Brennan J.

79 [2011] UKPC 36.

appointments process—which in any event was only nominal—did not taint the appeal proceedings. As Lord Kerr emphasised:

> The dual role of the minister is critical in the overall consideration of this case, in the Board's opinion. As Prime Minister he had an obvious responsibility to recover money that he believed had been wrongly diverted from public resources. And as the Minister of Finance he was obliged to make appointments to the Board. In his position of Prime Minister he can hardly be criticised for informing the public that he was determined to recover the money for the people of Belize. This is the stuff of politics. Simply because he had a statutory obligation to make appointments to the Board, he should surely not be muzzled from public comment about what he perceived to be irregularities in relation to money which he believed should have been used for public works.[80]

There are two important points in this passage. One is that the Prime Minister was obliged by statute to make the appointments. To hold that his appointees were tainted by his prior statements would be to frustrate the considered choice of the legislature to vest decision-making authority in an elected official. More broadly, the effect of a finding in favour of the Bank on the bias ground would have been to stifle public debate about financial irregularities; it would have impinged upon the ability of an elected official to make public statements about matters of public importance.[81] Here, as in *Gillies* and *Al-Hasan*, the outcome can be understood as having been influenced by administrative law values, as electoral legitimacy can be understood to have featured prominently in the Privy Council's analysis.

2.3 Retention of Discretion

2.3.1 The No-Delegation Principle

If X has been identified by statute as the decision-maker who may exercise a given power, can Y exercise the power, or influence X's exercise of the power? The law in this area 'deals with the extent to which an authority may permit another to exercise a discretion entrusted by a statute to itself'.[82] It has been said that the scope of a

[80] Ibid, [46].

[81] As was said in an Australian case:

> There may be cases in which a decision-maker, especially a minister, may properly have regard to a wide range of considerations of which some may be seen as bearing upon such matters as the political fortunes of the government of which the minister is a member and, thus, affect the minister's continuance in office.

Hot Holdings Pty Ltd v Creasy (n 5) [50] per Gaudron, Gummow and Hayne JJ. See also *Franklin v Minister of Town and Country Planning* (n 27).

[82] John Willis, '*Delegatus non potest delegare*' (1943) 21 *Canadian Bar Review* 257.

decision-maker's ability to delegate its powers is a matter of statutory construction which does not require 'some overarching theory about the propriety of delegation'.[83] Even though the particularities of statutory language will play an important role in any given case concerning the permissibility of delegation, the four values can be understood to influence the structure of the no-delegation principle.

To begin with, the no-delegation principle can be understood as being heavily influenced by judicial respect for the decisions of elected representatives. For the starting point here is that the administrative decision-maker identified by the legislature as the appropriate body in which to vest a discretionary power should exercise that power itself, not divest itself of the power,[84] unless it has express or necessarily implicit authority to make such a delegation.[85]

Consider the settled principle that a decision-maker identified by statute should not act under the dictation of another body. The primary concern here can be understood to be with the danger that an administrative decision-maker's failure to exercise the powers vested in it will thwart the considered choices of the legislature. *Roncarelli v Duplessis*[86] is a famous example. Here, the plaintiff's licence had been cancelled by the Quebec Liquor Commission. The cancellation power had been exercised on the orders of the Premier of Quebec (because of Roncarelli's links to the Jehovah's Witnesses). But the Premier had no statutory authority to cancel a licence; the power was exercisable only by the Commission. There was no 'authority to enable the respondent ... to direct the cancellation of a permit ... On the contrary, the intent and purpose of [the statute] appears to be to place the complete control over the liquor traffic in Quebec in the hands of an independent commission.'[87] A statutory body such as the Commission 'cannot abdicate its own functions and powers and act upon such direction' from a third party.[88] To do so would negate the choice of the province's elected representatives to vest the decision-making power in an identified administrative decision-maker (here, the Commission).[89] Electoral legitimacy can, accordingly, be understood to influence the no-acting-under-dictation principle.

[83] *Minister for Local Government v South Sydney City Council* [2002] NSWCA 288; (2002) 55 NSWLR 381, 424 per Mason P. See similarly, *Dainford Ltd v Smith* (1985) 155 CLR 342, 351 per Mason J. See e.g. *King-Emperor v Sarma* [1945] AC 14.

[84] See e.g. *Canada (Attorney-General) v Brent* [1956] SCR 318; *Hawke's Bay Raw Milk Producers Co-operative Co Ltd v New Zealand Milk Board* [1961] NZLR 218; *Victoria Police Pistol Club Inc v Keogh* [1991] 2 VR 277. Moreover, where a delegate has the power to sub-delegate his power to another body, that other body 'cannot delegate their power to some other person or body': *Allingham v Minister of Agriculture* [1948] 1 All ER 780, 781.

[85] See e.g. *Reference re Regulations (Chemicals) under War Measures Act* [1943] 1 DLR 248; *O'Reilly v State Bank of Victoria* (1983) 153 CLR 1; *Re Patterson, ex parte Taylor* [2001] HCA 51; (2001) 207 CLR 391.

[86] *Roncarelli v Duplessis* [1959] SCR 121.

[87] Ibid, 154 per Martland J.

[88] Ibid, 157. See also *H Lavender & Son Ltd v Minister of Housing and Local Government* [1970] 1 WLR 1231 and, to the same effect, *Kerridge v Girling-Butcher* [1933] NZLR 646; *McLoughlin v Minister for Social Welfare* [1958] IR 1; *State (Rajan) v Minister for Industry and Commerce* [1988] ILRM 231.

[89] In some statutory schemes, it may be perfectly legitimate for one decision-maker to dictate the outcome of a particular matter to another decision-maker, as this course of action may have been

Protection of individual interests may also be relevant in limiting the scope for delegation. A useful example is *Vine v National Dock Labour Board*.[90] The Board had the authority to allocate dock workers to stevedoring companies and had also been granted the express power to delegate its functions to local boards. Vine had been disciplined and sought, *inter alia*, a declaration that the Board could not delegate its disciplinary functions. Lord Somervell noted that '[i]n deciding whether a "person" has power to delegate one has to consider the nature of the duty and the character of the person'.[91] Here, because of the consequences of disciplinary action—'A man who has worked all his life in the docks may find himself precluded altogether from doing so'[92]—and because of the 'constitution of the Board'[93]—designed to balance the interests of employers and employees—the functions could not be delegated. To permit delegation would be to put at risk, as Viscount Kilmuir LC put it, 'the wise use' of the disciplinary powers.[94] In other words, to permit another body to exercise the power would be to risk frustrating the statutory scheme established by the legislature and to endanger the individual interests at stake.[95]

Judges can be understood, however, to have shown some solicitude for the concerns of effective and efficient public administration, permitting those identified by statute to take into account the views of others before coming to a final decision. Of course, statutory language continues to weigh heavily in the balance, and judges can be understood to have been careful not to evacuate the legislative designation of a given decision-maker of all meaning, but they can be understood as having aimed to strike a balance between respect for the considered choices of elected representatives on the one hand and the interests of effective and efficient public administration on the other.

permitted by the legislature. As was said in *Bread Manufacturers of New South Wales v Evans* (1981) 180 CLR 404, 429 per Mason and Wilson JJ:

> [T]he problem is not one which admits of an answer having a universal application. So much depends on a variety of considerations, for there are few cases in which the statute explicitly provides that the tribunal is bound to give effect to, or to give weight to, a ministerial direction. One must take into account the particular statutory function, the nature of the question to be decided, the character of the tribunal and the general drift of the statutory provisions in so far as they bear on the relationship between the tribunal and the responsible Minister . . .

See e.g. *Ankers v Attorney-General* [1995] 2 NZLR 595; *CPCF v Minister for Immigration and Border Protection* [2015] HCA 1; (2015) 255 CLR 514, 537 (French CJ) 631 (Gageler J).

90 [1957] AC 488.
91 Ibid, 512.
92 Ibid.
93 Ibid.
94 Ibid, 499.
95 See similarly, *Barnard v National Dock Labour Board* [1953] 2 QB 18, 40; *R (DS) v Secretary of State for the Home Department* [2019] EWHC 3046 (Admin) [67]–[72]. See also *Grange Developments Ltd v Dublin County Council (No 2)* [1986] IR 246 where divesting the democratically elected council members of a power relating to planning and development and placing it in the hands of an unelected official amounted to an unlawful delegation. By contrast, where less important administrative matters are delegated, the non-delegation rule is less likely to be violated: see e.g. *Flickinger v Superintendent of Mount Eden Prison* (1990) 6 CRNZ 552, 568.

In *Ellis v Dubowski*,[96] a licensing committee, acting under the Cinematograph Act 1909, attached the following condition to a licence: 'that no film be shown which has not been certified for public exhibition by the British Board of Film Censors.' The problem thereby created was that the Board was made 'the final dictator': 'a condition putting the matter into the hands of a third person or body not possessed of statutory or constitutional authority is ultra vires the committee.'[97] This concern was, however, tempered to some extent: if 'the condition had reserved to the committee the right to review the decisions of the Board, it would seem to be a reasonable condition.'[98] In other words, whilst acting under dictation would do violence to the considered view of the elected representatives who had adopted the statute in question, seeking outside advice to inform the final decision could enhance its accuracy, thereby better implementing the statutory scheme,[99] and achieving more efficient and effective decision-making by maximising the use of scarce decision-making resources.

A similar lesson can be drawn from *Jeffs v New Zealand Dairy Production and Marketing Board*,[100] sometimes associated with the 'rule against rubberstamping.'[101] Here, the Board had decided to investigate the supply of milk in a particular district. Three members of the Board were dispatched to the area to hold a public hearing. They subsequently prepared a report, with recommendations, which the Board approved without alteration. The advice of the Privy Council was that this arrangement was *ultra vires*:

> In some circumstances it may suffice for the board to have before it and to consider an accurate summary of the relevant evidence and submissions if the summary adequately discloses the evidence and submissions to the board. Unfortunately no such procedure was followed in this case. The committee was not appointed by the board, nor was it asked by the board to receive evidence for transmission to it. The committee's report did not state what the evidence was and the board reached its decision without consideration of and in ignorance of the evidence.[102]

Note, in particular, that the Board 'did not see the written statements' given at the hearing and was 'not informed of the evidence given.'[103] By contrast, 'it would have been a matter of procedure if the board had appointed a person or persons to hear

[96] [1921] 3 KB 621.
[97] Ibid, 625 per Lawrence CJ.
[98] Ibid.
[99] See similarly *Genmark Pharma v Minister for Health* [1998] 3 IR 111, 127 per Carroll J: 'An application for product authorisation for a medicinal product is by definition very technical and any Minister would require assistance to know what the salient points were. The applicant's solicitors ... did not dispute that the Minister was entitled to and, as a matter of common sense, ought to obtain expert advice.'
[100] [1967] 1 AC 551.
[101] *Videbeck v Auckland City Council* [2002] 3 NZLR 842, 861 per Heath J.
[102] *Jeffs v New Zealand Dairy Production and Marketing Board* (n 100), 569 per Viscount Dilhorne.
[103] Ibid, 567.

and receive evidence and submissions from interested parties for the purpose of informing the board of the evidence and submissions'.[104] Again, there can be understood to be a nod here to effective and efficient public administration, because the advice of the Privy Council makes clear the desirability of promoting the effective and efficient use of administrative resources by permitting the formation of sub-committees, as long as the final decision remains vested in the body identified by the legislature, apprised of all relevant material.

Two further cases provide strong support for the view that the decided cases on the no-delegation principle can be understood to memorialise the striking of a balance between administrative law values. Consider first *R (New London College) v Home Secretary*,[105] which addressed the lawfulness of an arrangement whereby the certification of a student's intention to study in the UK was made by educational institutions; the issuing of such a certificate by the Minister was a pre-requisite for a student visa. In the Supreme Court's view, the Minister had not unlawfully delegated her power to control entry into the country to educational institutions. The certificate served as 'strong but not conclusive evidence of some of the matters which are relevant upon the migrant's application for leave to enter or remain', the ultimate decision on which was taken by the Minister and her officials, with the illumination provided by the educational institution.[106] Having regard to the advice of a third party is acceptable,[107] and could plausibly be understood to further decisional accuracy and effective and efficient public administration by expanding the knowledge base of the decision-maker.[108]

To similar effect is *IWA v Consolidated-Bathurst Packaging Ltd*.[109] Here, an administrative decision-maker allowed general policy discussions amongst board members to take place after the hearing of individual cases but before final decisions were reached. The individuals affected by the decision had no knowledge of the discussions, still less the opportunity to respond to them. Gonthier J noted that 'nothing' in the governing statute gave 'the chairman, the vice-chairmen or other Board members the power to impose his opinion on any other Board member'.[110] Holding such general policy discussions as a means to achieve consistency in decisions was nonetheless held to be permissible.[111] This conclusion is unsurprising,

[104] Ibid, 568.
[105] [2013] UKSC 51; [2013] 1 WLR 2358.
[106] Ibid, [19].
[107] See also *R v Police Complaints Board, ex parte Madden* [1983] 1 WLR 447; *McInnes v Minister of Transport* [2001] 3 NZLR 11.
[108] Or, as in *King-Emperor v Benoari Lal Sarma* (n 83) 24–25, providing for local variations for the more effective implementation of the orders of a central authority. See also *R v Governor of Brixton Prison, ex parte Enahoro* [1963] 2 QB 455, 466.
[109] [1990] 1 SCR 282.
[110] Ibid, 333.
[111] On the virtues of such structures, see generally Roy Sainsbury, 'Administrative Justice: Discretion and Procedure in Social Security Decision-making' in Keith Hawkins ed, *The Uses of Discretion* (Clarendon Press, Oxford, 1991).

inasmuch as it can be understood to enhance effective and efficient public administration by treating like cases alike—thereby promoting consistent decision-making across differently constituted panels of the decision-maker—and greater congruence between the general policy views of the Board and the decisions of individual panels: 'Those affected by administrative decisions are entitled to expect that like cases will generally be treated alike and that outcomes will not depend merely on the identity of the individual decision maker.'[112] However, Gonthier J cautioned, 'this *de jure* situation must not be thwarted by procedures which may effectively compel or induce panel members to decide against their own conscience and opinions'.[113] Accordingly, participants in the high-level discussions could not lawfully descend into the factual minutiae of individual cases. He can be understood here as aiming to strike a balance between ensuring, on the one hand, that the decision-maker designated by the legislature took the decision in question and, on the other hand, effective and efficient public administration.[114]

Finally, it is notable, in terms of distinct bodies playing distinct roles, that administrative decision-makers 'enjoy much more flexibility' in terms of delegation than courts.[115] As with the no-bias principle, the retention of discretion principle operates quite differently in respect of administrative decision-makers than in respect of courts.[116]

2.3.2 The *Carltona* Exception

The no-delegation principle is subject to a very large exception, associated with the decision in *Carltona Ltd v Commissioners of Works*.[117] Pursuant to the *Carltona* exception, 'devised under the exigencies of administration in the United Kingdom in World War II',[118] but now part of the fabric of contemporary administrative law, a civil servant in a government department will be treated as the *alter ego* of the

[112] *Canada (Immigration and Citizenship) v Vavilov* 2019 SCC 65 [129].

[113] [1990] 1 SCR 282, 333. See e.g. *Shuttleworth v Ontario (Safety, Licensing Appeals and Standards Tribunals)* 2019 ONCA 518.

[114] See also *Canadian Association of Refugee Lawyers v Canada (Immigration, Refugee and Citizenship)* 2020 FCA 196.

[115] Mark Aronson, Matthew Groves and Greg Weeks, *Judicial Review of Administrative Action and Governmental Liability* 6th edn (Thomson Reuters, Sydney, 2017), [8.270]. On the relative lack of flexibility applied to judicial decision-making, see *R v Gateshead Justices, ex parte Tesco Stores Ltd* [1981] QB 470, 478–479.

[116] See also Joseph (n 7) 975: 'The question of whether to uphold sub-delegation is a contextual one. Multiple factors may need to be considered, including: the statutory language, objects and policy, the amplitude of the power, the importance of the decision and its effect on individuals, whether all or only part of the power is sub-delegated, the degree of supervision exercised over the delegate, and administrative efficiencies.' See similarly *Ex parte Forster; Re University of Sydney* [1963] SR (NSW) 723, 733. See also *Taylor v Public Service Board (New South Wales)* (1976) 137 CLR 208, 218–222 per Mason J.

[117] [1943] 2 All ER 560. See also *Buller Hospital Board v Attorney-General* [1959] NZLR 1259.

[118] *WT v Minister for Justice* [2015] IESC 73.

responsible minister. As a matter of law, decisions of civil servants are decisions of the minister. Thus where a statute identifies the minister as the decision-maker, a civil servant may in principle take the decision: 'If a decision is made on his behalf by one of his officials, then that constitutionally is the Minister's decision. It is not strictly a matter of delegation; it is that the official acts as the Minister himself and the official's decision is the Minister's decision.'[119]

At issue in *Carltona* was a wartime requisition of property under the authority of the respondents. One of the arguments raised was that the First Commissioner had not personally put his mind to the requisition in question. Lord Greene MR held that it was not necessary for the First Commissioner to do so, offering two lines of response[120] to the company's reliance on the 'simple and well-known principle of law' that the person identified by statute as the repository of a discretionary power should exercise it personally.[121]

First, the minister remains 'responsible' for decisions made on his behalf by officials, for '[i]t is he who must answer before Parliament for anything that his officials have done under his authority'.[122] The point here can be understood to be that the considered choice of the elected representatives that the power assigned to the minister should be exercised by the minister is respected in spirit by reference to the principle that the minister is, ultimately, responsible for the decision taken. This can be understood to sound in judicial concern for electoral legitimacy.

Ministerial responsibility was central, for example, to *R v Secretary of State for Social Services, ex parte Sherwin*.[123] It was held that a decision of the Benefits Agency (a so-called Next Steps Agency embedded in a government department[124]) was a decision of the Secretary of State. Under the framework agreement setting out its functions, the Agency was largely autonomous, with a chief executive who was responsible for day-to-day operations, but the minister remained accountable to Parliament. Moreover, the statutory power at issue was a power vested in the minister and it was exercised by a civil servant nominally employed by the minister. For these reasons, the *Carltona* principle applied.[125]

[119] *R v Skinner* [1968] 2 QB 700, 707. The *Carltona* exception may, nonetheless, be displaced by sufficiently clear statutory language: '[T]here will be some matters so obviously material to a decision on a particular project that anything short of direct consideration of them by the Ministers collectively would not be in accordance with the intention of the Act.' *CREEDNZ Inc v Governor-General* (n 24) 183. This case related to a cabinet decision but the point applies with equal force to any ministerial decision-making. See e.g. *Attorney General (Quebec) v Carrières Ste-Thérèse Ltée* [1985] 1 SCR 831; *Re Patterson, ex parte Taylor* (n 85).

[120] See also *O'Reilly v Commissioners of the State Bank of Victoria* (n 85) 11 per Gibbs CJ.

[121] Stephen Sedley, 'The Sound of Silence: Constitutional Law without a Constitution' (1994) 110 *Law Quarterly Review* 270, 272.

[122] [1943] 2 All ER 560, 563.

[123] (1996) 32 BMLR 1.

[124] See generally Mark Freedland, 'The Rule against Delegation and the *Carltona* Doctrine in an Agency Context' [1996] *Public Law* 19.

[125] *R v Secretary of State for Social Services, ex parte Sherwin* (n 123) 11.

Where, however, there is a 'constitutional separation' between the minister and the officials purporting to act on their behalf, the *Carltona* exception cannot apply.[126] For in the absence of clear lines of constitutional responsibility tying the minister to the officials, application of the *Carltona* exception would negate the considered choice of the elected representatives who approved the legislative scheme; at least where the minister remains responsible, one can say that the value of electoral legitimacy has not been ignored, as the minister has acted through officials 'for whose conduct [the minister] is accountable to the Legislature'.[127]

Second, the functions given to ministers by various statutes are 'so multifarious that no minister could ever personally attend to them'.[128] Lord Greene MR's concern here can be understood to be one for effective and efficient public administration: to require 'the minister in person [to] direct his mind to the matter' would mean '[p]ublic business could not be carried on'.[129] It is in the nature of modern government that ministers will not be able to turn their mind to every decision taken in their department: 'A Minister must perforce, from the necessity of the case, act through his departmental officials.'[130] This is further supported by the institutional expertise that departmental civil servants will be able to bring to bear on regulatory questions: 'The collective knowledge, technical as well as factual, of the civil servants in the department and their collective expertise are to be treated as the minister's own knowledge, his own expertise'.[131] This logic has been used to justify the *Carltona* exception—'a judicial recognition of the complexity of the administration of modern states'[132]—outside the context of government departments, for instance in the police force.[133] It can be understood as being supported

[126] *R (Bourgass) v Secretary of State for Justice* [2015] UKSC 54; [2016] AC 384 [64] and [50].

[127] *R v Harrison* [1977] 1 SCR 238, 245 per Dickson J.

[128] *Carltona v Commissioners of Works* (n 122) 563.

[129] Ibid.

[130] *Lewisham Metropolitan Borough and Town Clerk v Roberts* [1949] 2 KB 608, 629 per Jenkins J. See also *Minister for Aboriginal Affairs v Peko-Wallsend Ltd* (1986) 162 CLR 24, 38 per Mason J. As has been said by the Irish Supreme Court, 'When public officials are charged with administering a statutory scheme it may be difficult, if not impossible, for the Oireachtas to prescribe in legislation for every special circumstance of individuals who find themselves on the margins of such a scheme'. *Re Article 26 and the Health (Amendment) (No 2) Bill 2004* [2005] IESC 7; [2005] 2 IR 105, 172.

[131] *Bushell v Secretary of State for the Environment* [1980] UKHL 1; [1981] AC 75, 95, 28 per Lord Diplock. See also *R v Race Relations Board, ex parte Selvarajan* [1975] 1 WLR 1686. As McMenamin J has put it:

> In making administrative decisions, therefore, discretion is conferred on a minister, not simply as an individual, but rather as the person who holds office as head of a government department, which collectively holds a high degree of collective corporate knowledge and experience, all of which is imputed to the political head of the department. Frequently a minister's officials will prepare documents for consideration, consider objections, summarise memoranda, and outline a policy approach to be taken by the Minister as an integral part of the decision-making process.

WT v Minister for Justice (n 118) IESC 73.

[132] *WT v Minister for Justice* (n 118).

[133] *Director of Public Prosecutions v Haw* [2007] EWHC 1931 (Admin); [2008] 1 WLR 379 [29]; *Castle v Director of Public Prosecutions* [2014] EWHC 587 (Admin); [2014] 1 WLR 4279 [28]; *R (Hamill) v Chelmsford Justices* [2014] EWHC 2799 (Admin); [2015] 1 WLR 1798 [64]. See also *Commissioners of Customs and Excise v Cure & Deeley Ltd* [1962] 1 QB 340, 371 (taxation administration); *ex parte*

by a concern to promote effective and efficient public administration, using relevant expertise and all available resources to make better administrative decisions more swiftly.

There are, however, limitations to the scope of the *Carltona* exception. Again, administrative law values can be understood to influence the limitations. At issue in *R v Secretary of State for the Home Department, ex parte Oladehinde*[134] was whether immigration officers could lawfully be authorised by the Secretary of State to issue deportation orders. The House of Lords accepted that they could be so authorised, but added a limiting principle. Lord Griffiths could 'see no reason why [the minister] should not authorise members of [the immigration] service to take decisions under the *Carltona* principle *providing* they do not conflict with or embarrass them in the discharge of their specific statutory duties under the Act and that the decisions are suitable to their grading and experience'.[135] The point here can be understood to be that effective and efficient public administration would be not be achieved by permitting unqualified officials to make decisions in the minister's stead; accuracy might also be imperilled.[136] Indeed, it must 'be supposed that the Minister will select deputies and departmental officials of experience and competence', as '[a]ny other approach would but lead to administrative chaos and inefficiency'.[137] Relatedly, it seems that major policy decisions are to be taken by ministers,[138] which can be understood as sounding in respect for the role of the minister as an elected representative.

Where individual interests are at stake the *Carltona* exception is less likely to apply. As a general matter, 'the gravity of the consequences flowing from the

Forster; Re University of Sydney (n 116) 733 (university senate); *R v Harrison* (n 127) (Attorney General); *O'Reilly v Commissioners of the State Bank of Victoria* (n 85) (taxation administration); *Attorney-General (Cth) v Foster* (1999) 84 FCR 582 (Attorney General). See further cases involving senior officials in governmental departments (which, of course, might overlap with those in the previous list): see e.g. *Re Ahmad v Appeal Board established by the Public Service Commission* (1974) 51 DLR (3d) 470 (though cf *Re CAE Metal Abrasive Division of Canadian Bronze Co Ltd v Deputy Minister of National Revenue for Customs and Excise* [1985] 1 CTC 202); *Commissioners of Inland Revenue v Chesterfields Preschools Ltd* [2013] NZCA 53; [2013] 2 NZLR 679. Whether these cases are best classified as extensions of the *Carltona* exception or as applications of an implied statutory authority to delegate is a nice point, addressed in detail in Rory Gregson, 'When Should There Be an Implied Power to Delegate?' [2017] *Public Law* 408. See also Ann Chaplin, '*Carltona* Revisited: Accountability and the Devolution of Statutory Powers' (2007) 39 *Ottawa Law Review* 495.

134 [1991] 1 AC 254.

135 Ibid, 303. Emphasis added. See also *Ward v Governor of Portlaoise Prison* [2006] IEHC 297.

136 For this reason, it also makes sense that errors in the decision-making process can be imputed to the responsible minister (see e.g. *Daganayasi v Minister of Immigration* [1980] 2 NZLR 130, 149 per Cooke J; *Air Nelson Ltd v Minister of Transport* [2008] NZAR 139 [53]–[55]), though this will not always be possible, for instance because the responsible minister has taken a personal decision untainted by any errors by officials: see e.g. *Bancoult v Secretary of State for Foreign and Commonwealth Affairs (No. 3)* [2018] UKSC 3; [2018] 1 WLR 973 [45]–[49].

137 *R v Harrison* (n 127) 245–246 per Dickson J. See also Freedland (n 124) 22–24.

138 See e.g. *New South Wales Aboriginal Land Council v Minister Administering the Crown Lands Act* (2014) 88 NSWLR 125; *Re Buick's Application* [2018] NICA 26.

exercise of the power'[139] is 'a relevant consideration in a determination whether the *Carltona* principle has been displaced in a particular case'.[140] Consider *R (Bourgass) v Secretary of State for Justice*,[141] which concerned prisoners who had been sent to solitary confinement. Authority to segregate prisoners was provided by rule 45 of the *Prison Rules*, a statutory instrument. Further non-statutory guidance, issued by the Secretary of State, permitted operational managers within prisons to take segregation decisions. Given, however, that the *Rules* referred specifically to 'the authority of the Secretary of State', it was not lawful for senior prison officials to act in his stead. The 'apparent rationale' of rule 45 was to protect prisoners by providing for external review of segregation decisions by 'senior officials from outside the prison—in order to protect the prisoner against the risk of segregation for an unduly protracted period'.[142] Given the presence of important personal liberty interests, the ultimate conclusion that the function must be 'performed by an official from outside the prison' is unsurprising, inasmuch as it could easily 'be inferred that rule 45(2) is intended to provide a safeguard for the prisoner'.[143]

Although the workability of using individual interests to determine the scope of the *Carltona* exception has been doubted[144] and there are certainly cases involving very important individual interests where the *Carltona* exception has applied,[145] the suggestion I am making here is simply that the value of individual self-realisation can be understood to be relevant. That decisions relating to, say, personal liberty and thus going to the heart of individual self-realisation have been subject to the *Carltona* exception does not mean that individual interests must be irrelevant. For one thing, the importance of the individual interests at stake can certainly be understood as influencing the 'appropriate level of seniority' of the decision-maker: how far down the departmental hierarchy a decision can lawfully be made by a civil servant.[146] More generally, the suggestion is not that the presence of individual interests is not an absolute bar to the application of the *Carltona* exception but rather that where the individual interests at stake are more important, the *Carltona* exception is less likely to be applied.[147] This is borne out by the most recent leading case on the subject, *R v Adams*.[148] At issue here was whether a power

[139] *R v Adams* [2020] UKSC 19 [26] per Lord Kerr.
[140] *R v Adams* [2018] NICA 8 [46] citing *McCafferty's Application* [2009] NICA 59.
[141] *R (Bourgass) v Secretary of State for Justice* (n 126).
[142] Ibid, [80].
[143] Ibid, [88].
[144] See e.g. *Re Golden Chemical Products* [1976] Ch 300, 310 per Brightman J: 'A distinction between a case which involves a serious invasion of the freedom or property rights of the subject, and a case which involves a similar invasion that is not serious, seems to me to be impossibly vague.'
[145] See e.g. *R v Secretary of State for the Home Department, ex parte Doody* [1994] 1 AC 531 (prison tariff); *Tang v Minister for Justice* [1996] 2 ILRM 46 (deportation)
[146] *WT v Minister for Justice* (n 118).
[147] See also Joseph (n 7) 981: 'a minister personally must discharge legislative functions and make important decisions affecting individuals.'
[148] *R v Adams* (n 139).

to detain suspected terrorists indefinitely during the 'Troubles' in Northern Ireland could lawfully have been exercised by a junior minister rather than by the Secretary of State himself. For Lord Kerr, that '[t]he provision did nothing less than give the Secretary of State the task of deciding whether an individual should remain at liberty or be kept in custody, quite possibly for an indefinite period' militated in favour of concluding that Parliament intended 'such a crucial decision' should be taken by the Secretary of State personally.[149] Lastly, it can be fairly confidently suggested that courts are much more willing to apply the *Carltona* exception where administrative functions with little impact on individual interests are at issue.[150]

Accordingly, the *Carltona* exception can be understood to be influenced by administrative law values. Here they can be understood to operate in a complementary fashion, as the *Carltona* exception applies in such a way as to respect the importance of individual interests and effective and efficient public administration without compromising the obligation to give effect to the considered choices of elected representatives to vest power in a particular minister. In this respect, indeed, *Carltona* is as much a component of the no-delegation principle as it is an exception.[151]

[149] Ibid, [38].

[150] See e.g. *State (Keller) v Galway County Council* [1958] IR 142, 148 (chief medical officer can delegate physical examination of applicant for a grant, but not duty of forming the necessary opinion as to whether the applicant was substantially handicapped); *O'Reilly v Commissioners of the State Bank of Victoria* (n 85) 19 per Mason J, dissenting: 'The power to issue a s 264 notice may have a great impact on the affairs of individual persons. It is not like a power which, being purely administrative in nature or having no consequences of any significance, may perhaps be entrusted to another to exercise despite a statutory proscription against delegation or sub-delegation. It is a power the exercise of which involves a substantial area of discretion. Its exercise may not, therefore, be entrusted to a subordinate in the absence of a great degree of control by the authority'; *Webster v Taiaroa* (1987) 7 NZAR 1 (albeit drawing a distinction between a legislative act, which was not subject to the *Carltona* exception and administrative acts, which would be, rather than using the importance of the interests at stake as a touchstone); *DPP (Quigley) v Monaghan* [2007] IEHC 92, where Charleton J, discussing the DPP's power to prosecute, commented: 'In the District Court, members of An Garda Síochána may prosecute as common informers but they do so in the name of the Director of Public Prosecutions, as was done in this case. His authority does not need, perhaps, to be sought in every individual case as *his power to control prosecutions may be delegated in respect of relatively minor matters, through a list or other arrangement of an administrative kind*.' Emphasis added.

[151] In *obiter* comments in *R v Adams* (n 140) [25], Lord Kerr doubted the continued vitality of *Carltona*:

> It is unnecessary for the purposes of the present appeal to reach a firm conclusion on the question whether it is now established that there is a presumption that Parliament should be taken to have intended that the *Carltona* principle should apply. It is true that in *Oladehinde* Lord Griffiths said that a statutory duty placed on a minister may 'generally' be exercised by a member of his department, but I believe that he was not there proposing that there was a legal presumption to that effect. I am not persuaded that the authorities, apart from *McCafferty* and the decision of the Court of Appeal in the present case, have espoused that position. It is, of course, the case that Parliament legislates against the background that the *Carltona* principle is well-established. And it is also relevant that Parliament has shown itself on occasions willing to register the displacement of the principle in explicit terms. These considerations must influence the judgment as to whether, properly construed, a particular item of legislation is in keeping with the principle or not. But that does not amount, in my opinion, to the creation of a presumption in law that the principle must be taken to apply unless it has been removed by express statutory language.

2.3.3 Fettering of Discretion

It is trite law that an administrative decision-maker cannot fetter a discretionary power granted to it: 'After all, the existence of a discretion implies the absence of a rule dictating the result in each case; the essence of discretion is that it can be exercised differently in different cases. Each case must be looked at individually, on its own merits.'[152] Where the legislature vested a discretionary power in an administrative decision-maker it would be inconsistent with this considered legislative choice for the administrative decision-maker to bind itself as to how the power will be exercised in future cases, unless—and this is an important point, discussed further below[153]—the statute expressly or by necessary implication permits the decision-maker to do so.[154]

It has been argued that legislative intent cannot be the basis for the no-fettering principle, because the mere existence of a discretionary power tells us nothing about how the power is to be exercised and, indeed, it might make sense for a power to be exercised to adopt an inflexible rule, to more effectively achieve the overall statutory objectives.[155] But the generally accepted *starting point*, which

These comments are in tension with the common understanding of the *Carltona* principle, that a civil servant in a government department will be treated as the *alter ego* of the responsible minister. See n 117. On the common understanding, the *Carltona* principle does not create presumptions but merely recognizes the constitutional reality that ministers act through their civil servants (and, given the exigencies of modern administration, *must* act through their civil servants). On occasion, statutory language will make it clear that ministers may not properly so act, a conclusion which may be supported by the individual interests at stake (as in *Bourgass* and *Adams*). But it is unhelpful in determining what ministers can and cannot do to think of the *Carltona* principle as a 'legal presumption' or to invoke the jurisprudential background against which Parliament has been legislating. Simply put, civil servants *are* the minister, unless a personal decision of the minister is *required*.

[152] David P Jones and Anne S de Villars, *Principles of Administrative Law*, 5th edn (Thomson Reuters, Toronto, 2009) 198.

[153] See the discussion and cases at nn 186–192.

[154] The no-fettering principle applies as much to determinations made by an adjudicator as to exercises of discretionary power: see e.g. *Canadian Association of Refugee Lawyers v Canada (Citizenship and Immigration)* 2019 FC 1126. But the term 'fettering of discretion' is so embedded in the common law consciousness that I am too timorous to abandon it: for any reference to discretion, please understand that determinations are also included.

[155] See e.g. Denis Galligan, 'The Nature and Functions of Policy within Discretionary Power' [1976] *Public Law* 332; Adam Perry, 'The Flexibility Rule in Administrative Law' (2017) 76 *Cambridge Law Journal* 375. See also Chris Hilson, 'Judicial Review, Policies and the Fettering of Discretion' [2002] *Public Law* 111, 129:

> In some cases, the desired aim may require totally individualised decision-making, unencumbered by policies; in others, a policy or rule may be desirable but only if exceptions are provided for (and possibly spelled out); and in yet others, the end will only be achievable if a rigid rule with no exceptions is in place. There should, in other words, be shoes for all occasions, not one size fits all.

See also Aileen McHarg, 'Administrative Discretion, Administrative Rule-making, and Judicial Review' (2017) 70 *Current Legal Problems* 267, 295, arguing that confusion 'as to the [no-fettering] rule's doctrinal basis perhaps reflects the fact that, as a matter of principle, there is simply no justification for any presumption in favour of administrative discretion'. This is perhaps true if one conceives of the infers from the existence of a statutory discretion that its future exercise should not be fettered, seems unobjectionable to me as long as one recognises the possibility that fettering can be expressly or necessarily implicitly authorised in some statutory schemes. Both the starting point, and the possibility of its alteration by express or implicit statutory language, can be understood as sounding in respect for the considered choice of the legislature to vest a given discretionary power in a given decision-maker.

In any event, this is only a starting point for analysis. In fact, the current position is quite nuanced. There is no 'general presumption either for or against the legitimacy of administrative rule-making', but the no-fettering principle operates instead 'as a means of judicial control over the *degree of structuring* of discretion that is appropriate in particular contexts'.[156] Both its scope and limitations can be understood in terms of administrative law values.

2.3.3.1 Values, Soft Law and Fettering

In general, adopting a policy to guide future exercises of discretion, as opposed to an inflexible rule which would determine the outcome of individual decisions, is entirely appropriate. Although administrative bodies generally enjoy only those powers expressly granted (or that are necessarily implicit to express powers)[157] they have the ability to adopt 'soft law'[158] instruments to guide[159] the exercise of their discretionary powers:[160] 'A person or agency who is exercising discretion as to how to use a statutory power ... may formulate a policy or make a limiting rule as to the future exercise of his discretion ... provided that he listens to any applicant who has something new to say.'[161]

no-fettering principle as (itself) an inflexible rule, but I hope the analysis below reveals that the current state of the law is (as McHarg herself has it) much more nuanced than that.

156 McHarg, (n 155) 273.

157 *Attorney-General v Great Eastern Railway Co* (1880) 5 App Cas 473, 478 per Lord Shelborne.

158 By which I mean 'non-legislative instruments such as policy guidelines, technical manuals, rules, codes, operational memoranda, training materials, interpretive bulletins', including instructions delivered more informally, 'through oral directive or simply as a matter of ingrained administrative culture'. Lorne Sossin, 'Discretion Unbound: Reconciling the *Charter* and Soft Law' (2002) 45 *Canadian Public Administration* 465, 466–467.

159 *Re Drake v Minister for Immigration and Ethnic Affairs (No 2)* (1979) 2 ALD 634; (1979) 24 ALR 577, 640–641; *Ainsley Financial Corp v Ontario Securities Commission* (1994) 21 OR (3d) 104, 108–109.

160 See e.g. *R (New London College) v Home Secretary* [2013] UKSC 51; [2013] 1 WLR 2358.

161 *R (Gujra) v Crown Prosecution Service* [2012] UKSC 52; [2013] 1 AC 484 [76] per Lord Kerr. See similarly *Applicant S214 of 2002 v Attorney-General* [2004] FCA 1635 [16]. Something similar can be said of administrative decision-makers' power to contract. As long as the contract does not frustrate the operation of a particular statutory provision, as in *Ayr Harbour Trustees v Oswald* (1883) 8 App Cas 623, a concern for effective and efficient public administration can be understood to predominate and permit the entering into of contractual relations designed to achieve the decision-maker's statutory objectives. See e.g. *Birkdale Electricity Supply Co Ltd v Corporation of Southport* [1926] AC 355; *Petrocorp Exploration Ltd v Minister of Energy* [1991] 1 NZLR 641; *Rosborough v Cork City Council* [2008] IEHC 94; [2008] 4 IR 572; *Friends of Turitea Reserve Society Inc v Palmerston North City Council* [2008] 2 NZLR 661.

Permitting the adoption of soft law instruments has salutary benefits.[162] The use of soft law can be understood as promoting effective and efficient public administration, by making it easier for administrative decision-makers to discharge their functions. Adopting soft law instruments can 'enable an agency to deal with a problem comprehensively and proactively, rather than incrementally and reactively on a case-by-case basis',[163] setting out general guidance to ensure that like cases are treated alike: 'to achieve an acceptable level of consistency in administrative decisions is particularly important for tribunals exercising discretion, whether on procedural, evidential or substantive issues, in the performance of adjudicative functions.'[164] In this way 'fruitless applications involving expense and expenditure of time might be avoided'.[165] Moreover, once one acknowledges that sometimes '[b]linkered and individualised decision-making would be a recipe for maladministration'[166] the resultant benefits to efficiency and effectiveness are easy to perceive: 'It would be inimical to good administration and to consistency in decision making to oblige all decision makers to treat each decision entirely on its own, without reference to previous decisions or to criteria designed to serve the public interest.'[167] It is unsurprising, incidentally, that courts have held that any such policy must be operated consistently and is not to be departed from unless there is a 'good reason' to do so,[168] because a policy is likely to represent a

[162] See generally *Nzolameso v City of Westminster* [2015] UKSC 22; [2015] HLR 22 [40]–[41] per Lady Hale; *Thamotharem v Canada (Minister of Citizenship and Immigration)* 2007 FCA 198; [2008] 1 FCR 385.

[163] *Thamotharem v Canada (Minister of Citizenship and Immigration* (n 162) [55] per Evans JA. Indeed, such 'instruments may be put in place relatively easily and adjusted in the light of day-to-day experience, they may be preferable to formal rules requiring external approval and, possibly, drafting appropriate for legislation' (ibid).

[164] [2008] 1 FCR 385 [62]. See similarly *Hesham Ali (Iraq) v Home Secretary* [2016] 1 WLR 4799 [15] per Lord Reed:

> Decision-making in relation to immigration and deportation is not exhaustively regulated by legislation. It also involves the exercise of discretion, and the making of evaluative judgments, by the Secretary of State and her officials. A perennial challenge, in such a situation, is to achieve consistency in decision-making while reaching decisions which are appropriate to the case in hand. The solution generally lies in the adoption of administrative policies to guide decision-making: something which the courts have accepted is legitimate . . .

See also *Surinakova v Minister for Immigration, Local Government & Ethnic Affairs* (1991) 33 FCR 87, 98 per Hill J; *Criminal Bar Association of New Zealand Inc v Attorney-General* [2013] NZCA 176; [2013] NZAR 1409, 1440.

[165] *British Oxygen Co Ltd v Minister of Technology* [1971] AC 610, 631 per Viscount Dilhorne.

[166] *Plaintiff M64/2015 v Minister for Immigration and Border Protection* [2015] HCA 50; (2015) 258 CLR 173, 198 per Gageler J.

[167] *McCarron v Kearney* [2010] IESC 28; [2010] 3 IR 302, 322 per Fennelly J. See also Robert Baldwin, *Rules and Government* (Oxford University Press, Oxford, 1995), 13; *Canada (Immigration and Citizenship) v Vavilov* (n 112) [130].

[168] *Mandalia v Home Secretary* [2015] UKSC 59; [2015] 1 WLR 4546, citing *R (Nadarajah) v Secretary of State for the Home Department* [2005] EWCA Civ 1363 [68]. See also *Keogh v Criminal Assets Bureau* [2004] IESC 32; [2004] 2 IR 159; Yoav Dotan, 'Why Administrators Should be Bound by Their Policies' (1997) 17 *Oxford Journal of Legal Studies* 23, 23–31.

considered memorialisation of the considerations relevant to making a particular type of decision; as such, departures from the policy call for justification.[169]

In terms of individual self-realisation, soft law allows an administrative decision-maker's position to be publicised to the world at large, thereby enabling 'members of the public to predict how an agency is likely to exercise its statutory discretion and to arrange their affairs accordingly'.[170] Such instruments can empower individuals by giving them more knowledge about the administrative decision-making apparatuses they encounter, treating them with respect and increasing their ability to order their affairs.[171] Put briefly, 'people will know where they stand'.[172] Indeed, the English courts have held that any policy touching sufficiently important interests will have to be made available in some form to those subject to it.[173] Judges' willingness to permit the adoption of soft law instruments can, accordingly, be understood as having been influenced by their solicitude for individual self-realisation, given that soft law has the capacity to make administrative decisions more predictable and decision-making structures more transparent.[174]

But soft law may not harden into a rule. Judicial willingness to permit the development of soft law can be understood to be tempered by concerns for the self-realisation of individuals who come into contact with the administrative decision-maker. While it will undoubtedly be 'helpful to applicants for permits to know in general terms what the policy and practice of the Minister will be',[175] an administrative decision-maker cannot 'shut its ears' to an individual who wishes to argue that the policy should be revised:[176] 'What the authority must not do is to refuse to listen at all.'[177] To so refuse would be to compromise the ability of the individual concerned to participate in the decision-making process, failing to treat them with respect and reducing their ability to order their affairs. Moreover, where important individual interests are at stake, a policy will have to be relatively

[169] See e.g. *Canada (Attorney General) v Honey Fashions Ltd* 2020 FCA 64 [38].

[170] *Thamotharem v Canada (Minister of Citizenship and Immigration* (n 162) [55].

[171] Richard Titmuss, 'Welfare "Rights", Law and Discretion' (1970) 42 *Political Quarterly* 113, 126.

[172] *R (Purdy) v Director of Public Prosecutions* [2009] UKHL 45; [2010] 1 AC 345 [54] per Lord Hope of Craighead. See similarly *Drake v Minister for Immigration & Ethnic Affairs* (n 159) 641 per Brennan J.

[173] *R (Lumba) v Home Secretary* [2011] UKSC 12; [2012] 1 AC 245 [35] per Lord Dyson: 'The individual has a basic public law right to have his or her case considered under whatever policy the executive sees fit to adopt provided that the adopted policy is a lawful exercise of the discretion conferred by the statute. There is a correlative right to know what that currently existing policy is, so that the individual can make relevant representations in relation to it'; *R (Reilly) v Work and Pensions Secretary* [2013] UKSC 68; [2014] AC 453 [65] per Lord Neuberger and Lord Toulson: 'Fairness therefore requires that a claimant should have access to such information about the scheme as he or she may need in order to make informed and meaningful representations to the decision-maker before a decision is made.' See also Kenneth Culp Davis, *Discretionary Justice: A Preliminary Inquiry* (Louisiana State University Press, Baton Rouge, 1969).

[174] See also *Minister for Home Affairs v Brown* [2020] FCAFC 21 [113].

[175] *Maple Lodge Farms Ltd v Canada* [1982] 2 SCR 2, 7.

[176] *R v Port of London Authority, ex parte Kynoch Ltd* [1919] 1 KB 176, 183.

[177] *British Oxygen Co Ltd v Minister of Technology* (n 165) 625 per Lord Reid. See e.g. *Rendell v Release on Licence Board* (1987) 10 NSWLR 499.

flexible.[178] Accordingly, the contemporary law on the no-fettering principle can be understood as striking 'a balance'[179] between individual interests and effective and efficient public administration:

> [A] Ministry or large authority may have had to deal already with a multitude of similar applications and then they will almost certainly have evolved a policy so precise that it could well be called a rule. There can be no objection to that, provided the authority is always willing to listen to anyone with something new to say.[180]

As long as an individual can be heard as to why a policy applies or does not apply to them, or as to why a policy should be revised, the efficiency and effectiveness gains from proceeding pursuant to guidelines are not outweighed by concerns about potential negative impact on individuals.

2.3.3.2 Judicial Review of Soft Law

These soft law instruments operate in something of a legal grey area. They are not *binding*, strictly speaking—hence the use of 'soft'—but they are nonetheless *legal*, in the sense that they are designed to influence behaviour—hence the use of 'law'. Common law courts have had some difficulty in reviewing administrative action that has been influenced by soft law: '[a]s a concept, soft law tends to expose the inadequacy of traditional categories of legal analysis because it effectively regulates behaviour but is not binding in the manner of primary or delegated legislation.'[181] It is nonetheless clear that judicial review will be available in some situations and, furthermore, that administrative law values can be understood to influence the scope of judicial review of soft law.

First, any soft law instrument must not be applied as if it were a rule. The decision-maker must give 'proper, genuine and realistic consideration to the merits of the case' and the decision-maker must 'be ready in a proper case to depart from any applicable policy'.[182] If an administrative decision-maker were 'not to hear any application of a particular character by whomsoever made', this would amount to an unlawful fetter on a discretionary power:[183] 'a tribunal which is called upon to exercise a discretion does not perform its duty if it acts in blind obedience to a rule

[178] See e.g. *R v Secretary of State for the Home Department, ex parte Venables and Thompson* [1998] AC 407.

[179] *Thamotharem v Canada (Minister of Citizenship and Immigration* (n 162) [55] per Evans J.

[180] *British Oxygen Co Ltd v Minister of Technology* (n 165) 625 per Lord Reid.

[181] Greg Weeks, *Soft Law and Public Authorities: Remedies and Reform* (Hart, Oxford, 2016), 98. See especially *Gillick v West Norfolk and Wisbech Health Authority* [1986] AC 112.

[182] *Khan v Minister for Immigration and Ethnic Affairs* (1987) 14 ALD 291, 292 per Gummow J (these quotes are from a headnoted summary of Gummow J's reasons).

[183] *R v Port of London Authority, ex parte Kynoch* (n 176) 184 per Bankes LJ.

or policy that it had previously adopted.'[184] As the decision-maker would not be 'fairly judging all the issues which are relevant to each individual case as it comes up for decision', decisional accuracy would likely suffer.[185]

Only in circumstances where the 'necessary implication'[186] of a given statutory scheme is that a discretionary power can be fettered by an inflexible rule or where it would be inappropriate to require a decision-maker to undertake a decision 'wholly anew' on each occasion[187] will concerns about faithful implementation of legislative choices prove unavailing.[188] For instance, in *My Noodle Ltd v Queenstown Lakes District Council*,[189] a blanket policy setting a 21-hour limit on liquor licences was justified because the decision-maker was 'entitled to give precedence to the overriding statutory object' of establishing a reasonable system of control over the sale and supply of liquor to the public with the aim of contributing to the reduction of liquor abuse: 'If the Authority considered (as it did) that reduced trading hours would help reduce liquor abuse then, logically, any restriction on trading hours must be a blanket provision that applies to all liquor outlets (subject to the consideration of special individual circumstances).'[190] It is nonetheless notable that the decision-maker 'did not close its mind to possible departures from the policy'.[191] Consider also *Wetzel v District Court of New South Wales*,[192] where a body responsible for the distribution of mining claims had adopted an inflexible rule of requiring miners to attend the registry in person to collect relevant documentation. The purpose of doing so was to ensure that applicants did indeed reside at their stated address (and that they in fact existed), with a particular view to ensuring that no person held more than two mining claims in a specified mining division. This was held to be appropriate in the circumstances, though Priestley JA

[184] *Re Clarkson, ex parte Australian Telegram and Phonogram Officers' Association* (1982) 39 ALR 1, 9 per Gibbs CJ.

[185] *Stringer v Minister of Housing and Local Government* [1971] 1 WLR 1281, 1289 per Cooke J. As Fox and Franki JJ observed in *Howells v Nagrad Nominees Pty Ltd* (1982) 43 ALR 283, 307:

> Where the power given relates to the consideration of individual cases, it is not to be denied that the predominant aspect must be the consideration of the particular case. The merits of that case must be considered genuinely and realistically; there must always be a readiness to depart from policy. The policy does a dis-service to those who have to measure it against the individual situation if it is expressed in dogmatic or mandatory terms.

See e.g. *R (DS) v Secretary of State for the Home Department* (n 95) [64].

[186] *R (Sandiford) v Secretary of State for Foreign and Commonwealth Affairs* [2014] UKSC 44; [2014] 1 WLR 2697 [62].

[187] *Minister for Immigration and Multicultural Affairs v Lia Legeng* [2001] HCA 17; (2001) 205 CLR 507, 566 per Hayne J.

[188] See e.g. *Wetzel v District Court of New South Wales* (1998) 43 NSWLR 687; *R v Nottingham City Council, ex parte Howitt* [1999] COD 530; *R v Chief Constable of South Yorkshire Police, ex parte LS* [2004] UKHL 39; [2004] 1 WLR 2196 [58]–[60]; *R (Nicholds) v Security Industry Authority* [2006] EWHC 1792 (Admin); [2007] 1 WLR 2067; *My Noodle Ltd v Queenstown Lakes District Council* [2010] NZCA 224; [2010] NZAR 152. See further Hilson (n 155) 117–120.

[189] [2010] NZCA 224; [2010] NZAR 152.

[190] Ibid, 169 per Glazebrooke J.

[191] Ibid.

[192] (1998) 43 NSWLR 687.

emphasised that an allegation of fettering would call for justification from the administrative decision-maker that application of the inflexible rule was appropriate in the individual case.

But such examples are relatively unusual. As well as undermining the intention of the legislature in most cases and undercutting the value of electoral legitimacy, applying soft law inflexibly would mean a decision-maker would not be 'always willing to listen to anyone with something new to say', which would cut against the important interests of individuals subject to the jurisdiction of the decision-maker.[193] Accordingly, 'a decision made solely by reference to the mandatory prescription of a guideline, despite a request to deviate from it in the light of the particular facts, may be set aside, on the ground that the decision maker's exercise of discretion was unlawfully fettered'.[194]

Second, any soft law instrument must be consistent with the general law under which the decision-maker operates.[195] For instance, in *Ishaq v Canada (Citizenship and Immigration)* an administrative rule (contained in an operational manual) banning the wearing of face coverings at citizenship ceremonies was unlawful because it was inconsistent with delegated legislation guaranteeing the greatest possible religious liberty in the conduct of such ceremonies.[196] To similar effect is the decision of the House of Lords in *R (Bapio Action Ltd) v Home Secretary*.[197] Here, the Health Secretary sought to restrict the number of non UK/EEA doctors working in the National Health Service. Her means of doing so, however, was to issue non-statutory guidance (her attempt to convince the Home Office to amend the Immigration Rules having come to nothing). To issue guidance in this way had the effect that 'a new term, unwritten and formally unauthorised, was being silently introduced into their permissions'.[198] In these cases, respect by the courts for the intention of elected representatives as given effect in the statutory provisions at issue—the value of electoral legitimacy—can again be understood to have loomed large.

Judicial judgement will always be necessary in determining whether judicial intervention would be appropriate on a particular set of facts involving soft law.[199] The question was neatly put by Wyn Williams J in *R (Suppiah) v Home Secretary*: 'it

[193] *British Oxygen Co Ltd v Minister of Technology* (n 165) 625 per Lord Reid. See generally Perry (n 155).

[194] *Thamotharem v Canada (Minister of Citizenship and Immigration* (n 162) [62] per Evans JA.

[195] See e.g. *Gillick v West Norfolk and Wisbech Area Health Authority* (n 181) AC 112; *Robinswood Pty Ltd v Federal Commissioner of Taxation* (1998) 39 ATR 305; *R v Secretary of State for the Environment, ex parte Tower Hamlets London Borough Council* [1993] QB 632.

[196] 2015 FC 156; (2015) 381 DLR (4th) 541.

[197] [2008] UKHL 27; [2008] 1 AC 1003.

[198] Ibid, [15] per Lord Bingham. See also [36] per Lord Rodger.

[199] In Australia, the appropriateness of subjecting soft law to judicial review absent an individualised decision affecting the applicant has been doubted. *Director of Animal and Plant Quarantine v Australian Pork Ltd* (2005) 146 FCR 368; *Patsalis v New South Wales* [2012] NSWCA 307; (2012) 81 NSWLR 742 and see generally Aronson, Groves and Weeks, (n115) chapter 3.8.

seems to me that there is clear and binding authority for the proposition that a policy which is in principle capable of being implemented lawfully but which nonetheless *gives rise to an unacceptable risk of unlawful decision-making* is itself an unlawful policy'.[200] But the judgement can be understood as falling to be exercised within a framework constructed by administrative law values.

Consider, finally, the discordant note struck by *R (Sandiford) v Foreign and Commonwealth Secretary*.[201] A British citizen accused by the Indonesian authorities of drug trafficking, an offence which carries the death penalty in that jurisdiction, wanted the British government to fund her defence. But the Foreign Secretary had adopted a blanket policy of not defraying legal expenses of British nationals who find themselves on the wrong end of the law while overseas. This was an exercise of the prerogative power over foreign affairs, not a statutory power.

The question for the courts was whether the published policy fettered the discretion of the minister. At the Court of Appeal, Lord Dyson MR concluded that, in matters prerogative, the rule against fettering discretion does not apply. As a previous bench of the Court of Appeal had put it in *R (Elias) v Secretary of State for Defence*, 'it is within the power of the decision-maker to decide on the extent to which the power is to be exercised in, for example, setting up a scheme. He can decide on broad and clear criteria and either that there are no exceptions to the criteria in the scheme or, if there are exceptions in the scheme, what they should be.'[202] Lord Dyson MR's analysis was endorsed on appeal. Lord Carnwath and Lord Mance put the point this way:

> [P]rerogative powers have to be approached on a different basis from statutory powers. There is no necessary implication, from their mere existence, that the State as their holder must keep open the possibility of their exercise in more than one sense. There is no necessary implication that a blanket policy is inappropriate, or that there must always be room for exceptions, when a policy is formulated for the exercise of a prerogative power.[203]

In other words, the concerns that lead courts to insist that statutory discretionary powers remain unfettered simply do not apply to prerogative powers. This oversimplifies the law relating to fettering of discretion, where respect for the decisions of elected representatives, as memorialised in legislation, is only one consideration relevant to understanding the structure of the law.[204] Indeed, their Lordships made

200 [2011] EWHC 2 (Admin) [137]. Emphasis added. For some of the complexities which might arise, especially in situations where a decision-maker has a degree of choice or flexibility in administering the policy, see *R (Bayer plc) v NHS Darlington CCG* [2020] EWCA Civ 449 [196]–[208], where there were (per Rose LJ, [214]) 'modes of implementation that [were] both lawful and realistic' and the decision-maker was not constrained by the policy as to its preferred mode of implementation.

201 n 186.

202 [2005] EWHC 1435 (Admin); [2006] 1 WLR 3213 [191].

203 *R (Sandiford) v Foreign and Commonwealth Secretary* (n 186) [62].

204 See Chapter 2.3.3.

no mention at all of the importance of protecting individual interests or effective and efficient public administration. *Sandiford* has been criticised for this reason,[205] and while it is perhaps a rare example of the judges not striking a balance between competing considerations, it may equally simply be an outlier apt to be distinguished or overruled at the next available opportunity.[206]

2.4 Conclusion

I have sought to demonstrate in this chapter that the basic principles relating to the no-bias principle and retention of discretion in contemporary administrative law can be understood in terms of administrative law values: individual self-realisation, good administration, electoral legitimacy and decisional autonomy. Across these areas of judicial review of administrative action, the protection of individual interests, the ensuring of effective and efficient public administration, the giving of effect to legislative choices and electoral mandates, and the maintaining of distinct roles for courts and administrative decision-makers can be understood as structuring administrative law and influencing the disposition of individual cases. In general, these considerations function in complementary fashion and, where they might potentially come into conflict, judges can be understood as having struck a balance between them, giving each as much effect as possible to each without emptying the others of substance altogether. This is a theme which will recur across the coming chapters.

[205] See Paul Daly, 'Royal Treatment: The Special Status of the Crown in Administrative Law' (2017) 22 *Review of Constitutional Studies* 81; Perry (n 155).

[206] See e.g. the fate of the unloved decision in *Rederiaktiebolaget Amphitrite v The King* [1921] 3 KB 500 (permitting the Crown to renege on a contract on the basis that it would have fettered prerogative power) when it came up for detailed consideration in *Searle v Commonwealth of Australia* [2019] NSWCA 127.

3
Procedural Fairness

The object of discussion in this chapter is the contemporary form of the second of the two rules of natural justice mentioned in the introduction to Chapter 2: *audi alteram partem*. In today's administrative law lexicon, *audi alteram partem* has become 'procedural fairness' or the 'duty of fairness'. The basic principle of these interchangeable terms is that an individual is entitled to 'some kind of hearing' before an administrative decision-maker, but not necessarily a hearing with the traditional trappings of a court.[1]

Quite how the contemporary duty of fairness should be understood has been the subject of controversy. In earlier times the administrative law world was much simpler: the rules of natural justice applied with full force to 'judicial' decision-making; whilst fairness obligations did not attach at all to 'administrative' or 'legislative' decisions. Those days are long gone, the tripartite classification consigned to history in the mid-20th century and replaced by a context-sensitive approach.[2] But the (alleged) lost certainty of the old is sometimes lamented; the new approach has been criticised for depending in its application on judges' ideological predispositions;[3] and some of those charged with following it have raised the concern that it may provoke the 'nightmare of a Tennysonian "wilderness of single instances"',[4] in which the outcome of any given case is impossible to predict. Such concerns have merit, but only to a point: the overall structure of the contemporary law of procedural fairness is undoubtedly contextual, but significant case law has accrued around exceptions to the duty of fairness and the individual procedural rights the duty protects. Context still matters, but in many respects the exceptions and individual procedural rights are more like relatively well-defined grounds of review, subject to distinct tests; judges are thus not roaming blindly in the wilderness for they have sufficient navigational guides with which to find their way.

To continue to flesh out my argument that the contemporary law of judicial review of administrative action can be understood in terms of the four values

[1] Henry Friendly, 'Some Kind of Hearing' (1975) 123 *University of Pennsylvania Law Review* 1267.

[2] See generally David Mullan, '"Fairness"—The New Natural Justice' (1975) 25 *University of Toronto Law Journal* 281.

[3] See e.g. Martin Loughlin, 'Procedural Fairness: A Study of the Crisis in Administrative Law Theory' (1978) 28 *University of Toronto Law Journal* 215, setting out, in an article which remains descriptively useful today, a variety of possible approaches judges who are more or less 'activist' and 'formalist' might take.

[4] *R (L) v West London Mental Health NHS Trust* [2014] EWCA Civ 47; [2014] 1 WLR 3103 [72] per Beatson LJ.

Understanding Administrative Law in the Common Law World. Paul Daly, Oxford University Press. © Paul Daly 2021.
DOI: 10.1093/oso/9780192896919.003.0003

I introduced in Chapter 1, I will first discuss the general structure of procedural fairness, noting how judicial solicitude for individual interests, effective and efficient public administration, the decisions of elected representatives and the maintenance of distinct roles for distinct bodies illuminates the general structure of the duty of fairness. Second, I will briefly discuss exclusions to the duty of fairness, again presenting them in terms of administrative law values. Third, I will discuss individual procedural rights—such as the right to notice and the right to legal representation—with a view to highlighting how these too can be understood in terms of individual self-realisation, good administration, electoral legitimacy and decisional autonomy.

It is appropriate to say a word at this point about two competing theoretical justifications that are often offered in support of the contemporary law of procedural fairness, the instrumental and the dignitarian.[5] Some take the view that the duty of fairness is instrumental, that its sole role and purpose is to enhance the accuracy of decisions.[6] Inasmuch as individuals are treated fairly, in an instrumental sense, they are given those rights and obligations set out by statute:

> The upshot should be a decision which is made by faithfully applying the statutory criteria, while respecting and giving effect to any other values and standards relevant in that context. A person whose application is dealt with in that way is treated fairly, and the procedures which lead to that result are fair procedures.[7]

Others argue that the duty of fairness requires administrative decision-makers to treat individuals with concern and respect; the fact that individuals can participate in decision-making processes that affect them has, on this view, an independent value distinct from the accuracy of the decision reached,[8] 'reflecting the citizen's status as an autonomous moral agent':

> The greater the litigant's participation—the stronger his control over the nature of the proceedings—the greater the moral authority of the outcome. Where he has heard the justification for an administrative act, presented in its most favourable light, and has been permitted to show its deleterious effect on his own interests, he is normally bound to accept the judgment of an unbiased arbiter, granting his assent.[9]

[5] See e.g. Matthew Groves and Greg Weeks, 'The Legitimacy of Expectations About Fairness: Can Process and Substance be Untangled?' in Bell et al eds, *Public Law Adjudication in Common Law Systems: Process and Substance* (Hart, Oxford, 2016). See also *SZRUI v Minister for Immigration* [2013] FCAFC 80 [5].

[6] See generally Denis Galligan, *Due Process and Fair Procedures* (Clarendon, Oxford, 1996).

[7] Ibid, 54.

[8] See generally TRS Allan, *Constitutional Justice: A Liberal Theory of the Rule of Law* (Oxford University Press, Oxford, 2001), 77–87.

[9] Ibid, 87. See e.g. *R (Pathan) v Secretary of State for the Home Department* [2020] UKSC 41; [2020] 1 WLR 4506 [126] per Lord Kerr and Lady Black: 'utility is not the only yardstick by which to measure the

My view is that '[the] justifications for procedural fairness are both instrumental and intrinsic':[10] decisional accuracy *and* the protection of individual interests can be understood to play an important role in the law of procedural fairness. As will become clear, however, I do not agree, first that either instrumental or dignitarian considerations trump the other or, second, that instrumental or dignitarian considerations are exhaustive of the concerns which can be understood to have influenced the contemporary scope and content of the duty of fairness.[11] Rather, the four values of individual self-realisation, good administration, electoral legitimacy and decisional autonomy can be understood as, in combination and in balance, illuminating the modern law of procedural fairness.[12]

3.1 The General Structure of the Duty of Fairness

To begin with, the courts recognise that the procedures appropriate to administrative decision-making may legitimately be different from judicial procedures. What is 'fair' for the purposes of administrative proceedings need not be modelled on the trial-type procedures followed by the courts, which are not the 'gold standard' against which administrative decision-makers are to be measured.[13] This is 'is an area of broad principle, not precise rules' drawn from judicial process:[14]

duty to act fairly in communicating to an individual why . . . a decision adverse to their interests has been or is to be taken' and ibid, [52].

[10] *Assistant Commissioner Condon v Pompano Pty Ltd* [2013] HCA 7; (2013) 252 CLR 38, 107 per Gageler J.

[11] See also Joanna Bell, *The Anatomy of Administrative Law* (Hart, Oxford, 2020), chapter 4.

[12] The Irish Supreme Court has recently written of the multiplicity of justifications for procedural fairness:

> The first is that an impartial decision-maker and an opportunity for the person affected to put forward his comments both help to promote an "appropriate" result. The second is that the duty to give reasons will assist the affected person in discerning whether the decision was valid or invalid in substance. The third is described as being "a matter of satisfaction and dignity to the individual" that he should have his say before a decision is taken against him by a government agency, or, in other words, have his "day in court". Finally, it is said that an open and consistent procedure in which the decision-maker is seen to be impartial is necessary to maintain the confidence of the general public in the institutions of government *O'Brien v Tribunal of Inquiry into Payments to Haughey and Lowry* [2016] IESC 36; [2017] 3 IR 501, 549 per O'Malley J, citing Gerard Hogan, David Gwynn Morgan and Paul Daly, *Administrative Law in Ireland* 4th ed (Roundhall, Dublin, 2010).

These can be understood, respectively, in terms of electoral legitimacy (by virtue of a more accurate implementation of the legislative design created by the elected representatives), decisional autonomy (inasmuch as the courts will be better able to fulfil their reviewing role), individual self-realisation and good administration (by promoting trust in government).

[13] *Kelly v Nova Scotia Police Commission* 2006 NSCA 27, 43 Admin LR (4th) 260 [21] per Cromwell JA. Cf *SAAP v Minister for Immigration and Multicultural and Indigenous Affairs* [2005] HCA 24; (2005) 228 CLR 294, 300 per Gleeson CJ: 'judicial procedure ought to be an example of fairness in action, and it is not surprising to find some aspects of that procedure taken up for some administrative purposes'.

[14] *Royal Australasian College of Surgeons v Phipps* [1999] 3 NZLR 1, 16 *per curiam*.

'the underlying premise is not one or more black-letter rules, but the notion of fairness'.[15]

It might be thought, as McTiernan and Taylor JJ had it in *Mobil Oil Australia Pty Ltd* v *Federal Commissioner of Taxation* 'that within the limits of its statutory authority it is for the Board and for the Board alone to regulate the conduct of proceedings before it'.[16] But if taken literally, the result would be to wall off decision-makers' procedural choices from judicial oversight; it would be to accord absolute priority (rather than weight) to the decisional autonomy of administrative decision-makers and, in turn, cause the judicial role to contract completely.

By contrast, in *Prassad v Canada (Minister of Employment and Immigration)*, Sopinka J stated that administrative decision-makers 'are considered to be masters in their own house', *but* 'subject to the proviso that they comply with the rules of fairness …' (and any applicable statutory provisions).[17] The latter approach, which reflects the contemporary state of the art, can be understood as permitting courts to give weight where appropriate to the importance of individual interests, accurate decision-making and effective and efficient public administration. As Byles J put it in the landmark case of *Cooper v Wandsworth Board of Works*, if the 'justice of the common law' so requires, the courts 'will supply the omission of the legislature', engraving additional procedural protections onto the statutory scheme,[18] where 'the statutory procedure is insufficient to achieve justice …'[19] Procedural requirements may only be implied into a statutory scheme by the courts where 'to require additional steps would not frustrate the apparent purpose of the legislation'.[20] For example, in *Cooper*, requiring the Board to give the owner notice of the proposed demolition and an opportunity to make representations would neither have displaced the Board as the primary decision-maker nor caused the court to trespass on the merits of the Board's ultimate decision on whether to demolish the property. The concern here can be understood to be not to frustrate the operation of the statutory scheme as adopted by the elected representatives in the legislature.

Judicial concern for the achievement of more accurate decision-making can be understood to support the affording of participatory rights to individuals liable

[15] *TCL Air Condition (Zhongshan) Co Ltd v Castel Electronics Pty Ltd* [2014] FCAFC 83; (2014) 232 FCR 361, 388.

[16] [1964] ALR 517; (1963) 113 CLR 475, 491.

[17] [1989] 1 SCR 560, 568–569. See similarly *TA Miller Ltd v Minister for Housing and Local Government* [1968] 1 WLR 992, 995 per Lord Denning MR: 'A tribunal of this kind is master of its own procedure, *provided that the rules of natural justice are applied*'; *Kiely v Minister for Social Welfare (No 2)* [1977] IR 267, 281 per Henchy J: 'Tribunals exercising quasi-judicial functions are frequently allowed to act informally—to receive unsworn evidence, to act on hearsay, to depart from the rules of evidence, to ignore courtroom procedures, and the like—*but they may not act in such a way as to imperil a fair hearing or a fair result.*' Emphasis added.

[18] *Cooper v Wandsworth Board of Works* (1863) 14 CB 180.

[19] *Wiseman v Borneman* [1971] AC 297, 308 per Lord Reid.

[20] Ibid.

to be affected by a decision. This reduces the risk of error,[21] thereby giving better effect to the statutory scheme established by elected representatives. One of the 'virtues of procedurally fair decision-making is that it is liable to result in better decisions, by ensuring that the decision-maker receives all relevant information and that it is properly tested':[22]

> As everybody who has anything to do with the law well knows, the path of the law is strewn with examples of open and shut cases which, somehow, were not; of unanswerable charges which, in the event, were completely answered; of inexplicable conduct which was fully explained; of fixed and unalterable determinations that, by discussion, suffered a change.[23]

Indeed, procedural fairness 'promote[s] congruence between the actions of decision-makers and the law which should govern their action'.[24] Even in so-called application cases, where an individual has applied for a benefit, privilege or status, a measure of fairness is required, if only to ensure that the decision-maker has sufficient information on which to form a judgment about whether to grant the individual that which is sought.[25] This can be understood to be supported by judicial solicitude for accurate administrative decision-making, given that faithful application of the statutory scheme developed by the legislature will be more likely if the decision-maker has elicited relevant information from the individual or individuals concerned.

Concern for decisional accuracy can be understood as flowing from judicial respect for electoral legitimacy, ensuring respect for the considered choices of elected representatives.[26] However, this value will not invariably point towards unlimited procedural protections. First, administrative decision-makers located 'closer to the

[21] See e.g. *Nicholson v Haldimand-Norfolk Regional Board of Commissioners of Police* [1979] 1 SCR 311, 328.

[22] *Osborn v The Parole Board* [2013] UKSC 61; [2014] 1 AC 1115 [67] per Lord Reed. See also *May v Ferndale Institution* 2005 SCC 82; [2005] 3 SCR 809 [117–118], where a majority of the Court made reference to the need to allow individuals a means of 'understanding' a decision-making process so that they could make a 'meaningful response' to the case against them, and 'rebut the evidence relied upon'.

[23] *John v Rees* [1970] Ch 345, 402 per Megarry J. Nonetheless, '[t]he hearing will not have been unfair if it has caused no substantial prejudice to the party claiming to be aggrieved': *Sheridan v Stanley Cole (Wainfleet) Ltd* [2003] EWCA Civ 1046; [2003] 4 All ER 1181, 1191 per Ward LJ. See further Chapter 5.6.

[24] *Osborn v The Parole Board* (n 22) [70] per Lord Reed.

[25] See e.g. *Re HK* [1967] 2 QB 617, 630 per Lord Parker CJ:

> [E]ven if an immigration officer is not in a judicial or quasi-judicial capacity, he must at any rate give the immigrant an opportunity of satisfying him of the matters in the subsection, and for that purpose let the immigrant know what his immediate impression is so that the immigrant can disabuse him. That is not, as I see it, a question of acting or being required to act judicially, but of being required to act fairly.

[26] An obvious point is that where a procedural right is granted by statute, it must be given full force and effect by any administrative decision-maker. See e.g. *Innisfil Township v Vespra Township* [1981] 2 SCR 145.

executive end of the spectrum', whose 'primary purpose is to develop, or supervise the implementation of, particular government policies', 'may require little by way of procedural protections'.[27] The mere fact that a decision is taken by an elected official does not, in and of itself, reduce the level of procedural protection,[28] but where the decision is to be taken on policy grounds by someone with a line of accountability to the legislature (and onwards to the electorate), the courts will attach fewer procedural obligations.[29] Second, in determining the content of the duty of procedural fairness in any given case, the 'terms of the statute which creates the function, the nature of the function and the administrative framework in which the statute requires the function to be performed' will be 'material factors', which may increase the extent of the duty of fairness but which may equally decrease it:[30] 'The role of the particular decision within the statutory scheme and other surrounding indications in the statute help determine the content of the duty of fairness owed when a particular administrative decision is made.'[31] Similarly, in situations where the legislature has entrusted a decision-maker with a measure of discretion, reviewing courts must factor this legislative choice into the procedural fairness calculus,[32] almost certainly to reduce the applicable procedural protections (for these are to be left, to some degree, to the discretion of the decision-maker).

Judicial imposition of a duty of fairness can be understood to promote individual self-realisation. On the one hand, someone affected by a decision is likely to feel a 'sense of injustice' if they do not have a say in the decision-making process;[33] we should not 'underestimate the feelings of resentment of those who find that a decision against them has been made without their being afforded any opportunity to influence the course of events.'[34] On the other hand, '[i]n the modern state the decisions of administrative bodies can have a more immediate and profound

[27] *Bell Canada v Canadian Telephone Employees Association* 2003 SCC 36; [2003] 1 SCR 884 [21]. Emphasis added. See also *South Australia v O'Shea* (1987) 163 CLR 378. See further Colleen Flood and Lorne Sossin, 'The Contextual Turn: Iacobucci's Legacy and the Standard of Review in Administrative Law' (2007) 57 *University of Toronto Law Journal* 581.

[28] See e.g. *Errington v Minister of Health* [1935] 1 KB 249.

[29] See e.g. *Franklin v Minister of Town and Country Planning* [1948] AC 87; *FAI Insurances Ltd v Winneke* (1982) 151 CLR 342, 369–371; *Imperial Oil Ltd v Quebec (Minister of the Environment* 2003 SCC 58; [2003] 2 SCR 624.

[30] *National Companies and Securities Commission v News Corporation Ltd* (1984) 156 CLR 296, 326 per Brennan J. See also *Mobil Oil Australia Pty Ltd v Federal Commissioner of Taxation* (1963) 113 CLR 475, 504 per Kitto J.

[31] *Baker v Canada (Minister of Citizenship and Immigration)* [1999] 2 SCR 817 [24] per l'Heureux-Dubé J.

[32] See e.g. *Local Government Board v Arlidge* [1915] AC 120, 144; *R v Secretary of State for the Home Department, ex parte Doody* [1994] 1 AC 531, 561; *Baker v Canada (Minister of Citizenship and Immigration)* (n31) [31]. See further Bruce Dyer, 'Determining the Content of Procedural Fairness' (1993) 19 *Monash University Law Review* 165; Peter Cane and Leighton McDonald, *Principles of Administrative Law. Legal Regulation of Governance*, 2nd edn (South Melbourne, Oxford University Press, 2012), 125.

[33] *Osborn v The Parole Board* (n 22) [68] per Lord Reed.

[34] *John v Rees* (n 23) 402. See also *New Brunswick (Minister of Health and Community Services) v G (J)* [1999] 3 SCR 46 [125] per L'Heureux-Dubé J, dissenting:

impact on people's lives than the decisions of courts' and thus their ability to order their affairs.[35] The 'justice' referred to in *Cooper* is associated with decisional accuracy but also with protecting individual interests: the subject of *Cooper*, indeed, was a property right in a house which the Board had demolished without prior warning to the owner.

These concerns for individual self-realisation can be understood to support a broad scope for procedural fairness, which has been conceived of as 'a general right' which arises 'autonomous of the operation of any statute'.[36] This formulation, drawn from a decision of the Supreme Court of Canada, evokes a concern for the protection of individual interests, transcendent of the intricacies of the statutory scheme at issue.[37]

Judicial concern that individuals should be treated with respect and facilitated in ordering their affairs is unsurprising in this context. Procedural fairness cases invariably involve a person (occasionally a legal person) who contends that their legal position has been modified, by the exercise of 'a power ... apt to affect the interests of an individual in a way that is substantially different from the way in which it is apt to affect the interests of the public at large';[38] that they have been 'subjected to pains or penalties'.[39] That procedural rights are very much personal to the individual is underscored by the principles that procedural rights may be waived[40] and that where the individual is *au fait* with the allegations against them,

> The determination of [the existence of a right to counsel] must take into account the important value of meaningful participation in the hearing, taking into account the rights affected, and the powerlessness that a reasonable person in the position of the claimant may legitimately feel when faced with the formal procedures and practices of the justice system.

35 *R v Higher Education Funding Council, ex parte Institute of Dental Surgery* [1994] 1 All ER 651, 667. And consider the words of Denning LJ in *Russell v Duke of Norfolk* [1949] 1 All ER 109, 119:

> [The] penalty of disqualification [from racing] is the most severe penalty that the stewards can inflict. It is the same penalty as that which is imposed on persons guilty of corrupt practices. It disqualifies the trainer from taking any part in racing and thus takes away his livelihood. Common justice requires that before any man is found guilty of an offence carrying such consequences, there should be an inquiry at which he has the opportunity of being heard.

See most notably *Ridge v Baldwin* [1964] AC 40; *Goldberg v Kelly*, 397 US 254 (1970), 264. But see also how a concern for individuals' livelihood has extended to decisions affecting their academic prospects and credentials, as in *Khan v University of Ottawa* (1997) 34 OR (3d) 535.

36 *Knight v Indian Head School, Division No 19* [1990] 1 SCR 653, 668.

37 Others might be tempted to link the duty of procedural fairness to legislative intent. But see *Ainsworth v Criminal Justice Commission* (1992) 106 ALR 11, 16–17, justifying the imposition of a duty of procedural fairness on alternate bases: arising from the operation of the relevant statutory provisions, failing which on the basis of 'the general law'.

38 *Kioa v West* (1985) 62 ALR 321, 373 per Brennan J. See also *Annetts v McCann* (1990) 170 CLR 596, 598 per Mason CJ, Dean and McHugh JJ.

39 *Selvarajan v Race Relations Board* [1976] 1 All ER 12, 19 per Lord Denning MR.

40 See e.g. *Carroll v Minister for Agriculture and Food* [1991] 1 IR 230. See also *R v Secretary of State for the Home Department, ex parte Al-Mehdawi* [1990] 1 AC 876, where the applicant had entrusted matters to his legal advisors, who had failed to communicate effectively with him, and was held to be unable to make out a claim of breach of natural justice.

procedural protections may appropriately be diminished.[41] These features can be understood to sound in the value of individual self-realisation, given how they relate to the freedom to choose not to be treated in a particular way by the state and to the relative absence of an effect on important interests when the individual concerned knows already why an administrative decision-maker proposes to make a given decision.

Consistent with the suggestion that judicial solicitude for individual interests can be understood to influence the extent of the duty of fairness in any given case, the greater the impact on the individual of the decision, the greater the procedural protection the individual should receive:[42] 'The more important the decision is to the lives of those affected and the greater its impact on that person or those persons, the more stringent the procedural protections that will be mandated.'[43] The greater the effect, one might say, the more the value of individual self-realisation is served by according robust procedural rights. As Lord Atkin remarked in *General Medical Council v Spackman*, 'I cannot think that the procedure which may be very just in deciding whether to close a school or an insanitary house is necessarily right in deciding a charge of infamous conduct against a professional man.'[44] On rare occasions, a benefit or privilege applied for will be of such importance to the individual as to impose a duty of fairness on the decision-maker.[45] Conversely, where the impact of a decision is relatively limited or qualified, less will be required by way of procedural protection.[46] For instance, the withdrawal of a licence to engage in a regulated profession will typically have more far-reaching consequences for an individual than the refusal of an initial application for a licence, and will thus require more by way of procedural protection:[47] 'the claims of natural justice are particularly strong where a party is being deprived of a right previously enjoyed, especially if it involves loss of livelihood.'[48] Where a licence has already been granted, the

[41] See e.g. *Wiseman v Borneman* (n 19); *Stevenson v United Road Transport Union* [1977] ICR 893, 905.

[42] See e.g. *Murdoch v New Zealand Milk Board* [1982] 2 NZLR 108, 115 ('The more drastic the consequences of a decision of a tribunal may be, the more strictly should the Courts insist on compliance with principles of natural justice').

[43] *Baker v Canada (Minister of Citizenship and Immigration)* (n 31) [25].

[44] [1943] AC 627, 638.

[45] *R v Secretary of State for the Home Department, ex parte Fayed* [1998] 1 WLR 763, 773 per Lord Woolf MR:

> Apart from the damaging effect on their reputations of having their applications refused the refusals have deprived them of the benefits of citizenship. The benefits are substantial. Besides the intangible benefit of being a citizen of a country which is their and their families' home, there are the tangible benefits which include freedom from immigration control, citizenship of the European Union and the rights which accompany that citizenship—the right to vote and the right to stand in parliamentary elections.

[46] *Wiseman v Borneman* (n 19).

[47] See generally *McInnes v Onslow-Fane* [1978] 1 WLR 1520. See also *R v Gaming Board for Great Britain, ex parte Benaim* [1970] 2 QB 417.

[48] *Secretary of State for Health, ex parte United States Tobacco International Ltd* [1992] QB 353, 370 per Taylor LJ. See also *R v Secretary of State for the Environment, ex parte Brent London Borough Council* [1982] QB 593.

individual has been able to order their affairs on the basis that they would continue to hold the licence into the future—their autonomy is thus engaged. By contrast, an applicant for a licence does not typically have a comparable interest.[49] In addition, the withdrawal of a licence will generally carry the implication that the licence-holder is, in some way, unfit to hold a licence and thereby cast doubt on their character in a way that a failed application for a licence does not.[50] Judicial solicitude for individual self-realisation can be understood to be very important in determining the extent of procedural protection required in a given case.

If fair procedures do indeed lead to more accurate results (as is reasonable to assume) the outcome will be a more faithful implementation of the statutory scheme put into operation by the legislature, whilst also respecting the interests of the individual concerned, by permitting them to participate in the decision-making process. Consider, for instance, this passage from *Mahon v Air New Zealand*, a Privy Council case dealing with an alleged lack of fairness in a public inquiry into an air disaster: 'any person represented at the inquiry who will be adversely affected by the decision to make the finding *should not be left in the dark* as to the risk of the finding being made and thus deprived of any *opportunity to adduce additional material of probative value* ...'[51] The first highlighted passage has a dignitarian focus, with its emphasis on the individual not being 'left in the dark', whereas the second highlighted passage emphasises the utility of 'additional ... probative' material being placed before the decision-maker, thereby enabling a more accurate decision to be taken. Similarly, as Deane J noted in *Kioa v West*, a case concerning the deportation of an unlawful immigrant, a matter traditionally thought to be within the absolute discretion of the executive, there are a variety of benefits to imposing procedural protections even on broadly drawn discretionary powers:

> ... the fact that the basis of a deportation order is merely that the person in question is a prohibited immigrant will not deprive the potential deportee of his ordinary right to a prior and adequate opportunity of being heard and of seeking to answer or avoid the reasons which appear to favour his deportation: he might wish to dispute his status as a prohibited immigrant; he might wish to raise particular matters which might arguably warrant the exercise of some special discretion in his favour or rebut particular matters which might be taken into account as weighing against the exercise of such a discretion; he might wish to challenge the wisdom or justice of the administrative policy in pursuance of which it is proposed to order that he be deported.[52]

[49] See e.g. *R (Khatun) v Newham London Borough Council* [2003] EWHC 2326 (Admin); [2005] QB 37 [31]–[32] (albeit dealing with an application for a benefit).

[50] *McInnes v Onslow-Fane* (n 47) 1532. To borrow from Oliver Wendell Holmes, if even a dog knows the difference between being tripped over and being kicked, a licensee certainly appreciates the difference between the refusal to grant a licence and the decision to withdraw a licence.

[51] [1984] AC 808, 821 per Lord Diplock.

[52] (1985) 159 CLR 550, 633.

Pushed to their logical conclusion, the values of individual self-realisation and electoral legitimacy would counsel almost unlimited procedural protections to promote individual interests and decisional accuracy. However, the courts can be understood to have balanced these values against others.

Judicial sensitivity to concerns for effective and efficient public administration can be understood to ensure that procedural protections are not so onerous as to unduly limit administrative decision-makers' flexibility and allocation of decision-making resources:[53] 'If there were too much elaboration of procedural safeguards, nothing could be done simply and quickly and cheaply.'[54] Of course, a '"fair" process inevitably slows matters down and costs the taxpayer money'[55] and '[a]t some point the benefit of an additional safeguard to the individual affected by the administrative action and to society in terms of increased assurance that the action is just, may be outweighed by the cost'.[56] There is thus a need to strike 'a balance between the need for expedition' and the interests of the individual in knowing and answering the case against them.[57] Accordingly, considerations of effective and efficient public administration can be understood to justify a reduction in the intensity of the procedural obligations placed on a decision-maker: 'the more burdensome and far-reaching the consequences, the more carefully must be scrutinised the rule that is said to produce them.'[58] Thus it was necessary to have regard, in determining the level of fairness appropriate to a decision to classify a prisoner as highly dangerous (with knock-on consequences for the prisoner's liberty), the 'practical considerations which must apply to the proper running of a prison'.[59] In general, courts are attentive to concerns for effective and efficient decision-making. As long ago as the early 20th century, courts recognised that administrative decision-makers need not follow trial-type procedures. Rather, '[t]hey can obtain information in any way they think best, always giving a fair opportunity to those who are parties in the controversy for correcting or contradicting any relevant statement prejudicial to their view'.[60]

[53] Cf the comments of McMahon J in *Khan v Health Service Executive* [2008] IEHC 234: 'To those involved in administration, adherence to fair procedure standards may appear cumbersome, irritating and even irksome on some occasions. Undoubtedly, the necessary adherence may slow down the administrators and may not be conducive to efficiency. But that is the way it is. The battle between fair procedures and efficiency has long since been fought and fair procedures have won out.'

[54] *Pearlberg v Varty* [1972] 1 WLR 534, 547 per Lord Pearson.

[55] *Canada (Attorney General) v Mavi* 2011 SCC 30; [2011] 2 SCR 504 [40] per Binnie J.

[56] *Mathews v Eldridge* 424 US 319 (1976) per Powell J. The reader will, I hope, forgive the citation to an American case which puts the point irresistibly well. See similarly *R (Refugee Legal Centre) v Secretary of State for the Home Department* [2004] EWCA Civ 1481; [2005] 1 WLR 2219 [8] per Sedley LJ. See also Paul Craig, *Administrative Law* 8th edn (Sweet and Maxwell, London, 2016) 352–353.

[57] *Wiseman v Borneman* (n 19) 308 per Lord Reid

[58] *McInnes v Onslow-Fane* (n 47) 1533 per Megarry J. Cf *Barratt v Howard* [2000] FCA 190; (2000) 96 FCR 428 and *Jarratt v Commissioner of Police for New South Wales* [2005] HCA 50; (2005) 224 CLR 44, where the Commissioner argued (unsuccessfully) that a statutory duty to operate 'effectively, efficiently and economically' eliminated the duty of fairness.

[59] *R v Secretary of State for the Home Department, ex parte McAvoy* [1998] 1 WLR 790, 799 per Lord Woolf MR.

[60] *Board of Education v Rice* [1911] AC 179, 182 per Lord Loreburn LC.

For instance, in *Local Government Board v Arlidge*, an early example of judicial modification of the rules of natural justice to fit the realities of the modern administrative state, individual interests were engaged because the Board's acts would 'affect the property and rights of individuals'.[61] But considerations of effectiveness and efficiency can be understood to have been invoked to justify the imposition of 'principles of substantial justice'[62] rather than the rigid rules of natural justice: 'When, therefore, Parliament entrusts it with judicial duties, Parliament must be taken, in the absence of any declaration to the contrary, to have intended it to follow the procedure which is its own, and is necessary if it is to be capable of doing its work efficiently.'[63] Disclosure of evidence received by the Board could impose a 'serious impediment ... upon that frankness which ought to obtain among a staff accustomed to elaborately detailed and often most delicate and difficult tasks', which would be 'inconsistent ... with efficiency [and] practice' as well as 'the true theory of complete parliamentary responsibility for departmental action': 'if administration is to be beneficial and effective, it must be the master of its own procedure.'[64] *Arlidge* supports the proposition that a concern for effective and efficient public administration can be understood to be relevant in calibrating the content of procedural fairness in any given case.

Accordingly, the content of procedural fairness depends on the particular decision-making context: 'what the requirements of fairness demand ... depends on the character of the decision-making body, the kind of decision it has to make and the statutory or other framework in question'.[65] As to the content of procedural fairness, 'the so-called rules of natural justice are not engraved on tablets of stone'.[66] Context, when it comes to procedural fairness, is everything.[67] This contextual analysis can be understood, as I have explained, in terms of administrative law values. Concerns for decisional autonomy support the basic point that it is for administrative decision-makers to design procedures appropriate to the purposes they seek to achieve. Where these procedures do not adequately respect the individual interests at stake, or the search for decisional accuracy, the courts will supplement them. But where procedures would be too onerous—given the stakes—courts will baulk at requiring them.

[61] [1915] AC 120, 150 per Lord Moulton.
[62] Ibid, 140 per Lord Parmoor.
[63] Ibid, 132 per Viscount Haldane.
[64] Ibid, 137 per Lord Shaw of Dunfermline.
[65] *Lloyd v McMahon* [1987] 1 AC 625, 702 per Lord Bridge of Harwich. See also *Mobil Oil Australia Pty Ltd v Federal Commissioner of Taxation* (n 30) 503–504; *Webster v Auckland Harbour Board* [1987] 2 NZLR 129; *Flanagan v University College Dublin* [1988] IR 724; *R (L) v West London Mental Health NHS Trust* [2014] 1 WLR 3103; *P v Minister for Justice and Equality* [2019] IESC 49.
[66] *Lloyd v McMahon* (n 65) 702 per Lord Bridge of Harwich.
[67] See e.g. *Russell v Duke of Norfolk* (n 35) 118.

3.2 Exceptions to the Duty of Fairness

There are several exceptions to the duty of fairness, which can be understood in terms of administrative law values. Two preliminary comments are in order. First, whether the exceptions are categorical in nature is doubtful. as Estey J unwittingly put it, in a Supreme Court of Canada decision which recognised an exclusion in respect of legislative action: 'It is *always* a question of construing the statutory scheme *as a whole* in order to see to *what degree*, if any, the legislator intended the principle to apply'.[68] Second, it is extremely rare for the duty of fairness to be excluded in its entirety. More often, the content of the duty of fairness will be reduced – not entirely eliminated – because of the relative force of administrative law values.

3.2.1 Legislative Decisions

Most prominently, legislative action has traditionally not been subject to the safeguards of procedural fairness. Where primary legislation is concerned, 'parliamentary tradition' and the doctrine of parliamentary sovereignty limit due process to the cut and thrust of parliamentary debate.[69] As Holmes J once put it, in such situations, individuals' 'rights are protected in the only way that they can be in a complex society, by their power, immediate or remote, over those who make the rule'.[70] And it has regularly been said that, where administrative action is legislative in nature, procedural fairness is excluded.[71]

Respect for the role of elected representatives can be understood as supporting the suggestion that 'plainly legislative' action carries no procedural fairness obligations.[72] Justificatory arguments have also been based on accountability to the legislature.[73] More convincing, however, certainly as applied to administrative action taken by unelected officials, are the concerns for effective and efficient public administration that feature prominently in this area. For instance, in *Attorney General of Canada v Inuit Tapirisat*, the Supreme Court of Canada considered the

[68] *Attorney General of Canada v Inuit Tapirisat* [1980] 2 SCR 735, 755. Emphasis added. See also *Bread Manufacturers of New South Wales v Evans* (1981) 180 CLR 404, 414–417 per Gibbs CJ, doubting the utility of classifying administrative action as executive or legislative and concluding, after a detailed consideration of the statutory scheme under review, that the *audi alteram partem* principle did not apply.

[69] See e.g. *Authorson v Canada (Attorney General)* [2003] 2 SCR 40 [37].

[70] *Bi-Metallic Investment Co v State Board of Equalization* 239 US 441 (1915), 445.

[71] This was an aspect of the scope of the prerogative writs generally: *R v Wright, ex parte Waterside Workers' Federation of Australia* (1955) 93 CLR 528, 541–542.

[72] *Bates v Lord Hailsham* [1972] 3 All ER 1019, 1024 per Megarry J. See e.g. *Cassidy v Minister for Industry and Commerce* [1978] IR 297; *Reference Re Canada Assistance Plan (BC)* [1991] 2 SCR 525; *Gorman v Minister for the Environment* [2001] 2 IR 414.

[73] *Wilson v Esquimalt and Nanaimo Railway Company* [1922] 1 AC 202, 213: 'The appointed authority for dealing with the matter, it must be remembered, was the Executive Government of the Province directly answerable to the Legislature . . .'

'practicality'—or lack thereof—of providing individual ratepayers with procedural rights prior to a decision of the national cabinet on the tariffs chargeable for telephone calls.[74] Permitting thousands of individuals to make submissions to a small deliberative body about the relatively technical matter of telephone tariffs would have imposed significant costs without obviously advancing the effective operation of the statutory scheme. Similarly, in *CREEDNZ v Governor-General*, McMullin J resisted the imposition of procedural obligations on the executive in the context of legislation providing for streamlined procedures for projects of national importance because doing so 'would involve delay and would frustrate the very purpose of legislation which is intended to provide for the prompt consideration of proposed works of national importance'.[75] The concerns found in these two cases (which involved bodies composed of elected representatives but whose lessons apply more broadly) do not necessarily oust the duty of fairness, but they certainly justify a loosening of its constraints: 'The larger the class of persons reasonably expected to be affected, the less the likelihood that procedural fairness will be attracted and, if it is, the lower the likely content of the duty'.[76]

Another way to understand the removal of procedural protections in cases involving legislative decisions is that individual interests are simply not engaged in a meaningful way by a decision affecting the public at large. Significant individual interests are not at stake in, say, the setting of national telephone tariffs, which involves complex economic calculations about the rate of return on investment to be expected by utilities companies and imposes *de minimis* costs on individuals.[77] On this approach, the duty of procedural fairness attaches only to a decision 'which directly affects the person (or corporation) individually and not simply as a member of the public or a class of the public'.[78] But where action that is legislative in form touches a small number of people, reviewing courts happily impose procedural protections, the better to protect the individual interests at stake.[79] And, more generally, the English courts have begun to recognise a common-law duty to consult those affected by 'legislative' action, typically triggered by a legitimate expectation of consultation where a benefit is to be withdrawn from a group.[80] Notably, the

[74] [1980] 2 SCR 735, 754 per Estey J. See also *FAI Insurances Ltd v Winneke* (n 29).

[75] [1981] 1 NZLR 172, 206. See also *Bread Manufacturers of New South Wales v Evans* (n 68).

[76] *Castle v Director General, State Emergency Service* [2008] NSWCA 231 [6] per Basten JA.

[77] Cf *Manitoba (Hydro-Electric Board) v Manitoba (Public Utilities Board)* 2020 MBCA 60.

[78] *Salemi v Minister for Immigration & Ethnic Affairs (Cth) (No 2)* (1977) 137 CLR 396, 452 per Jacobs J.

[79] See e.g. *Re Mountcharles' Estate* [1935] IR 163 (although note that despite its use of the language of natural justice, the Supreme Court seemed to see the matter as one of *vires*); *Homex Realty v Wyoming (Village)* [1980] 2 SCR 1011, 1031 ('purported culmination of an *inter partes* dispute conducted on adversarial lines . . .'); *Bank Mellat v Her Majesty's Treasury (No 2)* [2013] 3 WLR 179; *Garda Representative Association v Minister for Public Expenditure and Reform* [2016] IECA 18 [45] per Hogan J. Cf. *Environmental Defence Society Inc v South Pacific Aluminium Ltd* [1981] 1 NZLR 146, 148 per Cooke J, expressing doubt about whether a court could quash an Order in Council.

[80] *R (Moselely) v Haringey London Borough Council* [2014] UKSC 56; [2014] 1 WLR 3947. See e.g. *R (Article 39) v Secretary of State for Education* [2020] EWCA Civ 1577.

point that 'the demands of fairness are likely to be somewhat higher when an authority contemplates depriving someone of an existing benefit or advantage than when the claimant is a bare applicant for a future benefit' can, again, be understood in terms of judicial solicitude for individual interests.[81] Where none are in play at all, the duty of fairness is not engaged but the greater the extent to which a general measure targets or interferes with the individual interests of identifiable persons, the more onerous the procedural obligations imposed.[82]

3.2.2 Emergencies

At the very least, where there is an emergency, 'one is at the low end of the duties of fairness'.[83] Often, 'the apparently urgent or emergency nature of the decision' will justify the abrogation of procedural rights.[84] At issue in *White v Redfern* was the procedure under the Public Health Act 1875 for the seizure and destruction of food 'diseased or unsound or unwholesome or unfit for the food of man'. Field J was mindful of the urgent nature of decisions taken under these provisions:

> The practice of selling unsound meat is, as every one who reads the newspapers must know, a great evil, which requires prompt and stringent measures for its repression. To prevent the evil it is obvious that it may be necessary that very rapid and summary proceedings should be taken.[85]

Effective and efficient—that is to say, in this case, rapid—public administration can be understood to have been central here. As 'the paramount object would appear to be the speedy destruction of a noisome and unwholesome thing', it was unnecessary to give notice to the owner of the spoiled meat.[86] Moreover, giving effect to the considered choices of elected representatives as memorialised in the statutory scheme can be understood to have supported the judge's concern that acceding to

[81] *R v Devon County Council, ex parte Baker* [1995] 1 All ER 73, 91 per Brown J, quoted with approval in *R (Moselely) v Haringey London Borough Council* (n 80) [27]. See also *Burke v Minister for Labour* [1979] IR 354; *R (Article 39) v Secretary of State for Education* (n 80) [85]. See generally Geneviève Cartier, 'Procedural Fairness in Legislative Functions: The End of Judicial Abstinence?' (2003) 53 *University of Toronto Law Journal* 217.

[82] See also *R (Article 39) v Secretary of State for Education* (n 80) [84], per Baker LJ where 'established practice' was relevant to the duty of consultation imposed in that case: holding officials to published policies can be understood in terms of good administration. See Chapters 2.3.3.1 and 8.2.2.

[83] *R v Secretary of State for Transport, ex parte Pegasus Holdings (London) Ltd* [1988] 1 WLR 990, 1000 per Schiemann J.

[84] *Cardinal v Director of Kent Institution* [1985] 2 SCR 643, 655 (prison segregation).

[85] (1879) 5 QBD 15, 17.

[86] Ibid, 18.

the owner's argument 'would throw such obstacles in the way of [the Act's] operation as might almost make it a dead letter'.[87]

Those concerned about the implications of depriving an individual of property without due process can comfort themselves, as Field J. did, with the possibility that compensation would have been payable under other provisions of the Act[88] (and, perhaps, with the knowledge that emergency action is sometimes taken to protect the rights of third parties[89]). It is not necessarily the case, moreover, that the existence of an emergency will justify the removal of procedural protections altogether.[90] At the very least, consistent with the importance of safeguarding individual interests, additional procedures may be required subsequent to an emergency decision.[91]

[87] Ibid, 19 per Manisty J. See also *R v Birmingham City Council, ex parte Ferrero Ltd* [1993] 1 All ER 530, 542 per Taylor LJ, where a duty to consult prior to the removal by a local authority of dangerous objects from sale under section 14 of the Consumer Protection Act 1987 was rejected, as '[t]here would be a danger that although the authority reasonably suspected goods were dangerous they would feel bound to delay serving a notice until they consulted the trader whereas, without a duty to consult, they would have served forthwith. Valuable time would be lost and danger could result'; *CREEDNZ v Governor-General* [1981] 1 NZLR 172, 177 per Cooke J, where it would have been impossible to provide for a hearing for property owners affected by the granting of consent for projects of national importance prior to the triggering by the executive of a procedure designed to facilitate strategically important projects 'without doing violence to the scheme of the Act'; and *O'Callaghan v Commissioners of Public Works* [1985] ILRM 364, where it was held that the Commissioners had acted legitimately in making, without notice, a preservation order in respect of a 2,000-year-old fort the plaintiff farmer seemed intent on destroying.

[88] (1879) 5 QBD 15, 17.

[89] See e.g. *R v Secretary of State for Transport, ex parte Pegasus Holdings (London) Ltd* (n 83) 1000, where in the context of a suspension of permission to foreign pilots to operate commercial aircraft in the United Kingdom, Schiemann J commented: 'one has to bear in mind the magnitude of the risk, by which I mean not so much the high percentage chance of it happening but the disastrous consequences of what would happen if something did happen. It is the old problem that one has with installations of nuclear power, or vehicles such as aeroplanes carrying a large number of people, that, if something goes wrong, then very many lives will be lost.'

[90] See e.g. *R (Shoesmith) v Ofsted* [2011] EWCA Civ 642 [60] per Maurice Kay LJ, where the 'degree of urgency' arising from the fact that 'vulnerable children' were involved had to be balanced against the 'catastrophic consequences' for the applicant of being removed from her job.

[91] See e.g. *Cardinal v Director of Kent Institution* (n 84); *Midwood v Paremoremo Medium Security Prison Superintendent* [1991] 1 NZLR 442, 445; *R v Life Assurance and Unit Trust Regulatory Organisation Ltd, ex parte Ross* [1993] QB 17, 52–53. See also *Ozepulse Pty Ltd v Minister for Agriculture Fisheries and Forestry* [2007] FCA 1601; (2007) 98 ALD 287, 301 per Emmett J: 'urgency will not of itself exclude the right to procedural fairness, although it may, in particular circumstances, reduce the content of the right to procedural fairness'. In *CREEDNZ v Governor-General* (n 87) 177 per Cooke J, as the very purpose of the National Development Act 1979 was to streamline planning procedures for projects of national importance, it was 'only to be expected that some rights will be done away with in the process'. It was also said, by Richardson J (at 191), to be 'of some significance in evaluating the scheme of the provision from the viewpoint of natural justice that . . . the provisions of the Act [can] be applied to a proposed work only where the elaborate criteria set out are satisfied to the statutory standards reflected in a positive finding that the work is likely to be in the national interest and . . . meet[s] the exacting test of essentiality'. Note, however, that the individuals affected would have been able to participate in a public inquiry subsequent to the initiation of the fast-track procedure.

3.2.3 Legislative Ouster

Hovering over all procedural fairness issues—save for situations in which a procedural right is constitutional in nature—is the prospect of legislative intervention. The legislature 'may certainly exclude or limit the application of the general rules' of procedural fairness, as long as it does so 'clearly and expressly',[92] but '[s]uch an intention is not to be assumed nor is it to be spelled out from indirect references, uncertain inferences or equivocal considerations. The intention must satisfactorily appear from express words of plain intendment'.[93] Where procedural rights—in whole or in part[94]—are excluded or compromised by express statutory language, the other values cannot come to the rescue.[95] This might be thought to privilege the giving of effect to legislative intent to the exclusion of other considerations. However, first, the exacting requirement that there be 'a strong manifestation of ... statutory intention' to exclude the duty of procedural fairness can be understood as being influenced by the concerns that would arise if no procedural protections were available to affected individuals[96]—it can be understood, itself, as the result of a balance being struck between different values. Second, judges are in any event extremely reluctant to conclude that procedural fairness rights have successfully been ousted: 'Statutory protections are minima, not maxima, and the courts will supplement the procedures by reference to common law standards of fairness.'[97]

Consider also the unusual case of *CPCF v Minister for Immigration and Border Protection*.[98] A ship with asylum seekers on it was intercepted by an Australian customs ship, which took the passengers aboard before eventually disembarking

[92] *Wiseman v Borneman* (n 19) 318 per Lord Wilberforce.

[93] *Commissioner of Police v Tanos* (1958) 98 CLR 383, 396 per Dixon CJ and Webb J.

[94] See e.g. *Maynard v Osmond* [1976] 3 WLR 711.

[95] Arguments may also be based on necessary implication from express statutory language. Compare e.g. *Roberts v Parole Board* [2005] UKHL 1; [2005] 2 AC 738 with *R v Secretary of State for the Home Department, ex parte Doody* (n 32) 562. See also *Grech v Minister of Immigration* (1991) 105 ALR 107, where there was no duty of fairness in respect of a power of arrest, given that the whole purpose of arresting an individual is to bring them within the judicial system.

[96] *Kioa v West* (n 38) 347 per Mason J. See e.g. *Fraser v State Services Commission* [1984] 1 NZLR 116, 121; *R v Secretary of State for the Home Department, ex parte Fayed* (n 45) 773–777; *Re Minister for Immigration and multicultural Affairs, ex parte Miah* [2001] HCA 22; (2001) 206 CLR 57; *R (West) v Parole Board* [2005] UKHL 1; [2005] 1 WLR 350 [29]; *Saeed v Minister of Immigration and Citizenship* [2010] HCA 23; (2010) 241 CLR 252, 258.

[97] Philip Joseph, *Constitutional and Administrative Law in New Zealand* 4th edn (Thomson Reuters, Wellington, 2014), 1028. See generally Matthew Groves, 'Exclusion of the Rules of Natural Justice' (2013) 39(2) *Monash University Law Review* 285. See also *Furnell v Whangarei* [1973] 2 NZLR 705, where the statutory and regulatory code for the discipline of teachers was so comprehensive that it could not be supplemented by the requirements of procedural fairness but where what was at issue was not a final decision; *Plaintiff S10/2011 v Minister for Immigration and Citizenship* [2012] HCA 31; (2012) 246 CLR 636, where no fairness requirements attached to a highly discretionary ministerial power to grant visas to those who had failed to meet the statutory criteria, a situation where any applicant would already have gone through an elaborate (and perfectly procedurally fair) decision-making process.

[98] [2015] HCA 1; (2015) 255 CLR 514.

them into immigration detention on the Cocos Islands. Before the High Court of Australia it was unsuccessfully argued that some sort of hearing should have been given to the passengers when they were brought aboard the Australian vessel, because the individuals might have been able to provide information about final destinations that would be dangerous for them. Procedural fairness was held to be incompatible with the legislative framework but the reasons for this conclusion were subtle and context-sensitive. The requirements of procedural fairness were said to be 'essentially practical' and dependent on 'the legislative framework and the circumstances of the particular case'.[99] The maritime officers on the Australian vessel were acting under the direction of the Minister in consultation with other members of the executive,[100] which was 'permissible' in this particular context.[101] The result was that 'there was no occasion under the statute for a maritime officer to consult with the plaintiff as to the destination to which he was to be compulsorily removed'.[102] As French CJ described it, there was 'no appropriate administrative framework to afford ... a meaningful opportunity to be heard'.[103] In general, any discretion the maritime officer might have had was pre-empted by the directions from on high.[104] Given the importance accorded to the ministerial directions, the decision seems to rest on a nexus of statutory language and executive action that simply rendered procedural fairness inappropriate at the moment of detention.

3.3 Procedural Fairness Rights

The contemporary law of procedural fairness is context-sensitive.[105] In general the issue to be addressed in this section is: 'What procedural protections, if any, are necessary for this particular decision-making process?'[106] And, again, in general the answer is such procedures 'as would provide reasonable fairness in all of the circumstances'.[107] But this question is not to be asked and answered simply by reference to context: more particular considerations attach to individual procedural fairness rights. I will focus on the particularities in this section, using administrative law values to elucidate them.

99 Ibid, [306] per Kiefel J.
100 See e.g. ibid, [38] per French CJ, describing the direction as 'decisive'.
101 Ibid, [364] per Gageler J.
102 Ibid, [500] per Keane J.
103 Ibid, [52].
104 Ibid, [501] per Keane J.
105 See Chapter 3.1.
106 Mullan (n 2) 315. Any of these rights can be regulated by statute, in which case respect for the considered choices of elected representatives requires close attention to the statutory provisions in question. This discussion focuses on the general common law principles relating to procedural fairness rights. In some cases, these may assist courts in determining the contours of procedural fairness rights regulated by statute.
107 *International Vessels Ltd v Minister for Marine (No 2)* [1991] 2 IR 93, 102 per McCarthy J.

3.3.1 Scope of Procedural Fairness

The touchstone in this area is whether a decision has modified, in a meaningful way, the legal position of the individual or individuals concerned. Where once remedies were restricted to decisions, taken 'judicially', having an impact on 'rights',[108] they may now be issued in respect of decisions affecting 'the rights, interests, property, privileges, or liberties of any person'.[109] Accordingly, 'what is decisive is the nature of the power, not the character of the proceeding which attends its exercise'.[110] It has also been suggested that the appropriate question for a court to ask is whether there is a 'real risk that a party's rights will be interfered with in the event that there is an adverse decision';[111] interference here includes a decision 'capable of [having] material practical effects on the exercise and enjoyment of the rights'.[112]

Two decisions are especially instructive, one older, one more recent.[113] In *Re Pergamon Press*[114] inspectors had been appointed by the Board of Trade under the Companies Act 1948 to investigate the conduct of those involved in a failed takeover bid. For various reasons, including the initiation of litigation in the United States, several of those involved did not wish to cooperate with the inspectors. The inspectors applied to the courts to move matters along. This was not a judicial review application, but it was nonetheless part of Lord Denning MR's conclusion that

[108] *R v Electricity Commissioners, ex parte London Electricity Joint Committee Company (1920) Ltd* [1924] 1 KB 171.

[109] *Martineau v Matsqui Institution Disciplinary Board (No 2)* [1980] 1 SCR 602, 623 per Dickson J, dissenting. See e.g. *Schmidt v Secretary of State for the Home Department* [1969] 2 Ch 149 (immigration); *Daganayasi v Minister of Immigration* [1980] 2 NZLR 130 (immigration); *Chief Constable of the North Wales Police v Evans* [1982] 1 WLR 1155 (probationary police officer); *Mahon v Air New-Zealand Ltd* [1984] AC 808, 820 (public inquiry influencing one's 'career or reputation'); *Irvine v Canada (Restrictive Trade Practices Commission)* [1987] 1 SCR 181 (regulatory investigation); *Annetts v McCann* (n 38) (coroner inquiry); *Ramsever v Mahon* [2005] IESC 82; [2006] 1 IR 216 (coroner inquiry).

[110] *Ainsworth v Criminal Justice Commission* (n 37) 17 per Mason CJ, Dawson, Toohey and Gaudron JJ. As Mason J explained in *FAI Insurances Ltd v Winneke:*

> The fundamental rule is that a statutory authority having power to affect the rights of a person is bound to hear him before exercising the power ... The application of the rules is not limited to cases where the exercise of the power affects rights in the strict sense. It extends to the exercise of a power which affects an interest or a privilege ... or which deprives a person of a 'legitimate expectation' ... in circumstances where it would not be fair to deprive him of that expectation without a hearing.

(n 29) 360, citations omitted.

[111] *Dellway Investments Ltd v National Asset Management Agency* [2011] 4 IR 1, 204 per Murray CJ, approving the High Court.

[112] Ibid, 327 per Fennelly J.

[113] See also *Lower Hutt City Council v Bank* [1974] 1 NZLR 545 (procedural fairness applicable to road closure decision); *Barreau du Québec c Khan* 2011 QCCA 792 (procedural fairness applicable to examinations process for entry to a regulated profession).

[114] [1971] Ch 388. See similarly *Hot Holdings Pty Ltd v Creasy* (1996) 185 CLR 149. But see also *Ainsworth v Criminal Justice Commission* (n 37), where certiorari was held not to be available in respect of a report imposing reputational damage on the applicant, albeit that the High Court of Australia did give declaratory relief in respect of a breach of procedural fairness. It has been said that 'the precise scope of the test laid down in *Ainsworth* and *Hot Holdings* is not easy to identify and apply' (*Patsalis v Attorney General for New South Wales* (2013) 85 NSWLR 463, 474 per Basten JA).

the rules of natural justice applied, even to an investigation which would not, of itself, modify the legal rights and obligations of those involved:

> [The inspectors] have to make a report which may have wide repercussions. They may, if they think fit, make findings of fact which are very damaging to those whom they name. They may accuse some; they may condemn others; they may ruin reputations or careers. Their report may lead to judicial proceedings. It may expose persons to criminal prosecutions or to civil actions. It may bring about the winding up of the company, and be used itself as material for the winding up ... Even before the inspectors make their report, they may inform the Board of Trade of facts which tend to show that an offence has been committed ... When they do make their report, the Board are bound to send a copy of it to the company; and the board may, in their discretion, publish it, if they think fit, to the public at large. Seeing that their work and their report *may lead to such consequences*, I am clearly of the opinion that the inspectors must act fairly.[115]

Here, the focus can be understood to be on the interests of those whose reputations might be sullied by the investigative process.

In the more recent case, *Dellway Investments Ltd v National Asset Management Agency*,[116] the Irish Supreme Court held that the transfer of a mortgage from a financial institution to a regulatory body with slightly more extensive powers than the bank was a decision attracting procedural fairness guarantees. The Agency argued that it had simply assumed the responsibilities of the financial institutions, leaving the applicants with precisely the same contractual rights and obligations as before; indeed, the 'asset' being transferred was the financial institution's, not the applicants'. But the Supreme Court rejected this argument, on the basis that the Agency had, by virtue of statute, powers that a bank does not have.[117] As Fennelly J put it: 'The consequence of an acquisition decision is to make a substantial change in the way in which the applicants are in a position to exercise their property rights. Their ability to manage their properties

[115] [1971] Ch 388, 399. Emphasis added. See also *Brettingham-Moore v St Leonards Municipality* (1969) 121 CLR 509; *In re Haughey* [1971] IR 217; *State (Shannon Atlantic Fisheries Ltd) v McPolin* [1976] IR 93; *Hot Holdings Pty Ltd v Creasy* (n 114); *Peters v Davison* [1999] 2 NZLR 164; *Royal Australasian College of Surgeons v Phipps* (n 14). Compare *R v Sloan* [1990] 1 NZLR 474 but note that its authority is questionable: *University of Auckland v Tertiary Education Commission* [2004] 2 NZLR 668. In general, this is an area in which 'no bright lines can be drawn': *Saraceni v Australian Securities and Investments Commission* (2013) 211 FCR 298, 313 per Jacobson and Gilmour JJ (FCAFC).

[116] (n 111).

[117] Its enabling statute permitted it to specified certain rights and obligations that were not transferred; it enjoyed, in general, privileges and immunities that a transferee of a mortgage would not normally have; it could seek a vesting order in relation to a property rather than the appointment of a receiver, as a mortgagee ordinarily would; and it had additional privileges and immunities in relation to the applicants' equity of redemption, something greatly cherished by common law courts. See generally (n 111) 359–372.

independently is reduced.'[118] Note that there was no suggestion that the Agency would actually use its additional powers to modify the applicants' legal position; there existed only the possibility of such modification at some point in the future. Again, the interests of the individuals concerned—here, relating to control of property and commercial freedom—can be understood as having been central to the analysis.[119]

Moreover, where no obligation of procedural fairness attaches to a preliminary decision, it will typically be the case that fair procedures will be supplied subsequently, as Geoffrey Lane LJ explained in *Lewis v Heffer*:

> In most types of investigation there is in the early stages a point at which action of some sort must be taken and must be taken firmly in order to set the wheels of investigation in motion. Natural justice will seldom if ever at *that* stage demand that the investigator should act judicially in the sense of having to hear both sides. No one's livelihood or reputation at that stage is in danger. But the further the proceedings go and the nearer they get to the imposition of a penal sanction or to damaging someone's reputation or to inflicting financial loss on someone the more necessary it becomes to act judicially, and the greater the importance of observing the maxim audi alteram partem.[120]

The availability of procedural protections subsequent to the initiation of a decision-making process makes the extension of procedural fairness to preliminary decisions in cases such as *Pergamon Press* and *Dellway* all the more notable. So anxious are courts to safeguard the interests of individuals that they insist on fairness from the earliest possible stage, even though the individual would benefit from robust procedural protection before a final decision was taken. This was clear in *Rees v Crane*, where the fact that further investigations would be conducted before a final decision was taken in respect of an allegation that a sitting judge was unfit to hold office did not obviate the need for procedural fairness, given the 'considerable publicity' generated by a preliminary decision to suspend the judge (on full pay), 'which subsequent revocation of the suspension would not necessarily dissipate'.[121] Evidently, the protections available at a preliminary stage will not be especially extensive (and a concern for effective and efficient public administration can be understood to be operative here) but the important point is that they are available at all.

[118] Ibid, 331. Emphasis deleted.
[119] See also *Fletcher (as Liquidators of Octaviar Administration Pty Ltd) v Anderson* [2014] NSWCA 450.
[120] [1978] 1 WLR 1061, 1078–1079. Emphasis original.
[121] [1994] 2 AC 173, 194. See also *Dunnes v Maloney* [1999] 3 IR 542.

3.3.2 Notice and Comment

The right to notice is 'the most elementary protection'.[122] The right carries with it a requirement that the reason proposed for acting against the individual be disclosed, along with 'the essential facts and findings alleged to constitute that reason' and a correlative opportunity to comment: the provision of 'a reasonable opportunity of presenting his response to that notice'.[123] This can include providing a reasonable time for the preparation of a response to the notice[124] and to any matters added subsequently.[125] It includes an adjournment of proceedings in appropriate circumstances to facilitate properly informed presentation of the issues.[126] An applicant may even have a right of reply to arguments raised by the other side, though this is a consideration that will typically arise only in an adjudicative setting.[127] In the unusual case of *R (Pathan) v Secretary of State for the Home Department*,[128] notice of a decision to revoke his employer's certificate of sponsorship was required in order to permit the applicant to take steps to make alternative arrangements. Even though the applicant, who was an economic migrant, could make no relevant submissions about the revocation of certification, his case could be 'regarded as akin to the conventional procedural fairness situation of an applicant being allowed to make further submissions with a view to improving the chances of his application

[122] *Malloch v Aberdeen Corporation* [1971] 1 WLR 1578, 1582 per Lord Reid. See similarly ibid, 1598. See also *Re Haughey* [1971] IR 217; *Kioa v West* (n 38); *Supermarchés Jean Labrecque Inc v Québec (Tribunal du Travail)* [1987] 2 SCR 219; *TV3 v Independent Radio and Television Commission* [1994] 2 IR 439; *C (K) v College of Physical Therapists (Alberta)* (1999) 72 Alta LR (3d) 77.

[123] *State (Gleeson) v Minister for Defence* [1976] IR 280, 296 per Henchy J. See e.g. *Royal Australasian College of Surgeons v Phipps* (n 14); *Gribbles Pathology (Vic) Pty Ltd v Cassidy* [2002] FCA 859; (2002) 122 FCR 78, 104; *R (Afzal) v Election Court* [2005] EWHC Civ 647; [2005] LGR 823, 844; *R (Bourgass) v Secretary of State for Justice* [2015] UKSC 54; [2015] 3 WLR 457 [100–101].

[124] See e.g. *R v Thames Magistrates' Court, ex parte Polemis* [1974] 1 WLR 1371, 1375 per Lord Widgery CJ; *Goyal v Canada (Minister of Employment & Immigration)* (1992) 4 Admin LR (2d) 159.

[125] See e.g. *Rich v Christchurch Girls' High School Board of Governors (No 1)* [1974] 1 NZLR 1, 9.

[126] See e.g. *Priddle v Fisher & Sons* [1968] 1 WLR 1478 but compare *Macdonald v Institute of Chartered Accountants of British Columbia* (2010) 295 BCAC 217 [52] per Kirkpatrick JA, where the request for an adjournment 'was not genuine but simply a further attempt to delay the already prolonged process'. It has been suggested that administrative resources will legitimately weigh heavily in the balance when determining whether to grant an adjournment. See also David Jones and Anne de Villars, *Principles of Administrative Law* 6th edn (Edmonton, Carswell, 2014), 342: 'Request for an adjournment must frequently be balanced against the value of continuing with the hearing in a timely fashion, particularly where the administrative tribunal has a public interest mandate.' Delay in the administrative process might, in and of itself, represent a breach of procedural fairness, due to the deleterious effects on the applicant, but such cases will be exceedingly rare. For discussion see *Flynn v An Post* [1987] IR 68; *Blencoe v British Columbia (Human Rights Commission)* [2000] 2 SCR 307; *NAIS v Minister for Immigration and Multicultural and Indigenous Affairs* [2005] HCA 77; (2005) 228 CLR 470; *Gillen v Commissioner of An Garda Síochána* [2012] IESC 3; [2012] 1 IR 574; *Abrametz v Law Society of Saskatchewan* 2020 SKCA 81.

[127] See e.g. *Communications, Energy and Paperworkers Union of Canada Local 141 v Bowater Mersey Paper Co Ltd* 2010 NSCA 19; (2010) 3 Admin LR (5th) 261 and note that there was no entitlement 'to a progress report ... on the interim cogency of the opponent's submission' ([54] per Fichaud JA).

[128] (n 9).

succeeding'.[129] Had he been notified, he would have had a 'real and distinct advantage' in terms of ordering his affairs[130] in view of 'a major disruption' to his life and that of his family,[131] a point which can be understood in terms of individual self-realisation.

The right is personal to the individual and, as such, will not be violated where the individual 'knew perfectly well' the allegations against her.[132] That the right is personal to the individual suggests it can be understood as being grounded in the protection of individual interests.[133] Indeed, the objective of the right has been said to be to give individuals a 'fair crack of the whip'.[134]

The gravitational force of any duty to disclose information will not be identical in all circumstances.[135] Final decisions implicating individual interests,[136] for instance, will require, because of their effect on those concerned, a higher degree of disclosure than preliminary proceedings where a privilege to engage in economic activity is involved.[137] This does not require an explicit attempt to balance liberty interests versus economic privileges but can be understood simply as reflecting the

[129] Ibid, [103] per Lord Kerr and Lady Black.

[130] Ibid, [105] per Lord Kerr and Lady Black. See also ibid, [139] per Lord Kerr and Lady Black:

> It can be argued that the making of submissions on the decision to be taken is integral to the decision-making process, whereas the opportunity to avoid the effect of an adverse outcome by taking a course not directly connected to that process is not. But why should this make a difference to the characterisation of the duty? Again, the notion of what is fair holds the key. If there is a duty to allow representations to be made for the purpose of bringing about a result favourable to the representor, why should it not also be fair to allow the affected person to have the chance by a different means to secure that outcome? In both cases the duty to act fairly involves allowing the opportunity to influence the result. And in both cases, in our opinion, the duty is properly to be regarded as a procedural duty.

[131] Ibid, [126] per Lord Kerr and Lady Black. See also [69] per Lady Arden, referring to the 'profound influence on the life of the applicant'.

[132] *Russell v Duke of Norfolk* (n 35) 117 per Tucker LJ. See e.g. *Davis v Carew-Pole* [1956] 1 WLR 833, 839–840; *Gallagher v Revenue Commissioners (No 1)* [1991] 2 IR 370, 374. But this proposition must be applied with caution: see e.g. *R (Balajigari) v Secretary of State for the Home Department* [2019] EWCA Civ 673; [2019] 1 WLR 4647, where the allegation was of dishonesty; Underhill LJ responded with a hypothetical question at [160]:

> [W]e do not believe that it was fair that Mr Kawos should have been expected to give detailed and definitive answers to an accusation of dishonesty without any prior notice. The contrary view seems to us to depend on the assumption that he must have known what the Secretary of State had in mind and should therefore have come prepared to face an interview in which he would have to give a detailed explanation of the original error in order to rebut an allegation of dishonesty; but if he was in fact innocent—which is the very question which the Secretary of State had to decide—why should he have anticipated any such thing?

[133] It has been said, in addition, that where an administrative decision-maker 'is aware that an order it might make could have a detrimental effect on the rights, interests or obligations of someone who is not an immediate party to the proceedings, it should ordinarily inquire whether the person wishes to be heard on the matter'. *Waitemata Health v Attorney-General* [2001] NZFLR 1122, 1150 per Tipping J.

[134] *Fairmount Investments Ltd v Secretary of State for the Environment* [1976] 2 All ER 865, 874 per Lord Russell of Killowen.

[135] *P v Minister for Justice and Equality* (n 65) [4.5–4.6].

[136] See e.g. *May v Ferndale Institution* (n 22).

[137] See e.g. *Strauts v College of Physicians & Surgeons (British Columbia)* (1997) 94 BCAC 254.

fact that individual interests are engaged to a greater extent in the former than in the latter case.

An affected individual must have 'a fair opportunity to make any relevant statement which he may desire to bring forward and a fair opportunity to correct or controvert any relevant statement brought forward to his prejudice',[138] the purpose of which can be understood as ensuring that relevant material is placed before the decision-maker, with a view to improving the accuracy of the final decision.[139] In *R v Hull Prison Board of Visitors, ex p. St-Germain (No 2)*, where prisoners suspected of involvement in a prison riot had been subjected to disciplinary proceedings, the prospect of a 'very substantial loss of liberty' (engaging autonomy interests) and the need to establish 'the vital facts at issue' (engaging the accuracy of the final decision) compelled the conclusion that the prisoners had, as a matter of fairness, the right to introduce evidence.

But a concern for effective and efficient public administration can also be found in the same case. Geoffrey Lane LJ noted that it was perfectly proper for the chairman of a prison disciplinary proceeding to require questions to be put through him for fear that otherwise arguments might break out[140] and, in principle, to 'limit the number of witnesses', for instance because the prisoner by calling a large number of witnesses meant to 'render the hearing of the charge virtually impracticable'.[141] In addition, it is well established that administrative decision-makers are not under any positive obligation to seek out relevant information[142]—to require

[138] *De Verteuil v Knaggs* [1918] AC 557, 560 per Lord Parmoor. See also *O'Callaghan v Mahon (No 1)* [2006] 2 IR 42 and *Ogawa v Minister for Immigration and Citizenship* [2011] FCA 1358; (2011) 199 FCR 51, 58 per Flick J, laying out a set of considerations relevant to assessing the adequacy of notice, but also emphasising (58–59) that '[a]ny assessment must necessarily be made by reference to the facts and circumstances of each individual case'.

[139] See e.g. *Board of Trustees of the Maradana Mosque v Mahmud* [1967] 1 AC 13, 24–25; *Fairmount Investments Ltd v Secretary of State for the Environment* (n 134) 1260 per Viscount Dilhorne ('it was contrary to natural justice for his decision to confirm the order to be based to a very considerable extent on an opinion, which investigation might have shown to be erroneous ... ') and, 1265–1266 per Lord Russell of Killowen; *Fraser v State Services Commission* (n 96) 124; *Marlborough Harbour Board v Goulden* [1985] 2 NZLR 378, 381–382. This right can, however, be waived: *Watson v BC Securities Commission* 1999 BCCA 625 [14].

[140] [1979] 1 WLR 1401, 1406:

> Those who appear before the board of visitors on charges are, ex hypothesi, those who are serving sentences in prison. Many such offenders might well seek to render the adjudications by the board quite impossible if they had the same liberty to conduct their own defences as they would have in an ordinary criminal trial. In our judgment the chairman's discretion is necessary as part of a proper procedure for dealing with alleged offences against discipline by prisoners.

[141] Ibid, 1406. See similarly *Bailey v A'Hearn* (1968) 13 FLR 199, 205–206 (Cth Industrial Court); *Egan v Governor of Wheatfield Prison* [2014] 1 IR 64 [27].

[142] See e.g. *Keogh v Criminal Assets Bureau* [2004] 2 IR 159, 176; *Puloutele v Minister of Immigration* [2006] NZHC 1091 [27–28]; *Sriskandarajah v United States of America* [2012] SCC 70; [2012] 3 SCR 609 [29–30]; *EK (Ivory Coast) v Secretary of State for the Home Department* [2014] EWCA Civ 1517; [2015] Imm AR 367 [32–35]; *SZSYG v Minister for Immigration* [2015] FCA 1319 [23–24]; *R (Pathan) v Secretary of State for the Home Department* (n 9) [108]. Of course, 'different considerations may arise' once information is in the possession of a decision-maker, such that fairness may require disclosure: *ATP15 v Minister for Immigration and Border Protection* [2016] FCAFC 53; (2016) 241 FCR 92,

them to do so would impose potentially costly and time-consuming obligations. In a similar vein, and sensibly, '[a] defect in any notice (whether relating to content, period or service) can be cured by providing any necessary further details and granting further time for the preparation of responses';[143] this can be understood to support the efficient use of scarce decision-making resources.

There is an instructive discussion of notice in *May v Ferndale Institution*.[144] The applicants, who were serving life sentences, had been transferred to a medium-security prison from a minimum-security facility. A reclassification exercise, based on feeding information about the applicants into a scoring matrix, prompted the decision to transfer them. At issue was whether the failure to disclose details of the underlying components of the scoring matrix was a breach of procedural fairness and of a statutory disclosure requirement. A majority of the Supreme Court of Canada held that it was, for two reasons. First, the applicants had been 'deprived of information essential to understanding the computerised system which generated their scores', knowing only 'what the factors were' but unaware of 'how values were assigned to them or how those values factored into the generation of the final score'.[145] The issue here was that the applicants were kept in the dark about a decision implicating fundamental liberty interests.[146] Second, it was not possible to formulate 'a meaningful response to a reclassification decision without information explaining how the security rating is determined', which raised the risk of an inaccurate reclassification decision being reached.[147] The Court can be understood to have been concerned about protecting the value of individual self-realisation and facilitating the accurate implementation of the legislative scheme designed by elected representatives.

Where the disclosure of information would imperil third parties, courts have greater scope to refuse disclosure. As Lord Denning MR explained, in the context of an application for a licence to run a gaming club, the regulator was obliged to gather relevant information, but was not required to 'tell the applicant the source of their information, if that would put their informant in peril or otherwise be contrary to the public interest'.[148] In such a situation, both the applicant and the third

108 per Flick J, dissenting. Although Flick J was dissenting, the case turned on the interpretation of a statutory provision, and his general proposition is sound.

[143] Mark Aronson, Matthew Groves and Greg Weeks, *Judicial Review of Administrative Action and Governmental Liability* 6th edn (Thomson Reuters, Sydney, 2017) [8.170].
[144] 2005 SCC 82; [2005] 3 SCR 809.
[145] Ibid, [117].
[146] Ibid, [101], stressing the 'importance' of the decision for the applicants.
[147] Ibid, [118].
[148] *R v Gaming Board for Great Britain, ex parte Benaim* (n 47) 431. See also *Ansett Transport Industries Ltd v Minister for Aviation* (1987) 72 ALR 469, 498–499 (commercially sensitive information); *Edwards v Toime* [2009] NZAR 47, 61 (legal professional privilege); *Roberts v Parole Board* (n 95) [48]. In *National Companies and Securities Commission v News Corporation* (n 30) 323–324, disclosure was limited so as not to frustrate the statutory purpose of an investigative process relating to alleged breaches of securities law. But here the investigative process was to be succeeded by a more formal proceeding, at which disclosure would, of course, be required.

party can be understood to have a concern for their self-realisation.[149] Rather than engage in a straightforward balancing of the relative importance of the competing interests,[150] Lord Denning MR adopted a compromise position: 'the board ought in every case to be able to give to the applicant sufficient indication of the objections raised against him such as to enable him to answer them'.[151] In other words, rather than assign an absolute priority to the applicant's interest on the one hand or the informant's interest on the other, the focus was on ensuring that the applicant had enough information to enable him to respond—to be informed 'in more or less general terms of the gist of the reasons'[152]—thereby increasing the likelihood of a more accurate decision being reached.[153] Where requiring disclosure would help to produce a decision more faithful to the statutory scheme, courts will be more willing to find a breach of the duty of fairness as a result of non-disclosure.[154] It is notable, however, that the rules which apply to disclosure of information in the judicial process do not apply in respect of administrative decision-making processes, a point which can be understood in terms of judicial solicitude for the decisional autonomy of administrative decision-makers.[155]

Lastly, a requirement of even-handedness follows from the basic requirements of notice and comment: 'the judge or whoever has to adjudicate must not hear evidence or receive representations from one side behind the back of the other'.[156]

[149] In addition, future informants might not come forward if their confidence is not respected, thereby inhibiting effective and efficient public administration. See e.g. *Ansett Transport Industries Ltd v Minister for Aviation* (n 148) 498–499; *ENZA Ltd v Apple and Pear Export Permits Committee* [2001] 3 NZLR 456, 462.

[150] See e.g. *Re K (An Infant)* [1965] AC 201.

[151] *R v Gaming Board for Great Britain, ex parte Benaim* (n 47) 431. See also *R v Secretary of State for the Home Department, ex parte McAvoy* (n 59).

[152] *R (Bourgass) v Secretary of State for Justice* (n 123) [103] per Lord Reed. See similarly *Applicant VEAL of 2002 v Minister for Immigration and Multicultural and Indigenous Affairs* [2005] HCA 72; (2005) 225 CLR 88, noting at 98, the 'public interest in ensuring that information that has been or may later be supplied by an informer is not denied to the Executive government when making its decisions'.

[153] See also *Roberts v Parole Board* (n 95) [76] per Lord Woolf [109] per Lord Steyn, and [143] per Lord Carswell.

[154] See e.g. *Pitt Polder Preservation Society v Pitt Meadows (District)* (2000) 189 DLR (4th) 219.

[155] See e.g. *P v Minister for Justice and Equality* (n 65) [4.23] per Clarke CJ:

> ... in judicial proceedings, a court cannot have regard, in coming to its ultimate conclusion on the merits, to materials or evidence which were not available generally to the parties. It does not necessarily follow that, in all circumstances, a balancing of competing interests would necessarily lead to the same conclusion in the context of a purely administrative decision making process which did not involve the administration of justice itself. Likewise, it is not for a court to rule on whether materials need to be disclosed except in proceedings in which the lawfulness of an administrative decision is challenged. Such questions are at least initially matters for the administrative decision maker, subject only to review by the courts on the grounds of lawfulness.

[156] *Kanda v Government of Malaya* [1962] AC 322, 337. See e.g. *Denton v Auckland City* [1969] NZLR 256; *Volkswagen Northern Ltd v Alberta (Industrial Relations Board)* (1964) 49 WWR 574; *Kane v Board of Governors of University of British Columbia* [1980] 1 SCR 1105; *Killiney and Ballybrack v Minister for Local Government (No. 1)* (1978) 112 ILTR 9; *Mercier v Canada* (1994) 167 NR 241; *Kiely v Minister for Social Welfare (No. 2)* (n 17); *O'Sullivan v Law Society* [2012] IESC 21. See also *Kioa v West* (n 38) 628–629 per Brennan J.

Strikingly, and supporting the view that procedural fairness is concerned not just with effectiveness and efficiency and decisional accuracy but also with the protection of individual interests, '[t]he court will not inquire whether the evidence or representations did work to his prejudice'; it is 'sufficient that they *might* do so'.[157] Where a court intervenes on the basis of a 'risk' of 'prejudice' to the individual,[158] rather than the actualisation of the danger, it is difficult to maintain that only considerations of efficacy, efficiency and accuracy are relevant.

3.3.3 Oral Hearing

There is no 'general rule that procedural fairness requires an administrative decision-maker to afford a person affected by the decision an oral hearing in every case'.[159] In delineating the circumstances in which an oral hearing will be required as a matter of procedural fairness, the courts can be understood to have struck a balance between the protection of individual interests and the accurate implementation of statutory schemes.[160] In *Lloyd v McMahon*,[161] the House of Lords can be understood to have relied heavily on the latter consideration in concluding that councillors who had been held personally liable by a local government auditor for financial losses incurred by Liverpool City Council were not entitled to an oral hearing prior to the imposition of liability. The crux of the issue was that the councillors' case, being based on 'a large volume of documentary material, clearly lent itself more aptly to written than oral presentation'.[162] This was emphatically not a case 'where an oral hearing would clearly be essential in the interests of fairness', for instance because there was a dispute about the underlying facts,[163] doubt

[157] *Kanda v Government of Malaya* (n 156) 337. Emphasis added.

[158] Ibid, 337.

[159] *Minister for Immigration and Border Protection v WZARH* [2015] HCA 40; (2015) 256 CLR 326, 336 per Kiefel, Bell and Keane JJ.

[160] Effective and efficient public administration can also be understood to have exerted an influence in this area, inasmuch as requiring an oral hearing of all issues will generally be cumbersome and delay the decision-making process. See e.g. *Branch-Allen v Easther* [2016] TASSC 29; (2016) 217 LGERA 147 (Supreme Court of Tasmania), 175 per Blow CJ, where what was at issue was an investigation into an allegedly dysfunctional local authority, 'an inquiry whose subject-matter is so wide that an oral hearing involving a full investigation of every disputed allegation and every asserted error of judgment would simply not be feasible.'

[161] [1987] AC 625.

[162] Ibid, 706 per Lord Bridge of Harwich. See also *Mobil Oil Canada Ltd v Canada-Newfoundland Offshore Petroleum Board* [1994] 1 SCR 202, 225–226 per Iacobucci J, where a written hearing would have been adequate to address the issue, a proposed interpretation of the decision-maker's governing statute and *White v New Zealand Stock Exchange (No 2)* [2002] NZAR 342, 354–355 per Richardson P where most applications for membership of the Exchange would involve 'a straightforward decision on the papers in which the Board would, of course, exercise its judgment as to whether, having regard to the applicant's past conduct and his references, it could satisfy itself that the applicant would carry out his or her responsibilities as a member and stockbroker honestly and diligently … and would meet the standard of conduct of members …'

[163] See e.g. *Heatley v Tasmanian Racing and Gaming Commission* (1977) 137 CLR 487, 516. See also *Re Haughey* [1971] IR 217, where the seriousness of the allegations (with implications for the applicant's

existed about the credibility of one of the individuals involved,[164] or (albeit that this is likely to be unusual) the individual concerned would be unable to participate effectively through writing;[165] circumstances in which the accuracy of the decision could be put at risk by a failure to hear the individual in person. Here, an oral hearing would have added nothing of value, because through the written procedure the councillors were 'afforded ample opportunity to express their views, and the auditor was enabled to reach a decision in the light of every defence which it was possible for the appellants to urge'.[166]

The importance of the individual interests at stake can, however, be understood to justify the requirement of holding an oral hearing in some cases, as Lord Reed made clear in *Osborn v Parole Board:*

> The board should also bear in mind that the purpose of holding an oral hearing is not only to assist it in its decision-making, but also *to reflect the prisoner's legitimate interest in being able to participate in a decision with important implications for him*, where he has something useful to contribute. An oral hearing should therefore be allowed where it is maintained on tenable grounds that a face to face encounter with the board, or the questioning of those who have dealt with the prisoner, is necessary to enable him or his representatives to put their case effectively or to test the views of those who have dealt with him.[167]

There is an ambiguity in this passage, in that the highlighted portion reflects a concern for interests personal to the prisoner, whereas the subsequent clause suggests that considerations of accuracy are paramount, in that an oral hearing will only be granted where the prisoner has 'something useful to contribute', presumably so as to enhance the accuracy of the final decision. The fairest reading of this passage, however, is that these considerations *and* those of individual interest should

good name) counted in favour of an oral hearing. See further *R (West) v Parole Board* (n 96) per Lord Bingham of Cornhill (though see also [35], where his Lordship suggested that even where important facts are not in dispute the Board 'may well be greatly assisted' by an oral hearing, because the undisputed facts 'may be open to explanation or mitigation, or may lose some of their significance in the light of other new facts'; this case, it is worth emphasising, involved individuals who were recalled to prison having been released, a significant interference with individual interests: see further *Osborn v Parole Board* (n 22) [83] per Lord Reed).

[164] [1987] AC 625, 696 per Lord Keith of Kinkel. See e.g. *Khan v University of Ottawa* (n 35); *SUN v Refugee Applications Commissioner* [2013] 2 IR 555; *Minister for Immigration and Border Protection v WZARH* (n 159) 338–339; *Cadillac Investments Ltd v Northwest Territories (Labour Standards Board)* (1993) 24 Admin LR (2d) 81 [18].

[165] *Chen v Minister for Ethnic Affairs* (1994) 121 ALR 83, 90–91.

[166] [1987] AC 625, 715 per Lord Templeman.

[167] [2013] UKSC 61; [2014] 1 AC 1115 [82]. Emphasis added. It is also possible that a statute will expressly or by necessary implication provide for an oral hearing. See e.g. *Estate Agents Board v Nakic* [1983] 2 VR 570 (Supreme Court of Victoria), where the best reading of the statutory references to 'hearing' was that an oral hearing was required for applications to the Board.

be understood to be relevant—indeed, interlinked—given Lord Reed's concern to highlight the importance to the prisoner of being able to participate in a process going to the heart of his or her liberty interests.[168] This can be understood to be an example of the value of individual self-realisation, supported by electoral legitimacy in the form of decisional accuracy, outweighing (without entirely negativing) the value of good administration inasmuch as the holding of an oral hearing is inevitably costly in terms of time and other scarce resources.

3.3.4 Cross-examination

In general, evidence received by an administrative decision-maker need not be 'tested by cross-examination'; it is sufficient that the decision-maker 'give[s] the other side a fair opportunity of commenting on it and of contradicting it'.[169] This approach can be understood in terms of a judicial desire not to compromise effective and efficient public administration: '[cross-examination] increases the length, formality and cost of proceedings; it may accentuate conflict; and, if there are many parties involved, it may make the proceedings quite unmanageable.'[170]

There will, nonetheless, be some issues of such importance 'that one cannot afford to have them dealt with by a court which is not particular about its procedure',[171] such as, for instance, allegations of 'serious' professional misconduct with the potential to impact an individual's good name and ability to earn a livelihood.[172] A concern for the accurate implementation of the statutory scheme can

[168] See also *Koia v Waitangi Tribunal* [2011] NZHC 47 [94] per Dobson J: 'The nature and extent of a right of reply depends on the scale of the issues involved, the nature of the Court or Tribunal, the relative components of fact and law in the contested issues, the pace at which the proceeding is expected to be progressed and a range of other matters ...' These factors can be understood as sounding in respect for individual interests and a concern for effective and efficient public administration.

[169] *TA Miller Ltd v Minister for Housing and Local Government* (n 17). See similarly *R v War Pensions Entitlement Appeal Tribunal, ex parte Bott* (1933) 50 CLR 228, 248–250; *Kavanagh v Chief Constable of Devon and Cornwall* [1974] QB 624; *O'Rourke v Miller* (1985) 156 CLR 342, 353 per Gibbs CJ 360–361 per Wilson J; *Rawson Finances Pty Ltd v Commissioner of Taxation* [2013] FCAFC 26; (2013) 296 ALR 307, 350–351.

[170] Mark Aronson, Matthew Groves and Greg Weeks, Judicial Review of Administrative Action and Governmental Liability 6th ed. (Thomson Reuters, Sydney, 2017) [8.370] (citations omitted).

[171] *R v Milton Keynes Justices, ex parte R* [1979] 1 WLR 1062, 1063 per Lord Widgery CJ (a case involving care proceedings). See also *Ramsay v Australian Postal Commission* [2005] FCA 640; (2005) 147 FCR 39, 47. This includes the interests of third parties: 'The prime instance where cross-examination will be necessary to satisfy the demands of natural justice is when the reputation of a third person or organisation is in issue': *Badger v Whangarei Refinery Expansion Commission of Inquiry* [1985] 2 NZLR 688, 705 per Barker J. See *a contrario Wolfe v Robinson* [1962] OR 132, where there was no right to cross-examine as individual interests were held not be engaged, on the basis that the underlying administrative proceeding (an inquest) would not produce binding legal effects. Although a similar result is unlikely to be reached today, the focus on individual interests (or the lack thereof) as influencing the right to cross-examination in administrative proceedings is instructive.

[172] *Finch v Goldstein* (1981) 36 ALR 287, 304 per Ellicott J. See e.g. *Borges v Fitness to Practice Committee* [2004] 1 IR 103.

also be understood to support a right to conduct cross-examination in some cases, especially where there are hotly contested issues of fact which could be teased out by a robustly adversarial proceeding.[173]

In a Canadian case involving a regulatory investigation on matters of competition law, the Supreme Court of Canada was explicit about the need to strike a balance between what I would describe as good administration and individual self-realisation:

> *Courts must, in the exercise of this discretion [to require additional procedures], remain alert to the danger of unduly burdening and complicating the . . . investigative process.* Where that process is in embryonic form engaged in the gathering of raw material for further consideration, the inclination of the courts is away from intervention. *Where, on the other hand, the investigation is conducted by a body seized of powers to determine, in a final sense or in the sense that detrimental impact may be suffered by the individual, the courts are more inclined to intervene.*[174]

Understood in terms of administrative law values, the first highlighted passage underlines the Court's concern not to impede effective and efficient public administration by disincentivising or rendering unduly burdensome preliminary investigations designed to ensure the smooth operation of a regulatory regime.[175] Similarly, questions or lines of questioning can be excluded, in the interests of expeditious decision-making, albeit that 'it is plain that cross-examination can be so excluded or abridged or interfered with that there will be a denial of natural justice'.[176] The second highlighted passage emphasises that where individual interests are engaged to the point where 'detrimental impact' may be suffered, the right to cross-examination is more likely to arise.[177]

[173] See e.g. *Jackson v Region 2 Hospital Corp.* (1994) 24 Admin LR (2d) 220; *R v Hull Prison Board of Visitors, ex parte St-Germain (No 2)* (n 140) 1409; *Australian Postal Commission v Hayes* (1989) 87 ALR 283, 289; *Bell v Victoria University of Wellington* [2010] NZHC 2200 [195–196]. See also *Barrier Reef Broadcasting Pty Ltd v Minister for Post and Telecommunications* (1978) 19 ALR 425, 445–447, where the right to cross-examine was inferred from a statutory scheme which provided for a court-like process.

[174] *Irvine v Canada (Restrictive Trade Practices Commission)* (n 109) 235 per Estey J. See also the factors enumerated per Estey J.

[175] See e.g. *Del Zotto v Minister of National Revenue* [2000] 4 FC 321.

[176] *R v Dobson, ex parte ANM* (1975) 15 ACTR 33, 36 per Fox J.

[177] See e.g. *R v Hull Prison Board of Visitors, ex parte St-Germain (No 2)* (n 140) 1408, 1411 per Geoffrey Lane LJ, emphasizing the 'substantial' liberty interests at stake and their relevance to the degree of fairness required. See also *Re Hirt and College of Physicians and Surgeons (British Columbia)* (1986) 34 DLR (4th) 331; *Beckner v Minister for Immigration, Local Government and Ethnic Affairs* (1991) 30 FCR 49. Contrast *R v Commission for Racial Equality, ex parte Cottrell and Rothon* [1980] 1 WLR 1580, 1587.

3.3.5 Rules of Evidence

As if to reflect the distinction between judicial and administrative decision-making, a fundamental feature of the law relating to evidence in administrative proceedings is that 'technical rules of evidence ... form no part of the rules of natural justice', with the emphasis instead on the probative value of the material in question:

> The requirement that a person exercising quasi-judicial functions must base his decision on evidence means no more than it must be based upon material which tends logically to show the existence or non-existence of facts relevant to the issue to be determined, or to show the likelihood or unlikelihood of the occurrence of some future event the occurrence of which would be relevant.[178]

An administrative decision-maker may thus consider 'any material which is logically probative even though it is not evidence in a court of law'.[179] This judicial solicitude for the introduction of and reliance on probative material can be understood in terms of a concern for decisional autonomy and accurate decision-making. Similarly, great leeway is given to administrative decision-makers to rely on background information and knowledge derived from the exercise of their functions.[180] However, a decision-maker should 'exercise care' in doing so, given that

[178] *R v Deputy Industrial Injuries Commissioner, ex parte Moore* [1965] 1 QB 456, 488 per Diplock LJ. See similarly *Kiely v Minister for Social Welfare (No 2)* (n 17); *Mahon v Air New-Zealand Ltd* (n 109); *Re Minister for Immigration and Cultural Affairs, ex parte Applicant S154/2002* (2003) 77 ALJR 1909; *Alberta (Workers' Compensation Board) v Alberta (Workers' Compensation Board Appeals Commission)* (2005) 258 DLR (4th) 29 [62–66]. See also *May v Ferndale Institution* (n 22) [89–93] (rules of disclosure developed for criminal proceedings not applicable in an administrative setting).

[179] *Kavanagh v Chief Constable of Devon and Cornwall* (n 169) 633 per Lord Denning MR. This principle is sometimes given a statutory basis: see e.g. *Mooring v Canada (National Parole Board)* [1996] 1 SCR 75 [29]. In the *Kavanagh* case, the Crown Court heard an appeal from the refusal of the Chief Constable to grant a shotgun certificate and registration as a firearms dealer to the applicant. Lord Denning commented, at 633:

> It seems to me that the Crown Court is in the same position as the court of quarter sessions. The Crown Court is to try cases according to the same rules as the court of quarter sessions used to do. The court of quarter sessions, when trying criminal cases, applied the rules of evidence applicable to criminal cases. But from time immemorial the court of quarter sessions exercised administrative jurisdiction. When so doing, the justices never held themselves bound by the strict rules of evidence. They acted on any material that appeared to be useful in coming to a decision, including their own knowledge. No doubt they admitted hearsay, though there is nothing to be found in the books about it.

[180] See e.g. *Starr v Minister of Pensions* [1946] 1 KB 345, 353; *Christchurch District Licensing Agency Inspector v Karara Holdings Ltd* [2003] NZAR 752, 767–768; *Scorgie v Minister for Immigration and Citizenship* [2008] FCAFC 101 [36–44] (albeit addressing a discrete statutory provision). See generally Matthew Groves, 'The Power of an Administrative Tribunal to Inform Itself' (2015) 22 *Australian Journal of Administrative Law* 236.

the applicant will not have an opportunity to contest the information and knowledge, further underscoring the importance of accurate decision-making.[181]

Effective and efficient public administration can also be understood to be significant in restraining the extent to which such background information and knowledge can be put in issue before an administrative decision-maker. *Bushell v Secretary of State for the Environment*[182] is instructive. A local inquiry was held into the routing of a motorway. One of the elements relied on by the inspector in coming to his conclusions was a central government report on traffic volumes, a report based on various assumptions and statistical models. Lord Diplock accepted that fairness required that those opposed to the motorway project have a right to 'be given sufficient information . . . to enable them to challenge the accuracy of any facts and the validity of any arguments', that supporters 'should also be heard' and that 'those adversely affected by the modification should be given an opportunity of stating their reasons for objecting to it'.[183] Yet these individual interests[184] could only be given limited space because of the 'expense and inconvenience to other parties to the inquiry which would be caused by any resulting prolongation of it', a consideration which can be understood as sounding in concern for effective and efficient public administration:

[181] *Peel Law Association v Pieters* 2013 ONCA 396; (2013) 363 DLR (4th) 598 [120] per Juriansz JA. Reliance on one's lay knowledge of scientific processes (relating, for instance, to the absorption of alcohol in the human body) has been especially liable to provoke judicial intervention. *Huerto v College of Physicians & Surgeons (Saskatchewan)* (1996) 34 Admin LR (2d) 159; *Dennis v British Columbia (Superintendent of Motor Vehicles)* (2000) 82 BCLR (3d) 313. See more generally JA Smillie, 'The Problem of "Official Notice": Reliance by Administrative Tribunals on the Personal Knowledge of their Members' [1975] *Public Law* 64, 70–71, drawing a useful distinction between general background knowledge, which need not be disclosed to the parties for their observations and specific sources, which must be disclosed:

> Where an adjudicator proposes to rely upon his knowledge of facts which are capable of being attributed to specific identifiable sources, those facts should be disclosed to the parties for comment and rebuttal regardless of the purpose for which they are to be used. Where specific factual knowledge of this kind is relied upon it should be immaterial for purpose of disclosure whether the knowledge leads the tribunal to reject evidence which was not challenged at the hearing, or whether it merely provides a basis for a choice between two conflicting and evenly balanced lines of evidence. In both cases reliance on such facts will involve the introduction of new matters which the parties could not reasonably have been expected to anticipate; it will not be difficult for the tribunal to communicate such details to the parties; and because the sources of the tribunal's knowledge can be clearly identified the parties may be able to prove that the tribunal's information is inaccurate, or argue persuasively that the information is not properly applicable to the present case.

See e.g. *Dekker v Medical Board of Australia* [2014] WASCA 216 [66–69]; *Ville de Saint-Lambert v Wade* 2020 QCCA 1322 [12–18].

[182] [1980] UKHL 1; [1981] AC 75.

[183] Ibid, 96.

[184] See e.g. *Report of the Franks Committee on Administrative Tribunals and Enquiries* (Cmnd 218, 1957) [269], describing the purpose of a local inquiry as 'to ensure that the interests of the citizens closely affected should be protected by the grant to them of a statutory right to be heard in support of their objections, and to ensure that thereby the Minister should be better informed of the facts of the case'.

> Proceedings at a local inquiry at which many parties wish to make representations without incurring the expense of legal representation, and cannot attend the inquiry throughout its length ought to be as informal as is consistent with achieving those objectives. To 'over-judicialise' the inquiry by insisting on observance of the procedures of a court of justice which professional lawyers alone are competent to operate effectively in the interests of their clients would not be fair.[185]

As Lord Lane put it, the result of permitting cross-examination would have been 'an even lengthier hearing without any appreciable advantage'.[186] Moreover, an attack on the policy of central government would not have been appropriate, as a local inquiry was no place to impugn the 'reliability and statistical validity' of a model applied nationwide:[187] to permit such an attack would have undermined the efficient use of scarce resources.

3.3.6 Legal Representation

There is no general right to legal representation in administrative proceedings. Concerns for effective and efficient public administration can be understood to account for the reluctance to allow lawyers to actively represent clients in a non-court setting. The presence of lawyers, it has been suggested, is inimical to the swift resolution of matters arising before administrative decision-makers: 'If legal representation were allowed, it would mean considerable delay'[188] and, potentially, cost.[189] Moreover, in some circumstances '[j]ustice can often be done ... better by a good layman than by a bad lawyer', as long as 'no points of law are likely to arise ... '[190]

Nonetheless, administrative decision-makers have the discretion to allow individuals to be represented by lawyers in proceedings before them.[191] This discretion is to be exercised by reference to principles, helpfully summarised in

[185] *Bushell v Secretary of State for the Environment* (n 182) 97 per Lord Diplock.

[186] Ibid, 122.

[187] Ibid, 100. Compare *Innisfil (Township) v Vespra (Township)* (n 26), where examination of a government policy was permitted, but strictly in the context of its application to local conditions.

[188] *Fraser v Mudge* [1975] 1 WLR 1132, 1133 per Lord Denning MR. See also *Barry v Review Group and the Minister for Justice, Equality and Law Reform* [2001] 4 IR 167, 169–170.

[189] *Enderby Town Football Club Ltd v Football Association Ltd* [1971] 1 Ch 591, 608 per Lord Denning MR.

[190] Ibid, 605 per Lord Denning MR. Interpreters, by contrast, are more likely to contribute to the effective, efficient and accurate implementation of the statutory scheme. See e.g. *Attorney-General v Udompun* [2005] 3 NZLR 204.

[191] *Maynard v Osmond* [1977] QB 240, 252 per Lord Denning MR; *R v Secretary of State for the Home Office, ex parte Tarrant* [1985] QB 251, 282; *R v Board of Visitors of Her Majesty's Prison, The Maze, ex parte Hone* [1988] AC 379, 394; *X v McDermott* (1994) 51 FCR 1, 12; *Drew v Attorney-General* (2001) 6 HRNZ 368; [2002] 1 NZLR 58 [70]; *WABZ v Minister for Immigration and Multicultural Affairs* [2004] FCAFC 30; (2004) 134 FCR 271, 295; *Garvey v Minister for Justice, Equality and Law Reform* [2006] 1 IR 548, 559.

the prison context in *R v Secretary of State for the Home Office, ex parte Tarrant*, which can be understood in terms of the values I have laid out.[192] First, the 'seriousness of the charge and of the potential penalty',[193] factors that go to the importance of the individual interests at stake.[194] Second, '[w]hether any points of law are likely to arise',[195] such that representation by a lawyer would assist the decision-maker in reaching a more accurate decision. Third, '[t]he capacity of a particular prisoner to present his own case'.[196] As Lord Denning MR once put it, with characteristic flair:

> It is not every man who has the ability to defend himself on his own. He cannot bring out the points in his own favour or the weaknesses in the other side. He may be tongue-tied or nervous, confused or wanting in intelligence. He cannot examine or cross-examine witnesses. We see it every day. A magistrate says to a man: 'You can ask any questions you like'; whereupon the man immediately starts to make a speech. If justice is to be done, he ought to have the help of someone to speak for him. And who better than a lawyer who has been trained for the task?[197]

The underlying concerns here can be understood to be for the individual to be able to participate effectively in a matter of importance to them; for decision-makers to receive effective submissions, so as to favour 'swift and speedy decisions';[198] and for reaching accurate decisions. Finally, the fourth and fifth factors can be taken together: both 'procedural difficulties' and[199] '[t]he need for reasonable speed in making their adjudication' can be understood, straightforwardly as being concerned with effective and efficient public administration. Accordingly, the discretionary decision to grant or refuse legal representation in any given administrative decision-making process can be understood to require a balance to be struck between the values of individual self-realisation, good administration and electoral legitimacy.

[192] See also *Cains v Jenkins* (1979) 42 FLR 188, 198 per JB Sweeney and St John JJ; *Li Shi Ping v Minister for Immigration, Local Government and Ethnic Affairs* (1994) 35 ALD 557, 570; *New Brunswick (Minister of Health and Community Services) v G (J)* [1999] 3 SCR 46 [75]; *Drew v Attorney-General* (n 191) [71]. It has been suggested that very similar principles should apply to non-legal representation. See *Damjanovic v Maley* [2002] NSWCA 230; (2002) 55 NSWLR 149 [69–88].

[193] *R v Secretary of State for the Home Office, ex parte Tarrant* (n 191) 285 per Webster J. See e.g. *Flanagan v University College Dublin* (n 65).

[194] See also *Majar v Northern Land Council* (1991) 37 FCR 117, 138.

[195] *R v Secretary of State for the Home Office, ex parte Tarrant* (n 191) 285 per Webster J.

[196] Ibid, 285 per Webster J. See e.g. *Drew v Attorney-General* (n 191).

[197] *Pett v Greyhound Racing Association Ltd* [1969] 1 QB 125, 132 per Lord Denning MR. See similarly *Krstic v Australian Telecommunications Commission* (1988) 20 FCR 489, 491.

[198] *Fraser v Mudge* (n 188) 1135 per Roskill LJ. See also *Enderby Town Football Club Ltd v Football Association Ltd* (n 189) 608; *In re Scott* (2001) 10 Tas R 148 [3].

[199] *R v Secretary of State for the Home Office, ex parte Tarrant* (n 191) 286 per Webster J.

3.3.7 Reasons

In most common law jurisdictions,[200] there is no general duty to give reasons.[201] Militating against a right to reasons are concerns which can be understood in terms of judicial solicitude for efficient and effective administrative decision-making:

> These include the possibility that an additional burden will be cast on administrative officers and that increased cost and delay may be entailed and the further possibility that ... [a right to reasons] might in some cases induce a lack of candour on the part of the administrative officers concerned.[202]

There are, however, important exceptions to this general exclusionary rule, which sound in administrative law values.[203]

First, in cases where an appeal has been provided for by statute, a duty to provide reasons is an uncontroversial corollary of the legislative decision to provide a means of appeal, for the giving of reasons 'enables a litigant dissatisfied with a decision to more readily consider whether there are grounds of appeal'.[204] In the absence of reasons to protest against, the right of appeal would be nugatory. For instance, under Ireland's planning legislation, the planning authority is required

[200] Ireland is a notable exception: see *Mallak v* The *Minister for Justice, Equality & Law Reform* [2012] 3 IR 297 but see also my comments to n 227–230.

[201] See e.g. *R v Gaming Board for Great Britain, ex parte Benaim* (n 47); *R v Awatere* [1982] 1 NZLR 644; *Wingfoot Australia Partners Pty Ltd v Kocak* [2013] HCA 43; (2013) 252 CLR 480.

[202] *Public Service Board of New South Wales v Osmond* (1986) 159 CLR 656, 668 per Gibbs CJ. See also *Bell v Victoria University of Wellington* (n 173) [78] per Clifford J, in the context of a university discipline case involving alleged plagiarism: 'The [Disciplinary Appeals Committee] is not a judicial body, and is comprised of academics rather than lawyers. In my judgment, this properly impacts on the extent of the reasons that are to be expected in its decisions. DAC decisions, in fact, usually comprise little more than one page. The courts should, in my view, avoid overly formalising and legalising expert academic decision-making processes in this area. Requiring decisions of bodies such as the DAC to be in the form that is expected from the courts themselves, or from more formal quasi-judicial decision-makers such as professional regulatory bodies, would tend to have that very effect'.

[203] For a useful overview of the supposed benefits of a right to reasons see *Singh v Chief Executive Officer, Department of Labour* [1999] NZAR 258, 626–263 per Keith J. Already at the end of the last century the Privy Council wondered whether these exceptions had swallowed the rule: 'There is certainly a strong argument for the view that what were once seen as exceptions to a rule may now be becoming examples of the norm, and the cases where reasons are not required may be taking on the appearance of exceptions.' *Stefan v General Medical Council* [1999] 1 WLR 1293, 1301. See also Mark Elliott, "Has the Common Law Duty to Give Reasons Come of Age Yet?" [2011] *Public Law* 56. The analysis below certainly suggests that the exceptions are wide enough to swallow the rule, but with the content of the duty to give reasons carefully calibrated by reference to administrative law values: see text to nn 221–224 below. This suggests that even if the exceptions have gobbled up the rule the consequences are not as drastic as one might fear.

[204] *Potter v New Zealand Milk Board* [1983] NZLR 620, 624 per Davison CJ. See also *Norton Tool Co v Tewson* [1973] 1 WLR 45; *Public Service Board of New South Wales v Osmond* (n 202) 664–665; *Gurusinghe v Medical Council of New Zealand* [1989] 1 NZLR 139, 162; *Stefan v General Medical Council* (n 203) 1300 (PC); *Rawson v Minister for Defence* [2012] IESC 26 [6.5]. Of course, where there is no appeal and a decision is thus final, reasons might be even more valuable: see e.g. *Baker v Canada (Minister of Citizenship and Immigration)* (n 31) [24].

to give reasons in respect of each condition imposed on an application for planning permission.[205] It has been said that the object of this provision is to enable the applicant to obtain 'such information as may be necessary and appropriate for him firstly to consider whether he has got a reasonable chance of succeeding in appealing against the decision of the planning authority and, secondly, to enable him to arm himself for the hearing of such appeal'.[206] This can be understood to sound in respect for the considered choices of elected representatives, ensuring that the appeal right they decided to make available is in fact a meaningful one.

Second, concerns for accurate decision-making can be understood to underlie the principle that where a decision is so 'aberrant' that it 'cries out for reasons',[207] reasons will be required. A good example is provided by *Oakley v South Cambridgeshire District Council*,[208] where a local authority's decision to grant planning permission for a football stadium on green belt land against the advice of the planning officer gave 'rise to an important onus of justification on the part of the decision-maker'.[209] It has, indeed, been suggested in general terms that reasons may lead to more accurate decision-making by helping 'to concentrate the mind of the Tribunal upon the issues for determination':[210] 'Reasons, it has been argued, foster better decision making by ensuring that issues and reasoning are well articulated and, therefore, more carefully thought out'.[211] Even the process of formulating reasons might have a salutary effect on the decision-maker, as 'without [a right to reasons] there is a risk that some supposed fact which [the individual] could controvert, some opinion which he could challenge, some policy which he could argue against, might wrongly go unanswered'.[212] Reasons may also lead to more accurate appellate conclusions, as reasons permit a body sitting on appeal or review to 'know what principles of law have been applied and to consider whether such were correct'.[213]

Third, where a decision 'has important significance for the individual', reviewing courts will impose a duty on administrative decision-makers to give reasons: 'It would be unfair for a person subject to a decision ... so critical to their future not to be told why the result was reached'.[214] This can be understood to be supported by judicial solicitude for individual self-realisation: 'Those affected may be more likely to feel they were treated fairly and appropriately if reasons are given',[215] 'thereby

[205] Planning and Development Act 2000, s 34(10)(a).

[206] *State (Sweeney) v Minister for the Environment* [1979] ILRM 35, 37 per Finlay P.

[207] *R v Higher Education Funding Council, ex parte Institute of Dental Surgery* [1994] 1 WLR 242, 257, 263.

[208] [2017] EWCA Civ 71; [2017] 2 P & CR 4.

[209] Ibid, [79] per Sales LJ.

[210] *Potter v New Zealand Milk Board* (n 204) 624 per Davison CJ.

[211] *Baker v Canada (Minister of Citizenship and Immigration)* (n 31) [39].

[212] *R v Secretary of State for the Home Department, ex parte Doody* (n 32) 563 per Lord Mustill.

[213] *Potter v New Zealand Milk Board* (n 204) 624 per Davison CJ.

[214] *Baker v Canada (Minister of Citizenship and Immigration)* (n 31) [43]. See similarly *R v Secretary of State for the Home Department, ex parte Doody* (n 32)

[215] *Baker v Canada (Minister of Citizenship and Immigration)* (n 31) [39] per L'Heureux-Dubé J.

contributing to a more willing acceptance of the decision'.[216] Moreover, the exercise of government power 'is less likely to be, *or to appear to be arbitrary*, if the decision maker formulates and provides reasons for his decision'.[217]

Finally, reasons may be necessary to permit the courts to perform their distinct function of reviewing the lawfulness of administrative action. For instance, the Irish Supreme Court recognised a right to reasons where the decision-maker's failure to provide any meant it was not possible for the individual 'to ascertain whether he has a ground for applying for judicial review and, by extension, not possible for the courts effectively to exercise their power of judicial review'.[218] Similarly, in *R v Secretary of State for the Home Department, ex parte Doody*, Lord Mustill was concerned that an individual could not without access to the reasons mount an 'effective attack' on a sentencing decision taken by the executive—'I think it important that there should be an effective means of detecting the kind of error which would entitle the court to intervene . . .'[219]—a concern that outweighed the worry about respecting the legislative choice to accord the decision-maker an unfettered discretion. Omitting reasons 'makes it more difficult to assess how the tribunal has reached its conclusion and whether it is correct' or, in the present context, lawful.[220] This can be understood to be supported by a concern to preserve the decisional autonomy of reviewing courts.

Where reasons are required on one or more of the foregoing bases, they must adequately reveal the basis of the decision,[221] an exercise that must be conducted contextually,[222] such that (we might understand) the more powerful the values pulling in favour of a duty to give reasons in a particular case, the more detailed the reasons will have to be;[223] the standard 'can vary markedly with the context'.[224] Put

[216] *Taxquet v Belgium* (2012) 54 EHRR 26 [91].

[217] *Public Service Board of New South Wales v Osmond* (n 202) 675 per Deane J. Emphasis added. See further TRS Allan, 'Procedural Fairness and the Duty of Respect' (1998) 18 *Oxford Journal of Legal Studies* 497.

[218] *Mallak v Minister for Justice* (n 200) [65].

[219] *R v Secretary of State for the Home Department, ex parte Doody* (n 32).

[220] *Auckland Standards Committee 3 of New Zealand Law Society v W* [2011] 3 NZLR 117, 123 per Duffy J. See also *Canada (Immigration and Citizenship) v Vavilov* 2019 SCC 65 [81].

[221] See e.g. *Singh v Chief Executive, Department of Labour* (n 203) 258. It has been said in Australia that a statement of reasons 'is not invalid merely because it employs a verbal formula that is routinely used by persons making similar decisions': *Minister for Immigration and Ethnic Affairs v Wu Shan Liang* (1996) 185 CLR 259, 266 per Brennan CJ, Toohey, McHugh and Gummow JJ.

[222] See e.g. *Uprichard v Scottish Ministers* [2013] UKSC 21 [44]: 'In considering the adequacy of the reasons given for a decision, it is necessary to take account of a number of matters, including the nature of the decision in question, the context in which it has been made, the purpose for which the reasons are provided and the context in which they are given.' See further *Clarke Homes Ltd v Secretary of State for the Environment* (1993) 66 P & CR 263; *South Buckinghamshire District Council v Porter* [2004] UKHL 33; [2004] 1 WLR 1953.

[223] See also *Bell v Victoria University of Wellington* (n 173) [78], where considerations of effective and efficient public administration can be understood to have pulled against imposing an onerous duty to give reasons.

[224] *Wingfoot Australia Partners Pty Ltd v Kocak* (n 201) 498 per French CJ, Crennan, Bell, Gageler and Keane JJ.

another way, the greater the force of the values in any given case, the more detailed the reasons will have to be.

The influence that administrative law values can be understood to exert on the right to reasons is exemplified by the decision of the UK Supreme Court in *Dover District Council v CPRE Kent*.[225] The underlying issue involved an application for planning permission in the Kent Downs, an Area of Outstanding Beauty. Against the advice of its professional advisers, the local authority granted the application, no doubt heavily influenced by the positive economic impact the development was expected to have.[226]

Although he accepted that there is no general duty to give reasons at common law, Lord Carnwath took the view that reasons will be required where they are necessary to permit the courts to scrutinise the underlying decision appropriately, 'to allow effective supervision by the courts'.[227] Lord Carnwath favoured effective supervision as the general rationale for a common law obligation to give reasons—a rationale sounding in decisional autonomy. In his view, the obligation could be justified in the present case on the basis that 'openness and *fairness to objectors* required the members' reasons to be stated'.[228] Openness as a rationale in this instance is consistent with effective supervision as a general rationale for a duty to give reasons. Indeed, the 'widespread public controversy' and departure from the expert recommendations 'made it impossible to infer the reasons from [the members'] report or other material available to the public'.[229] It is also consistent with a concern for accurate administrative decision-making. But *fairness* to objectors is a different rationale. It is difficult to relate it to the effective supervision of the decision-making process. It relates more to the need to respond to objectors as rational beings whose engagement in the process deserves respect—a concern to respect individual interests—or to the need to promote public confidence in the process, ensuring its effective and efficient operation. The framework for Lord Carnwath's analysis, therefore, can be understood to be formed by the administrative law values I have developed.

In setting out with even greater precision the circumstances in which reasons will be required, Lord Carnwath can again be understood as giving effect to administrative law values:

> Typically they will be cases where ... permission has been granted in the face of substantial public opposition and against the advice of officers, for projects which

[225] [2018] 1 WLR 108.

[226] It was conceded that the local authority had breached its obligation under the applicable European Union regulations to set out 'the main reasons and considerations' for its decision (ibid, [64]), but the question of remedy was unresolved, which led Lord Carnwath to canvass the various European and domestic sources for an obligation to give reasons.

[227] Ibid, [54].

[228] Ibid, [57]. Emphasis added.

[229] Ibid.

> involve major departures from the development plan, or from other policies of recognised importance ... Such decisions call for public explanation, not just because of their immediate impact; but also because ... they are likely to have lasting relevance for the application of policy in future cases.[230]

Accordingly, these considerations act as qualifications to the potentially limitless scope of the effective supervision rationale for a reason-giving requirement. But the considerations do not all map neatly onto the effective supervision rationale. The references to 'major departures' and 'policies of recognised importance' do seem to relate to effective supervision. But 'substantial public opposition' evokes respect for the interests of individuals who engaged in the decision-making process and 'application of policy' suggests that the accurate, effective and efficient operation of the decision-making process should be borne in mind. In summary, Lord Carnwath's analysis can be understood as a microcosm of the right to reasons: an attempt to use the values of decisional autonomy, good administration, electoral legitimacy and individual self-realisation in a complementary way to structure an important aspect of the contemporary duty of fairness in administrative law.

3.4 Conclusion

The journey in this chapter through the contemporary law of procedural fairness has been designed to demonstrate that whether one considers the structure of the duty of fairness, exclusions from it or individual procedural fairness rights, the four values of individual self-realisation, good administration, electoral legitimacy and decisional autonomy help to illuminate this important area of administrative law. Demonstrating that judges can be understood to have used the values of individual self-realisation, good administration, electoral legitimacy and decisional autonomy to draw the contours of procedural fairness—sometimes in a complementary fashion, sometimes striking a balance between them in situations of potential conflict—has been my primary goal in this chapter.

But I hope also to have demonstrated that as far as the duty of fairness is concerned, one need not make a binary choice between an instrumentalist and dignitarian explanation for the contemporary law of procedural fairness: in fact, both instrumentalist and dignitarian considerations can be understood to have influenced the current structure of the law.

On the one hand, dignitarian considerations can be understood to be important: the greater the effect on individual interests, the more extensive (other things being equal) the procedural protections required as a general matter, as we

[230] Ibid, [59].

have seen in respect of the scope of procedural fairness, and with regard to specific procedural rights, such as the right to legal representation and the right to reasons. On the other hand, however, instrumental considerations can be understood to exert significant gravitational force across the field of procedural fairness: decisional accuracy is a prominent concern, as is the concern for good administration, which manifests itself in the form of judicial reluctance to compromise the effective and efficient functioning of administrative decision-making processes.

And the value of decisional autonomy—which does not feature in the contest between dignitarians and instrumentalists—can be understood to be of overarching significance to the law of procedural fairness (in that the duty of fairness is not to be modelled on judicial trial-type procedures) and is influential too in the important areas of evidence in administrative proceedings and the right to reasons. Here, as everywhere in the law of judicial review of administrative action, the subject cannot be reduced to one single meta-value, meta-concept or meta-principle. There is, rather, a plurality of values which taken together illuminate administrative law.

4
Substantive Review

Even where a decision is taken in an appropriate way in terms of the requirements of institutional structures and procedural fairness, the decision may nonetheless be unlawful. How intensively judges should scrutinise procedurally proper administrative decisions is a question that has bedevilled courts and commentators for decades. In contemporary parlance, this area of administrative law is known as 'substantive review'. It is the realm of 'merits', not procedure. Those reared in earlier eras will be more familiar with terms such as '*Wednesbury* unreasonableness'[1] and 'irrationality', but today's watchwords are 'scope' and 'intensity'.[2] Contemporary courts and commentators are preoccupied with 'the extent to which review of the merits, traditionally limited to *Wednesbury* unreasonableness, should be expanded into more intensive reasonableness review, or new substantive grounds of review, or both'.[3] Under the broad umbrella of 'substantive review', I group three particular areas of administrative law: jurisdictional issues (including review for error of law); irrationality; and the doctrines of relevancy and propriety. Failure to meet the standards of substantive review in any of these areas means the decision at issue will be held to be unlawful.

This chapter addresses areas of law where there are significant divergences—certainly at the level of detail—between Commonwealth jurisdictions. On relevancy and propriety, the differences are not especially marked (save perhaps for Canada, where the doctrine of 'deference' has an important role to play[4]) but on jurisdictional issues and irrationality there are fierce disputes (intra—and inter-national) and daunting doctrinal thickets. 'Jurisdiction' is plagued by conceptual and analytical controversy,[5] carries different meanings in different

[1] For a formulation similar to Lord Greene MR's, see *Buck v Bavone* (1976) 135 CLR 110, 118.

[2] See generally Hanna Wilberg and Mark Elliott eds, *The Scope and Intensity of Substantive Review: Traversing Taggart's Rainbow* (Hart, Oxford, 2015).

[3] Hanna Wilberg and Mark Elliott, 'Introduction' in *The Scope and Intensity of Substantive Review: Traversing Taggart's Rainbow* (Hart, Oxford, 2015), 1. See also Rebecca Williams, 'Structuring Substantive Review' [2017] *Public Law* 99, 100, suggesting that jurists' attention could fruitfully be focused on two issues: 'namely *what in substance* is alleged to have gone wrong with the decision, and *how intensively* that issue is to be reviewed'.

[4] See e.g. *Dr Q v College of Physicians and Surgeons of British Columbia* 2003 SCC 19; [2003] 1 SCR 226; *Canada (Citizenship and Immigration) v Vavilov* 2019 SCC 65 [108]–[111]. But for sceptical comment see Hanna Wilberg, 'Deference on Relevance and Purpose: Wrestling with the Law/Discretion Divide' in Hanna Wilberg and Mark Elliott eds, *The Scope and Intensity of Substantive Review: Traversing Taggart's Rainbow* (Hart, Oxford, 2015).

[5] Paul Craig, *Administrative Law*, 8th edn (Sweet and Maxwell, London, 2016), chapter 16; Paul Daly, *A Theory of Deference in Administrative Law: Basis, Application and Scope* (Cambridge University Press, Cambridge, 2012), chapter 6.

Understanding Administrative Law in the Common Law World. Paul Daly, Oxford University Press.
DOI: 10.1093/oso/9780192896919.003.0004

jurisdictions[6] and is, sometimes, simply obscure;[7] and in Canada (and, tentatively, in England), deference is paid by courts to some administrative decision-makers' interpretations of law.[8] Irrationality was once synonymous with *Wednesbury* unreasonableness, in the sense that a decision-maker could not lawfully take a decision so unreasonable no reasonable decision-maker could take it, but many have argued (and some judges have accepted) that it should be supplanted by proportionality review.

Accordingly, the analysis in this chapter will be conducted at a higher level of abstraction than the analysis in the other chapters.

First, I will argue that administrative law values are useful in distinguishing jurisdictional from non-jurisdictional issues and in understanding debates about 'deference'. Here, 'jurisdictional issues' is shorthand for decisions which attract close judicial scrutiny, approximating to what Canadians call 'correctness review'; it is more likely that the reviewing court will intervene and substitute its judgement for that of the administrative decision-maker on the 'jurisdictional' issue identified. By contrast, 'non-jurisdictional issues' refers to situations in which judicial intervention is much less likely, as courts will only intervene to correct a serious mistake in respect of the 'non-jurisdictional' issue identified. A metaphor might help: there is a spectrum running from 'jurisdictional' to 'non-jurisdictional', with judicial intervention much more likely at the 'jurisdictional' pole than at the 'non-jurisdictional' pole; administrative law values, I will suggest, help to identify different points on this spectrum.

Second, I will argue that administrative law values are useful in understanding rationality review—in particular, in calibrating the range of reasonable responses, a key concept in the contemporary approach to irrationality. It is notable that in respect of irrationality, although differences remain, there has been a significant degree of convergence in recent years, making my task in this chapter much easier. Note also that here rationality has a technical legal meaning which is distinct from its colloquial sense.[9]

Third, I will argue that the structure of relevancy and propriety can be understood as being influenced by administrative law values. As such, I move from

[6] The Canadian courts have abolished the category of jurisdictional error entirely. See *Canada (Citizenship and Immigration) v Vavilov* (n 4) [65]–[68]. In Australia, by contrast, it is said that whether an issue is jurisdictional is a matter of construction. See e.g. *Timbarra Protection Coalition v Ross Mining* (1999) 46 NSWLR 55 [37]–[39]; *Canberra Tradesmens' Union Club Inc v Minister for Environment* (2000) 183 ALR 137, 146–147; *Plaintiff M70/2011 v Minister for Immigration and Citizenship (Malaysian Declaration Case)* [2011] HCA 32; (2011) 244 CLR 144, 194–200.

[7] The Irish law is 'in an unsatisfactory, uneven and dated condition' and awaits 'a reserved Supreme Court judgment which will definitively review the present state of the law dealing with jurisdictional error ...'. James O'Reilly, 'Errors of Fact and Errors of Law as Grounds for Judicial Review' (2012) 48 *Irish Jurist* (NS) 1, 5.

[8] See Chapter 4.1.4.

[9] See generally Hasan Dindjer, 'What Makes an Administrative Decision Unreasonable?' (2021) 84 *Modern Law Review* 265.

the most difficult terrain for my approach—'jurisdiction'—to the friendliest—relevancy and propriety—by passing though the domains of deference (slightly less friendly) and abuse of discretion (slightly more friendly). Lastly, this chapter's demonstration that a plurality of values can be understood to influence the contemporary law of substantive review refutes any suggestion that the notion of 'jurisdiction' is a meta-concept, meta-principle or meta-value capable of unifying the field of administrative law.

4.1 Jurisdictional Issues

Quite what constitutes a 'jurisdictional' issue is a matter of controversy, 'based on differing views about the proper balance of power between courts and agencies . . .'[10] At first glance, the value of electoral legitimacy seems to point in one direction, those of good administration and decisional autonomy in another.

Where an exercise of a power by an administrative decision-maker is conditional upon the existence of some state of facts, the common law courts have historically engaged in *de novo* review to ensure that the facts do indeed exist.[11] When the legislature grants authority to an administrative decision-maker, the authority will perforce be limited,[12] as the decision-maker must act within the jurisdiction it has been granted.[13] What legitimises the proposition that jurisdiction is limited is that the legislature has set the limits out in statute. An error relating

[10] Paul Craig, 'Ultra Vires and the Foundations of Judicial Review' (1998) 57 *Cambridge Law Journal* 63, 76. See further Ivan Hare, 'The Separation of Powers and Judicial Review for Error of Law' in Christopher Forsyth and Ivan Hare eds, *The Golden Metwand and the Crooked Cord: Essays on Public Law in Honour of Sir William Wade QC* (Clarendon, Oxford, 1998), 113. Issues as to jurisdiction arise both in relation to particular administrative decisions and general rules and regulations adopted under statutory authority:

> Subordinate legislation will be held by a court to be invalid if it has an effect, or is made for a purpose, which is *ultra vires*, that is, outside the scope of the statutory power pursuant to which it was purportedly made. In declaring subordinate legislation to be invalid in such a case, the court is upholding the supremacy of Parliament over the Executive. *That is because the court is preventing a member of the Executive from making an order which is outside the scope of the power which Parliament has given him or her by means of the statute concerned.* Accordingly, when, as in this case, it is contended that actual or intended subordinate legislation is *ultra vires*, it is necessary for a court to determine the scope of the statutorily conferred power to make that legislation.

R (Public Law Project) v Lord Chancellor [2016] UKSC 39; [2016] 3 WLR 387 [23] per Lord Neuberger. Emphasis added. See also *Kennedy v Incorporated Law Society of Ireland* [2002] 2 IR 458, 486.

[11] See e.g. *R v Commissioners for Special Purposes of the Income Tax* (1888) 21 QBD 313, 319 per Lord Esher MR. See similarly *R v Shoreditch Assessment Committee, ex parte Morgan* [1910] 2 KB 859, 880.

[12] 'It is a contradiction in terms to create a tribunal with limited jurisdiction and unlimited power to determine such limit at its own will and pleasure': *R v Shoreditch Assessment Committee, ex parte Morgan* (n 11) 880 per Farwell LJ; 'any grant of jurisdiction will necessarily include limits to the jurisdiction granted, and any grant of a power remains subject to conditions': *Union des employés de service, local 298 v Bibeault* [1988] 2 SCR 1048, 1086 per Beetz J.

[13] DM Gordon, 'Conditional or Contingent Jurisdiction of Tribunals' (1959–1963) 1 *University of British Columbia Law Review* 185, 197.

to a jurisdictional issue 'results in a decision which has been made in fact lacking characteristics necessary for it *to be given force and effect by the statute* pursuant to which the decision-maker purported to make it'.[14] When the courts decide 'whether or not the fact exists',[15] they are merely giving effect to the wishes of the legislature as set out in statute.[16] Indeed, it has been said to be imperative that they police the boundaries of jurisdiction, for a decision-maker 'cannot, by a wrong decision with regard to [a jurisdictional fact], give itself jurisdiction which it would not otherwise possess'.[17] Thus in *R v London Rent Tribunal, ex parte Honig*, Lord Goddard CJ felt obliged to determine whether a contract existed between a landlord and a tenant in order to ensure that the Tribunal could indeed exercise its power to reduce the tenant's rent 'because it was only if there was a contract that they could exercise the jurisdiction which the Act of Parliament has given them'.[18] This point can be understood in terms of respect for the considered choices of elected representatives to establish an administrative decision-maker and to set bounds on its powers.

Equally, however, it has been said that the circumstances permitting a reviewing court to 'intervene by way of judicial review to correct errors of fact must be extremely rare'.[19] Reticence to countenance aggressive oversight of factual issues echoes the traditional reluctance of Commonwealth courts to interfere in judicial review with first-instance decision-makers' assessment of evidence:[20] 'want of evidence on matter of fact' is not a basis for judicial intervention;[21] only where there is no evidence at all can judicial review be countenanced.[22] Nor are reviewing courts permitted to reweigh the factors considered by the administrative decision-maker.[23] A concern to preserve some decisional autonomy for administrative

[14] *Hossain v Minister for Immigration and Border Protection* [2018] HCA 34; 264 CLR 123 [24] per Kiefel CJ, Gageler and Keane JJ.

[15] Peter Hogg, 'The Jurisdictional Fact Doctrine in the Supreme Court of Canada: *Bell v Ontario Human Rights Commission*' (1971) 9 *Osgoode Hall Law Journal* 203, 210.

[16] See e.g. *Gedeon v Crime Commission (NSW)* [2008] HCA 43; (2008) 236 CLR 120, 139.

[17] *R v Lincolnshire Justices, ex parte Brett* [1926] 2 KB 192, 201 per Atkin LJ, citing Halsbury's Laws of England. See also *Parisienne Basket Shoes Pty Ltd v Whyte* (1938) 59 CLR 369, 391; *Killeen v Director of Public Prosecutions* [1998] 1 ILRM 1, 8.

[18] [1951] 1 KB 641, 646. See similarly *R v Blakeley; ex parte Association of Architects, Engineers, Surveyors and Draughtmen of Australia* (1954) 82 CLR 54, 91–92.

[19] *Ryanair Ltd v Flynn* [2000] 3 IR 240, 264 per Kearns P. See e.g. *Australian Broadcasting Tribunal v Bond* (1990) 94 ALR 11, 37–40; *Minister for Immigration and Multicultural Affairs v Rajamanikkam* [2002] HCA 32; (2002) 190 ALR 402, 408–409 and 412–415 per Gleeson CJ, 429–431 per Gaudron and McHugh JJ; *Wandsworth London Borough Council v A* [2000] 1 WLR 1246, 1255–1256.

[20] *R v Nat Bell Liquors Ltd* [1922] 2 AC 128, 151–152 per Lord Sumner . See also *R v Governor of Brixton Prison, ex parte Armah* [1968] AC 192, 234 per Lord Reid.

[21] *Ex parte Hopwood* (1850) 15 QB 121, 128 per Patteson J.

[22] See e.g. *Minister for Immigration and Multicultural Affairs v Rajamanikkam* (n 19).

[23] See e.g. *Tesco Stores v Secretary of State for the Environment* [1995] UKHL 22; [1995] UKHL 22; [1995] 1 WLR 759, 764 per Lord Keith of Kinkel and 780 per Lord Hoffmann; *Canada (Citizenship and Immigration) v Khosa* 2009 SCC 12; [2009] 1 SCR 339 [61]. Cf Paul Craig, 'The Nature of Reasonableness Review' (2013) 66 *Current Legal Problems* 131.

decision-makers can be understood to support judicial reticence to correct alleged factual errors.

Concern for accurate and effective and efficient decision-making can also be understood to be relevant, because 'very considerable difficulties can and do arise when the dispute is in a specialised area and the facts themselves are in dispute and the subject matter of claim and counterclaim'.[24] The complex, technical issues on which the advantages of a specialist decision-maker over a court—staffed, as common law courts are, by generalist judges—are most marked when factual assessments,[25] sometimes relating to uncertain future events,[26] are involved.[27] Moreover, for courts to retry contested factual issues in judicial review proceedings would be very difficult given the nature of the courts' jurisdiction, which is 'not designed to raise issues of fact for the High Court to determine *de novo*'.[28] To do otherwise would significantly increase the cost and length of administrative litigation.[29]

On the one hand, then, having regard to the value of electoral legitimacy, judges in judicial review cases can correct factual errors relating to the outer boundaries of administrative decision-makers' powers. On the other hand, judicial interference with factual findings should be limited, a point which can be understood in terms of decisional autonomy and good administration.

That the values seem to point in different directions can, at an abstract level, help to illuminate why jurisdiction is such a difficult area of the law. Moreover (and more helpfully), in concrete cases, the values can be understood to influence why judges are more or less reluctant to classify a given issue as 'jurisdictional'. The argument in this section is that in understanding why courts classify some issues as 'jurisdictional'—with the result that the reviewing court will scrutinize the matter closely and perhaps even substitute its judgement for that of the decision-maker—and others as 'non-jurisdictional'—in which case a reviewing court will, at most, assess the rationality of the conclusion under review—the values of individual self-realisation, good administration, electoral legitimacy and decisional autonomy can be understood to be influential. In brief: the stronger the individual interests

[24] *Ryanair Ltd v Flynn* (n 19) 266 per Kearns P.

[25] See e.g. *Canada (Attorney General) v Public Service Alliance of Canada* [1993] 1 SCR 941, 962 per Cory J; *Canada (Director of Investigation and Research v Southam* [1997] 1 SCR 748, 773–774 per Iacobucci J.

[26] See e.g. *R (Lord Carlile of Berriew QC) v Secretary of State for the Home Department* [2014] UKSC 60; [2015] 1 AC 945 [51] (Lord Sumption) and [75] (Lord Neuberger). See generally Stephen Breyer, *Breaking the Vicious Circle: Toward Effective Risk Regulation* (Cambridge, Harvard University Press, 1993), 42–43; Adrian Vermeule, 'Rationally Arbitrary Decisions in Administrative Law' (2015) 44 *Journal of Legal Studies* 475.

[27] *R v London Rent Tribunal, ex parte Honig* [1951] 1 KB 641, 646–647 per Lord Goddard CJ.

[28] *R v Fulham, Hammersmith and Kensington Rent Tribunal* [1951] 2 KB 1, 11 per Devlin J.

[29] See e.g. *R (Cart) v Upper Tribunal* [2011] UKSC 28; [2012] 1 AC 663, albeit a case concerned with legal error, not factual error, but the points therein made about the desirability of proportionate dispute resolution on institutional grounds apply *a fortiori* to factual issues.

at stake and the more objectively worded the statutory provision at issue, the more likely it is that a given issue is 'jurisdictional' (be it factual or legal in nature or somewhere in between). Conversely, in respect of the application of vague statutory terms, involving complex allocative judgements by expert administrative decision-makers, it is more likely that a given issue will be treated as 'non-jurisdictional'. From a practical perspective, the difference between an issue being characterised as 'jurisdictional' or as 'non-jurisdictional' is a difference in the intensity of judicial review, ranging from correctness review at one extreme to some form of rationality review at the other extreme. Administrative law values can be understood as influencing where a given judge will place a given issue on this spectrum.

4.1.1 Electoral Legitimacy and Decisional Autonomy

Respect for the decisions of elected representatives can be understood to have significant traction in this area. To allow judges to second-guess determinations of fact and policy where 'Parliament has entrusted the decision-making power' to an administrative body would be to frustrate legislative intent as manifested in statutory language.[30] An example is *State (Attorney General) v McGivern*,[31] where the legislature had employed broad language relating to the licensing of liquor sales, specifically the words 'special occasion'. O'Daly J held that the breadth of the language used meant that this and similar terms used in the licensing context 'range over a wide variety of circumstances, [and] their very imprecision is of itself a mark that their meaning is being committed to the [administrative decision-maker] as part of his substantive jurisdiction'.[32] Accordingly, any error in determining whether an applicant for an exemption from the licensing laws had demonstrated a 'special occasion' would be an error within jurisdiction (and, as such, an unreviewable non-jurisdictional error). The point here is that use of broadly worded statutory terms, which give scope for factually infused policy judgements by front-line decision-makers, are less likely to be characterised as jurisdictional.[33]

Consider in this light *R v Hillingdon London Borough Council, ex parte Puhlhofer*,[34] where the relevant statutory term was broad. At issue was individuals' entitlement to housing under the Housing (Homeless Persons) Act 1977, an entitlement that would not arise if they already had 'accommodation'. The House of Lords concluded that whether one was in 'accommodation' was a question of fact

[30] *R v Hillingdon London Borough Council, ex parte Puhlhofer* [1986] AC 484, 518 per Lord Brightman.

[31] Unreported, Irish Supreme Court (Ireland), 25 July 1961.

[32] Here, the administrative decision-maker was an inferior court judge. See also *Australia Heritage Commission v Mount Isa Mines Ltd* (1997) 187 CLR 297, 303–304.

[33] See similarly *State (Abenglen Properties Ltd) v Dublin Corporation* [1984] IR 381, 399–400.

[34] [1986] AC 484.

and that a local authority's conclusion on the matter was not subject to intrusive judicial oversight:

> Where the existence or non-existence of a fact is left to the judgment and discretion of a public body and that fact involves a broad spectrum ranging from the obvious to the debatable to the just conceivable, it is the duty of the court to leave the decision of that fact to the public body to whom Parliament has entrusted the decision-making power save in a case where it is obvious that the public body, consciously or unconsciously, are acting perversely.[35]

It was thus significant not only that Parliament had entrusted local authorities with the making of accommodation decisions, but that Parliament had employed a term—'accommodation'—that has a 'broad spectrum' of meaning; proper attention to the considered view of elected representatives as manifested in statutory language required the court to give significant breadth to local authorities. As has been said in Australia, 'if the matter is one requiring evaluative judgment, it is more likely that the legislature intended that the officer form an opinion as to the contingency', and that close scrutiny by the courts would thus be inappropriate.[36]

Similarly, in *Katz Group Canada Inc v Ontario (Health and Long-Term Care)*,[37] the Supreme Court of Canada was faced with an argument that delegated legislation introduced to decrease the price of prescription drugs was *ultra vires* because it failed to achieve its stated purposes. The Court adopted a hands-off approach, noting that 'although it is possible to strike down regulations as *ultra vires* on this basis ..., "it would take an egregious case to warrant such action"'.[38] The Court can be understood to have been conscious of the pre-eminent role of the identified decision-maker in developing delegated legislation in a fast-moving regulatory environment.[39] In addition, the claims by drug companies that they had a 'right' to market their products fell on deaf ears: the individual interests at stake were not especially pressing, because it is 'somewhat ethereal to speak of a commercial "right" to trade in a market as highly regulated as is the pharmaceutical market ...'[40]

More generally, judicial willingness to review factual error too readily might blur the lines between the distinct roles of the courts and administrative decision-makers: 'To expose all findings of fact, or the generality of them, to judicial review would expose the steps in administrative decision-making to comprehensive review by the courts and thus bring about a radical change in the relationship between the executive and judicial branches of government.'[41] Concern for the decisional

[35] Ibid, 518 per Lord Brightman.
[36] *Barrick Australia v Williams* (2009) 74 NSWLR 733 [26] per Basten JA.
[37] 2013 SCC 64; [2013] 3 SCR 810.
[38] Ibid, [28] citing *Thorne's Hardware Ltd v The Queen* [1983] 1 SCR 106, 111.
[39] *Katz Group Canada Inc v Ontario (Health and Long-Term Care)* (n 37) [41].
[40] Ibid, [44].
[41] *Australian Broadcasting Corporation v Bond* (n 19) 27 per Mason CJ.

autonomy of administrative decision-makers can, accordingly, be understood to support the statement of an Irish judge that the application of a broadly worded discretionary power, by an administrative decision-maker who is familiar with the operation of a given statutory scheme, is 'probably... unimpeachable in law'.[42] The qualifier 'probably' is important. As Sachs LJ said in *Commissioners of Customs and Excise v Cure and Deeley Ltd*, the use of broad statutory language does not 'necessarily make that authority the sole judge of what are its powers as well as the sole judge of the way in which it can exercise such powers as it may have';[43] understood in terms of administrative law values, a concern to maintain distinct roles for courts and administrative decision-makers counsels in favour of at least some judicial oversight even of broadly worded exercises of discretion. Non-jurisdictional is, in other words, not synonymous with non-justiciabile (where matters are shielded entirely from judicial review).

4.1.2 Good Administration

Whereas considerations of electoral legitimacy and decisional autonomy can be understood to tend to point to the classification of a given issue as 'non-jurisdictional', considerations of good administration and individual self-realisation can often be understood to militate in favour of a finding that an impugned decision, or part of it, is 'jurisdictional'.[44]

Courts are much more willing to classify as 'jurisdictional' those facts which have the characteristics of 'objectivity' and 'essentiality',[45] 'distinguished by their clear-cut and identifiable character', and thus can be proven by reference to documentary evidence without the sort of live testimony that judicial review proceedings are not designed to accommodate.[46] Considerations of relative expertise—and, by extension, a concern for effective and efficient public administration—can be understood to be operative here.

A values-based interpretation of *R (A) v Croydon London Borough Council*[47] supports the proposition that in situations where the statutory language is clear

[42] *Hussain v Minister for Justice, Equality and Law Reform* [2013] 3 IR 257, 265 per Hogan J.

[43] [1962] 1 QB 340, 366–367.

[44] But not inevitably. In *R v Hillingdon London Borough Council, ex parte Puhlhofer* (n 30), Lord Brightman expressed concern about the 'prolific' use of court proceedings to enforce the 1977 Act and, in view of the difficult balancing act that local authorities had to perform in providing accommodation, urged 'great restraint' in giving leave to bring judicial review applications. [1986] AC 484, 518. The concern here can be understood to be for the efficient and effective operation of the legislation by local authorities.

[45] *Timbarra Protection Coalition Inc v Ross Mining NL* (n 6) 64 per Spigelman CJ.

[46] *(Attorney General) v McGivern* (n 31). Unsurprisingly, time limits seem particularly likely to be classified as jurisdictional. See e.g. *Bank of Scotland (Ireland) v Employment Appeals Tribunal* [2002] IEHC 119; *Fitzwilton v Mahon* [2008] 1 IR 712.

[47] [2009] UKSC 8; [2009] 1 WLR 2557.

and the courts are not at a disadvantage relative to administrative decision-makers in terms of expertise, judges will patrol jurisdictional boundaries more vigilantly. Section 20 of the Children Act 1989 imposes a duty on local authorities to provide accommodation, in defined circumstances, to 'any child in need within their area'. Lady Hale rejected the argument that the local authority's determination as to whether a person is a 'child in need' was not jurisdictional, drawing a distinction between the question of 'need', which would require 'a number of different value judgments' to which 'there are no clear cut right or wrong answers',[48] and the question of whether a person is a 'child', where '[t]here is a right or a wrong answer' and which is of a type of question that 'regularly come[s] before the courts'.[49] The question of 'need' would require an evaluative judgement, by a decision-maker much more expert in such matters than a court, and would accordingly not be suitable for intensive scrutiny in the form of the application of a correctness standard or *de novo* judicial review. Whereas the issue of whether an individual is a 'child' is much more suitable for judicial resolution without regard for the conclusions of the administrative decision-maker on that issue. As has been said by the High Court of Australia:

> The weight to be given to the opinion of the tribunal in a particular case will depend upon the circumstances. These will include such matters as the field in which the tribunal operates, the criteria for appointment of its members, the materials upon which it acts in exercising its functions and the extent to which its decisions are supported by disclosed processes of reasoning.[50]

A concern to give effect to legislative intent can be understood to be operative here alongside a concern for effective and efficient public administration: there is a focus on the statutory language and the relative institutional competence of courts and decision-makers ; the greater the decision-maker's expertise relative to the court and the less clear-cut the statutory term at issue, the more democratic legitimacy and good administration weigh in favour of treating the matter as non-jurisdictional.

Buck v Bavone[51] is another helpful example. This case involved a potato grower in South Australia, who was charged with the unlawful sale of potatoes under South Australian legislation. As the potato grower was not registered under the Potato Marketing Act 1948–1973 (SA), he was not entitled to sell his produce. For the most part the decision of the High Court of Australia turned on a constitutional

[48] Ibid, [26].
[49] Ibid, [27].
[50] *City of Enfield v Development Assessment Commission* (2000) 199 CLR 135, 154–155. See also *R v Blakeley; ex parte Association of Architects, Engineers, Surveyors and Draughtmen of Australia* (n 18) 92; *R v Ludeke; ex parte Queensland Electricity Commission* (1985) 159 CLR 178, 183–184.
[51] (1976) 135 CLR 110.

issue—whether the Act was an unconstitutional restraint of trade[52]—but in the course of his judgment, Gibbs J engaged in a helpful extended discussion of jurisdictional issues. He drew a distinction between matters of 'opinion or policy or taste' (the reviewability of which is extremely limited) and 'particular matters of objective facts', where more thoroughgoing judicial review will be performed.[53] Here, the matters as to which the regulatory body had to be satisfied were 'clearly defined' and left no room for 'judgment' about the 'fitness of the applicant' or matters of 'policy'.[54] All that had to be determined were simple matters of fact relating to 'whether the applicant will grow potatoes, and whether they are being grown or will be grown for sale'.[55] Accordingly, 'an erroneous decision . . . on such a question could be readily reviewed by the courts'.[56] Indeed, in this case, it was possible to conclude, based on the documentary evidence, that the potato grower's freedom to engage in interstate trade had not been infringed, in that he could have successfully applied for registration under the Act.[57] Understood in terms of the considerations I have laid out, the clear-cut, objective language and the availability of sufficient documentary evidence justified intrusive judicial review of such questions to give effect to the statutory scheme adopted by the legislature, without compromising effective and efficient administration.

4.1.3 Individual Self-realisation

Where important individual interests are engaged, courts are more likely to find that a given issue is 'jurisdictional'. A line of Irish cases involving 'jurisdictional' issues in which individual interests were very much at stake supports this proposition, running from *State (Holland) v Kennedy*, which involved the imposition of a custodial sentence on a young offender,[58] through taxation cases such as *Kennedy v Hearne*[59] and *Royal Dublin Society v Revenue Commissioners*,[60] to *Foley v Judge Murphy*,[61] another case involving a decision with implications for personal liberty.[62]

[52] Section 92 of the Australian Constitution provides: 'On the imposition of uniform duties of customs, trade, commerce, and intercourse among the States, whether by means of internal carriage or ocean navigation, shall be absolutely free'.

[53] *Buck v Bavone* (n 51) 119.

[54] Ibid.

[55] Ibid.

[56] Ibid.

[57] Ibid, 119, 120. See similarly Stephen J at 126 and Mason J at 131.

[58] [1977] IR 193.

[59] [1988] IR 481 (issuing to sheriff of tax enforcement notice).

[60] [2000] 1 IR 270 (misinterpretation of licensing code had with consequent effect on the right (constitutionally protected in Ireland) to earn a livelihood.

[61] [2005] 3 IR 574.

[62] See also the *Malaysia Declaration Case* (n 6), where a ministerial declaration under s 198A(3)(a) of the Migration Act 1958 (Cth) was held to be a jurisdictional issue even though the declaration covered a wide variety of matters relating to the protection of the rights of refugees in Malaysia,

It is worth considering the leading English case of *Khawaja v Home Secretary*[63] in this regard. Here, the House of Lords had to consider the definition of 'illegal entrant' in section 33 of the Immigration Act 1971, for under this provision two immigrants who had been living in the United Kingdom had been detained on the basis that they had not previously disclosed material facts to immigration officials. The case involved 'grave issues of personal liberty',[64] so much so that their Lordships were persuaded to depart from one of their own recent decisions. In *R v Secretary of State for the Home Department, ex parte Zamir*,[65] it had been held that the determination as to whether an immigrant was an 'illegal entrant' was *not* jurisdictional. This created a 'a draconian power of arrest and expulsion based upon [the immigration officer's] own decision of fact which, if there was any evidence to support it, cannot be examined by any judicial process until after it has been acted on . . .'.[66] For his part, Lord Scarman was 'convinced that the *Zamir* reasoning gave insufficient weight to the important—I would say fundamental—consideration that we are here concerned with, the scope of judicial review of a power which inevitably infringes the liberty of those subjected to it'.[67] In other words, individual interests can be understood to have been paramount, such that any individual subject to removal proceedings could challenge his or her classification as an 'illegal entrant' before the courts.

The importance of individual interests can also be understood to be operative in cases in which courts have read down broadly worded discretionary powers capable of being used to interfere with the exercise of individual rights.[68] An example

specifically: '(i) . . . access, for persons seeking asylum, to effective procedures for assessing their need for protection; and (ii) . . . protection for persons seeking asylum, pending determination of their refugee status; and (iii) . . . protection to persons who are given refugee status, pending their voluntary repatriation to their country of origin or resettlement in another country; and (iv) [meeting] relevant human rights standards in providing that protection . . .'. At issue was whether the plaintiff asylum seekers could lawfully be removed, under the declaration, from Australia to Malaysia.

63 [1984] AC 74.
64 Ibid, 97 per Lord Fraser of Tullybelton.
65 [1980] AC 930.
66 *Khawaja v Home Secretary* (n 63) 120 per Lord Bridge of Harwich.
67 Ibid, 109. In his speech, Lord Wilberforce justified treating the question of whether the immigrants were 'illegal entrants' as jurisdictional by making an analytical distinction between 'two parts' of the decision to resort to s 33 of the 1971 Act, the determination as to whether an immigrant is an 'illegal entrant' (a jurisdictional matter reviewable by the courts) being distinct from the decision whether, in all the circumstances, to actually remove the 'illegal entrant'. Ibid, 99–101. This may very well be the formal basis for the decision—but as I have stressed, my goal in this book is to provide an interpretation (not a description) of the decided cases. The best interpretation of *Khawaja* is that individual interests were centrally important to the analysis.
68 See e.g. *The State (Lynch) v Cooney* [1982] IR 337, 360; *Buck v Comcare* (1996) 66 FCR 359, where workers' compensation payments 'necessary to secure the basic amenities of life in modern society' were at issue (364–365 per Finn J); *Lord Allen of Liverpool v Secretary of State for the Home Department* [2008] EWCA Civ 443; [2008] 1 WLR 2341. Cf *Liversidge v Anderson* [1942] AC 206 but note that the dissenting view of Lord Atkin is now to be preferred as an accurate statement of the applicable legal principles: it is 'now orthodox' (*George v Rockett* (1990) 170 CLR 104, 122. See also *Nakkuda Ali v Jayaratne* [1951] AC 66, 76–77 and the *Malaysia Declaration Case* (n 6)).

is *R (UNISON) v Lord Chancellor*.[69] Here, the United Kingdom Supreme Court had to determine whether fees imposed in respect of employment claims, which must be brought in the tribunal system, were unlawful. Under section 42 of the Tribunals, Courts and Enforcement Act 2007, the Lord Chancellor has the power to prescribe fees. Exercising this power, the Lord Chancellor introduced a Fees Order, which prescribed steep fees for those who wished to access the tribunal system to enforce employment rights. The goal was to shift the costs of operating the system from taxpayers to users. It bears noting that the sums at stake in employment disputes are typically modest, such that the Fees Order had a significant deterrent effect.

The importance of the individual interests at stake and the need to preserve the distinct role of the judiciary can be understood to have influenced the Court's interpretation of the scope of the power, and ultimately the result that the Fees Order was *ultra vires*. To begin with, '[t]he constitutional right of access to the courts' has to be protected.[70] Here, moreover, the enforcement mechanism provided for by statute allowed claims to be brought which would 'enable legislation to have the deterrent and other effects which Parliament intended, provide authoritative guidance as to its meaning and application, and underpin alternative methods of dispute resolution'.[71] In addition, it was clear that 'any hindrance or impediment by the executive' of the right of access to the courts 'requires clear authorisation by Parliament'.[72] As a result, the Court explained in a series of passages which can be understood to be infused by concerns for individual interests, that if the delegated legislation created 'a real risk that persons will effectively be prevented from having access to justice', it would be *ultra vires*.[73] Indeed, 'even where primary legislation authorises the imposition of an intrusion on the right of access to justice, it is presumed to be subject to an implied limitation ... [that] ... the degree of intrusion must not be greater than is justified by the objectives which the measure is

[69] [2017] 3 WLR 409. See also *O'Brien v Personal Injuries Assessment Board* [2007] 1 IR 328 (restrictions on legal representation in formal, quasi-judicial proceedings); *Ahmed v Her Majesty's Treasury (No 1)* [2010] UKSC 2; [2010] 2 WLR 378 (statutory instrument freezing assets); *Trial Lawyers Association of British Columbia v British Columbia (Attorney General)* 2014 SCC 59; [2014] 3 SCR 31 [70]–[79] per Cromwell J (court fees set out in subordinate legislation preventing access to justice). See also *Reference re Section 6 of the Time Limits and Other Periods Act (COVID-19) (CA)* 2020 FCA 137 [17].

[70] *R (UNISON) v Lord Chancellor* (n 69) [66]. This was said to be 'inherent in the rule of law', but on my approach to administrative law values it is better understood as relating to the value of decisional autonomy. At issue here, admittedly, was access to a tribunal, not a court, though of course an individual dissuaded by the fees from accessing the tribunal would not later be in a position to invoke the appellate or supervisory jurisdiction of the courts. Cf *Prairies Tubulars (2015) Inc v Canada (Border Services Agency)* 2021 FC 36. In any event, in the United Kingdom (which includes England and Wales), 'the general assumption seems to be that tribunals do essentially the same thing as courts' (Peter Cane, *Administrative Tribunals and Adjudication* (Hart, Oxford, 2009), 139).

[71] Ibid, [72]; see also [103]–[104].

[72] Ibid, [78].

[73] Ibid, [87].

intended to serve'.[74] On the facts, the Fees Order 'effectively prevent[ed] access to justice, and [was] therefore unlawful'.[75]

It is also worth noting that there is now greater judicial willingness to review factual matters (even where these are not 'jurisdictional'), previously considered to be entirely within the bailiwick of the administrative decision-maker,[76] especially in cases involving significant individual interests.[77] In *A v Criminal Injuries Compensation Board*,[78] a case in which the Board rejected a claim by an alleged rape victim without having had regard to an important medical report, putting her credibility in issue on a matter of fundamental personal importance, the impugned decision was quashed on the ground of unfairness.[79] And in *E v Secretary of State for the Home Department*, Carnwath LJ justified the introduction of 'a separate ground of review' of error of fact 'on the principle of fairness'.[80] This is best understood in terms of individual self-realisation.[81] Error costs in this regime are extraordinarily high, as failed asylum seekers wrongly returned to their country of origin are at grave risk of physical danger.[82] Concern for important individual interests can thus be understood as militating in favour of more intensive judicial review of factual matters in some circumstances.

4.1.4 Deference on Questions of Law

In most of the jurisdictions under consideration it is now accepted that where an administrative decision-maker commits an error of law by interpreting the law incorrectly, a reviewing court may intervene.[83] *Anisminic v Foreign Compensation*

[74] Ibid, [88].

[75] Ibid, [98]. See similarly *R v Lord Chancellor, ex parte Witham* [1998] QB 575; *R v Secretary of State for the Home Department, ex parte Simms* [2000] 2 AC 115.

[76] *R v Nat Bell Liquors Ltd* (n 20). See also *R v Governor of Brixton Prison, ex parte Armah* (n 20) 234. But see now, generally, Paul Daly, 'Facticity: Judicial Review of Factual Error in Comparative Perspective' in Cane et al eds, *The Oxford Handbook of Comparative Administrative Law* (Oxford University Press, Oxford, 2020) and further Paul Craig, 'Judicial Review, Appeal and Factual Error' [2004] *Public Law* 788; Rebecca Williams, 'When Is an Error Not an Error? Reform of Jurisdictional Review of Error of Law and Fact' [2007] *Public Law* 793; Christopher Forsyth and Emma Dring, 'The Final Frontier: The Emergence of Material Error of Fact as a Ground for Judicial Review' in Forsyth et al eds, *Effective Judicial Review: A Cornerstone of Good Governance* (Oxford University Press, Oxford, 2010).

[77] See also *Donegan v Dublin City Council* [2012] 3 IR 600 (applicant's rights under Article 8 of the European Convention on Human Rights engaged).

[78] [1999] 2 AC 330.

[79] Ibid, 347.

[80] [2004] EWCA Civ 49; [2004] QB 1044 [63]. See also *R v Secretary of State for the Home Department, ex parte Bugdaycay* [1987] AC 514, 531.

[81] See also Edward Lui, '"Fairness" for Mistake of Fact: A Mistake in Fact' [2020] *Public Law* 428.

[82] See also the *Malaysia Declaration Case* (n 6), where the issue was sending asylum seekers from Australia to Malaysia, which was not their country of origin but which did not (the asylum seekers argued) have a sufficiently robust system of refugee protection.

[83] See e.g. *Bulk Gas Users Group v Attorney General* [1983] NZLR 129; *City of Enfield v Development Assessment Commission* (n 50) 199 CLR 135. The Irish position is in a state of flux but for general support for the proposition in the text see e.g. *State (Holland) v Kennedy* [1977] IR 193 and cf *Killeen v*

Commission[84] was a watershed case. A majority of the House of Lords held that an error in interpreting an Order in Council justified judicial intervention. Concern for giving effect to legislative intent can be understood to have weighed heavily in the balance. As Lord Pearce put it, administrative decision-makers must 'confine themselves within the powers specially committed to them on a true construction of the relevant Acts of Parliament'.[85] When courts intervene to keep an administrative decision-maker within boundaries established by legislation—to ensure the 'very effectiveness' of statute[86]—this represents 'simply an enforcement of Parliament's mandate to the tribunal'.[87] It is now widely accepted that the logic of *Anisminic* means that errors of law will generally justify judicial intervention.[88]

A statute might, however, grant significant power to an administrative decision-maker, which a court paying due respect to the value of electoral legitimacy would be obliged to take into account:

> The legislature may entrust the tribunal or body with a jurisdiction, which includes the jurisdiction to determine whether the preliminary state of facts exists as well as the jurisdiction, [and] on finding that it does exist, to proceed further or do something more ... [In such a case] it is an erroneous application of the [jurisdictional error] formula to say that the tribunal cannot give themselves jurisdiction by wrongly deciding certain facts to exist, because the legislature gave them jurisdiction to determine all the facts, including the existence of the preliminary facts on which the further exercise of their jurisdiction depends ...[89]

Their Lordships were well aware of these nuances. For Lord Wilberforce, for instance, while the 'essential point' of *Anisminic* is that a tribunal exercises 'derived

Director of Public Prosecutions (n 17) (where the error of law complained of was treated as jurisdictional but the possibility of an error of law being beyond judicial review was also countenanced). This position once prevailed in Canada too: *Metropolitan Life Insurance Co v International Union of Operating Engineers* [1970] SCR 425.

84 [1969] 2 AC 147.

85 Ibid, 194. See further Chapter 6.4.

86 *R (Cart) v Upper Tribunal* [2009] EWHC 3052; [2010] 1 All ER 908 [38] per Laws LJ

87 *Anisminic v Foreign Compensation Commission* (n 84) 196. See similarly *R v Northumberland Compensation Appeal Tribunal, ex parte Shaw* [1952] 1 KB 338, 346.

88 See e.g. *In re A Company* [1981] AC 374, 383 per Lord Diplock: 'The break-through made by [*Anisminic*] was that, as respects administrative tribunals and authorities, the old distinction between errors of law that went to jurisdiction and errors of law that did not, was for practical purposes abolished'; *R v Hull University Visitor, ex parte Page* [1993] AC 682, 701 per Lord Browne-Wilkinson: 'In my judgment the decision in [*Anisminic*] rendered obsolete the distinction between errors of law on the face of the record and other errors of law by extending the doctrine of ultra vires'; *R (Cart) v Upper Tribunal* [2011] UKSC 28; [2012] 1 AC 663 [18] per Baroness Hale of Richmond: '[*Anisminic*] removed the distinction between error of law and excess of jurisdiction'.

89 *R v Income Tax Special Commissioners, ex parte Cape Copper Mining Company* (1888) 21 QBD 313, 319–320 per Lord Esher MR. See e.g. *Tithe Redemption Commission v Wynne* [1943] KB 756.

authority' and is thus subject to limitations set out by the legislature in statute, '[t]here is always an area, narrow or wide, which is the tribunal's area'.[90]

Indeed, it is possible to build a deferential approach to judicial review of administrative action on these foundations. In Canada, where deference to administrative decision-makers is embraced, the courts recognise the importance of respecting the 'tribunal's area': 'Courts, while exercising their constitutional functions of judicial review, must be sensitive ... to the necessity of avoiding undue interference with the discharge of administrative functions in respect of the matters *delegated to administrative bodies by Parliament and legislatures*'.[91] Statutes are treated as relevant information which carve out a space for administrative decision-makers or which inform the degree of deference courts ought to accord to administrative decision-makers.[92] The legislative choice to grant authority to administrative decision-makers can thereby be respected.[93] As Lord Wilberforce acknowledged in *Anisminic*, determining the 'extent of the interpretatory power conferred upon the tribunal' should not be done with 'any necessary predisposition towards one that questions of law, or questions of construction, are necessarily for the courts'.[94] Ultimately, 'when a reviewing court considers the scope of a decision-making power or the jurisdiction conferred by a statute, [it] *strives to determine what authority was intended to be given to the body in relation to the subject-matter*'.[95]

The authority thereby granted is not absolute, however. The courts still police the limits of powers granted by legislatures, but they do so mindful of the need to respect the autonomy of administrative decision-makers. For example, the Supreme Court of Canada has emphasised that a deferential standard of review permits judicial intervention where the administrative decision is not based on 'rational and logical' reasoning[96] or is inadequately 'justified in relation to the constellation of law and facts that are relevant to the decision'.[97] This can be understood as judicial insistence upon the maintaining of distinct roles for courts—reviewing for legality, rationality and procedural fairness—and administrative decision-makers—taking first-instance decisions on the merits, as well as they possibly can. Moreover, while

[90] *Anisminic v Foreign Compensation Commission* (n 84) 207.

[91] *Dunsmuir v New Brunswick*, 2008 SCC 9 [2008] 1 SCR 190 [27]. Emphasis added.

[92] Peter L Strauss, '"Deference" is Too Confusing—Let's Call Them "Chevron Space" and "Skidmore Weight"' (2012) 112 *Columbia Law Review* 1143.

[93] See especially *Canada (Citizenship and Immigration) v Vavilov* (n 4) [23]:

> Where a court reviews the merits of an administrative decision (i.e., judicial review of an administrative decisions other than a review related to a breach of natural justice and/or the duty of procedural fairness), the standard of review it applies must reflect the legislature's intent with respect to the role of the reviewing court, except where giving effect to that intent is precluded by the rule of law. The starting point for the analysis is a presumption that the legislature intended the standard of review to be reasonableness.

[94] *Anisminic v Foreign Compensation Commission* (n 84) 209.

[95] *Dunsmuir v New Brunswick* (n 91) [29] per Bastarache and LeBel JJ. Emphasis added. See also *Canada (Citizenship and Immigration) v Vavilov* (n 4) [108]–[109].

[96] *Canada (Citizenship and Immigration) v Vavilov* (n 4) [102].

[97] Ibid, [105].

matters on which administrative decision-makers have particular expertise should be reviewed on a deferential standard,[98] some questions should be left for the courts. Non-deferential correctness review on constitutional questions, questions of central importance to the legal system and questions of overlapping jurisdiction 'respects the unique role of the judiciary in interpreting the Constitution and ensures that courts are able to provide the last word on questions for which the rule of law requires consistency and for which a final and determinate answer is necessary'.[99]

A deferential approach can be buttressed by considerations relating to effective and efficient public administration. To defer to administrative decision-makers is to defer to expert bodies which can deal efficiently with complex issues, sometimes relying on input from interested parties. Such bodies can exercise their functions with 'cheapness, accessibility, freedom from technicality, expedition and expert knowledge of their particular subject'.[100] For the Supreme Court of Canada, the demonstrated expertise of administrative decision-makers justifies a deferential approach by reviewing courts,[101] who should be slower to interfere in the context of a 'discrete and special administrative regime in which the decision maker has special expertise'.[102]

It is true that in the rest of the common law world there is significant judicial resistance to deference on questions of law. It has been said, for instance, that a decision-maker's 'expertise and the specialised nature of its functions do not clothe it with any wider power to determine its statutory jurisdiction than is enjoyed by other administrative decision-makers, and its conclusions on [legal questions] are entitled to no greater deference on a review or appeal'.[103] Nonetheless, the picture is not quite as straightforward as is portrayed by the famous statement that it 'is emphatically the province and duty of the judicial department to say what the law is'.[104]

To begin with, there are limited exceptions to the proposition that all errors of law are reviewable. In *R v Hull University Visitor, ex parte Page*, the Visitor was

[98] Ibid, [27].

[99] Ibid, [53]. See also *Dunsmuir v New Brunswick* (n 91) [58]; Louis LeBel, 'De *Dunsmuir* à *Khosa*' (2010) 55 *McGill Law Journal* 311.

[100] *Report of the Franks Committee on Administrative Tribunals and Enquiries* (Cmnd 218, 1957), 9.

[101] *Canada (Citizenship and Immigration) v Vavilov* (n 4) [93].

[102] *Dunsmuir v New Brunswick* (n 91) [55]. In *Dunsmuir* [49] the Supreme Court of Canada also endorsed Professor Mullan's recognition of the 'reality that, in many instances, those working day to day in the implementation of frequently complex administrative schemes have or will develop a considerable degree of expertise or field sensitivity to the imperatives and nuances of the legislative regime'. David J Mullan, 'Establishing the Standard of Review: The Struggle for Complexity?' (2004) 17 *Canadian Journal of Administrative Law and Practice* 59, 93. See also *Canada (Citizenship and Immigration) v Vavilov* (n 4) [93].

[103] *Société Coopérative de Production SeaFrance SA v Competition and Markets Authority* [2015] UKSC 75 [31] per Lord Sumption.

[104] *Marbury v Madison* (1803) 5 US (1 Cranch) 137 (1980), 178. See especially *City of Enfield v Development Assessment Commission* (n 50).

required to make determinations about a 'peculiar, domestic law'[105] and, in doing so, was not subject to judicial review for error of law. Lord Browne-Wilkinson's reasons for so concluding can be understood to sound in administrative law values. Effective and efficient public administration was relevant: a visitor applies 'not the general law of the land but a peculiar, domestic law of which he is the sole arbiter and of which the courts have no cognisance'[106] and so has an edge on the courts in terms of relative expertise; moreover, the visitorial jurisdiction is 'an informal system which produces a speedy, cheap and final answer to internal disputes . . .'[107] A concern to keep the judicial and administrative domains somewhat distinct can also be understood to have been operative: the ordinary 'constitutional basis'[108] of judicial review for error of law was absent because the 'special status of a visitor springs from the common law recognising the right of the founder [of a private organisation] to lay down such a special law subject to adjudication only by a special judge, the visitor.'[109] Here, the appropriate role of the courts was more restricted than in the case of review of administrative decision-makers.

Inferior courts may also have a special status as far as review for error of law is concerned.[110] In an expansive discussion of the modern doctrine of jurisdictional error in *Re Racal Communications*, Lord Diplock praised what he saw as the advances made in *Anisminic* but warned his colleagues 'not [to] be astute to hold that Parliament did not intend the inferior court to have jurisdiction to decide for itself the meaning of ordinary words used in the statute to define the question which it has to decide.'[111] One way of understanding this warning is that the expertise of inferior courts on questions of law will be likely to approach that of the superior courts. Similarly, in the litigation concerning the scope of review of decisions of the Upper Tribunal, created by the Tribunals, Courts and Enforcement Act 2007, there was a generalised judicial reluctance to mandate plenary review of the Tribunal's interpretations of law,[112] because, variously, of the Tribunal's evident expertise and Parliament's desire to create a unified, judicialised dispute resolution mechanism. It is also worth recalling what Lord Denning MR said about judicial review of tribunal appeals on social welfare benefits:

105 (n 88) 702.
106 Ibid.
107 Ibid, 704.
108 Ibid, 702.
109 Ibid, 700.
110 See e.g. in Ireland *Killeen v Director of Public Prosecutions* (n 17), countenancing error of law within jurisdiction in the context of an inferior court and, semble, *Craig v South Australia* (1995) 184 CLR 163, albeit that in *Kirk v Industrial Relations Commission (NSW)* [2010] HCA 1; (2010) 239 CLR 531 the High Court of Australia doubted the workability of a distinction between administrative tribunals and inferior courts. See also the discussion in *R (Privacy International) v Investigatory Powers Tribunal* [2019] UKSC 22; [2019] 2 WLR 1219.
111 (n 88) 383.
112 *R (Cart) v Upper Tribunal* [2009] EWHC 3052 (Admin); [2011] QB 120 and [2012] 1 AC 663 (Supreme Court).

> The courts should not enter into a meticulous discussion of the meaning of this or that word in the [Supplementary Benefit] Act [1966]. They should leave the tribunals to interpret the Act in a broad reasonable way, according to the spirit and not to the letter ... The courts should only interfere when the decision of the tribunal is unreasonable in the sense that no tribunal acquainted with the ordinary use of language could reasonably reach that decision.[113]

Moreover, not every error of law will invalidate an administrative decision, a point which can be understood in terms of administrative law values and as a manifestation of deference in another form. This point is often considered in terms of a distinction between 'mandatory' and 'directory' statutory provisions. The distinction has been deprecated by the High Court of Australia,[114] the House of Lords[115] and the Supreme Court of Canada[116] but has been retained in Ireland. It is designed to serve a similar function to the distinction between jurisdictional and non-jurisdictional error, namely, assisting a court in 'interpreting a statute to determine whether invalidity was the intended result'[117] and hence in determining whether an error should be treated as being fatal to the validity of an administrative decision:

> If the requirement which has not been observed may fairly be said to be an integral and indispensable part of the statutory intendment, the courts will hold it to be truly mandatory, and will not excuse a departure from it. But if, on the other hand, what is apparently a requirement is in essence merely a direction which is not of the substance of the aim and scheme of the statute, non-compliance may be excused.[118]

In determining whether to treat an error as a breach of a mandatory or merely directory provision, the materiality of the error—in terms of its consequences for the operation of the statutory scheme[119] —will be a key

[113] *R v Preston Supplementary Benefits Appeal Tribunal, ex parte Moore* [1975] 1 WLR 624, 631–632. See also *R v National Insurance Commissioner, ex parte Stratton* [1979] QB 361, 368–369.

[114] *Project Blue Sky Inc v Australian Broadcasting Authority*) (1998) 194 CLR 355.

[115] *R v Soneji* [2006] AC 340.

[116] *British Columbia (Attorney General) v Canada (Attorney General)* [1994] 2 SCR 41.

[117] Boughey J and Burton-Crawford L, 'Reconsidering R. *(on the application of Cart) v Upper Tribunal* and the rationale for jurisdictional error' [2017] *Public Law* 592, 601.

[118] *State (Elm Developments Ltd) v An Bord Pleanála* [1981] ILRM 108, 110 per Henchy J. See also Robert Macaulay, James Sprague, and Lorne Sossin, *Practice and Procedure Before Administrative Tribunals*, vol 3 (looseleaf) 22 [126]–[126.1]:

> Where a provision is imperative it must be complied with. The consequence of failing to comply with an imperative provision will vary depending on whether the imperative direction is mandatory or directory. Failing to comply with a mandatory direction will render any subsequent proceedings void while failing to comply with [a] directory command will not result in such invalidation (although the person to whom the command was directed will not be relieved from the duty of complying with it.

[119] See e.g. *Society Promoting Environmental Conservation v Canada (Attorney General)* [2003] 4 FC 959 [27] per Evans JA: 'The relevant question was whether invalidating administrative action for breach

consideration.[120] One way to understand the mandatory/directory distinction is to think of it in terms of the importance of the error in question: only a serious error, which undermines the statutory scheme or interferes with individual rights or other legal values,[121] will be treated as mandatory and, therefore, as having invalidated the decision; whereas a relatively immaterial error will not invalidate the decision;[122] invalidity, after all, would have significant administrative consequences and risk frustrating good administration,[123] such that minor errors should not be taken as invalidating decisions and prompting further expenditure of scarce resources (or, in extreme cases, administrative chaos). Even, in other words, if the language of deference is absent from the law reports of some jurisdictions, the concept may (on one view) be glimpsed nonetheless.

Consider, finally, the decision of the House of Lords in *R v Monopolies and Mergers Commission, ex parte South Yorkshire Transport*.[124] At issue was the interpretation of section 64 of the Fair Trading Act 1973. A deal involving the acquisition by a bus company of local bus services in South Yorkshire, Derbyshire and Nottinghamshire was referred to the Commission for a determination as to whether the merger concerned a 'substantial part of the United Kingdom'. On investigating the merger, the Commission concluded that although the area in question represented a tiny percentage of the geographical territory of the United Kingdom, it was sufficiently economically and culturally significant to count as 'substantial' for the purposes of the 1973 Act. The Commission's recommendation that the purchaser divest itself of the companies it had acquired was challenged in judicial review proceedings. In the House of Lords, Lord Mustill noted that the

of the statute would be inconvenient or unjust, or would otherwise be inconsistent with the purposes of the legislation'.

120 See also *Wei v Minister for Immigration and Border Protection* (2015) 257 CLR 22, 32.

121 See e.g. *R v Immigration Appeal Tribunal, ex parte Jeyeanthan* [2000] 1 WLR 354, 360 per Lord Woolf MR: 'In the majority of cases, whether the requirement is categorised as directory or mandatory, the tribunal before whom the defect is properly raised has the task of determining what are to be the consequences of failing to comply with the requirement in the context of all the facts and circumstances of the case in which the issue arises. In such a situation that tribunal's task will be to seek to do what is just in all the circumstances'.

122 See e.g. the list of factors set out by Evans JA in *Society Promoting Environmental Conservation v Canada (Attorney General)* (n 119) [35] and Gerard Hogan, David Morgan and Paul Daly, *Administrative Law in Ireland* 5th edn (Roundhall, Dublin, 2019) [12–75]:

> A court addressing this issue will have to ask two questions. First, was the provision mandatory or directory? Second, should the violation of the provision be tolerated or not? The first question is essentially an exercise in discerning legislative intent, in the abstract; the second more a matter of judicial policy as applied to the facts of particular cases. In general, the stronger the legislative intent ... and the more serious the consequences of the violation, the more compelling the argument will be to invalidate the impugned decision. Conversely, where legislative intent is weaker and the consequences of non-compliance are relatively harmless, the party arguing that non-compliance should be excused will ordinarily win the day. Of course, most cases are likely to fall somewhere in between these two extremes.

123 See further Chapter 5.6.

124 [1993] 1 WLR 23.

term 'substantial part' is 'protean' and 'accommodates a wide range of meanings'.[125] Indeed, the term was 'so imprecise that different decision-makers, each acting rationally, might reach differing conclusions when applying it to the facts of a given case', such that the court was 'entitled to substitute its own opinion for that of the person to whom the decision has been entrusted only if the decision is so aberrant that it cannot be classed as rational'.[126] Here, '[e]ven after eliminating inappropriate senses of "substantial" one is still left with a meaning broad enough to call for the exercise of judgment rather than an exact quantitative measurement' and the Commission's conclusion was 'well within the permissible field of judgment'.[127] Where a term 'does have a correct meaning and one meaning alone', a court will insist upon it, but that was not the case here.[128] Proper attention to statutory language opened up a discretionary range of judgment within which the Commission could roam. In other words, even if the courts have 'the last word' on matters of statutory interpretation, some statutory terms will be so broad as to vest significant discretionary authority in the administrative decision-makers they empower;[129] this might not be 'deference, Canada-style', but it certainly resembles it, and can be understood to be supported by respect for the considered choices of elected representatives to leave the elaboration of the vague term in the hands of an expert body. This conclusion also makes sense from the perspective of effective and efficient public administration—the Commission is plainly better equipped than a court to determine the economic effects of the absorption by a larger company of smaller operators; judicial interference on economic matters might, indeed, impede the efficient and effective regulation of competition by the Commission.[130]

Accordingly, even in jurisdictions which reject Canada-style deference, traces of the concept can nonetheless be discerned, with administrative law values illuminating its manifestations.

Furthermore, nothing in the foregoing forecloses the possibility that courts might, in some circumstances, give *some* weight[131] to interpretations of law developed by administrative decision-makers,[132] just as they may in respect of other jurisdictional issues where an administrative decision-maker's expertise relative to the court and the breadth of its statutory mandate so suggest. It is notable in this

[125] Ibid, 29.
[126] Ibid, 32.
[127] Ibid, 32–33.
[128] Ibid, 32.
[129] See also *Pong Marketing and Promotions Inc v Ontario Media Development Corporation* 2018 ONCA 555 [44]–[52].
[130] See also *Dowty Boulton Paul Ltd v Wolverhampton Corporation (No 2)* [1976] Ch 13, 26 per Russell LJ, where the interpretation of the term 'not required' (for the purposes of local authority property purchases) gave rise to 'matters both of degree and of comparative needs, as to which there can be no question but that the local authority is better qualified than the court to judge, assuming it to be acting bona fide and not upon a view that no reasonable local authority could possibly take'.
[131] Daly (n 5), chapter 1.
[132] See e.g. *Rhuppiah v Secretary of State for the Home Department* [2018] UKSC 58 [43].

regard that common law courts have suggested, in the context of statutory appeals from administrative decision-makers to the courts, that a measure of deference may be appropriate where the administrative decision-maker has more subject-matter expertise than the reviewing courts.[133]

The point here is not that other common law jurisdictions should necessarily follow Canada's lead but that the exceptions to the conventional view that questions of law are for the courts can be understood in terms of the same values which support a generalised deferential approach, and, moreover, that close study may in fact support the conclusion that administrative decision-makers enjoy a zone of interpretive freedom even though there is no Canada-style doctrine of deference in place.[134]

4.2 Abuse of Discretion

The common law has for centuries subjected discretion to law. Administrative decision-makers' proceedings must, Coke CJ told us long ago, 'be limited and bound with the rule of reason and law'.[135] The same is true today. Even in Australia, notwithstanding the constitutional restriction on the ability of reviewing courts to engage in 'merits' review, a legal limitation of reasonableness is implied into statutory grants of discretionary power to public bodies,[136] because '[t]he legislature is

[133] See e.g. *Canada (Director of Investigation and Research) v Southam Inc* (n 25); *Henry Denny and Co (Ireland) Ltd v Minister for Social Welfare* [1998] 1 IR 34 (albeit that in Ireland this only extends to mixed questions of fact and law and not to pure questions of law); *Planet Energy (Ontario) Corp v Ontario Energy Board* 2020 ONSC 598 [31]. In England and Wales, such considerations have also given rise to the suggestion that courts should not lightly entertain appeals from specialist administrative tribunals: see e.g. *Cooke v Secretary of State for Social Security* [2001] EWCA Civ 734; [2002] 3 All ER 279 [16] per Hale LJ:

> It is also important that such appeal structures have a link to the ordinary court system, to maintain both their independence of government and the sponsoring department and their fidelity to the relevant general principles of law. But the ordinary courts should approach such cases with an appropriate degree of caution. It is quite probable that on a technical issue of understanding and applying the complex legislation the Social Security Commissioner will have got it right. The Commissioners will know how that particular issue fits into the broader picture of social security principles as a whole. They will be less likely to introduce distortion into those principles. They may be better placed, where it is appropriate, to apply those principles in a purposive construction of the legislation in question. They will also know the realities of tribunal life. All of this should be taken into account by an appellate court when considering whether an appeal will have a real prospect of success.

[134] For empirical analysis of this issue in the context of European Union competition law, see Pablo Ibanez Colomo, *The Shaping of EU Competition Law* (Cambridge University Press, Cambridge, 2018). If there is significant deference to administrative decision-makers in practice, such empirical evidence further strengthens the case for developing a generalised principle of deference on questions of law.

[135] *Rooke's Case* (1598) 5 Co Rep 99b.

[136] See e.g. *Kruger v The Commonwealth* (1997) 190 CLR 1, 36 per Brennan CJ: '[W]hen a discretionary power is statutorily conferred on a repository, the power must be exercised reasonably, for the legislature is taken to intend that the discretion be so exercised'; *Abebe v The Commonwealth* (1999) 197 CLR 510, 554 per Gaudron J: '[I]t is difficult to see why, if a statute which confers a decision-making power is silent on the topic of reasonableness, that statute should not be construed so that it is an

taken to intend that a discretionary power, statutorily conferred, will be exercised reasonably'.[137] Action that is legally unreasonable is *ultra vires*, because it falls outside the four corners of the statutory authorisation granted by the legislature. As with Lord Greene MR's classic formulation of *Wednesbury* unreasonableness, even where the decision-maker has interpreted the law correctly, considered the appropriate factors and, in good faith, exercised its powers for a proper purpose, it is not at liberty 'to be arbitrary or capricious or to abandon common sense'.[138]

Rather than relying on clear-cut distinctions between 'law' and 'fact', 'jurisdictional' and 'non-jurisdictional' or 'quasi-judicial' and 'administrative' decisions,[139] contemporary courts and commentators are concerned with the intensity with which administrative decisions ought to be scrutinised, consistent with the general trend on apex courts towards the development of context-sensitive, multi-factoral tests, in both public and private law.[140] Common law courts have introduced significant nuance to *Wednesbury* unreasonableness: 'in fact the courts, while broadly adhering to the monolithic language of *Wednesbury*, have to a considerable extent in recent years adopted variable standards of review'.[141]

4.2.1 Contemporary Characteristics

Contemporary substantive review for abuse of discretion has three characteristics across the common law world.[142] First, as the United Kingdom Supreme Court has put it, it treats the 'classic judicial review investigation' as whether the impugned administrative decision 'lay within the range of reasonable responses'.[143] In two

essential condition of the exercise of that power that it be exercised reasonably, at least in the sense that it not be exercised in a way that no reasonable person could exercise it.' The principle extends further, as Edelman J explained in *Minister for Immigration and Border Protection v SZVWF* [2018] HCA 30 [132] referencing wills, deeds and contracts: 'The implication of reasonableness is not unique to statutes. When a legal power is conferred by an instrument, it is often implied that the legal power will be exercised reasonably.'

137 *Minister for Immigration and Citizenship v Li* [2013] HCA 18; (2013) 249 CLR 332, 362 per Hayne, Kiefel and Bell JJ. See also *Attorney General (NSW) v Quin* (1990) 170 CLR 1, 36.

138 *Minister for Immigration and Citizenship v Li* (n 137) 351 per French CJ.

139 See generally Dean Knight, *Vigilance and Restraint in the Common Law of Judicial Review* (Cambridge University Press, Cambridge, 2018).

140 See generally Brice Dickson, 'Apex Courts and the Development of the Common Law' in Paul Daly ed, *Apex Courts and the Common Law* (University of Toronto Press, Toronto, 2019). See also Jason Varuhas, 'Taxonomy and Public Law' in Mark Elliott, Jason Varuhas and Shona Wilson-Stark eds, *The Unity of Public Law? Doctrinal, Theoretical and Comparative Perspectives* (Hart, Oxford, 2018); 'The Socialisation of Private Law: Balancing Private Right and Public Good' (2021) 137 *Law Quarterly Review* 141.

141 Sir John Laws, '*Wednesbury*', in Christopher Forsyth and Ivan Hare eds, *The Golden Metwand and the Crooked Cord* (Oxford University Press, Oxford, 1998), 185, 186–187.

142 See generally Paul Daly, 'Substantive Review in the Common Law World: *AAA v Minister for Justice* in Comparative Perspective' (2019) 1 *Irish Supreme Court Review* 105.

143 *Michalak v General Medical Council* [2017] UKSC 71; [2017] 1 WLR 4193 [21–22] per Lord Kerr. See similarly *Refugee Council of New Zealand v Attorney-General (No 1)* [2002] NZAR 717 [111];

key decisions in *Dunsmuir* and *Vavilov*, the Supreme Court of Canada has articulated a standard of reasonableness review which applies 'both to the process of articulating the reasons and to outcomes', looking to 'the existence of justification, transparency and intelligibility within the decision-making process'[144] such that contextual '[e]lements of the legal and factual contexts of a decision operate as constraints on the decision maker in the exercise of its delegated power'.[145] All administrative decisions are potentially subject to this framework, including decisions which interfere with constitutional rights[146] (though in such circumstances, 'reasonableness requires proportionality'[147]) and those which contain interpretations of law[148] (though here the range might be so narrow as to contain only one answer, upon which a reviewing court can insist[149]). I have argued that these Canadian developments can and should inform English administrative law.[150]

There is high authority in Australia—where a reviewing court may intervene on the basis of legal unreasonableness when a decision-maker has 'committed a particular error in reasoning, given disproportionate weight to some factor or reasoned illogically or irrationally'[151]—for the proposition that the Supreme Court of Canada's formulation of the reasonableness standard can assist Australian courts charged with applying the concept of legal unreasonableness.[152] Indeed, 'the new Australian approach to reasonableness seems to share much in common with Canadian developments, so that Canadian law might provide guidance to Australia in these respects'.[153] Even the 'broader view' articulated in *Vavilov* can provide guidance.[154]

Minister for Immigration and Citizenship v Li (n 137) 375; *Catalyst Paper Corp v North Cowichan (District)* 2012 SCC 2; [2012] 1 SCR 5 [18]; *YY v Minister for Justice and Equality* [2017] IESC 61 [70].

[144] *Dunsmuir v New Brunswick* (n 91) [47].

[145] *Canada (Citizenship and Immigration) v Vavilov* (n 4) [105].

[146] *Doré v Barreau du Québec* 2012 SCC 12; [2012] 1 SCR 395. Save where the constitutional validity of a law is frontally attacked, in which case the administrative tribunal's conclusions will be subject to correctness review, as in *Saskatchewan (Human Rights Commission) v Whatcott* 2013 SCC 11; [2013] 1 SCR 467.

[147] *Loyola High School v Quebec (Attorney General)* 2015 SCC 12; [2015] 1 SCR 613 [38].

[148] This has been the position since *CUPE v New Brunswick Liquor Corporation* [1979] SCR 227. For discussion see Matthew Lewans, *Administrative Law and Judicial Deference* (Hart, Oxford, 2016).

[149] *McLean v British Columbia (Securities Commission)* 2013 SCC 67; [2013] 3 SCR 895 [38].

[150] Paul Daly, 'Convergence and Divergence in English and Canadian Administrative Law' in Swati Jhaveri and Michael Ramsden eds, *Judicial Review of Administrative Action across the Common Law World: Origins and Adaptations* (Cambridge University Press, Cambridge, 2021).

[151] *Minister for Immigration and Citizenship v Li* (n 137) 366 per Hayne, Kiefel and Bell JJ.

[152] Ibid, 375 per Gageler J. See also *Minister for Immigration and Border Protection v SZVWF* (n 136) [10] per Kiefel CJ ('a decision made in the exercise of a statutory power is unreasonable in a legal sense when it lacks an evident and intelligible justification') [82] per Nettle and Gordon JJ; *ABT17 v Minister for Immigration and Border Protection* [2020] HCA 34 [20], [72], [126].

[153] Janina Boughey, *Human Rights and Judicial Review in Australia and Canada: The Newest Despotism?* (Hart, Oxford, 2017), 238.

[154] *ABT17 v Minister for Immigration and Border Protection* (n 152) [127] per Edelman J.

Courts in New Zealand and Ireland have, too, found utility in the 'range' concept.[155] In Ireland, for instance, judicial review is 'flexible and expansive'[156] and the Supreme Court has made clear[157] that the question to ask in judicial review applications is 'whether the applicant has discharged the onus of proof to show that there was a risk of ill-treatment such that the decision made fell outside the range of the decision[s] that were reasonably open to the Minister'.[158]

Second, it is 'flexible',[159] 'context-specific'[160] and 'invariably fact dependent',[161] with a broader or narrower range of reasonable responses depending on the interplay of a variety of factors.[162] I deal with this point in further detail below.

Third, the concept of proportionality is relevant to determining whether an impugned decision falls inside or outside the range of possible, acceptable outcomes.[163] There has been lively debate in recent years about whether *Wednesbury* should be supplanted by a proportionality test.[164] Participants in the debate have

[155] *Isaac v Minister of Consumer Affairs* [1990] 2 NZLR 606; *Waitakere City Council v Lovelock* [1997] 2 NZLR 385.

[156] *NM (DRC) v Minister for Justice, Equality and Law Reform* [2016] IECA 217 [37]; *AAA v Minister for Justice and Equality* [2017] IESC 80 [26].

[157] *YY v Minister for Justice and Equality* (n 143).

[158] *XX v Minister for Justice and Equality* [2016] IEHC 377 [134] per Humphreys J. The citation was to a decision of the Minister, which cited in turn to Humphreys J's exposition of the relevant principles. Nonetheless, O'Donnell J described it as 'a clear and correct statement of the law' (*YY v Minister for Justice and Equality* (n 143) [70]).

[159] *Pham v Secretary of State for the Home Department* [2015] UKSC 19; [2015] WLR 159 [60]. See similarly *NM (DRC) v Minister for Justice, Equality and Law Reform* (n 156) [37]; *AAA v Minister for Justice* (n 156) [26].

[160] *Minister for Immigration and Border Protection v SZVWF* (n 136) [52] per Gageler J.

[161] *Minister for Immigration and Border Protection v Singh* [2014] FCAFC 1 [42].

[162] See e.g. *Institute of Chartered Accountants of New Zealand v Bevan* [2003] 1 NZLR 154 [53–54] per Keith J; *Minister for Immigration and Citizenship v Li* (n 137), 363–364; *Canada (Minister of Transport, Infrastructure and Communities) v Jagjit Singh Farwaha* 2014 FCA 56; [2015] 2 FCR 1006 [88–91]; *R (Rotherham Metropolitan Borough Council) v Secretary of State for Business, Innovation and Skills* [2015] UKSC 6 [169]; *Pham v Home Secretary* (n 159) [107] per Lord Sumption; *Canada (Citizenship and Immigration) v Vavilov* (n 4) [105]–[138].

[163] See e.g. *Isaac v Minister of Consumer Affairs* (n 155), 636 per Tipping J; *Waitakere City Council v Lovelock* (n 155) 407–408; *Meadows v Minister for Justice, Equality and Law Reform* [2010] 2 IR 701, 723; *PO and SO v Minister for Justice and Equality* [2015] 3 IR 164, 204; *McCloy v New South Wales* [2015] HCA 34; (2015) 325 ALR 15, 19; *Law Society of British Columbia v Trinity Western University* 2018 SCC 32; [2018] 2 SCR 293 [57]–[59]. See also *Kim v Minister of Justice* [2019] NZCA 209 [45]–[47].

[164] It is variously said that the more structured methodology of proportionality is superior to the methodology of *Wednesbury*: Jeffrey Jowell and Anthony Lester, 'Proportionality: Neither Novel nor Dangerous' in Jeffrey Jowell and Dawn Oliver eds, *New Directions in Judicial Review* (Stevens and Sons, London, 1988); Paul Craig 'Unreasonableness and Proportionality in UK Law' in Evelyn Ellis ed, *The Principle of Proportionality in the Laws of Europe* (Oxford University Press, Oxford, 1999); that the law would be simplified if proportionality, already used in European Union law cases and human rights adjudication, were adopted as the general common law ground of review: Craig (n 5), and (more recently) that proportionality has deep historical roots in the common law: Paul Craig, 'Proportionality and Judicial Review: A UK Perspective' in Stephan Vogenauer and Stephen Weatherill eds, *General Principles of Law: European and Comparative Perspectives* (Hart, Oxford, 2017). It has been said in response that properly understood *Wednesbury* has its own structure: Paul Daly, '*Wednesbury's* Reason and Structure' [2011] *Public Law* 238; that *Wednesbury* preserves an appropriate balance between decision-making autonomy and judicial intervention, which would be upset by the introduction of more intrusive proportionality review: Lord Irvine of Lairg, 'Judges and Decision-Makers: The Theory and Practice of *Wednesbury* Review' [1996] *Public Law* 59; and that deferential *Wednesbury* review and

been quite concerned by the relative merits and demerits of proportionality and *Wednesbury* as mechanisms for reviewing administrative decisions. Interestingly, however, although partisans in the substantive review debate typically advocate either that proportionality should sweep the board or that proportionality and *Wednesbury* (usually in a modified form) should both be retained and kept distinct, the trend in the common law world has been to merge the two. The UK Supreme Court has recognised, for instance, that '[b]oth reasonableness review and proportionality involve considerations of weight and balance, with the intensity of the scrutiny and the weight to be given to any primary decision maker's view depending on the context'.[165] It is a short journey from this understanding to a recognition of the need for 'a flexible approach to principles of judicial review',[166] where what matters is 'the strength of the justification or the breadth of the decision-maker's margin of judgment'.[167] In other jurisdictions too, the concepts of reasonableness and proportionality have begun to merge. In Canada, 'reasonableness requires proportionality'[168] where fundamental rights are engaged; in Australia, proportionality may (it seems) be considered in the course of the inquiry into legal unreasonableness (although there do not seem to be any concrete examples);[169] and in Ireland and New Zealand proportionality is part of the overall inquiry into the reasonableness of a decision.[170]

4.2.2 Variation in the Range of Reasonable Outcomes

The intensity of substantive review varies from case to case, depending on the interaction of a variety of contextual factors. As has been said, in Canada the 'range will

less deferential proportionality review serve different functions: Jason Varuhas, 'Against Unification' in Mark Elliott and Hanna Wilberg eds, *The Scope and Intensity of Substantive Review: Traversing Taggart's Rainbow* (Hart, Oxford, 2015), though see Paul Craig's rejoinder in *UK, EU and Global Administrative Law: Foundations and Challenges* (Cambridge University Press, Cambridge, 2015), 260–271.

165 *Kennedy v Charity Commission (Secretary of State for Justice intervening)* [2014] UKSC 20; [2015] AC 455 [54]. See generally Craig (n 23).

166 *Pham v Home Secretary* (n 159) [60] per Lord Carnwath.

167 Ibid, 109. This chimes with Lord Neuberger of Abbotsbury MR's (as he then was) comment, made in the EU law context, that '[t]he breadth of the margin of appreciation in relation to any decision thus depends on the circumstances of the case and, in particular, on the identity of the decision-maker, the nature of the decision, the reasons for the decision, and the effect of the decision'. *R (Sinclair Collis Ltd) v Secretary of State for Health* [2011] EWCA Civ 437; [2012] QB 394 [200], cited by Lord Carnwath in *R (Rotherham Metropolitan Borough Council) v Secretary of State for Business, Innovation and Skills* [2015] UKSC 6.

168 *Loyola High School v Quebec (Attorney General)* (n 147) [38] per Abella J and see further text to n 188 on 'harsh consequences'.

169 *McCloy v New South Wales* (n 163) 19 per French CJ, Kiefel, Bell and Keane JJ.

170 *Isaac v Minister of Consumer Affairs* (n 155) 636 per Tipping J; *Waitakere City Council v Lovelock* (n 155) 407–408; *Meadows v Minister for Justice, Equality and Law Reform* (n 163) 723; *PO and SO v Minister for Justice and Equality* (n 163) 204.

necessarily vary',[171] because reasonableness 'takes its colour from its context',[172] falling to 'be assessed in the context of the particular type of decision making involved and all relevant factors'.[173] To put the point another way, 'reviewing courts can afford the administrative decision-maker hardly any margin or no margin of appreciation, a moderate margin, or a broad margin'.[174] In New Zealand, while review of the merits 'is to be avoided',[175] the standard of substantive review 'may vary with context'.[176] Australian courts have said that legal unreasonableness is 'context-specific'[177] and 'invariably fact dependent',[178] requiring an 'evaluative judgement' by the reviewing court,[179] such that in all cases, 'the precise content of an implication of reasonableness, where it is implied, will be based upon the context, including the scope, purpose, and real object of the statute'.[180]

Around the common law world, in cases involving broad statutory grants of discretionary authority to regulate economic activity, on the one hand, the intensity of review of abuse of discretion is more relaxed; whereas on the other hand, in cases involving detailed statutory schemes with little room for interpretive manoeuvre and important individual interests at stake, judges will engage in exacting review of the administrative action in question. Sometimes, the range of possible, acceptable outcomes will be so constrained by the relevant contextual factors as to admit of *only one* reasonable outcome.[181] This varying intensity of review can be understood in terms of individual self-realisation, good administration, electoral legitimacy and decisional accuracy.

4.2.2.1 Individual Self-realisation

When rights or important individual interests are in play, the range of reasonable outcomes will be narrower:[182]

[171] *Wilson v Atomic Energy Agency of Canada* 2016 SCC 29; [2016] 1 SCR 770 [22].

[172] *Canada (Citizenship and Immigration) v Khosa* (n 23) [59].

[173] *Catalyst Paper Corp v North Cowichan (District)* (n 143) [18]. See also *Canada (Citizenship and Immigration) v Vavilov* (n 4) [107].

[174] *Canada v Kabul Farms Inc* 2016 FCA 143 [24]. See also *Canada (Citizenship and Immigration) v Vavilov* (n 4) [110].

[175] *Canterbury Regional Council v Independent Fisheries Ltd* [2012] NZCA 601; [2013] 2 NZLR 57 [22].

[176] *Quake Outcasts v Minister of Canterbury Earthquake Recovery* [2017] NZCA 332; [2017] 3 NZLR 486, 509. See also *Kim v Minister of Justice* (n 163) [45–47].

[177] *Minister for Immigration and Border Protection v SZVWF* (n 136) [52] per Gageler J.

[178] *Minister for Immigration and Border Protection v Singh* (n 161) [42].

[179] *Minister for Immigration and Border Protection v Stretton* [2016] FCAFC 11 [5] per Allsop CJ.

[180] *Minister for Immigration and Border Protection v SZVWF* (n 136) [134] per Edelman J.

[181] See e.g. *In re G (Adoption: Unmarried Couple)* [2009] AC 173 [144]; *McLean v British Columbia (Securities Commission)* (n 133) [38]; *Michalak v General Medical Council* (n 143) [37].

[182] *R v Secretary of State for the Home Department, ex parte Khawaja* (n 63); *R v Secretary of State for the Home Department, ex parte Bugdaycay* (n 80) 531; *R v Secretary of State for the Home Department, ex parte Brind* [1991] AC 696, 748–749; *R v Ministry of Defence, ex parte Smith* [1996] QB 517, 554; *Pham v Home Secretary* (n 159) [108]; *Law Society of British Columbia v Trinity Western University* (n 163) [57]; *Kim v Minister of Justice* (n 163) [45]–[47]; *Canada (Citizenship and Immigration) v Vavilov* (n 4) [127].

> Whether a reviewing Court considers a decision reasonable and therefore lawful, or unreasonable and therefore unlawful and invalid, depends on the nature of the decision: *upon who made it*; by what process; what the decision involves (ie its subject matter and the level of policy content in it) *and the importance of the decision to those affected by it, in terms of its potential impact upon, or consequences for, them.*[183]

It has even been suggested, in this vein, that the 'humanity and dignity of the individual will inform the conclusion, necessarily to a degree evaluative, as to whether the decision bespeaks an exercise of power beyond its source'.[184]

The *locus classicus* of England's so-called 'sub-*Wednesbury*' standard is *R v Secretary of State for the Home Department, ex parte Bugdaycay*,[185] but the best expression of the more demanding standard is *R v Ministry of Defence, ex parte Smith* (a case brought by members of the British military who had been harassed pursuant to an anti-homosexual army policy):

> The court may not interfere with the exercise of an administrative discretion on substantive grounds save where the court is satisfied that the decision is unreasonable in the sense that it is beyond the range of responses open to a reasonable decision-maker. But in judging whether the decision-maker has exceeded this margin of appreciation the human rights context is important. The more substantial the interference with human rights, the more the court will require by way of justification before it is satisfied that the decision is reasonable in the sense outlined above.[186]

This formulation speaks for itself. What is significant for present purposes is that the 'sub-*Wednesbury*' standard is triggered by the presence of an important right or interest, and that its intensity is influenced by the extent of the interference with the right or interest.

183 *Wolf v Minister for Immigration* [2004] NZAR 414 [47] per Wild J.

184 *Minister for Immigration and Border Protection v Stretton* (n 179) [9] per Allsop CJ.

185 *R v Secretary of State for the Home Department, ex parte Bugdaycay* (n 80) 531 per Lord Bridge (see also *R v Secretary of State for the Home Department, ex parte Brind* (n 182) 748–749 per Lord Bridge).

186 *R v Ministry of Defence, ex parte Smith* (n 182) 554 per Sir Thomas Bingham MR (quoting, with approval, the submission of David Pannick QC). See also Paul Craig, 'Judicial Review and Anxious Scrutiny: Foundations, Evolution and Application' [2015] *Public Law* 60, but note the comments of Lord Sumption in *Pham v Home Secretary* (n 159) [106], describing the *Smith* approach as 'in substance a proportionality test, but with the important difference that the court declined to judge for itself whether the decision was proportionate, instead asking itself whether a rational minister could think that it was'. See also Mark Elliott, 'The Human Rights Act 1998 and the Standard of Substantive Review' [2001] *Cambridge Law Journal* 301, 305, suggesting that the 'defining feature' of *Wednesbury* review is that a court 'may simultaneously conclude that a decision which infringes an individual's human rights is incoherent and lacking in adequate justification, but that it is not unlawful'; *R (Daly) v Secretary of State for the Home Department* [2001] 2 AC 532 [32].

Similarly, the Supreme Court of Canada has noted the 'heightened responsibility'[187] on administrative decision-makers 'in cases where the consequences of the decision for the affected party are particularly severe or harsh':[188]

> Where the impact of a decision on an individual's rights and interests is severe, the reasons provided to that individual must reflect the stakes ... [I]f a decision has particularly harsh consequences for the affected individual, the decision maker must explain why its decision best reflects the legislature's intention. This includes decisions with consequences that threaten an individual's life, liberty, dignity or livelihood.[189]

This feature of the law can be understood as being influenced by judicial concern for individual self-realisation: where important individual interests are engaged by an administrative decision, the standard of review is more exacting; more is required from the decision-maker 'by way of justification'.

4.2.2.2 Good Administration

It has been said that 'there is a continuum of approaches to judicial review, which will be of greater or less intensity according to the nature of the case and especially the respective competence and experience of the decision-maker and of the Court'.[190] Accordingly, in *R v Chief Constable of Sussex, ex parte International Trader's Ferry*, where the Chief Constable had struck a balance in allocating police resources to quell disruptive protests, deference was due: 'He knows through his officers the local situation, the availability of officers and his financial resources [and] the other demands on the police in the area at different times.'[191] Similarly, a minister has access to the 'collective knowledge, experience and expertise of all those who serve the Crown in the department',[192] which helps to explain why ministerial decisions on matters within departmental expertise are typically accorded significant deference by the courts. In such circumstances, the range of reasonable outcomes will be broader.

Polycentricity,[193] according to which problems 'cannot be resolved independently and sequentially' but are 'interdependent and a choice from one set of alternatives has implications for preferences within other sets of alternatives',[194] will also contribute to expanding the range of reasonable outcomes,[195] as will complex

[187] *Canada (Immigration and Citizenship) v Vavilov* (n 4) [135].
[188] Ibid, [134].
[189] Ibid, [133].
[190] *Progressive Enterprises Ltd v North Shore City Council* [2006] NZRMA 72 [70] per Baragwanath J.
[191] [1999] 2 AC 418, 430 per Lord Slynn of Hadley.
[192] *Bushell v Environment Secretary* [1980] UKHL 1; [1981] AC 75, 95 per Lord Diplock.
[193] Lon Fuller, 'The Forms and Limits of Adjudication' (1978) 92 *Harvard Law Review* 3553.
[194] Anthony Ogus, *Regulation: Legal Form and Economic Theory* (Clarendon Press, Oxford, 1994), 117.
[195] See e.g. *R v Cambridge Health Authority, ex parte B* [1995] 1 WLR 898, 906.

situations that require evaluative judgement on the part of decision-makers.[196] But on more strictly legal issues involving concepts with which judges are familiar, or at least no less expert than the primary decision-maker, the range of reasonable outcomes will be narrower.[197]

In *R v Cambridge Health Authority, ex parte B*,[198] a young child was grievously ill with leukaemia. Her doctors thought further treatment would be unjustified, in view of the suffering it would cause and the low likelihood of success. Her father sought the opinion of other experts, who suggested that an aggressive course of treatment, if followed, might have a 20 per cent chance of success. But the treatment was available only in the private sector, at high cost. The health authority was unwilling to fund the treatment. Although Laws J had quashed its decision to refuse to fund at first instance, the Court of Appeal allowed an appeal by the health authority. One particularly important aspect of Sir Thomas Bingham MR's reasons for allowing the appeal related to the allocation by the health authority of its scarce resources: 'Difficult and agonising judgments have to be made as to how a limited budget is best allocated to the maximum advantage of the maximum number of patients',[199] judgements best made by administrative decision-makers, not the courts: 'it would be totally unrealistic to require the authority to come to the court with its accounts and seek to demonstrate that if this treatment were provided for B. then there would be a patient C. who would have to go without treatment. No major authority could run its financial affairs in a way which would permit such a demonstration.'[200] Judicial solicitude for effective and efficient public administration can be understood as influencing the analysis.

4.2.2.3 Electoral Legitimacy

Judicial respect for the considered choices of elected representatives can be understood to play an important role in setting the range of reasonable decisions. Courts should be guided by 'the scope and purpose of the statute conferring the discretionary power and its real object'.[201] The range of reasonable outcomes may be 'circumscribed' by reference to 'the rationale of the statutory regime',[202] or the legislature might have specified 'a recipe of factors to be considered', narrowing 'the range of options the decision-maker legitimately has'.[203] Indeed, as Lord

[196] See e.g. *Tervita Corporation v Commissioner of Competition* 2013 FCA 28; 360 DLR (4th) 717 [148]; *R (Lord Carlile of Berriew QC) v Home Secretary* [2014] UKSC 60; [2015] AC 945 [32]; *Youssef v Secretary of State for Foreign and Commonwealth Affairs* [2016] UKSC 3; [2016] 2 WLR 509 [50].

[197] See e.g. *Canada (Canadian Human Rights Commission) v Canada (Attorney General)* 2011 SCC 53; [2011] 3 SCR 471; *Canada (Citizenship and Immigration) v Vavilov* (n 4) [115]–[124].

[198] *R v Cambridge Health Authority, ex parte B* (n 195).

[199] Ibid, 906.

[200] Ibid.

[201] *Minister for Immigration and Citizenship v Li* (n 137) 364 per Hayne, Kiefel and Bell JJ.

[202] *Catalyst Paper Corp v North Cowichan (District)* (n 143) [25].

[203] *Canada (Minister of Transport, Infrastructure and Communities) v Jagjit Singh Farwaha* (n 162) [91]; *Canada (Citizenship and Immigration) v Vavilov* (n 4) [111].

Wilberforce put it in *Anisminic*, 'it may be apparent that Parliament is itself directly and closely concerned with the definition and delimitation of certain matters of comparative detail and has marked by its language the intention that these shall accurately be observed'.[204] Equally, however, powers might have been granted in broad terms, to a democratically accountable or expert decision-maker, such that the range of reasonable outcomes will be relatively large.[205] Broad statutory language empowers decision-makers, making the range of reasonable outcomes relatively broader.[206] In all events, one can understand courts to be requiring proper attention to the considered choices of elected representatives.

Beyond this, where policy decisions are taken by elected representatives, the range of reasonable outcomes will generally be broader. So-called 'super-*Wednesbury*' cases, where the standard of review is dialled down, such that judicial review is less exacting, have tended to involve democratically legitimate decision-makers and/or complex areas of regulation, such that considerations of effective and efficient public administration and respect for the decisions of elected representatives can be understood to be influential. Two well-known examples are *Nottinghamshire County Council v Environment Secretary*[207] and *R v Environment Secretary, ex parte Hammersmith and Fulham London Borough Council*.[208] Both cases involved a procedure whereby ministerial decisions on certain local authority finance matters were to be approved by a resolution of the House of Commons. The process thus involved the decision of an elected official and subsequent approval by popularly elected representatives. The local authorities sought to impugn the expenditure guidance issued by the Minister pursuant to this procedure. They were unsuccessful, because the judges applied a less-exacting-than-usual standard of review. The point was made most clearly in the *Hammersmith and Fulham* case, by Lord Bridge of Harwich:

> The formulation and the implementation of national economic policy are matters depending essentially on political judgement. The decisions which shape them are for politicians to take and it is in the political forum of the House of Commons that they are properly to be debated and approved or disapproved on their merits.[209]

[204] *Anisminic v Foreign Compensation Commission* (n 84) 209–210. See also *R (Privacy International) v Investigatory Powers Tribunal* (n 110) [205].

[205] See e.g. *Re: Sound v Canadian Association of Broadcasters* 2017 FCA 138 [40]. See also *Forest Ethics Advocacy Association v Canada (National Energy Board)* 2014 FCA 245 [69].

[206] See e.g. *Pong Marketing and Promotions Inc v Ontario Media Development Corporation* (n 129) [48]–[52]. See also Chapter 4.1.4.

[207] [1986] AC 240.

[208] [1991] 1 AC 521.

[209] Ibid, 597. In the *Nottinghamshire* case, Lord Scarman said:

> We are in the field of public financial administration and we are being asked to review the exercise by the [Minister] of an administrative discretion which inevitably requires a political judgment on his part and which cannot lead to action by him against a local authority unless that action is first approved by the House of Commons.

Nottinghamshire County Council v Environment Secretary (n 207) 247.

The courts can be understood in such cases as being concerned with ensuring respect for the electoral mandates of the decision-makers in question and avoiding undue interference by non-expert courts in matters beyond their ken. Thus, in *Hammersmith and Fulham*, 'since the statute [had] conferred a power on the Secretary of State which involves the formulation and implementation of national economic policy', the decision was 'not open to challenge on the grounds of irrationality short of the extremes of bad faith, improper motive or manifest absurdity'.[210]

R (Lord Carlile) v Home Secretary[211] is another example. A group of parliamentarians invited an Iranian dissident to London. The Home Secretary had already excluded the dissident from the United Kingdom and refused to admit her for the meeting. The Home Secretary was especially concerned about the effects that admitting the dissident might have on relations with Iran. These could not, of course, be proved, but Lord Sumption nonetheless relied on them in upholding the Home Secretary's decision as a proportionate interference with freedom of expression:

> The executive's assessment of the implications of the facts is not conclusive, but may be entitled to great weight, depending on the nature of the decision and the expertise and sources of information of the decision-maker or those who advise her ... [T]here are cases where the rationality of a decision is the only criterion which is capable of judicial assessment. This is particularly likely to be true of predictive and other judgmental assessments, especially those of a political nature. Such cases often involve a judgment or prediction of a kind whose rationality can be assessed but whose correctness cannot in the nature of things be tested empirically ... [W]here the justification for a decision depends upon a judgment about the future impact of alternative courses of action, there is not necessarily a single 'right' answer. There may be a range of judgments which could be made with equal propriety, in which case the law is satisfied if the judgment under review lies within that range. A case like the present one is perhaps the archetypal example.[212]

Generally, the fact that a fundamental right protected by a constitutional instrument has been engaged increases the intensity of review, but examples can be found of the intensity of review being reduced to take account of countervailing considerations.[213] In *Lord Carlile*, the democratic bona fides and expertise of the Minister

[210] *R v Environment Secretary, ex parte Hammersmith and Fulham London Borough Council* (n 208) 597 per Lord Bridge.

[211] *R (Lord Carlile of Berriew QC) v Home Secretary* (n 196).

[212] Ibid, [32].

[213] See e.g. *R (Begum) v Governors of Denbigh High School* [2006] UKHL 15; [2007] 1 AC 100 (expertise of school authorities); *Alberta v Hutterian Brethren of Wilson Colony* 2009 SCC 37; [2009] 2 SCR 567 (expertise of authorities in relation to identity fraud).

were important in dialling down the intensity of review, which can be understood as being influenced by judicial respect for the role of elected representatives and judicial concern not to impede effective and efficient public administration.

4.2.2.4 Decisional Autonomy

There remains a fundamental distinction between 'appeal' and 'review' in the common law world. Judicial review of administrative action is concerned not with the merits of the decision under review but with whether it was reached in a lawful manner.[214] It is notable that recent developments in the law of substantive review have not caused a complete collapse of the distinction between appeal and review. Even on the contemporary approach, courts and administrative decision-makers retain distinct roles. In *Michalak v General Medical Council*,[215] Lord Kerr drew the conventional distinction between an appeal and a judicial review. Whereas an appellate body can, 'if it disagrees with [the] conclusions' of the first-instance decision-maker 'substitute its own', judicial review is 'a proceeding in which the legality of or the procedure by which a decision was reached is challenged'.[216] An appellate body adjudicating (say) on a discrimination complaint 'must confront directly the question whether discrimination has taken place' but a reviewing court is limited to asking whether the decision-maker 'had taken a decision which was legally open to it'.[217] An appeal involves a merits review, judicial review does not: 'An appeal is different from a review of the legal entitlement to make a decision; it involves an examination of what decision *should* be taken in the dispute between the parties.'[218]

Even the application of the proportionality test is leavened by considerations of separation of powers:

> ... it is important to start any debate on the subject with the clear understanding that a review based on proportionality is not one in which the reviewer substitutes his or her opinion for that of the decision-maker. At its heart, proportionality review requires of the person or agency that seeks to defend a decision that they show that it was proportionate to meet the aim that it professes to achieve. It does not demand that the decision-maker bring the reviewer to the point of conviction that theirs was the right decision in any absolute sense.[219]

214 See Chapter 1.2.
215 (n 143).
216 Ibid, [20].
217 Ibid, [22].
218 Ibid, [30]. Emphasis original. See similarly *Canada (Immigration and Citizenship) v Vavilov* (n 4) [12].
219 *Keyu v Foreign Secretary* [2015] UKSC 69; [2015] 3 WLR 1665 [272] per Lord Kerr.

Contemporary courts are more willing than their predecessors to scrutinise administrative action, making clear that there is no area of decisional autonomy free from judicial oversight—even on matters of high policy, arbitrariness will not be tolerated.[220] Accordingly, Lord Mance was rightly careful in *Michalak* not to 'circumscribe the development of judicial review or its ability to cater, in appropriate circumstances, for close examination of a claim on its merits'.[221] In many cases, a review will approximate an appeal. A review may even, where there is only one possible, acceptable outcome, have the same result as a successful appeal, namely, substitution of judgement by the hierarchical superior of the first-instance decision-maker. But that is likely to arise only in a limited set of circumstances.[222] It is, one might say, the exception that proves the rule.

4.2.2.5 Prerogative Powers

Judicial oversight of *exercises* of prerogative powers is typically conducted with great deference. In sensitive matters of policy, common law courts are reluctant to impose fetters on the discretion of the executive branch of government.[223] This can be understood as promoting effective and efficient public administration, with the executive given a relatively free hand in making decisions in complex, fast-moving areas of high policy.[224] As such, there are strong affinities between the review of prerogative powers and those areas of substantive review where decisions are subject to a broad range of reasonable outcomes. It would be wrong, moreover, to conclude that exercises of the prerogative are—notwithstanding occasional judicial statements to the contrary—entirely walled off from judicial oversight and, thus, non-justiciable.[225]

R (Bancoult) v Foreign Secretary (No. 2)[226] is instructive. Here, an Order in Council had been issued to prevent individuals from visiting the outer islands of the British Indian Ocean Territory without specific permission. The individuals had been forcibly removed from their homeland in 1968 to facilitate American military activity on Diego Garcia. By majority, the House of Lords held that the

[220] See especially *Minister for Immigration and Citizenship v Li* (n 137) 350–351 per French CJ; *Hupacasath First Nation v Canada (Foreign Affairs and International Trade Canada)* 2015 FCA 4; (2015) 379 DLR (4th) 737; *R (Miller) v Prime Minister* [2019] UKSC 41; [2020] AC 373.

[221] *Michalak v General Medical Council* (n 143) [37].

[222] See e.g. *Canada (Attorney General) v Impex Solutions Inc* 2020 FCA 171 [90].

[223] See generally Paul Daly, 'Justiciability and the "Political Question" Doctrine' [2010] *Public Law* 160.

[224] See e.g. Timothy Endicott, *The Stubborn Stain Theory of Executive Power: From Magna Carta to Miller* (Policy Exchange, London, 2017).

[225] Walling off only truly occurs where constitutional rules, such as parliamentary privilege, apply and even here the courts will assess the extent of the privilege claimed: see e.g. *Canada (House of Commons) v Vaid* 2005 SCC 30; [2005] 1 SCR 667; *R v Chaytor* [2010] UKSC 52; [2011] AC 684; *Canada (Board of Internal Economy) v Boulerice* 2019 FCA 33; [2019] 3 FCR 145.

[226] [2008] UKHL 61; [2009] AC 453. I borrow here from Daly, *A Theory of Deference in Administrative Law* (n5), chapter 7.

decision to refuse access to the Chagos Islands was not unlawful, irrational or procedurally improper.

On unlawfulness, Lord Rodger was prepared to accept in principle the possibility of review of the exercise of the prerogative power to make laws for the 'peace, order and good government' of British overseas territories, but held that he could not second-guess the use of the power in an individual case, 'simply because such questions are not justiciable', being 'for the determination of the responsible ministers rather than judges'.[227] Despite the use of the term justiciable—in the sense of non-justiciability—Lord Rodger's reasoning does not actually support a position that certain categories of decision are beyond judicial review. In fact, Lord Rodger accepted in principle that the decision was reviewable, but found that the power of the Queen in Council to pass colonial legislation under the prerogative was coextensive with the power of the Queen in Parliament to pass primary legislation: 'the legislation made for the colonies is in the same position as legislation made by Parliament for this country ... '[228] On the most plausible reading of his speech, Lord Rodger simply found that the power of the Queen in Council was very broad indeed and amounted to plenary law-making power.[229] If this interpretation is accurate, the exercise of the prerogative *was reviewed* by Lord Rodger. However, because of the sheer breadth of the power, the Order in Council was perfectly lawful and no relief could be afforded to the Chagossians. Indeed, in matters prerogative 'the boundaries of power may be more difficult to define and the evaluation of whether the action taken was within those boundaries cannot be conducted by reference to the relevant statute, its terms, scope and purpose'.[230] The best reading is that a ground of relief was not established; not that the exercise of the power was not reviewed.[231] Indeed, the other judges in the majority certainly did review the exercise of the power but, with the deference due to the executive in such circumstances, concluded that it was not unlawful. As Lord Hoffmann explained, given that the Chagossians had a primarily 'symbolic' interest in winning the right to return,[232] to be balanced against the British military interests at stake, the Order in Council was not irrational:

> Policy as to the expenditure of public resources and the security and diplomatic interests of the Crown are peculiarly within the competence of the executive and it seems to me quite impossible to say, taking fully into account the practical

[227] Ibid, [109].
[228] Ibid.
[229] See also Lord Carswell [130]: 'A court might understandably be strongly attracted to the view that a law which removes the Chagossians from their homeland cannot be said to be for the peace, order and good government of the colony. But it is not for the courts to declare the law invalid on that ground.'
[230] *Jabbour v Secretary of Home Affairs* [2019] FCA 452 [104] per Robertson J.
[231] See further Mark Elliott and Amanda Perreau-Saussine, 'Pyrrhic Public Law: *Bancoult* and the Sources, Status and Content of Common Law Limitations on Prerogative Power' [2009] *Public Law* 697.
[232] *R (Bancoult) v Foreign Secretary (No 2)* (n 226) [53].

> interests of the Chagossians, that the decision to reimpose immigration control on the islands was unreasonable or an abuse of power.[233]

It is clear, then, that exercises of prerogative power are subject to judicial review, with appropriate deference being afforded where the circumstances require it.[234]

4.2.2.6 Falling Outside the Range

In general, then, the values of individual self-realisation, good administration, electoral legitimacy and decisional autonomy can be understood to operate in a complementary fashion, shaping the range of reasonable outcomes in any given case where the applicant alleges abuse of a discretionary power.

In addition, in order to demonstrate that a decision falls outside the range, the applicant will need to identify one or more 'badges' of unreasonableness which suggest that the decision ought to be struck down by a reviewing court.[235] These badges can be understood in terms of administrative law values.

Violation of fundamental rights,[236] expropriation of property[237] and the imposition of 'harsh consequences' on individuals[238] are badges of unreasonableness which impose a justificatory burden on decision-makers. These badges involve important individual interests and thus engage the value of self-realisation. Where decisions are inconsistent,[239] illogical[240] or based on fundamental

[233] Ibid, [58]. See also [132] per Lord Carswell:

> Criticisms have been advanced of the validity of the reasons advanced on behalf of the United States for wanting to keep the whole of the Territory free from settlement, but even if it might be said that the concerns expressed appear exaggerated, the fact remains that the US clearly desired to keep a large clear area around the base. Decisions about how far to accommodate such concerns and wishes are very much a matter for ministers, who have access to a range of information not available to the courts and are accountable to Parliament for their actions. I think that courts should be more than a little slow to pin that butterfly to the wheel.

[234] See e.g. *R (Sandiford) v Foreign and Commonwealth Secretary* [2014] UKSC 44. The Canadian courts have suggested that prerogative powers may only be reviewed where 'rights' (and not 'privileges' are engaged): *Black v Canada (Prime Minister)* (2001) 54 OR (3d) 215; *Black v Advisory Council for the Order of Canada* 2012 FC 1234. But the rights/privileges distinction did not feature in the most recent leading case on the reviewability of the prerogative, *Hupacasath First Nation v Canada* (n 220).

[235] *Delios v Canada (Attorney General)* 2015 FCA 117; (2015) 100 Admin LR (5th) 301 [27] per Stratas JA.

[236] See e.g. *Saskatchewan (Human Rights Commission) v Whatcott* (n 146).

[237] See e.g. *Hall and Co Ltd v Shoreham-by-Sea Urban District Council* [1964] 1 WLR 240; *R v Hillingdon London Borough Council, ex parte Royco Homes Ltd* [1974] QB 720.

[238] *Canada (Citizenship and Immigration) v Vavilov* (n 4) [133].

[239] See e.g. *Drake v Minister for Immigration and Ethnic Affairs* (1979) 2 ALD 634; (1979) 24 ALR 577, 591; *R (L (A Minor)) v Governors of J School* [2003] UKHL 9; [2003] 2 AC 633; *R (O'Brien) v Independent Assessor* [2007] UKHL 10; [2007] 2 AC 312; *R (Gallaher Group Ltd) v Competition and Markets Authority* [2018] UKSC 25; [2019] AC 96 [43], [52]–[56], [63]; *Minister for Home Affairs v Brown* [2020] FCAFC 21 [113]; *Canada (Citizenship and Immigration) v Vavilov* (n 4) [129]–[132]. See also *Re Drake and Minister for Immigration and Ethnic Affairs (No 2)* (1979) 2 ALD 634, 640: with decisions 'which profoundly affect the interests of the [person] and his [or her] family and which are of relevance to the community at large, inconsistency born of the application of differing standards and values should be reduced as far as it is possible to do so'.

[240] See e.g. *Zenner v Prince Edward Island College of Optometrists* 2005 SCC 77; [2005] 3 SCR 645; *R (Rogers) v Swindon NHS Primary Care Trust* [2006] EWCA Civ 392; [2006] 1 WLR 2649; *R (Law*

misapprehensions about relevant evidence,[241] good administration is engaged, for inconsistent or illogical decision-making prevents the efficient and effective operation of public administration. And failure to accurately implement a statutory scheme[242] triggers concern for respect for the considered choices of elected representatives and thus sounds in the value of electoral legitimacy.[243]

Decisional autonomy is an overarching concern in respect of assessing whether the presence of a badge of unreasonableness justifies the conclusion that a decision is unlawful. Courts do not have a roving commission to identify unreasonable decisions and hold them to be unlawful; they must, indeed, 'avoid assuming a supervisory role or reviewing power over the merits of decisions taken administratively by the selected public authority'.[244] Good administration also counsels caution in undoing decisions which are the product of the demonstrated expertise of an administrative decision-maker.[245] Rather, the applicant bears the onus of demonstrating that there is a flaw in a decision,[246] at which point the reviewing court assesses whether the flaw is fatal.[247] In this way, the autonomy of the courts in assessing whether a decision falls within or without the range of acceptable, permissible outcomes and the autonomy of administrative decision-makers in making determinations on the merits are preserved.

4.2.3 A Note on Reasoned Decision-making

Increasingly, common law courts have moved towards imposing a requirement (de facto if not de jure) on administrative decision-makers to deliver

Society) v Legal Services Commission [2010] EWHC Admin 2550 (Admin); [2011] ACD 16; *Canada (Citizenship and Immigration) v Vavilov* (n 4) [102]–[104].

241 *Canada (Citizenship and Immigration) v Vavilov* (n 4) [126].

242 See e.g. *Halifax (Regional Municipality) v Canada (Public Works and Government Services)* 2012 SCC 29; [2012] 2 SCR 108; *Canada (Citizenship and Immigration) v Vavilov* (n 4) [108–110].

243 See further Daly (n 5) chapter 4.

244 *Re W (A Minor) (Wardship: Jurisdiction)* [1985] AC 791, 797 per Lord Scarman.

245 *Canada (Citizenship and Immigration) v Vavilov* (n 4) [93].

246 *R (Gallaher Group Ltd) v Competition and Markets Authority* (n 239) [42]–[44]; *Canada (Citizenship and Immigration) v Vavilov* (n 4) [75]. See also *Workplace Health, Safety and Compensation Commission v Allen* 2014 NLCA 42 [41] explaining (in the context of an interpretation of law) that the applicant has an 'onus in the present case to point to some reason, whether stemming from the facts or the words of the statute to question the reasonableness' of the decision; and *Delios v Canada (Attorney General)* (n 235) [21–27].

247 As an analytical matter, the flaw(s) identified must then be assessed in light of the reasons and evidence contained in the record before the reviewing court:

> Where a decision is indelibly tainted by a badge or badges of unreasonableness, judicial intervention will be more or less appropriate depending on the range of reasonable outcomes. For instance, the narrower the range, the more that will be required by way of explanation of the badge(s) of unreasonableness tainting the decision. Conversely, the wider the range, the less a reviewing court should require by way of explanation.

Paul Daly, 'Struggling Towards Coherence in Canadian Administrative Law: Recent Cases on Standard of Review and Reasonableness' (2016) 62 *McGill Law Journal* 527, 558.

reasoned decisions.[248] It is not enough for a decision to be 'in the ballpark' but the decision-maker must explain how they got to the ballpark, why they chose to go there and what considerations justified their choice of seat.[249] This is an emerging trend, but a consideration of recent Canadian experience demonstrates how administrative law values are useful in guiding development of the law.

Prior to its seminal decision in *Canada (Citizenship and Immigration) v Vavilov*, the Supreme Court of Canada had taken a relaxed approach to the review of reasons for decision, upholding decisions on the basis of reasons which *could have been offered* in support of the outcome, bootstrapping otherwise defective decisions by reference to new arguments or information.[250]

But this approach was unfair to individuals, who argued their cases before administrative decision-makers without knowing the decision-makers' position on key issues of interpretation and policy (for these could be added later, if the individual is unsatisfied and seeks judicial review). It was inimical to good administration, both because a decision-maker might be tempted to take a less rigorous approach to decision-making if it knows it can supplement its reasons later on, and because a court might impute to an administrative decision-maker a position that would frustrate the efficient and effective attainment of its statutory objectives. It was difficult to reconcile with the legislative choice to assign authority over an area of regulatory policy to an administrative decision-maker, because when a court is allowed to impute additional reasons to an administrative decision-maker it arrogates to judges the power to make judgement calls on issues central to the administrative decision-maker's statutory mandate. And it violated decisional autonomy by tempting judges to trespass into matters of administration.[251] The reversal of approach effected in *Canada (Citizenship and Immigration) v Vavilov* is, thus, consistent with administrative law values. This, indeed, is an example of administrative law values guiding the development of the law,[252] as they can be understood to have influenced the Supreme Court of Canada's change of approach.[253]

[248] See e.g. *Canada (Citizenship and Immigration) v Vavilov* (n 4); *ABT17 v Minister for Immigration* [2020] HCA 34 [127].

[249] See generally Paul Daly, '*Vavilov* and the Culture of Justification in Contemporary Administrative Law' (2021) *Supreme Court Law Review* (2d) (forthcoming).

[250] See especially *Newfoundland and Labrador Nurses' Union v Newfoundland and Labrador (Treasury Board)* 2011 SCC 62; [2011] 3 SCR 708.

[251] This passage appeared in Paul Daly, 'Reasons and Reasonableness in Administrative Law: *Delta Air Lines Inc. v Lukacs*' (2018) 31 *Canadian Journal of Administrative Law & Practice* 209.

[252] The use of administrative law values to guide the development of the law is considered in detail in Chapter 8. See also Chapter 7.6.

[253] See also *Delta Air Lines Inc v Lukács* 2018 SCC 2; [2018] 1 SCR 6.

4.3 Relevancy and Propriety

Failure to take into account a relevant factor, or the taking into account of an irrelevant factor, will justify judicial intervention:

> ... if it be shown that an authority exercising a power has taken into account as a relevant factor something which it could not properly take into account in deciding whether or not to exercise the power, then the exercise of the power, normally at least, is bad. Similarly, if the authority fails to take into account as a relevant factor something which is relevant, and which is or ought to be known to it, and which it ought to have taken into account, the exercise of the power is normally bad.[254]

A related principle is that failure to use a power for a purpose authorised by statute—and seeking instead to further some ulterior objective—will justify judicial intervention.[255] A decision-maker should not act 'so as to frustrate the policy and objects' of the legislation under which they operate.[256] It is thus unlawful for a minister to use a discretionary power 'in a manner which is not in accord with the intention of the statute which conferred it'.[257] Similarly, respect for the language chosen by the legislature to implement its policy goals can be understood to support the principle that taking into account irrelevant considerations or failing to take into account relevant considerations will lead a decision-maker into unlawfulness, as 'a power exercised outside the statutory power is unlawful'.[258] These basic principles can be understood to be supported by judicial concern for electoral legitimacy.

The law in this area can also be understood to be marked by an appreciation that the courts and administrative decision-makers have distinct functions. Relevancy and propriety are questions of law, for the courts,[259] whereas 'it is entirely for the decision maker to attribute to the relevant considerations such weight as he thinks fit',[260] subject to review for abuse of discretion (on the terms set out in Chapter 4.2).

[254] *Hanks v Minister of Housing and Local Government* [1963] 1 QB 999, 1020 per Megaw J.

[255] *Municipal Council of Sydney v Campbell* [1925] AC 338, 343 per Duff J.

[256] *Padfield v Minister of Agriculture, Fisheries and Food* [1968] AC 997, 1033 per Lord Reid; see similarly ibid, 1045 per Lord Hodson: 'The discretion must be exercised by the Minister in accordance with the intention of the Act ... '; ibid, 1054 per Lord Pearce: 'It was for the Minister to use his discretion to promote Parliament's intention'.

[257] Ibid, 1034 per Lord Reid. See also *Montréal (City) v Montreal Port Authority* 2010 SCC 14; [2010] 1 SCR 427; *Halifax (Regional Municipality) v Canada (Public Works and Government Services)* (n 242).

[258] *R v Secretary of State for Foreign Affairs, ex parte World Development Movement Ltd* [1995] 1 All ER 611, 622. See also *Swan Hill Corporation v Bradbury* (1937) 56 CLR 746, 757–758; *CREEDNZ Inc v Governor-General* [1981] 1 NZLR 172, 183.

[259] Cf Wilberg (n 4).

[260] *Tesco Stores v Secretary of State for the Environment* (n 23) 764 per Lord Keith of Kinkel.

A zone of autonomy exists within which decision-makers enjoy considerable liberty, as Lord Hoffmann explained in a planning case:

> The law has always made a clear distinction between the question of whether something is a material consideration and the weight which it should be given. The former is a question of law and the latter is a question of planning judgment, which is entirely a matter for the planning authority. Provided that the planning authority has regard to all material considerations, it is at liberty (provided that it does not lapse into *Wednesbury* irrationality) to give them whatever weight the planning authority thinks fit or no weight at all. The fact that the law regards something as a material consideration therefore involves no view about the part, if any, which it should play in the decision-making process.[261]

Meanwhile, substitution of judgement is forbidden.[262] There is also a basic requirement of materiality: the illegality must have had an effect on the final decision. Accordingly, 'where the court is quite satisfied that even though one reason may be bad in law, nevertheless the statutory body would have reached precisely the same decision on the other valid reasons', there is no basis for judicial intervention.[263] Again, this can be understood as protective of the autonomy of administrative decision-makers.

What of situations where there are mixed motives, that is, that the decision-maker relied on some irrelevant considerations or improper purposes but also took relevant considerations and proper purposes into account? The answer seems to be that as to propriety of purpose, it is only where the improper purpose is *dominant* that a decision will be invalid, but as to relevancy of considerations, it is sufficient to demonstrate a *substantial influence* on the final decision to justify a finding of invalidity.

As to propriety, 'the general rule is that [administrative] action will be lawful provided that the permitted purpose is the true and dominant purpose behind the act, even though some secondary or incidental advantage may be gained for some

[261] *Tesco Stores v Secretary of State for the Environment* (n 23) 780 per Lord Hoffmann. Similarly, Mason J (as he then was) pointed out in *Minister for Aboriginal Affairs v Peko Wallsend Ltd* (1986) 162 CLR 24, 40 that:

> In the context of judicial review on the ground of taking into account irrelevant considerations, this Court has held that where a statute confers a discretion which in its terms is unconfined, that factors that may be taken into account in the exercise of the discretion are similarly unconfined, except in so far as there may be found in that subject-matter, scope and purpose of the statute some implied limitation of the factors to which the decision maker may legitimately have regard.

See also, Lord Irvine of Lairg (n 164) 67; *Ashby v Minister of Immigration* [1981] 1 NZLR 222, 224 per Cooke J.

[262] *R v Somerset County Council, ex parte Fewings* [1995] 1 All ER 513, 515 per Laws J.

[263] *R v Broadcasting Complaints Commission, ex parte Owen* [1985] QB 1153, 1177 per May LJ. See also *Hanks v Minister of Housing and Local Government* (n 254) 1020 per Megaw J.

purpose which is outside the authority's powers'.[264] As to relevancy, however, the test is more relaxed: 'If the influence of irrelevant factors is established, it does not appear to be necessary to prove that they were the sole or even the dominant influence; it seems to be enough to prove that their influence was *substantial*.'[265]

The lower threshold for relevancy can be understood to be appropriate on the basis that a decision-maker would be able to take a decision afresh (based this time only on relevant considerations) once the matter has been remitted to it by the courts. By contrast, where a power has been exercised improperly, in order to achieve an ulterior motive, it will rarely be open to a decision-maker to re-make the decision in a lawful way. Conservation of the decisional autonomy of the administrative decision-maker can thus be understood as favouring more judicial restraint (and a higher threshold for intervention) where the allegation is one of impropriety of purpose than in situations involving alleged irrelevancy of considerations.

It is difficult to say much more in a general sense about relevant considerations and proper purposes.[266] They are, on the conventional approach, matters of statutory interpretation. As such, their application in a particular case will depend upon the peculiarities of the relevant statutory provisions, which are likely to be unique and unlikely to engage the general principles of administrative law.[267] As Lord Reid put it in *Padfield*, legal limits on discretion 'must be inferred from a construction of the Act read as a whole'.[268]

4.4 Conclusion

My task in this chapter has been to demonstrate that the values I have identified can be understood as illuminating the structure of the contemporary law of substantive review. In the area of relevant considerations and proper purposes it is relatively easy to make a convincing demonstration of the gravitational force of the values of electoral legitimacy and decisional autonomy. In the sections on jurisdictional error and abuse of discretion, where there is significant disagreement

[264] William Wade and Christopher Forsyth, *Administrative Law*, 11th edn (Oxford University Press, Oxford, 2014), 352, cited (from a previous edition) with approval in *R v Southwark Crown Court, ex parte Bowles* [1998] 2 WLR 715. See also *Westminster Corporation v London and North Western Railway Company* [1905] AC 426; *Earl Fitzwilliam's Wentworth Estates Co v Minister of Town and Country Planning* [1951] 2 KB 284.

[265] *R v Rochdale Metropolitan Borough Council, ex parte Cromer Ring Mill* [1982] 3 All ER 761, 770 per Forbes J. Emphasis added.

[266] For a helpful overview, see GDS Taylor, 'Judicial Review of Improper Purposes and Irrelevant Considerations' (1976) 35 *Cambridge Law Journal* 272.

[267] See also TRS Allan, 'Doctrine and Theory in Administrative Law: An Elusive Quest for the Limits of Jurisdiction' [2003] *Public Law* 429; Joanna Bell, *The Anatomy of Administrative Law* (Hart, Oxford, 2020), chapter 3.

[268] *R (on the application of Padfield and others) v Minister of Agriculture, Fisheries and Food and others* (n 256) 1033; it 'is a matter to be determined by looking at the Act and its scope and object in conferring a discretion ...' ibid, 1060 per Lord Upjohn.

within and across jurisdictions on what the law is and what it ought to be, I have not delved into detail in the way I have in other chapters. Nonetheless, by using the accepted distinction between 'jurisdictional error' (and its companion, 'correctness' review) and 'non-jurisdictional error' and the increasingly popular concept of a range of reasonable outcomes in respect of the exercise of discretionary powers, I have demonstrated that in calibrating the appropriate degree of judicial oversight of alleged jurisdictional errors and abuses of discretion, judges can be understood to have been influenced by administrative law values.[269] As to relevancy and propriety and abuse of discretion the values can be understood to operate in a complementary fashion; as to jurisdictional error, the courts can be understood to strike a balance between the values in choosing between *de novo* and deferential judicial review. Once more, a plurality of considerations helps to illuminate the contemporary law of judicial review of administrative action.

[269] I do not venture here any suggestion that the law relating to jurisdictional error and the law relating to abuse of discretion should be merged. Evidently, the contention that the same values can be understood to influence the law in both of these areas would militate in favour of the elimination of the distinction between them. This has occurred in Canada: see *Baker v Canada (Citizenship and Immigration)* [1999] 2 SCR 817 [51]–[56]. I have argued previously, on analytical grounds, that the distinction should be eliminated, but here note only that the analysis in the text further supports the argument advanced in that previous work: Daly (n 5) chapter 6.

5
Remedies

When an applicant for judicial review succeeds in demonstrating that an administrative decision was unlawful because it breached the principles of institutional structures, procedural fairness or substantive review, the court must then decide whether to grant a remedy. In this Chapter, I will, first, discuss the nature of the remedies available to a reviewing court, explaining how the different characteristics of the so-called 'prerogative writs' and their successors can be understood in terms of the values of individual self-realisation, good administration, electoral legitimacy and decisional autonomy. I will also highlight how judges' choices whether to issue a remedy and how to structure a remedy can also be understood as being influenced by these values. Second, I will address several aspects of judicial discretion *not* to grant a remedy. This discretion is also the subject of Chapter 6, 'Restrictions on Remedies'. There, however, I will be dealing for the most part with *general principles* relating to restrictions on access to the supervisory jurisdiction of the courts, whereas in the latter part of this chapter, I will be focusing on reasons for refusing a remedy which are *personal to the particular individual* seeking judicial intervention. Whilst there is a natural overlap between the topics of Chapters 5 and 6, the division between them can be justified in terms of this distinction between the particular and the general.

In Chapter 1, the term 'prerogative writs' was introduced. In fact, although the remedies associated with the term came of judicial age in the 17th century, the term itself seems to date from the 18th century. Lord Mansfield is widely credited with applying the term to the writs of certiorari, prohibition, mandamus, quo warranto, habeas corpus and prohibition. In truth, the nomenclature is misleading, for while it was 'convenient' to attribute them to the monarch (in whose name justice was done by the common law courts) the writs did not have royal origin.[1] Later, the remedies of the declaration (statutory in origin) and injunction (equitable in origin) also became associated with the control of administrative action by the common law courts.

In this chapter, I will discuss the modern forms of some of the prerogative writs—certiorari, prohibition and mandamus—and also declaratory and injunctive relief. Two of the older remedies, quo warranto and habeas corpus are

[1] John Baker, *An Introduction to English Legal History*, 4th edn (Oxford University Press, Oxford, 2002), 144.

Understanding Administrative Law in the Common Law World. Paul Daly, Oxford University Press. © Paul Daly 2021.
DOI: 10.1093/oso/9780192896919.003.0005

excluded for different reasons. Quo warranto has been eliminated in some jurisdictions[2] and is 'virtually obsolete'[3] even in those jurisdictions where it has not been abolished outright.[4] Habeas corpus, meanwhile, 'stands apart from the other prerogative remedies'.[5] Given its status as the 'Great Writ', designed to protect individual liberty, it is more procedurally and substantively flexible than the other remedies;[6] and, moreover, strays into the fields of constitutional law and criminal procedure, far beyond the territory covered by this book.[7]

Procedural reforms since the mid-20th century have reduced the significance of the prerogative writs. That said, some jurisdictions have continued to rely on the old prerogative writs even subsequent to introducing procedural reforms.[8] Others, such as England and Wales, abolished the writs but retained their essential forms. Part 54 of the *Civil Procedure Rules* there provides:

> The judicial review procedure must be used in a claim for judicial review where the claimant is seeking
>
> (a) a mandatory order [*mandamus*];
> (b) a prohibiting order [prohibition];
> (c) a quashing order [*certiorari*]; or
> (d) an injunction under section 30 of the Supreme Court Act 1981.

A tour through the hodgepodge of procedural provisions in the different jurisdictions would, however, be a distraction from the business of this chapter. Although there are significant differences of detail in how the remedies are made available by different jurisdictions across the common-law world, there is a very high degree of commonality in the range of remedies available and the circumstances in which they may be granted.

[2] See e.g. Administration of Justice (Miscellaneous Provisions) Act 1938, s 9.

[3] Gerard Hogan, David Gwynn Morgan and Paul Daly, *Administrative Law in Ireland* 5th edn (Roundhall, Dublin, 2019) [16]–[101].

[4] The discussion in *Marie v Wanderingspirit* 2003 FCA 385 [17]–[20] indicates that litigants in the Canadian federal courts prefer to ask for declaratory relief rather than quo warranto even though quo warranto is expressly provided for in the Federal Courts Act RSC 1985, c F-7, s 18(1)(a).

[5] Philip Joseph, *Constitutional and Administrative Law in New Zealand* 4th edn (Thomson Reuters, Wellington, 2014), 1163.

[6] The general view in England and Wales is, in the words of the Law Commission, that 'judicial review and habeas corpus are subject to a common principle and … the scope of review of these remedies is and should be essentially the same' (Law Com No 226 [11.10]). This desire for 'procedural uniformity' (Mark Aronson, Matthew Groves and Greg Weeks, *Judicial Review of Administrative Action and Governmental Liability* 6th edn (Thomson Reuters, Sydney, 2017) [14.150]) seems to be unique to that jurisdiction, however.

[7] For an authoritative treatment, see Judith Farbey QC, Robert Sharpe and Simon Attrill, *The Law of Habeas Corpus*, 3rd edn (Oxford University Press, Oxford, 2011).

[8] See e.g. Law Commission (New Zealand), *Review of Prerogative Writs* (Issues Paper 9, August 2008).

5.1 The Broad Scope of Declaratory Relief

In this and subsequent sections (up to 5.5), I discuss the remedies available for breach of the principles of institutional structures, procedural fairness and substantive review in terms of administrative law values. I begin with declaratory relief, where interference with the decisional autonomy of the administrative decision-maker is at a minimum and the influence of the values in shaping the remedy provided is easy to perceive. I then move through the remedies by reference to the increasing extent to which they encroach on decisional autonomy: certiorari, prohibition, mandamus and injunctive relief.

Declaratory relief is a statutory remedy[9] that provides 'a speedy and easy access to the Courts for any of His Majesty's subjects who have any real cause of complaint against the exercise of statutory powers by Government departments and Government officials . . .'[10] Already in the earliest days of its emergence as a forceful common law remedy it was said that proceeding by declaration can be 'highly convenient',[11] and indeed can 'guide' public bodies' 'action in the future'[12] (albeit that there was, also at an early stage, typically a concern for the wise husbandry of judicial resources[13]). Where 'a law has been contravened that should be publicly enunciated and formally made known', something declaratory relief facilitates.[14]

Considerations of effective and efficient public administration and giving effect to legislative choices can be understood to be at work here. Declarations allow the courts to give guidance as to the law set down by the legislature and thereby assist administrative decision-makers in the accurate, efficient and effective discharge of their duties,[15] as public bodies almost invariably comply with declarations duly made by the courts, which may indicate the practical utility—from the administrative decision-maker's perspective—of declaratory relief.[16]

[9] Common law courts did not have, prior to the Judicature Act 1873, the jurisdiction to issue declaratory relief: 'The remedies of the declaration and the injunction developed originally as private law remedies in the pre-Judicature Act Chancery Court'. Hogan, Morgan and Daly (n 3) [16-24]. Even the courts of equity were not formally given this authority until 1852: 15 & 16 Vict c 86, s 50 (though they could before then make declarations if they were giving consequential relief). For the history, see *De Smith's Judicial Review of Administrative Action* 8th edn (London, Sweet and Maxwell, 2016) [15-060]–[15-067]. As was pointed out: 'Nakedly to declare a right, without doing or directing anything else relating to the right, does not, I conceive, belong to the functions of this Court' (*Clough v Ratcliffe* (1847) 1 De G & S 164, 178–179 per Bruce VC). Cf *Ainsworth v Criminal Justice Commission* (1992) 175 CLR 564, 581 per Mason CJ, Dawson, Toohey and Gaudron JJ: 'It is now accepted that superior courts have inherent power to grant declaratory relief'; *Taylor v Attorney General* [2018] NZSC 104 [118] per Elias CJ.

[10] *Dyson v Attorney-General (No 1)* [1911] 1 KB 410, 423 per Farwell LJ.

[11] Ibid, 417.

[12] *Dyson v Attorney General (No 2)* [1912] 1 Ch 158, 166.

[13] See e.g. *Hanson v Radcliffe Urban District Council* [1922] 2 Ch 490, 507.

[14] *Wool Board Disestablishment Co Ltd v Saxmere Co Ltd* [2011] 2 NZLR 442, 472 per Hammond J.

[15] Declarations 'delineate, in a concrete way that binds all, the legal rights, the legal state of affairs or the legal status of parties before the Court when the delineation will have some practical use': *Entertainment Software Association v Society Composers* 2020 FCA 100 [105] per Stratas JA.

[16] *M v Home Office* [1994] 1 AC 377, 397 per Lord Woolf:

A useful example is *Pandion Haliaetus Ltd v Revenue Commissioners*,[17] where the applicant and respondents were at loggerheads over, first, the repayment of a sum withheld by the Commissioners on the basis that the applicant had been involved in a 'sham' tax avoidance scheme and, second, the procedural means by which the Commissioners could be compelled to repay the monies. Finding in favour of the applicant, Blayney J considered it would be 'eminently just and convenient' to issue declaratory relief because the alternative would be continued 'stalemate' in which neither party was sure as to its rights and obligations.[18]

Individual interests can also be understood to be relevant, for declaratory relief may be an excellent means of vindicating individual rights and interests without necessarily coercing an administrative decision-maker to act in a particular way (via mandamus), interfering in an ongoing decision-making process (via prohibition) or even undoing a previous decision (via certiorari).[19] In the *Dyson* case, the applicant challenged the legality of a procedure employed by the Commissioners of Inland Revenue to demand information from taxpayers about the value of their lands. As Fletcher Moulton LJ observed, there were significant advantages to proceeding by declaration rather than waiting to raise a collateral challenge[20] or simply complying with a demand thought to be illegal:

> So far from thinking that this action is open to objection . . . I think that an action thus framed is the most convenient method of enabling the subject to test the justifiability of proceedings on the part of permanent officials purporting to act under statutory provisions. Such questions are growing more and more important, and I can think of no more suitable or adequate procedure for challenging the legality of such proceedings. It would be intolerable that millions of the public should have to choose between giving information to the Commissioners which they have no right to demand and incurring a severe penalty.[21]

> . . . in ordinary circumstances ministers of the Crown and government departments invariably scrupulously observe decisions of the courts. Because of this, it is normally unnecessary for the courts to make an executory order against a minister or a government department since they will comply with any declaratory judgment made by the courts and pending the decision of the courts will not take any precipitous action.

[17] [1987] IR 309.

[18] Ibid, 321–322.

[19] See e.g. *Ainsworth v Criminal Justice Commission* (n 9); *Edwards v Santos Ltd* [2011] HCA 8; (2011) 242 CLR 421.

[20] See Chapter 6.3.

[21] [1912] 1 Ch 158, 168. See e.g. *Green v Law Society of Manitoba* 2017 SCC 20; [2017] 1 SCR 360, where a lawyer sought a declaration that the Society was not entitled to adopt a rule providing for mandatory continuing legal education with suspension as a sanction for non-compliance rather than waiting to challenge the Society's authority to impose a suspension for a breach of the rule.

Given the advantages of this remedy and the fact that it 'creates no legal obligation or direct legal sanction for breach',[22] it is unsurprising that the courts have taken a generous view of the scope of declaratory relief,[23] stopping only at the point where the matter is beyond the scope of judicial review[24] or the remedy of a declaration should be refused in the exercise of the court's discretion.[25]

Notably, declaratory relief can be tailored to the circumstances of a particular case. In cutting the cloth appropriately, administrative law values can be understood to be relevant. At issue in *R v Secretary of State for Social Services, ex parte Association of Metropolitan Authorities*[26] was the Minister's power to create a housing benefit scheme through regulations. This power was exercisable only after consultation with representative authorities, of which the Association was clearly one. Webster J held that the Minister had not 'consulted' with the Association within the meaning of the statute. But he refused to quash the regulations, because the failure to consult related only to the Association, not to the other representative authorities, whereas quashing them would cause administrative inconvenience:

> The regulations have been in force for about six months and, although their implementation creates difficulties for some at least of the housing authorities who have to administer them, those authorities must by now have adapted themselves

[22] Joseph (n 5) 1172. Cf *New Zealand Maori Council v Attorney-General* [1987] 1 NZLR 641 (declaration requiring the Crown to prepare and consult on a scheme for the protection of indigenous interests in state assets).

[23] In *Guaranty Trust Company of New York v Hannay & Co* [1915] 2 KB 536, it was held, for instance, that the existence of a right or cause of action is not a condition precedent to the granting of a declaration. Bankes LJ noted, in particular, 'having regard to general business convenience and the importance of adapting the machinery of the Courts to the needs of suitors I think the rule should receive as liberal a construction as possible' (at 572). See similarly *Sankey v Whitlam* (1978) 142 CLR 1, 23 per Gibbs ACJ, noting that in the context of declaratory relief the term 'right' must be 'used in a sense that is wide and loose'. And, in *Cooper v Wilson* [1937] 2 KB 309, having regard to how the power of the courts to issue declarations had been 'greatly extended', a declaration was available even where a writ of certiorari could have been sought (at 321). In England, the declaration now covers much the same ground as the prerogative writs. As Lord Diplock explained in *Grunwick Processing Laboratories Ltd v Advisory, Conciliation and Arbitration Service* [1978] AC 655, 695:

> ... where a statutory authority has acted ultra vires any person who would be affected by its act if it were valid is normally entitled ex debito justiciae to have it set aside, if he has proceeded by way of certiorari, or to have it declared void. If he has proceeded by way of an action for a declaration the court may exercise its discretion to refuse the remedy on grounds of laches or of acquiescence or maybe, though there appears to be no reported case of this, where the ultra vires act of the authority was induced by the unlawful acts of the complainant himself.

See also *Equal Opportunities Commission v Secretary of State for Employment* [1995] 1 AC 1, 36. The position in Australia is more complicated. See e.g. *Kronen v Federal Commissioner of Taxation* [2012] FCA 1463; (2012) 213 FCR 495, 503. But as Gaudron J observed in *City of Enfield v Development Assessment Commission* [2000] HCA 5; (2000) 199 CLR 135, 157: 'within the limits of their jurisdiction and consistent with their obligation to act judicially, the courts should provide whatever remedies are available and appropriate to ensure that those possessed of executive and administrative powers exercise them only in accordance with the laws which govern their exercise. The rule of law requires no less.' See also *Buttrose v Attorney General for New South Wales* [2015] NSWCA 221; (2015) 324 ALR 562, 566.

[24] See Chapter 7.

[25] *Hanson v Radcliffe Urban District Council* (n 13).

[26] [1986] 1 WLR 1.

> as best they can to those difficulties. If, however, the regulations were to be revoked all applicants who had been refused benefit because of the new regulations would be entitled to make fresh claims, and all authorities would be required to consider each such claim.[27]

Accordingly, Webster J made a declaration that the Minister had failed to discharge his duty of consultation in respect of the Association only, thereby avoiding the creation of additional burdens on decision-makers and incursions on their limited resources; this judicial reluctance to unnecessarily create extra administrative expense can be understood to be supported by a desire not to compromise effective and efficient public administration.[28]

To similar effect is *R v Monopolies and Mergers Commission, ex parte Argyll Group*,[29] which concerned a corporate takeover. A group of minority shareholders of the target company sought to quash the decision of the Trade and Industry Secretary to set aside a reference to the Commission about the propriety of the purchaser acquiring the target company. In the meantime, the purchaser submitted a fresh bid. In the circumstances, the Court of Appeal would have exercised its discretion to refuse relief to the applicants. Sir John Donaldson MR noted the need for the court to have 'a proper awareness of the needs of public administration' in exercising its discretion.[30] Among the relevant factors were speed of decision, decisiveness and finality: the financial public was 'entitled to rely upon the finality of the announced decision to set aside the reference . . .'.[31] Dillon LJ was even more emphatic that the interests of third parties weighed heavily in the balance, in that individuals would have relied on the Secretary of State's decision to set the reference aside and, were it to be quashed, a fresh reference could be made, causing uncertainty and 'serious detriment' to shareholders.[32] Giving effect to legislative choice can also be understood to have influenced the exercise of discretion, given the importance of the Secretary of State's role in the statutory scheme—he was, as Sir John Donaldson MR put it, 'the guardian of the public interest'.[33]

Commenting on *Argyll Group* in the later case of *R v Panel on Take-Overs and Mergers, ex parte Datafin plc*,[34] Sir John Donaldson MR said it was evidence of the

[27] Ibid, 15.

[28] See also *Agricultural, Horticultural and Forestry Industry Training Board v Aylesbury Mushrooms Ltd* [1972] 1 WLR 190 (failure to consult the mushroom industry led to a declaration that the regulations in question did not apply to the mushroom industry); *Talley's Fisheries Ltd v Minister of Immigration* HC Wellington CP201/93 (10 October 1995) (prospective declaration only in respect of the Minister's obligations under immigration law, for fear that a retrospective declaration could cause 'significant' damage to the fishing industry by upsetting settled expectations).

[29] [1986] 1 WLR 763.

[30] Ibid, 774.

[31] Ibid, 775.

[32] Ibid, 778–779.

[33] Ibid, 774.

[34] [1987] QB 815.

importance of effective and efficient public administration and the interests of third parties in the exercise of remedial discretion:

> That case also illustrates the awareness of the court of the special needs of the financial markets for speed on the part of decision-makers and for being able to rely upon those decisions as a sure basis for dealing in the market. It further illustrates an awareness that such decisions affect a very wide public which will not be parties to the dispute and that their interests have to be taken into account as much as those of the immediate disputants.[35]

Argyll Group thus provides support for the proposition that judicial choice about remedies can be understood as being influenced by values of individual self-realisation, good administration, electoral legitimacy and decisional autonomy.

5.2 Certiorari and Decisional Autonomy

Certiorari has long been the preferred remedy in successful judicial review applications. Where a decision is unlawful, the effect of certiorari is to quash the decision with retrospective effect: 'The function of certiorari is to quash the legal effect or the legal consequences of the decision or order under review.'[36] Certiorari involves minimal intrusion on the territory of an administrative decision-maker, because the administrative decision-maker will be able to retake a quashed decision: the 'usual form' is for the matter to be remitted for a fresh decision in accordance with the judgment of the reviewing court.[37] The least intrusive of the traditional remedies, from an administrative decision-maker's point of view, is certiorari, compromising decisional autonomy only to a limited extent.

Nowadays, declaratory relief will typically achieve the same result as certiorari, as the administrative decision-maker will consider the declaration to be an authoritative statement of the law. But applicants for judicial review often ask for decisions to be quashed and courts generally grant certiorari. The effect, if nothing else, is to authoritatively remove any vestiges of doubt about the legitimacy of the quashed decision and the extent to which it might have ongoing legal effects.

[35] Ibid, 840.

[36] *Ainsworth v Criminal Justice Commission* (n 9) 581 per Mason CJ, Dawson, Toohey and Gaudron JJ.

[37] *Maxstra Constructions Pty Ltd v Joseph Gilbert* [2013] VSC 243 [72] per Vickery J. See e.g. Rules of the Superior Courts (Ireland), Order 84, rule 26(4): 'Where the relief sought is an order of certiorari and the Court is satisfied that there are grounds for quashing the decision to which the application relates, the Court may, in addition to quashing it, remit the matter to the Court, tribunal or authority concerned with a direction to reconsider it and reach a decision in accordance with the findings of the Court'; Federal Courts Act RSC 1985, c F-7, s 18.1(3): 'On an application for judicial review, the Federal Court may ... (b) declare invalid or unlawful, or quash, set aside or set aside and refer back for determination in accordance with such directions as it considers to be appropriate, prohibit or restrain, a decision, order, act or proceeding of a federal board, commission or other tribunal.'

In England and Wales, CPR 54.19(2) allows the reviewing court to 'substitute its own decision for the decision to which the claim relates'. But the circumstances in which it may do so are set out in section 31 of the Senior Courts Act 1981 and are limited by section 31(5A) to the correction of errors of law by courts or tribunals where 'without the error, there would have been only one decision which the court or tribunal could have reached'. Mindful of the risk of over-interference in the domain of administrative decision-makers, judges are reluctant to reach for provisions that allow for substitution of judgement: '[substitutionary orders] should be issued against bodies in different decision-making hierarchies from that of the issuer only in instances where the issuer has some special qualification, competence or experience relevant to the making of the decision in question'.[38] Accordingly, it is unsurprising that the power of substitution of judgment is limited to situations where, once the error of law has been corrected there is only one possible outcome. As Professor Cane explains:

> To the extent that the power to make particular types of decisions has been given to a decision maker because it possesses certain qualifications, experience and competences, it would be wrong to give a power to revise that type of decision by making a substitutionary order to a body in a different decision-making hierarchy which lacked some or all of those qualifications, experience and competences.[39]

This point can be understood in terms of protecting the decisional autonomy of administrative decision-makers and, though perhaps to a lesser extent, of ensuring effective and efficient public administration and decisional accuracy (inasmuch as potentially ham-fisted intervention by a court poorly equipped to adjudicate on technical matters lying within the decision-maker's field of expertise might lead to an incorrect decision and/or upset the decision-maker's effective and efficient attainment of the objectives set out in statute).

5.3 Judicial Reluctance to Grant Prohibition

Prohibition is designed to prevent an administrative decision-maker from making an unlawful decision in the future. It has been said that prohibition and certiorari 'are complementary remedies, based upon common principles',[40] and that there is 'no difference in principle between certiorari and prohibition, except that the latter

[38] Peter Cane, 'The Constitutional Basis of Judicial Remedies in Public Law' in Peter Leyland and Terry Woods eds, *Administrative Law Facing the Future: Old Constraints & New Horizons* (Blackstone, London, 1997), 242, 262.

[39] Ibid, 242, 247.

[40] Joseph (n 5) 1150.

may be invoked at an earlier stage'.[41] Indeed, a prohibiting order will sometimes simply allow the decision-maker to 'look at the matter afresh', as in *R v Liverpool Corporation, ex parte Liverpool Taxi Fleet Operators' Association*,[42] where the distribution of new taxi licences was prohibited due to a failure to engage in prior consultation with those holding existing licences. Here, certiorari was not obviously appropriate, because the issuing of new licences was not outside the powers of the Corporation; the legal flaw was the failure to consult, which could be remedied by preventing the Corporation from going ahead with its plan without giving those affected an opportunity to be heard.[43]

However, relative to certiorari, prohibition countenances more of an interference with the decisional autonomy of the administrative decision-maker in question, given that it operates *prior* to a decision being taken. Granting the remedy of prohibition interferes with an administrative decision-maker's ability to be the 'master of its own process'.[44] A reviewing court will not be able to 'anticipate or direct what the findings' of the decision-maker will be and so, understood in terms of preserving the decisional autonomy of both the courts and the administrative decision-maker, it is better to let the administrative process run its course, reaching the best available decision on the merits before the courts consider its lawfulness.[45] Furthermore, given the early point at which it is being asked to intervene by way of prohibition, a reviewing court will be deprived of the administrative decision-maker's views on the issue in question[46] (and the record will probably be less fully developed[47]) and thus find itself in a sub-optimal position in terms of faithfully implementing the statutory scheme under review.[48] One judge summarised judicial disquiet with prohibition in succinct terms: 'Early judicial intervention risks depriving the reviewing court of a full record bearing on the issue ... encourages an inefficient multiplicity of proceedings in tribunals and courts; and may compromise carefully crafted, comprehensive legislative regimes.'[49] These concerns,

[41] *R v Electricity Commissioners, ex parte London Electricity Joint Committee Co* [1924] 1 KB 171, 206 per Atkin LJ; William Wade and Christopher Forsyth, *Administrative Law* 11th edn (Oxford University Press, Oxford, 2014), 509. See also *Re Wakim, ex parte McNally* (1999) 198 CLR 511, where the High Court of Australia granted prohibition rather than certiorari because of the third party interests that would have been affected by a quashing order.

[42] [1972] 2 QB 299, 309 per Lord Denning MR.

[43] See also the unusual case of *R v Greater London Council, ex parte Blackburn* [1976] 1 WLR 550, where the Council had been applying an unlawfully lax test to decisions regarding the licensing of pornographic films and a prohibiting order was issued to prevent it from applying an unlawfully lax test in the future.

[44] *Vancouver (City) v British Columbia (Assessment Appeal Board)* (1996) 135 DLR (4th) 48 [26] per Williams JA.

[45] *Phillips v Medical Council* [1992] ILRM 469.

[46] *Canada (Border Services Agency) v CB Powell Limited* 2010 FCA 61; [2011] 2 FCR 332 [32].

[47] *R v Federal Court, ex parte Western Australia National Football League (Inc)* (1979) 143 CLR 190, 206–207.

[48] See e.g. *R v Federal Court, ex parte Pilkington ACI (Operations) Pty* (1978) 142 CLR 113, 127 (albeit dealing with a prohibition of an inferior tribunal, not an administrative decision-maker).

[49] *Halifax (Regional Municipality) v Nova Scotia (Human Rights Commission)* 2012 SCC 10; [2012] 1 SCR 364 [36] per Cromwell J. See similarly *R v Ross-Jones, ex parte Green* (1984) 156 CLR 185, 222–225

which can be understood in terms of ensuring respect (via decisional accuracy) for the considered choices of elected representatives and effective and efficient public administration, allied to those for decisional autonomy, have caused common law courts to be reluctant about granting prohibition.[50]

As such, where there is a 'clear question of law' to resolve, the resolution of which will enhance accurate, effective and efficient decision-making, prohibition will be an appropriate remedy,[51] but on more complex matters, one can expect a reviewing court to stay its hand and wait for a final decision.[52]

5.4 The Limited Scope of Mandamus

From the perspective of an administrative decision-maker, mandamus involves greater interference with its functions than certiorari or prohibition. Mandamus lies in situations where there is a public duty owed to the applicant. A successful application for mandamus will result in a court ordering a decision-maker to take a particular course of action. Whereas '[t]he quashing order and a prohibiting order deal with wrongful action, a mandatory order deals with wrongful inaction'.[53] Failure to comply with a mandatory order is contempt of court.[54] Mandamus had humble origins[55] but has since become 'a comprehensive remedy for controlling the exercise of administrative discretions'.[56] Its scope could be very broad indeed: Lord Mansfield took the view that mandamus 'ought to be used upon all occasions where the law has established no specific remedy, and where in justice and good government there ought to be one'.[57] Such a broad approach would license significant interference with administrative decision-makers' freedom to act. Inasmuch as an order of mandamus might compel an administrative decision-maker to accord a particular benefit, status or privilege, this could be 'to usurp the

(albeit an inferior tribunal); *Rowland v An Post* [2017] 1 IR 355 [11]; *Thielmann v The Association of Professional Engineers and Geoscientists of the Province of Manitoba* 2020 MBCA 8 [76].

[50] See e.g. *R v Federal Court, ex parte Western Australia National Football League (Inc)* (n 47) 206–207. In situations where the impugned decision is interlocutory judicial review will be available only 'in the most exceptional circumstances' (*R v Association of Futures Brokers and Dealers Ltd, ex parte Mordens Ltd* (1991) 3 Admin LR 254, 263 per McCullough J).

[51] *R v Tottenham and District Rent Tribunal, ex parte Northfield (Highgate) Ltd* [1957] 1 QB 103, 108 per Lord Goddard LCJ.

[52] See also the discussion by Basten JA in *Police Integrity Commission v Shaw* (2006) 66 NSWLR 446 of the potential for flexibility in the granting of prohibition.

[53] Wade and Forsyth (n 41) 520.

[54] See e.g. *R v Poplar Borough Council, ex parte London County Council (No 2)* [1922] 1 KB 95 (failure of council to levy rates, because of poverty in the district).

[55] *Bagge's Case* (1615) 11 Co Rep 93b (mandamus to order Bagge's reinstatement to the Plymouth Corporation, from which he had been removed without observance of the rules of natural justice).

[56] SA de Smith, 'Wrongs and Remedies in Administrative Law' (1952) 15 *Modern Law Review* 189, 203.

[57] *R v Barker* (1762) 3 Burr 1265, 1267.

function of the Executive'.[58] Here, in particular, a court may 'unconsciously stray from its proper province of reviewing the propriety of the decision-making process into the forbidden territory of evaluating the substantial merits of a decision'.[59] Significant inroads could thereby be made into an administrative decision-maker's sphere of action.

The plea that 'mandamus goes to set a party in motion to do a thing, but not to prescribe the way in which it shall be done' rings somewhat hollow.[60] For since its emergence, mandamus has 'developed along more modest lines'[61] precisely because judges have been mindful of how intrusive the remedy can be, given its potentially 'startling scope'.[62] That judges should be more reluctant to grant mandatory orders was highlighted by Lord Wilberforce in the *Fleet Street Casuals* case. He referred to 'a rule of common sense, reflecting the different character of the relief asked for' based on the 'obvious' fact 'that the interest of a person seeking to compel an authority to carry out a duty is different from that of a person complaining that a judicial or administrative body has, to his detriment, exceeded its powers'.[63] *Chief Constable of the North Wales Police v Evans*[64] is instructive. The Chief Constable had, by making a threat, caused Evans to resign from the police force. The House of Lords held that the Chief Constable had acted unlawfully. Lord Brightman was uncomfortable about simply issuing a declaration to this effect: 'the matter cannot be satisfactorily left there. One must know what are the consequences that flow from the breach of duty'.[65] He did strongly indicate that Evans ought to be allowed to rejoin the police force, thus restoring the *status quo ante*. Nonetheless, an order of mandamus would not be appropriate:

> I feel that the choice of remedy is a difficult one. It is a matter of discretion. From the point of view of the respondent who has been wronged in a matter so vital to his life, an order of mandamus is the only satisfactory remedy. I have been much tempted to suggest to your Lordships that it would in the circumstances

[58] *New Zealand Association for Migration and Investments Inc v Attorney-General* [2006] NZAR 45, 56 per Randerson J. Indeed, it has been said, '[m]andamus is not available to compel the exercise of a discretion'. *Moran v Secretary to the Department of Justice and Regulation* [2015] VSC 593 [21] per McDonald J. This claim is probably too strong (and was based on High Court of Australia authority relating to a situation where statute expressly regulated a minister's power to make discretionary decisions: *Plaintiff M61/2010E v Commonwealth of Australia & Ors* [2010] HCA 41 [99]–[100].

[59] *R v Chief Constable of the Thames Valley Police, ex parte Cotton* [1990] IRLR 344, 352 per Bingham LJ. See similarly Cane (n 38) 242, 246.

[60] *R v Overseers of Halifax* (1841) 10 LJ MC 81. See also *R v War Pensions Entitlement Appeal Tribunal, ex parte Bott* (1933) 50 CLR, 242–243.

[61] Louis Jaffe and Edith Henderson, 'Judicial Review and the Rule of Law: Historical Origins' (1956) 72 *Law Quarterly Review* 345, 360.

[62] Edith G Henderson, *Foundations of English Administrative Law: Certiorari and Mandamus in the Seventeenth Century* (Harvard University Press, Cambridge, 1963), 72.

[63] *R v Inland Revenue Commissioners, ex parte National Federation of Self-Employed and Small Businesses Ltd* [1982] AC 617, 631.

[64] [1982] 1 WLR 1155.

[65] Ibid, 1175.

> be a remedy proper to be granted. But it is unusual, in a case such as the present, for the court to make an order of mandamus, and I think that in practice it might border on usurpation of the powers of the chief constable, which is to be avoided. With some reluctance and hesitation, I feel that the respondent will have to content himself with the less satisfactory declaration that I have outlined.[66]

A concern not to trespass in the domain of the Chief Constable can be understood to have been present here. Many years had elapsed since Evans' departure, such that reintegrating him into the force, familiarising him with new colleagues, techniques, guidelines, legislation and so on would not necessarily have been straightforward. The particularities were much better left to the decision-maker on the ground. This can be understood in terms of judicial reluctance to compromise the decisional autonomy of the police force.[67]

Conversely, a concern to ensure the effectiveness of the judicial role can be understood to have been influential in other cases where the courts have been reluctant to grant mandamus. For instance, that the exercise of the court's jurisdiction would be unavailing has been a reason to refuse to grant mandamus, as enforcing the mandamus there would be impossible because the body responsible for the statutory duty in question is 'virtually defunct'.[68]

The other administrative law values can also be understood to have been operative in cases in which judges have had to choose whether or not to grant mandamus. Respect for the decisions of elected representatives will often be in play in mandamus cases, though typically it will be rolled into the question whether there is an enforceable public duty in the first place, which depends on the interpretation of the statutory provision at issue,[69] against the backdrop of a requirement that the duty must be 'clearly and unambiguously expressed in the statute' to be enforceable by mandamus.[70]

66 Ibid, 1176.

67 See also *MacQueen v Frackelton* (1909) 8 CLR 673, 695; *R v Milton Keynes Justices, ex parte R* [1979] 1 WLR 1062, 1065.

68 *Re Bristol and North Somerset Railway Co* (1877) 3 QBD 10, 12 per Cockburn CJ. See also *R v Hampstead Borough Council, ex parte Woodward* (1917) 116 LT 213 (personal rather than public-spirited motives not enough to invoke the courts' jurisdiction); *R v National Dock Labour Board, ex parte National Amalgamated Stevedores and Dockers* [1964] 2 Lloyds LR 420 (remedy sought related to the Board's failure in the past, which it was not the court's role to remedy); *Minister for Labour v Grace* [1993] 2 IR 53 (mandamus not granted because to do so would have been a meaningless exercise).

69 See e.g. *R v Kerrier District Council, ex parte Guppys (Bridport) Ltd* [1977] 1 EGLR 25; *R v Lancashire County Council, ex parte Guyer* [1980] 1 WLR 1024.

70 *State (Sheehan) v Government of Ireland* [1987] IR 550, 562 per Henchy J. See also *R v Inner London Education Authority, ex parte Ali* (1990) 2 Admin LR 822, where the duty imposed on an education authority by the Education Act 1944, s 8 to secure sufficient school places was held not to be automatically breached where the authority, through no fault of its own and for a limited period, failed to comply with that duty; and *Environmental Defence Society Inc v Agricultural Chemicals Board* [1973] 2 NZLR 758, 767, where mandamus was not available for a decision, taken on the basis of relevant considerations on foot of an investigation, not to revoke or otherwise require a renewed application for a licence. Sometimes, a concern for giving effect to the considered choices of elected representatives might also be understood to stand in the way of a mandatory order. For instance, in *Cuming Campbell Investments Pty*

Judicial choice as to whether to combine mandamus with some other remedies can be understood to be influenced by a concern not to impede effective and efficient public administration. *R v Paddington Valuation Officer, ex parte Peachey Property Corporation Ltd*[71] involved a challenge to a valuation list, on the basis that the methodology employed had been hopelessly flawed. The applicants sought an order of mandamus compelling the officer to create a fresh list in a manner consistent with his statutory obligations. A difficulty was presented by the existence of the allegedly flawed list—did it have to be quashed, with the administrative chaos that this might entail, including repayment of rates had and received? Lord Denning MR took a common sense approach:

> No doubt if the list is in due course avoided, certiorari must eventually go to quash it. But I see no reason why a mandamus should not issue in advance of the certiorari ... If the existing list has been compiled on the wrong footing the court can order the valuation officer to make a new list on the right footing ... Once the new list is made and is ready to take effect, the court can quash the old list. In that case everything done under the old list will remain good. The rates that have been demanded and paid cannot be recovered back.[72]

This desire to avoid administrative chaos is a regular feature of difficult cases on remedies.[73] It is easy to understand this reluctance to upset the administrative applecart in terms of judicial solicitude for effective and efficient public administration.

Effective and efficient public administration can also be understood to be implicated where a public body with limited resources 'is doing all that it honestly and honourably can to meet the statutory obligation, and that its failure, if there be failure, to meet that obligation arises really out of circumstances over which it has no control'.[74] In such circumstances, which arose in *R v Bristol Corporation, ex parte Hendy*, regarding the duty to rehouse a tenant, mandamus would be 'improper', as it would effect a judicially mandated reallocation of the decision-maker's scarce resources, even though there were 'other persons not before the court who may have equal rights with the applicant and some of whom would certainly have equal

Ltd v Collector of Imposts (Vic) (1938) 60 CLR 741, mandamus was not available to compel a particular result, but it is perhaps notable that 'the statute expressly provide[d] a specific method of putting the collector right if he goes wrong', a justification for judicial reticence which can be understood in terms of respecting the statutory scheme established by the legislature (at 750 per Latham CJ).

71 [1966] 1 QB 380.

72 Ibid, 402. See similarly *Teys Australia Beenleigh Pty Ltd v Australasian Meat Industry Employees' Union* [2015] FCAFC 11; (2015) 230 FCR 565. See also *R (Shoesmith) v Ofsted* [2011] EWCA Civ 642 [119], [132]; *McCaffrey v Minister for Agriculture* [2017] IECA 246.

73 See further Chapter 5.6.

74 *R v Bristol Corporation, ex parte Hendy* [1974] 1 WLR 498, 503 per Lord Denning MR. See also *Brady v Cavan County Council* [1999] 4 IR 99.

moral claims'.[75] This can be understood to have been supported by judicial reluctance to compromise effective and efficient decision-making by the Corporation.

R v Peak Park Joint Planning Board[76] is also instructive. Here, the applicant had been appointed to a planning board, but the council that had appointed him later sought to rescind the appointment. It was held on judicial review that the applicant did not hold the office at pleasure, such that the purported rescission of the appointment was unlawful. However, an order of mandamus was refused on the basis that 'the form of the order may require day to day supervision and the detailed examination of circumstances ...',[77] which, one might say, would be liable to compromise the effective and efficient exercise by the Board of its duties.[78] Instead, an order of certiorari was granted to quash the purported removal of the applicant from the Board. In general, this judicial reluctance to require ongoing judicial monitoring of public bodies can be understood on the basis that to implement such an order would be inimical to effective and efficient public administration.[79]

But a public body cannot simply invoke the risk of interference with its decisional autonomy and/or the efficient use of its resources and leave it at that. In *R v Secretary of State for the Home Department, ex parte Phansopkar*,[80] the Home Office was ordered to treat an application for an immigration certificate in its London office rather than one of its Indian offices. Rather than apply in India for the certificate, which would have entitled her to join her husband (a British citizen) in England, the applicant came to London to apply. Although Lord Denning MR suggested that there 'ought ... to be a separate queue' in India for those in the position of the applicant,[81] which would seem to impinge significantly on the Home Office's ability to manage its resources, his point can be understood to be that invoking administrative convenience will not invariably avail a public body, especially where the alternative was to send the applicants back to India where they would face 'long delays' in receiving the certificates to which they were entitled; indeed, as Lawton LJ observed, the rights at issue were 'fundamental human rights—of husbands and wives to live together'.[82] It is also notable that there was no statutory barrier of any sort to the applications being considered by the Home Office in London,[83] and in fact, 'a very

[75] *R v Bristol Corporation, ex parte Hendy* (n 74) 503 per Lord Denning MR.

[76] (1976) 74 LGR 376.

[77] Ibid, 380 per Lord Widgery CJ.

[78] See also *Minister for Immigration and Citizenship v Li* [2013] HCA 18; (2013) 249 CLR 332, 358 per Hayne, Kiefel and Bell JJ, commenting that a statutory provision requiring decision-making to be 'fair, just, economic, informal and quick' was 'apt to apply to objectives but not to enforceable commitments, not the least because each pulls the Tribunal in a different direction'.

[79] See e.g. the comments of Lord Brown of Eaton-under-Heywood in *R (Walker) v Secretary of State for Justice* [2009] UKHL 22; [2010] 1 AC 553, 600–601. See also *R v Commissioner of the Metropolis, ex parte Blackburn* [1968] 2 QB 118 and *(No. 3)* [1973] QB 241.

[80] [1976] QB 606.

[81] Ibid, 622.

[82] Ibid, 623.

[83] Ibid, 624–625. As Scarman LJ explained at 628:

important part of the inquiry must be made in England'[84]—put in terms of administrative law values, the point can be understood to be that the accurate implementation of the considered choices of elected representatives would actually be facilitated by the granting of mandamus (whereas the nebulous concerns for good administration were insufficient to overcome the concrete impact on individual interests).

As in *Phansopkar*, judicial protection of individual interests will occasionally be a powerful consideration. A useful example is *D'Errico v Canada (Attorney General)*.[85] The applicant had suffered injuries in a car accident but was denied a disability pension, apparently on the basis that she had been taking yoga classes and working as a yoga instructor. Quite properly, Stratas JA noted that mandamus will only be issued in exceptional cases.[86] In determining that this case was exceptional, he can be understood to have been influenced by the four values of individual self-realisation, good administration, electoral legitimacy and decisional autonomy. First, he emphasised the importance of the claimed benefit to the applicant and the deleterious effects of further delay. The benefits were 'meant to address a very serious condition, one that prevents the earning of meaningful income to sustain oneself', yet the applicant had been waiting eight years for resolution of her claim.[87] Second, he focused on effective and efficient public administration. Ordinarily, administrative decision-makers reach appropriate outcomes more quickly and efficiently than courts. But remitting a matter for further decision where the outcome is obvious would hurt efficient decision-making, not help it.[88] Third, respecting the considered choices of elected representatives was not a pressing concern here: although the decision-maker had been designated by Parliament, it had not discharged its functions in a timely manner. And any concerns about directing the decision-maker to reach a particular outcome (thereby compromising its decisional autonomy) were outweighed by the need to protect individual interests

> If the Secretary of State wishes to compel these applicants to stand in that long queue waiting in India and Bangladesh he should say so in an appropriate immigration rule so that all who claim the right may know. Had I entertained any doubt I would have held without hesitation that the combination of Magna Carta and the European Convention would not permit in law the Secretary of State to maintain either of the two positions I have mentioned. Neither the statute nor the rules help him, and without clear and express provision in the statute or rule, there is no overriding that combination.

[84] Ibid, 622 per Lord Denning MR.

[85] 2014 FCA 95; (2014) 459 NR 167. See also *Canada (Public Safety and Emergency Preparedness) v LeBon* 2013 SCC 36; (2013) 444 NR 93; *Canada (Citizenship and Immigration) v Tennant* 2019 FCA 206.

[86] *D'Errico v Canada (Attorney General)* (n 85) [17].

[87] Ibid, [19]. See also *NAIS v Minister for Immigration and Multicultural and Indigenous Affairs* [2005] HCA 77; (2005) 228 CLR 470, suggesting per Gleeson CJ, 474, that 'mandamus may be an available remedy for dilatory behaviour' on the part of an administrative decision-maker. See similarly, 483 per Gummow J and see also *Hoey v Minister for Justice* [1994] 3 IR 329.

[88] See e.g. *Alberta (Information and Privacy Commissioner) v Alberta Teachers' Association* 2011 SCC 61; [2011] 3 SCR 654 [55] per Rothstein J: 'remitting the issue to the tribunal may undermine the goal of expedient and cost-efficient decision making, which often motivates the creation of specialized administrative tribunals in the first place.' See also *Canada (Minister of Citizenship and Immigration) v Vavilov* 2019 SCC 65 [142].

and promote effective and efficient public administration.[89] Lest it be thought that Stratas JA's conclusion was too strong, in that it eliminated altogether any zone of autonomy enjoyed by the administrative decision-maker, it was clear that *D'Errico* was one of those unusual cases where administrative decision-making authority 'could be exercised in only one way'.[90]

Consider, by way of contrast with *D'Errico*, *NAIS v Minister for Immigration and Multicultural and Indigenous Affairs*,[91] an 'exceptional'[92] or 'very exceptional'[93] case of undue delay, where five and a half years were allowed to elapse between a consideration of the applicants' refugee applications and a final determination by the Refugee Review Tribunal. The High Court of Australia issued an order of mandamus, but only to require the Tribunal to determine the application 'according to law'.[94] There being more than one option open to the Tribunal, an order of mandamus can be understood to have represented an inappropriate interference with the Tribunal's decisional autonomy even if its effect were to vindicate the individual interests involved.

Some courts have been tempted to make orders of mandamus virtually unobtainable. For instance, the Canadian Federal Court of Appeal laid out a long list of 'principal requirements'[95] for the granting of mandamus. This, however, is to push the law too far from the course it was set on by Coke CJ and Lord Mansfield.

[89] *D'Errico v Canada (Attorney General)* (n 85) [21].

[90] *Commissioner of State Revenue (Vic) v Royal Insurance Australia Ltd* (1994) 182 CLR 51, 81 per Mason CJ. See similarly *R v Special Commissioners of Income Tax* (1888) 21 QBD 313, 322. See also *Point Exhibition Theatre Co Ltd v Revenue Commissioners* [1993] 2 IR 551.

[91] *NAIS v Minister for Immigration and Multicultural and Indigenous Affairs* (n 87).

[92] Ibid, 505 per Kirby J.

[93] Ibid, 517 per Callinan and Heydon JJ.

[94] Ibid, 528. See similarly *Right to Life New Zealand Inc v Rothwell* [2006] 1 NZLR 531.

[95] *Apotex Inc v Canada (Attorney General)* [1994] 1 FCR 742:

1. There must be a public legal duty to act:
2. The duty must be owed to the applicant:
3. There is a clear right to performance of that duty, in particular:
   (a) the applicant has satisfied all conditions precedent giving rise to the duty;
   (b) there was (i) a prior demand for performance of the duty; (ii) a reasonable time to comply with the demand unless refused outright; and (iii) a subsequent refusal which can be either expressed or implied, e.g. unreasonable delay;
4. Where the duty sought to be enforced is discretionary, the following rules apply:
   (a) in exercising a discretion, the decision-maker must not act in a manner which can be characterized as 'unfair', 'oppressive' or demonstrate 'flagrant impropriety' or 'bad faith';
   (b) *mandamus* is unavailable if the decision-maker's discretion is characterized as being 'unqualified', 'absolute', 'permissive' or 'unfettered';
   (c) in the exercise of a 'fettered' discretion, the decision-maker must act upon 'relevant', as opposed to 'irrelevant', considerations;
   (d) *mandamus* is unavailable to compel the exercise of a 'fettered discretion' in a particular way; and
   (e) *mandamus* is only available when the decision-maker's discretion is 'spent'; i.e., the applicant has a vested right to the performance of the duty.
5. No other adequate remedy is available to the applicant
6. The order sought will be of some practical value or effect

A more generous approach is to be preferred: 'Instead of being astute to discover reasons for not applying this great constitutional remedy for error and misgovernment, we think it our duty to be vigilant to apply it in every case to which, by any reasonable construction, it can be made applicable.'[96] This 'reasonable construction' can be understood in determining whether to grant the remedy of mandamus to be influenced by administrative law values. There is, of course, nothing to prevent the courts from using these values to develop a more rule-based approach, rather than relying (as they tend to do) on contextual analysis. But the point for present purposes is that judges can be understood to be influenced by the protection of individual interests, effective and efficient public administration, respect for the decisions of elected representatives and maintaining distinct roles for administrative decision-makers and courts.

5.5 Injunctive Relief

Although injunctive relief is extremely intrusive, in that courts can order interim relief against a party to preserve the status quo pending a full hearing, its equitable origins account for the view that injunctive relief can be granted 'whenever required by justice'.[97] Injunctive relief can be granted pending the outcome of a trial or appeal, subject to the principles set out by Lord Diplock in *American Cyanamid v Ethicon Ltd*:[98] whether the applicant has a strong or merely an arguable case; the adequacy of damages as a remedy and the balance of convenience.

Respect for statutory edicts and individual interests can be understood to justify this form of relief against public bodies. For instance, in *Bradbury v Enfield London Borough Council*,[99] a case provoked by the move to a comprehensive secondary school system, such move triggered, the Court of Appeal held, a duty of consultation under the Education Act 1944. To the argument that ordering an injunction so close to the school year (set to start under the new arrangements) should not be ordered, Lord Denning MR replied strongly: 'Even if chaos should result, still the law must be obeyed'—but he did note his view that the prospect of chaos here was 'over-stated' and, indeed, would be lesser than if the new arrangements had

7. The Court in the exercise of its discretion finds no equitable bar to the relief sought
8. On a 'balance of convenience' an order in the nature of *mandamus* should (or should not) issue.

[96] *R v Hanley Revising Barrister* [1912] 3 KB 518, 529 per Darling J.

[97] *TV3 Network Ltd v Eveready New Zealand Ltd* [1993] 3 NZLR 435, 438 per Cooke P. See e.g. *R v Kensington and Chelsea Royal London Borough Council, ex parte Hammell* [1989] QB 518; *Dunne v CanWest TV Works Ltd* [2005] NZAR 577.

[98] [1975] AC 396.

[99] [1967] 1 WLR 1311.

to be undone at a future point.[100] In other words, the countervailing concerns for effective and efficient public administration did not weigh heavily in the balance against the implementation of the statutory scheme.[101]

The application of the *American Cyanamid* principles to administrative law was considered in detail in *Hoffman-La-Roche & Co v Trade and Industry Secretary*,[102] a case in which administrative law values can be understood to have been prominent. The operation of statutory machinery resulted in the making of a statutory instrument that had the effect of depressing the price of Valium and Lithium. Saddened by the potential loss of profits, the drug manufacturers sought to challenge the *vires* of the statutory instrument. Having been told by the manufacturers that they would not obey the terms of the statutory instrument, the Minister sought an injunction. Protecting constitutional fundamentals was most likely a consideration for the Crown, as, no doubt, were the costs the National Health Service would incur by paying higher prices for the drugs.

By majority, the House of Lords granted an injunction even though the Minister had refused to give an undertaking that he would make whole the losses incurred by the manufacturers in the event that their challenge to the *vires* of the statutory instrument were successful:

> The duty of the Crown to see that the law declared by the statutory instrument is obeyed is not suspended by the commencement of proceedings in which the validity of the instrument is challenged. Prima facie the Crown is entitled as of right to an interim injunction to enforce obedience to it. To displace this right or to fetter it by the imposition of conditions it is for the defendant to show a strong prima facie case that the statutory instrument is ultra vires.[103]

These concerns for giving effect to considered legislative choices meant it would be necessary to show 'special reason' why an injunction should not be granted, to use Lord Reid's terms:[104] 'the measure of the strength of the attack upon the statutory instrument must inevitably call for some consideration.'[105] Understood in terms of administrative law values, the individual interests would need to be very strong—perhaps overwhelming—to justify an injunction against the enforcement

[100] Ibid, 1324–1325. See also *Consumers Co-operative Society (Manaawtu) Ltd v Palmerston North City Council* [1984] 1 NZLR 1.

[101] Issues relating to such interim relief (which can be difficult to categorise: see e.g. *R v Education and Science Secretary, ex parte Avon County Council* [1991] 1 QB 558; *Okunade v Minister for Justice, Equality and Law Reform* [2012] 3 IR 152) are now generally dealt with by the provisions relating to the procedure for applying for judicial review in a given jurisdiction. See e.g. Order 84, rule 20(7)(a) of the Rules of the Superior Courts (Ireland).

[102] [1975] AC 295.

[103] Ibid, 367 per Lord Diplock.

[104] Ibid, 341.

[105] Ibid, 353 per Lord Morris of Borth-y-Gest.

of an extant law.[106] But here the case on the merits was weak. It was true, of course, that the Crown had a financial interest in ensuring that the order was respected pending a decision on its *vires*. But this was not enough to persuade a majority of their Lordships that no injunctive relief should be granted, given the negative effects for efficient and effective regulation:

> It is true that the appellants have proposed an ingenious scheme which they would undertake to operate if an interim injunction is refused. The effect of it would be that they would continue to charge the forbidden prices but that if the order were ultimately held to be intra vires they would repay the difference between the forbidden charges which they had made and the lower charges which they ought to have made. *The scheme would involve considerable practical difficulties and would probably not be fully effective*, but I shall not discuss those difficulties because the serious objection would remain that the law laid down in the order is to be disregarded until the case is decided.[107]

The net result is that, ordinarily, where the Crown or state seeks to rely on an extant regulation or decision, it can expect that the presumed validity of the underlying action will weigh heavily in the balance of convenience.[108]

5.6 Refusal of Relief

The 'starting point' is that there should be 'extremely strong reasons' to refuse relief[109] once a violation of one of the principles of institutional structures, procedural fairness or substantive review has been established: 'Subordinate legislation, executive orders and the like are presumed to be lawful. If and when, however, they are successfully challenged and found ultra vires, generally speaking it is as if they had never had any legal effect at all: their nullification is ordinarily retrospective rather than merely prospective.'[110] This starting point that relief will presumptively be

[106] See e.g. *Monsanto v Canada (Health)* 2020 FC 1053 [109]–[113].

[107] *Hoffman-La-Roche* (n 102) 342 per Lord Reid. Emphasis added.

[108] See similarly *Okunade v Minister for Justice, Equality and Law Reform* (n 101) 188 per Clarke J: 'significant weight needs to be placed into the balance on the side of permitting measures which are prima facie valid to be carried out in a regular and orderly way. Regulators are entitled to regulate. Lower courts are entitled to decide. Ministers are entitled to exercise powers lawfully conferred by the Oireachtas. The list can go on. All due weight needs to be accorded to allowing the systems and processes by which lawful power is to be exercised to operate in an orderly fashion.' See also *Campus Oil v Minister for Industry and Energy (No 2)* [1983] IR 88, 107; *State (Abenglen Properties Ltd) v Dublin Corporation* [1984] IR 381.

[109] *Air Nelson Ltd v Minister of Transport* [2008] NZAR 139, 155 per O'Regan J.

[110] *Mossell (Jamaica) Ltd v Office of Utilities Regulation and others* [2010] UKPC 1 [44] per Lord Philips. Emphasis added. See also *Bolton Metropolitan Borough Council v Secretary of State for the Environment* (1990) 61 P & CR 343, 353; *Berkeley v Secretary of State for the Environment* [2000] UKHL 36; [2001] 2 AC 603, 616.

available vindicates individual self-realisation by treating the applicant as someone deserving of concern and respect. For example, in *Secretary of State for the Home Department v JJ*, there were no circumstances justifying the refusal of a judicial review remedy to quash an unlawful control order which had significantly interfered with the applicant's liberty interests: it would have been 'contrary to principle to decline to quash an order, made without power to make it, which had unlawfully deprived a person of his liberty'.[111]

5.6.1 Starting Point: A Remedy Should be Provided

Granting of relief in respect of an unlawful decision is generally the starting point even if the breach was procedural in nature and might not have had a material impact on the decision reached:[112]

> [T]he denial of a right to a fair hearing must always render a decision invalid, whether or not it may appear to a reviewing court that the hearing would likely have resulted in a different decision. The right to a fair hearing must be regarded as an independent, unqualified right which finds its essential justification in the sense of procedural justice which any person affected by an administrative decision is entitled to have. It is not for a court to deny that right and sense of justice on the basis of speculation as to what the result might have been had there been a hearing.[113]

Concern for the protection of individual interests can be understood to be key to this analysis,[114] especially inasmuch as the 'viciousness' of the breach at issue

[111] [2007] UKHL 45 [27]. But compare Lord Hoffmann [53]: 'there seems to me no conceptual reason why Parliament should not say that if the exercise of a power is found to have been unlawful, the court shall have power to modify the order or direct the Secretary of State to modify it so as to make it lawful. The judge's failure to accept that he had these powers means that in my opinion he did not properly exercise his discretion'. Lord Carswell, at [85], emphasised the concerns raised by a deprivation of liberty. Note that in *Secretary of State for the Home Department v E* [2007] EWHC 233 [311] Beatson J stayed the effect of a quashing order for seven days to allow for an appeal. See similarly *Applicants A1 and A2 v Brouwer* (2007) 16 VR 612; *FX v Central Mental Hospital* [2012] IEHC 272; [2014] 1 IR 269. See also *Project Blue Sky Inc v Australian Broadcasting Authority* (1998) 194 CLR 355.

[112] There may be some overlap between remedial discretion and the content of procedural fairness in some of these cases. For example, if an individual is in some way undeserving of a remedy, it might be said that their conduct obviated any alleged breach of procedural fairness *or* that the court is entitled to exercise its discretion to refuse relief. See Wade and Forsyth (n 41) 425–426.

[113] *Cardinal v Director of Kent Institution* [1985] 2 SCR 643, 661 per Le Dain J. See also *R v Chief Constable of the Thames Valley Police, ex parte Cotton* (n 59) 352; *Hossain v Minister for Immigration*, [2018] HCA 34, [40] (Nettle J) and [72] (Edelman J). See similarly Cane (n 38) 242, 246.

[114] Though, reflecting the individual nature of these concerns, breaches of procedural fairness can be 'cured' through internal appellate mechanisms where 'the parties should fairly be taken to have accepted [the mechanisms] when they joined the association'. *Calvin v Carr* [1980] AC 574, 593 . See also the discussion in *Twist v Randwick Municipal Council* (1976) 136 CLR 106.

contributes to judicial willingness (or, where absent, unwillingness), to grant a remedy.[115] A majority of the Supreme Court of Canada took a strong line in *Lakeside Colony of Hutterian Brethren v Hofer*, a case involving individuals who were expelled from a religious sect because they had contravened the tenets of the group's faith:

> It must be remembered that natural justice requires procedural fairness no matter how obvious the decision to be made may be. It does not matter whether it was utterly obvious that [the individuals] would be expelled. Natural justice requires that they be given notice of a meeting to consider the matter, and opportunity to make representations concerning it. This may not change anything, but it is what the law requires.[116]

This was so, even though as McLachlin J pointed out in dissent: 'Like Luther with Rome, the problem lay not in unfair procedures or lack of opportunities for hearing; the problem lay rather in the fundamental divergence between the parties, a divergence which doomed any proceedings, no matter how just, to failure.'[117]

Bingham LJ also took a strong line in *R v Chief Constable of the Thames Valley Police, ex parte Cotton*[118] in respect of the idea that relief should not be granted where the decision-maker would have reached the same decision regardless of the error complained of: 'Unless the subject of the decision has had an opportunity to put his case it may not be easy to know what case he could or would have put if he had had the chance', because 'experience shows that that which is confidently expected is by no means always that which happens';[119] and, in any event, '[t]his is a field in which appearances are generally thought to matter'.[120] This can be understood to be supported by a desire to ensure accurate, effective and efficient administrative decision-making. After all, '[t]here is no better deterrent against lax public

[115] *Reid v Rowley* [1977] 2 NZLR 472, 485 per Cooke J. See similarly *Stefan v Minister for Justice* [2001] IESC 92; [2001] 4 IR 203, 218.

[116] [1992] 3 SCR 165, 222.

[117] Ibid, 233. See also *General Medical Council v Spackman* [1943] AC 627; *Annamunthodo v Oilfields Workers' Trade Union* [1961] AC 945.

[118] (n 59) 352. See also *R v Monopolies and Mergers Commission, ex parte Argyll Group* [1986] 2 All ER 257, 266.

[119] See also *John v Rees* [1970] Ch 345, 402 per Megarry J; *Meadowvale Stud Farm Ltd v Stratford County Council* [1979] 1 NZLR 342, 350; *International Finance Trust v New South Wales Crime Commission* [2009] HCA 49; (2009) 240 CLR 319, 380–381. Compare *Secretary of State for the Home Department v AF (No 2)* [2009] UKHL 28; [2010] 2 AC 269 [73] per Lord Hoffmann: 'Most lawyers will have heard or read of or even experienced such cases but most will also know how rare they are. Usually, if evidence appears to an experienced tribunal to be irrefutable, it is not refuted.' See also the comments of Lord Briggs in the unusual case of *R (Pathan) v Secretary of State for the Home Department* [2020] UKSC 41; [2020] 1 WLR 4056 [162–165] but note that Lord Briggs was in dissent and, indeed, that he was (in my view) justly criticised by his colleagues for confusing the principles of procedural fairness with the issue of judicial discretion to shape an appropriate remedy: see [72] per Lady Arden, [118]–[130] per Lord Kerr and Lady Black, [217] per Lord Wilson.

[120] (n 59) 352.

administration than the quashing of unlawful decisions'[121] and, all things being equal, public trust is more likely to be gained than lost by an insistence on procedural propriety.

Finally, in determining whether the same outcome would inevitably have been reached, there is a risk that a court might 'substitute its own view of the merits', thereby stepping into the shoes of the decision-maker and compromising its decisional autonomy.[122]

5.6.2 The Discretionary Nature of Judicial Review Remedies

Building on this generalised judicial distaste for standing idly by in the presence of an unlawful decision, it is sometimes suggested that, as a matter of logic and principle, administrative action that is tainted by illegality is void and that judges should not enjoy any discretion over the granting of remedies. Writing on *Her Majesty's Treasury v Ahmed (No 2)*,[123] Professor Forsyth argues that therein:

> ... classic administrative law learning, regarding jurisdiction as the basic organising principle of the subject, and the consequent voidness of invalid acts, is brought to bear on the subject of remedial discretion. The recognition that, where the court finds that an impugned act is invalid and so legally non-existent, it cannot thereafter lend that act legal effect de jure or de facto through the exercise of remedial discretion, since that would be to obfuscate its earlier judgment, is the crucial conceptual breakthrough.[124]

But it has always been the case that administrative law remedies are, with some exceptions, discretionary.[125] The prerogative writs were never 'writs of course; they cannot be had for the asking, but proper cause must be shown to the satisfaction

[121] Joseph (n 5) 1202.

[122] *Lawrence v Attorney General (Grenada)* [2007] UKPC 18; [2007] 1 WLR 1474 [65].

[123] [2010] UKSC 2; [2010] 2 AC 534.

[124] 'The Rock and the Sand: Jurisdiction and Remedial Discretion' [2013] JR 360. *Ahmed (No 2)*, it should be said, was a rather unusual case. The quashing (in *Her Majesty's Treasury v Ahmed (No 1)* [2010] UKSC 2; [2010] 2 WLR 378) of a regulatory scheme designed to permit the freezing of assets held by suspected terrorists created a problem, inasmuch as replacement provisions could not be put in place immediately, giving the individuals concerned the time to send their newly unfrozen assets overseas. The Treasury asked the Supreme Court to suspend the operation of its orders, a request which was ultimately refused. All sides agreed, however, that the effect of the decision in *Ahmed (No 1)* was to render the regulatory scheme *void ab initio* (see especially [5]–[7]). The question at issue in *Ahmed (No 2)* was the narrow one of whether the Supreme Court should acquiesce in an attempt to obfuscate the effects of *Ahmed (No 1)* [8]. To this narrow question, the majority answered, resoundingly, 'No'.

[125] *Dr Astley McLaughlin v A-G of the Cayman Islands* [2007] UKPC 50 [16]. Professor Forsyth elsewhere acknowledges, albeit with disdain, that courts have 'continued to exercise remedial discretion freely as if it were unexceptional to breathe life into an invalid act'. Wade and Forsyth (n 41) 598.

of a court why they should issue.'[126] Indeed, the expression *ex debito justitiae*, albeit Latin, 'has no magic virtue and cannot change a writ of grace into a writ of right nor destroy the discretion even in cases involving lack of jurisdiction.'[127] Judicial review is 'inherently discretionary'.[128]

5.6.3 Principled Grounds for Withholding a Remedy

Indeed, there are some judicial holdouts against the proposition that procedural breaches which make no difference to the substantive outcome will invariably result in a decision being quashed. As Lord Wilberforce noted in *Malloch v Aberdeen Corporation*, there must be 'something of substance which has been lost by the failure. The court does not act in vain.'[129] There are examples of courts refusing to grant relief where the breach complained of would not have made a material difference to the decision; indeed, courts have long used the so-called mandatory/directory distinction to justify the conclusion that a given breach of a statutory requirement was too technical to justify the grant of a remedy.[130] Consider, relatedly, the comments of May LJ in *R v Broadcasting Complaints Commission, ex parte Owen*, delivered in the context of a failure to take into account relevant factors, which can also be understood in terms of administrative law values:

> Where the reasons given by a statutory body for taking or not taking a particular course of action are not mixed and can clearly be disentangled, but where the court is quite satisfied that even though one reason may be bad in law, nevertheless

[126] SA de Smith, 'The Prerogative Writs' (1951) 11 *Cambridge Law Journal* 40, 42–45; See also Thomas Adams, 'The Standard Theory of Administrative Unlawfulness' (2017) 76 *Cambridge Law Journal* 289.

[127] *Harelkin v University of Regina* [1979] 2 SCR 561, 576 per Beetz J. See also *State (Cussen) v Brennan* [1981] IR 181, 195; *Seal v Chief Constable of the South Wales Police* [2007] UKHL 31; [2007] 1 WLR 1910 [33]; *Walton v Scottish Ministers* [2013] Env LR 16 [81], [103], [112] and [155]–[156]; *R (New London College) v Secretary of State for the Home Department* [2013] UKSC 51; [2013] 1 WLR 2358 [45]–[46]. For a particularly broad statement of the scope of judicial discretion in granting judicial review remedies see *Stefan v Minister for Justice Equality and Law Reform* (n 115) 217 per Denham J:

> In considering all the circumstances, matters including the existence of an alternative remedy, the conduct of the applicant, the merits of the application, the consequences to the applicant if an order of *certiorari* is not granted and the degree of fairness of the procedures, should be weighed by the court in determining whether *certiorari* is the appropriate remedy to attain a just result.

[128] *Martin v Ryan* [1990] 2 NZLR 209, 237 per Fisher J.

[129] [1971] 1 WLR 1579, 1595. See e.g. *R v Aston University Senate, ex parte Roffey* [1969] 2 QB 538, 559; *Wislang v Medical Practitioners Disciplinary Committee* [1974] 1 NZLR 29; *Brannigan v Davison* [1997] 1 NZLR 140, 149; *R (KM) v Cambridgeshire County Council* (2012) 126 BMLR 186 [38]; *Australian and International Pilots Association v Fair Work Australia* [2012] FCAFC 65; (2012) 202 FCR 200, 222, 229, and 242–243; *Walton v Scottish Ministers* (n 127) [113]; *Sami v Minister for Immigration and Border Protection* [2015] FCA 1496 [14].

[130] See generally Hogan, Morgan and Daly (n 3) chapter 12; Paul Daly, 'A Typology of Materiality' (2019) 26 *Australian Journal of Administrative Law* 134.

> the statutory body would have reached precisely the same decision on the other valid reasons, then this court will not interfere by way of judicial review.[131]

Whilst a desire to give effect to legislative choices can be understood to support the enforcement of the law relating to relevant factors, if the outcome of a given decision was not tarnished by a misapplication of the law, the value of electoral legitimacy evidently has less purchase.[132]

As we have seen, there is significant debate over the extent to which individual interests are at stake in cases of procedural errors which made no material difference to the outcome. In general, the better view seems to be that individual interests will invariably be compromised by a failure to hold a fair hearing and, accordingly, that a court should intervene to quash a decision tainted by procedural error. However, consistent with May LJ's comments in *Owen*, respect for legislative choice will occasionally lead a court to refuse to grant relief. In *Mobil Oil Canada Ltd v Canada-Newfoundland Offshore Petroleum Board*,[133] for example, although the applicant had established a breach of procedural fairness, the remedies sought were 'impractical'; compelling the decision-maker to reconsider its position would have been 'nonsensical' as it was 'bound in law' to reject the application because of the Court's disposition of other aspects of the case.[134] In these 'exceptional' circumstances, Iacobucci J concluded, relief would be inappropriate.[135] One can understand a judicial desire to accurately implement the statutory scheme as having stood in the applicant's way; one might also say that the court was concerned not to waste scarce administrative resources by ordering a reconsideration which would have cost time and money without materially altering the parties' positions.

Beyond the contested terrain of the 'makes no difference' principle there are ample examples of judges refusing to grant remedies in respect of unlawful decisions. It has justly been said, however, that the legitimacy of judicial discretion rests on the giving of reasons 'which make it clear that the discretion [is] being exercised in a selective and discriminatory manner, and neither arbitrarily nor idiosyncratically', for otherwise 'the rights of the parties could become, or at least appear, dependent upon judicial whim'.[136] Significant countervailing concerns will need to be present for a court to justify withholding relief: 'because such discretionary power may make inroads upon the rule of law, it must be exercised with the greatest care'.[137]

[131] [1985] QB 1153, 1177.

[132] See also *J & E Davy v Financial Services Ombudsman* [2010] IESC 30; [2010] 3 IR 324, 351 (inappropriate to order mediation at a late stage given the importance of expedition to the functioning of the statutory scheme) and 370 (requirement to give reasons in a particular form had to be considered with due regard to the 'requirement for informality').

[133] [1994] 1 SCR 202.

[134] Ibid, 228.

[135] Ibid. See also *Feng v Saskatchewan (Economy)* 2020 SKCA 6 [110]–[118].

[136] *Zamir and Woolf: The Declaratory Judgment* 3rd edn (Sweet and Maxwell, London, 2002) [4.005].

[137] *MiningWatch Canada v Canada (Fisheries and Oceans)* [2010] 1 SCR 6 [52] per Rothstein J.

Some of the reasons found in the decided cases for refusing relief are quite straightforward. For instance, the misconduct of the applicant might justify the withholding of a remedy.[138] Such cases can probably be best understood as turning on institutional considerations, relating to a desire to maintain the standing of the judiciary.

Other decisions in which the consequences of granting a remedy have been taken into account can, however, be understood in terms of judicial solicitude for effective and efficient public administration and individual interests (albeit those of third parties). For example, relief was refused in *R v Monopolies and Mergers Commission, ex parte Argyll Group* partly because of 'the probability that deals have been done in reliance on the validity of the decisions now impugned'.[139] In *Irish Permanent Building Society v Caldwell*, Barrington J openly refused to entertain the quashing of a decision providing a licence to a financial institution on the basis that doing so would cause administrative chaos and wreak havoc on innocent third parties who had dealt with the institution over many years.[140] Similarly, in *R (New London College) v Secretary of State for the Home Department*, Lord Carnwath was quite clear that he would have exercised remedial discretion to ensure that a finding of unlawfulness would not undo legal relationships that had been entered into on the basis of allegedly unlawful administrative action.[141]

Consider too *New Zealand Employers Federation v National Union of Public Employees*,[142] where the plaintiff sought an injunction against strike notices on the basis that the union in question had been registered (unlawfully) before new legislation had come into force. Richardson P 'weighed' on the one hand 'the plea to avoid administrative chaos' against, on the other, the 'requirement that statutory officers ensure they keep within their powers and are accountable in law' and the risk of creating 'undesirable uncertainty' for third parties, before concluding that granting relief 'would serve the important public purposes of vindicating the law and emphasising the proper scope of administrative anticipation of the coming into force of legislation'.[143] This can be understood as a straightforward balancing exercise, trying to achieve a balance between competing considerations. Accordingly, it

[138] *New Zealand Waterside Workers' Industrial Union of Workers v Dalglish* [1949] NZLR 783; *State (Vozza) v O'Floinn* [1957] IR 227; *Cock v Labour Relations Board* (1960) 26 DLR (2d) 127; *Wislang v Medical Practitioners Disciplinary Committee* (n 129); *SZQBN v Minister for Immigration and Citizenship* [2013] FCAFC 71.

[139] [1986] 2 All ER 257, 266. See also ibid, 272 per Neill LJ. Dillon LJ (at 269) referenced the possibility of 'serious detriment' to shareholders as a reason for refusing a remedy, primarily a reason which can be understood as sounding in concern for effective and efficient public administration though one which overlaps with a concern for the interests of individuals. See similarly *Kingsway Investments (Kent) Ltd v Kent County Council* [1971] AC 72, 91 per Lord Reid, dissenting.

[140] [1981] ILRM 242, 269–270. See also *MiningWatch Canada v Canada (Fisheries and Oceans)* (n 137) [52] per Rothstein J.

[141] [2013] 1 WLR 2358 [45]–[46]. See also *Unison Networks Ltd v Commerce Commission* [2006] NZCA 365 [87]; *Bertrand v Acho Dene Koe First Nation* 2021 FC 287 [103]

[142] (2001) 6 NZELC 98 ; [2002] 2 NZLR 54.

[143] Ibid, 66–67.

is difficult to speak in absolutes: as the New Zealand Court of Appeal commented in *Lower Hutt City Council v Bank*, 'expedience cannot be promoted to the stage of denying citizens fundamental rights'.[144]

To these cases of 'administrative chaos' must be added the notion that 'if, in the circumstances of the case, it would work an unfairness to third parties',[145] relief ought to be refused. Thus in *Re Wakim, ex parte McNally*, the High Court of Australia declined to quash an unlawful order, fearful of the third-party reliance interests that would be defeated by the issuance of a quashing order.[146] A straightforward example is *The State (Cussen) v Brennan*, where the Irish Supreme Court held that a health authority had unlawfully required that applicants for a position as a doctor be able to speak Irish, but refused to quash the appointment decision, as the successful candidate (and his family) and the health authority had been 'induced to make plans for the future and to enter into commitments from which they should not now be compelled to withdraw'.[147] Similarly, in *Barker v Queenstown Lakes District Council*, the New Zealand High Court refused to quash a legally defective consent notice as to land purchased by the applicant, because doing so would have removed a covenant designed to safeguard the applicant's neighbours' view of lake and mountainside scenery:

> The landscapes of the Queenstown area are of international quality. As the Environment Court has recognised, that quality in fact drives the economy of this resort area. The price paid for land enjoying the landscape amenity approximate to the town centre, is very high by New Zealand standards. This is not to say that if a property is worth a lot it is more deserving of protection but rather the Court must, in exercising its discretion by way of judicial review, balance competing interests including the effect on the amenity of a locality to all affected parties, and the extent of potential loss of value.[148]

The conclusion in these cases that individuals not involved in a decision-making process should not shoulder the burden of administrative unlawfulness can be understood in terms of judicial solicitude for the interests of third parties, inasmuch as granting a remedy would have interfered with their autonomy, by imposing costs on or reducing the amenity value of their activities or properties.

144 *Lower Hutt City Council v Bank* [1974] 1 NZLR 545, 551. There may, in this regard, be a distinction to draw between genuine administrative chaos (where remedial discretion can be exercised) and mere administrative inconvenience. Cf Oakey Coal Action Alliance Inc v New Acland Coal Pty Ltd [2021] HCA 2.

145 *McCaffrey v Minister for Agriculture* (n 72) [51] per Hogan J.

146 (1999) 198 CLR 511, 592.

147 [1981] IR 181, 197 per Henchy J.

148 [2006] NZAR 716, 731 per Fogarty J.

5.7 Severance

Finally, it is worth noting the principles on severability, as they are related to the refusal of relief. The authors of *De Smith's Judicial Review* set out the issue as follows:

> What if an act or decision is partly legal and partly illegal? Suppose that a public body has power to revoke a person's licence. It revokes X's licence, and proceeds to order that he shall be disqualified from applying for a new licence for five years. It has no power to impose such a disqualification. In this case, X will be able to obtain a quashing order in respect of the five-year disqualification, or a declaration that the disqualification is void; but the court can still hold that the revocation of his licence is valid, for the two limbs of the public body's order are severable from one another. Cases of partial invalidity are often more complicated than this because the good and the bad elements are not clearly distinct.[149]

One might take the view that severance is never appropriate, for it would involve interfering with the decisional autonomy of the administrative decision-maker in question: to allow planning permission to stand, for instance, shorn of its unlawful conditions, would be to impose upon a planning authority a result which it might not have reached had it known the conditions would be struck down.[150] Moreover, as Dawson J observed in *Re Dingjan*, 'to fashion a provision entirely different' from the one condemned as unlawful would be to exercise a legislative power[151]—a conclusion that carries particular weight in Australia due to the constitutionalised separation of powers but which also applies more broadly inasmuch as it is supported by a concern that judges should not trespass in the political domain. Accordingly, where severance could only be effected by modifying the text of a regulatory provision, this can only be done 'when the court is satisfied that it is effecting no change in the substantial purpose and effect of the impugned provision'.[152]

Sometimes, however, 'severance is the only sensible course',[153] as where invalidating an administrative decision in its entirety would cause administrative chaos, a point which can be understood in terms of judicial reluctance to compromise effective and efficient public administration: 'to strike down an entire

149 *De Smith's Judicial Review* (n 9) [5-155]–[5-156].

150 See e.g. *Pyx Granite Co v Ministry of Housing and Local Government* [1958] 1 QB 554, 578–579 per Hodson LJ. See also *Hall & Co v Shoreham-by-Sea UDC* [1964] 1 WLR 240; *R v Hillingdon London Borough Council, ex parte Royco Homes Ltd* [1974] QB 720; *Bord na Móna v Galway County Council* [1985] IR 205; *Potts v Invercargill City Council* [1985] 1 NZLR 609; *R v North Hertfordshire District Council, ex parte Cobbold* [1985] 3 All ER 486; *State (FPH Properties SA) v An Bord Pleanála* [1987] IR 698; *Ross v An Bord Pleanála* [2015] IEHC 256.

151 (1995) 183 CLR 323, 349. See also *Pidoto v Victoria* (1943) 68 CLR 87, 107–111 per Latham CJ, another case involving issues relating to constitutional validity.

152 *Director of Public Prosecutions v Hutchinson* [1990] 2 AC 783, 811 per Lord Bridge of Harwich. See e.g. *Transport Ministry v Alexander* [1978] 1 NZLR 306; *Harrington v Lowe* (1996) 190 CLR 311, 328.

153 *R v Secretary of State for the Home Department, ex parte Pierson* [1998] AC 539, 592 per Lord Steyn.

regulation because of a curable omission … would represent a triumph of logic over reason.'[154] Similarly, requiring a matter to be reheard in its entirety would drain scarce resources and, accordingly, 'the courts appear reluctant to set aside the whole of a formal court or tribunal hearing where it has a less destructive option'.[155] Indeed, in some planning cases, the result of severing unlawful conditions 'would be that the owner could do things on his land for which he never in fact obtained permission and that would be contrary to the intention of the statute'.[156]

There is significant merit to Devlin J's observation that 'the question to be asked is whether the bad part can be effectively severed from the good',[157] and we can understand the answer in any given case to depend on the striking of a balance between the values of good administration, electoral legitimacy and decisional autonomy, as in *R (National Association of Health Stores) v Department of Health*, where Sedley LJ took the view that '[i]f an omission can be made good without disrupting the existing, presumptively lawful, text' and 'appears to have done no harm', there was no reason why, 'instead of permitting the rule-maker to insert the missing brick, the entire structure should be pulled down'.[158]

5.8 Conclusion

The starting point for the last section of this chapter, on refusal of relief, was that the granting of a judicial review remedy is ordinarily automatic, even in respect of procedural failings which, if put right, would probably not have affected the final outcome. There are examples, however, of this 'makes no difference' principle being applied to refuse relief and, beyond that, of remedies being denied in the discretion of the court in view of the likely consequences of granting relief to the applicant for judicial review. Both the starting point and the deviations from the ordinary course of remedying unlawful administrative action can be understood in terms of administrative law values.

Similarly, the nature of the different remedies—certiorari, prohibition, mandamus, declaration and injunction—and judicial willingness or reluctance to grant them, can be understood in terms of the protection of individual interests, effective and efficient public administration, respect for the decisions of elected representatives and the preservation of the decisional autonomy of courts and administrative decision-makers. As the least intrusive of the old prerogative writs certiorari is the default remedy, rivalled only by the declaration, with courts progressively more

[154] *R (National Association of Health Stores) v Department of Health* [2005] EWCA Civ 154 [16] per Sedley LJ.
[155] Aronson, Groves and Weeks (n 6) [10.470]. See e.g. *State (McKeown) v Scully* [1986] ILRM 133.
[156] *Kingsway Investments (Kent) Ltd v Kent County Council* (n 139) 90 per Lord Reid, dissenting.
[157] *Potato Marketing Board v Merricks* [1958] 2 QB 316, 333.
[158] (n 154) [20].

reluctant to grant prohibition and mandamus, mindful (one might understand) of the increased level of interference these remedies occasion in the work of administrative decision-makers (engaging the value of decisional autonomy) and the risks they pose to effective and efficient public administration (engaging the value of good administration). Meanwhile, the structure of injunctive relief in administrative law can also be drawn by reference to administrative law values.

On occasion, as with the choice to issue mandamus, refuse relief in a given case or sever the unlawful component from an otherwise lawful decision, courts can be understood to have struck a balance between potentially conflicting values. More generally, the values can be understood to function in a complementary way to illuminate the choice of remedy in administrative law cases.

6
Restrictions on Remedies

This chapter follows naturally from the latter part of its predecessor. There I addressed judicial discretion to refuse a remedy on the ground that the breach of the principles of institutional structures, procedural fairness or substantive review did not have a material effect on the final decision or in view of the consequences a remedy would have for the public at large or third-party interests. Remedial discretion is, again, the subject of this chapter, but the focus is somewhat wider: whereas in Chapter 5 the discussion was of individualised reasons—relating to the particular decision-making process or particular decision—for refusing to grant a remedy, in this chapter the issues to be discussed are general principles restricting the granting of judicial review remedies; these are systemic in nature and not specific to the circumstances presented by individual applicants and the decisions they wish to challenge. Some overlap is, of course, to be expected, but the procedural requirements of promptness and permission; the principle that an applicant must exhaust alternative remedies before seeking judicial review; the bar on collateral attack; privative clauses; the principles relating to ripeness and prematurity and the obligation to demonstrate standing to seek judicial review are all general, in that they apply to each and every application for judicial review regardless of the particular factual and legal matrix.

For the most part, the restrictions take the form of a general principle—for instance, that an applicant for judicial review must exhaust alternative remedies—to which a relatively well-defined exception exists—for instance, that the alternative remedies in question must be effective and adequate to remedy the flaws the applicant complains of. These are, in other words, well-defined bars to judicial review remedies. This is not true across the board: the law relating to standing is notably fluid, for example, requiring relatively open-ended contextual analysis sensitive to the circumstances of each individual case. But it would be wrong to suggest that judges determining the scope of restrictions on remedies are cast adrift on an endless sea of context.

As in the other chapters, my argument will be that the law in relation to restrictions on remedies can be understood in terms of the values of individual self-realisation, good administration, electoral legitimacy and decisional autonomy. Judicial respect for the considered choices of elected representatives and judicial caution about imposing undue burdens on public administration can be understood to be particularly prominent in the justification of restrictions on access to remedies. These restrictions are rarely absolute, however, because judicial

Understanding Administrative Law in the Common Law World. Paul Daly, Oxford University Press. © Paul Daly 2021.
DOI: 10.1093/oso/9780192896919.003.0006

solicitude for decisional autonomy and, especially, individual interests can also be understood to exert traction in this area, typically to ensure that there is some possibility for individuals to access judicial review remedies in appropriate cases. Thus, despite the argument powerfully advanced by Professor Varuhas that 'the principal focus of common law review is not individual rights and interests, but ensuring public power is exercised properly for the public good', it is clear in my view that individual interests are of central importance to the law on restrictions on remedies, which has, *contra* Varuhas an 'individual-regarding nature'.[1] Here, as elsewhere in the contemporary law of judicial review of administrative action, the courts can be understood to employ a plurality of values in shaping the applicable legal principles.

6.1 Procedural Requirements

I briefly note some important procedural requirements associated with judicial review remedies, namely permission and promptness. My discussion here is cursory, as there are very detailed statutory and regulatory provisions governing these aspects of the judicial review procedure in the jurisdictions under discussion, but should nonetheless demonstrate that the basic principles relating to these procedural requirements can be understood in terms of administrative law values.

A permission requirement has long formed part of what is now the judicial review jurisdiction of the superior courts.[2] Lord Diplock's explanation of the requirement in *R v Inland Revenue Commissioners, ex parte National Federation of Self-Employed and Small Businesses Ltd* can be understood as being supported by considerations relating to effective and efficient public administration:

> The need for leave to start proceedings for remedies in public law is not new. It applied previously to applications for prerogative orders, though not to civil actions for injunctions or declarations. Its purpose is to prevent the time of the court being wasted by busybodies with misguided or trivial complaints of administrative error, and *to remove the uncertainty in which public officers and authorities might be left as to whether they could safely proceed with administrative action* while proceedings for judicial review of it were actually pending even though misconceived.[3]

[1] Jason Varuhas, 'Taxonomy and Public Law' in Mark Elliott, Jason Varuhas and Shona Wilson-Stark eds, *The Unity of Public Law? Doctrinal, Theoretical and Comparative Perspectives* (Hart, Oxford, 2018), 39, 67. See also Jason Varuhas, 'The Reformation of English Administrative Law? "Rights", Rhetoric and Reality' (2013) 72 *Cambridge Law Journal* 369.

[2] It is not omnipresent, however. See e.g. Philip Joseph, *Constitutional and Administrative Law of New Zealand* 4th edn (Thomson Reuters, Auckland, 2014), 1147, fn 3.

[3] [1982] AC 617, 642–643. Emphasis added. See also *G v Director of Public Prosecutions* [1994] 1 IR 374.

Promptness has always been another important requirement:[4] 'public authorities and third parties should not be kept in suspense as to the legal validity [of a decision] for any longer period than is absolutely necessary in fairness to the person affected by the decision'.[5] A concern for effective and efficient public administration and the protection of the interests of third parties can be understood as supporting this requirement, which is now typically memorialised in statute or rules of court as a maximum period of weeks or months within which a challenge to an administrative decision by way of judicial review must be initiated. When the time period has expired, the administrative decision-maker can safely turn its mind to other matters, supporting its effectiveness and efficient use of resources, whilst individuals can, for their part, safely rely on the decision in question, subject only to the small risk that an applicant for judicial review would be able to demonstrate sufficiently convincing circumstances to persuade a judge to extend the time limit.[6]

Consider *R v Rochdale Metropolitan Borough Council, ex parte Butterworth*,[7] where a challenge to an allocation of school places was held not to have been brought in a timely manner because it should have been brought before the beginning of the school year. The possibility of administrative chaos—with deleterious effects for effective and efficient public administration—was obvious: 'it is important to give early warning as to what is going on so that people can endeavour to conclude matters soon, so that the whole education system ... is not kept in suspense while legal proceedings drag on.'[8] In planning cases, promptness will typically be of the essence, because there will usually be third-party interests at issue. A developer is entitled to start developing as soon as permission has been granted, something that is difficult and costly to undo.[9] A useful example is *Turner v Allison*,[10] where the applicant sought to challenge the decision to change the zoning of land to permit the construction of a shopping centre. By the time litigation was initiated, almost a year had elapsed since the critical decision in the matter and work had already begun on the shopping centre: a remedy was refused.[11] The same factor has motivated courts to be stringent about promptness requirements in the public procurement context.[12]

4 *Swan v Secretary of State for Scotland* 1998 SC 479, 487 per Rodger P. See e.g. *R (Rainey) v Belfast Recorder* (1937) 71 ILTR 272.

5 *O'Reilly v Mackman* [1983] 2 AC 237, 280–281 per Lord Diplock.

6 For a useful discussion of provisions modelled on those in place in England and Wales, see *Maharaj v National Energy Corporation of Trinidad and Tobago* [2019] UKPC 5.

7 [2000] Ed CR 117.

8 *R v Leeds City Council, ex parte N* [1999] ELR 324, 334 per David Pannick QC.

9 See e.g. *Kelly v Leitrim County Council* [2005] 4 IR 404; *Finn-Kelcey v Milton Keynes Borough Council* [2009] Env LR 17.

10 [1971] NZLR 833.

11 See similarly *R v Stafford Justices* [1940] 2 KB 33. See also *R v Board of Broadcast Governors* (1962) 33 DLR (2d) 449 , a late challenge to the grant of a telecommunications licence, the grant of which had already prompted the holder to expend significant resources.

12 See e.g. *R (Nash) v Barnet London Borough Council* [2013] EWCA Civ 1004; *BAM PPP v Balfour Realty* [2017] IEHC 157.

Generally speaking, it would 'be contrary to public policy, and as such an abuse of the process of the court' to allow a person to attack an administrative decision otherwise than by way of an application for judicial review, because this would 'evade' provisions, such as the promptness and permission requirements which exist 'for the protection of' administrative decision-makers.[13] This point can be understood, following from the discussion earlier in this section, to sound in terms of effective and efficient public administration. It sometimes goes under the rubric of 'procedural exclusivity'. Set out in its most extreme form by the House of Lords in *O'Reilly v Mackman*,[14] it has been 'resisted' elsewhere in the common law world, where a clear distinction is drawn between the English and indigenous authorities.[15]

Yet even on the most extreme version of procedural exclusivity, if an individual seeks to assert individual interests which can be classified as private-law rights against a public body, he or she will not be required to launch judicial review proceedings:

> [W]here a litigant asserts his entitlement to a subsisting right in private law, whether by way of claim or defence, the circumstance that the existence and extent of the private right asserted may incidentally involve the examination of a public law issue cannot prevent the litigant from seeking to establish his right by action commenced by writ or originating summons, any more than it can prevent him from setting up his private law right in proceedings brought against him.[16]

A judicial desire to promote the protection of individual interests can be understood to support this exception.

Nevertheless, where effective and efficient public administration would be undermined because the case involves 'a claim for judicial review with only a thin pretence to a private wrong', designed to circumvent procedures put in place for the

[13] *O'Reilly v Mackman* (n 5) 285 per Lord Diplock. See also the judgment of Charleton J in *Dún Laoghaire Rathdown County Council v West Wood Club* [2019] IESC 43.

[14] *O'Reilly v Mackman* (n 5) 285 per Lord Diplock.

[15] *Earthquake Commission v Insurance Council of New Zealand Inc* [2014] NZHC 3138; [2015] 2 NZLR 381, 433–434. See e.g. Paul Daly, 'The Constitutionalisation of English Judicial Review in Ireland: Continuity and Change' in Michael Ramsden and Swati Jhaveri eds, *Judicial Review of Administrative Action across the Common Law World: Origins and Adaptations* (Cambridge University Press, Cambridge, 2021). The very notion of procedural exclusivity has been strongly challenged (see e.g. Dawn Oliver, *Common Values and the Public-Private Divide* (Butterworths, London, 1999); John Allison, *A Continental Distinction in the Common Law: A Historical and Comparative Perspective on English Public Law* rev edn (Cambridge University Press, Cambridge, 2000)) but for good or ill it remains a feature of contemporary administrative law.

[16] *Roy v Kensington and Chelsea and Westminster Family Practitioner Committee* [1992] 1 AC 624, 628–629 per Lord Bridge of Harwich. Of course, quite what one classifies as a 'private law right' is a difficult question. Indeed 'it seems unlikely that much general guidance will ever be available on the question of which rights are private law rights' for the purposes of navigating the divide between public law and private law: Peter Cane, 'Private Rights and Public Procedure' [1992] *Public Law* 193, 197.

benefit of administrative decision-makers, courts will use their inherent powers to prevent an inappropriate claim from proceeding.[17]

The arguments in favour of (and against) permitting an individual to raise a public law defence in civil proceedings (rather than requiring the individual to bring a separate judicial review application) rest on similar considerations. Situations may arise where, for example, a defendant sued for breach of contract by a public body seeks to assert that the contract was unlawful. The coercive power of the courts will not lightly be brought to bear on any individual, least of all an individual who claims that the administrative act upon which a civil action is based was unlawful and invalid. As Lord Fraser of Tullybelton observed in *Wandsworth London Borough Council v Winder*, 'the arguments for protecting public authorities against unmeritorious or dilatory challenges to their decisions have to be set against the arguments for preserving the ordinary rights of private citizens to defend themselves against unfounded claims'.[18] This point can be understood in terms of individual self-realisation. Moreover, it is dangerous to assume 'that public law elements are exceptional and separable in an essentially private law relationship'.[19] Indeed, where a public body can rely on a defence based on a statutory provision—invoking, one might say, the considered choice of the elected representatives sitting in the legislature—it could simply raise the defence in an ordinary action.[20] Again, however, where raising a defence to a civil action is designed to circumvent the promptness and permission requirements (which can be understood as posing a threat to effective and efficient public administration), it will be an abuse of process to raise it.[21]

6.2 Exhaustion of Alternative Remedies

A court may refuse to grant a judicial review remedy where the applicant has failed to exhaust alternative remedies, such as, most commonly, appeal rights provided for by statute: 'it has always been a principle that certiorari will go only where there is no other equally effective and convenient remedy'.[22]

Some commentators have an intense dislike of judicial ability to refuse relief on this basis:

[17] *Canada (Attorney General) v TeleZone Inc* [2010] 3 SCR 585 [78].

[18] [1985] AC 461, 509. See also *Dunlop v Woollahra Municipal Council* [1982] AC 158, 172.

[19] Gillian Morris and Sandra Fredman, 'Public or Private? State Employees and Judicial Review' (1991) 107 *Law Quarterly Review* 298, 306.

[20] This proposition is consistent with the approach taken in *Davy v Spelthorne Borough Council* [1984] AC 262.

[21] See e.g. *Dún Laoghaire Rathdown County Council v West Wood Club* [2017] IECA 213. On appeal, an intervening decision of the Court of Justice of the European Union meant that the Supreme Court did not have to address this point in terms: [2019] IESC 43.

[22] *R v Hillingdon London Borough Council, ex parte Royco Homes Ltd* [1974] QB 720, 728 per Lord Widgery CJ.

> In principle there ought to be no categorical rule requiring the exhaustion of administrative remedies before judicial review can be granted. A vital aspect of the rule of law is that illegal administrative action can be challenged in the court as soon as it is taken or threatened. *There should be no need first to pursue any administrative procedure or appeal in order to see whether the action will in the end be taken or not.* An administrative appeal on the merits of the case is something quite different from judicial determination of the legality of the whole matter.[23]

The authors' concern, as evidenced by the highlighted passage, is with the effect on individual interests. How dare the courts, they ask, refuse to vindicate individual interests? But where the courts insist on the exhaustion of alternative remedies, their reasons for doing so are typically grounded in the other administrative law values. A useful statement of the exhaustion principle can be found in the following passage from the speech of Lord Scarman in *R v Inland Revenue Commissioners, ex parte Preston*:

> [A] remedy by way of judicial review is not to be made available where an alternative remedy exists. This is a proposition of great importance. Judicial review is a collateral challenge: it is not an appeal. Where Parliament has provided by statute appeal procedures ... it will only be very rarely that the courts will allow the collateral process of judicial review to be used to attack an appealable decision.[24]

As Lord Templeman explained, in cases involving taxation matters, 'the remedy of the taxpayer lies in the appeal procedures' before bodies with 'wide knowledge and experience of fiscal law and practice' provided for by statute.[25] A concern for effective and efficient public administration can be understood to support the principle that judicial review processes 'should not be allowed to supplant the normal statutory appeal procedure' save in 'exceptional' circumstances.[26]

Questions about exhaustion 'usually arise[] in the context of statutory schemes and if Parliament directly or indirectly has provided for an appeals procedure, it is not for the court to usurp the functions of the appellate body'.[27] Judicial insistence on the exhaustion of alternative remedies provided by statute can be understood as being supported by a desire to ensure the faithful implementation of the statutory scheme: 'The reason for this approach is ... that it must be presumed that the

[23] William Wade and Christopher Forsyth, *Administrative Law*, 11th edn (Oxford University Press, Oxford, 2014), 600. Emphasis added.

[24] [1985] AC 835, 852.

[25] Ibid, 862.

[26] Ibid.

[27] *R v Panel on Take-overs and Mergers, ex parte Guinness plc* [1990] 1 QB 146, 177 per Lord Donaldson of Lymington MR. See also *R (Davies) v Financial Services Authority* [2003] EWCA Civ 1128; [2004] 1 WLR 185 [31]; *R (Lim) v Home Secretary* [2007] EWCA Civ 773; *R (C) v Financial Services Authority* [2013] EWCA Civ 677 [37].

Oireachtas, in establishing a form of statutory appeal, intended that such an appeal was to be the means by which, ordinarily, those dissatisfied with an initial decision might be entitled to have the initial decision questioned.'[28] Unsurprisingly, it has been said that this provides 'vital constitutional underpinning' for the obligation to exhaust alternative remedies:[29] 'When Parliament enacts a remedy with the clear intention that this should be pursued in place of judicial review, it is appropriate to have regard to the considerations giving rise to that intention.'[30] A concern for respecting considered legislative choices can be understood to be engaged here.[31]

Considerations of effective and efficient public administration and decisional accuracy can also be relevant: 'Appellate bodies may be better or equally well equipped to handle disputes of fact than a court operating the judicial review mechanisms [and may be] prepared and able to re-hear evidence and witnesses and determine questions of fact [and so] may be a better check on inadequate decisions than judicial review.'[32] As Professor Craig summarises: 'The courts have been mindful not to usurp Parliament's choice where it has established a special statutory mechanism to adjudicate on a particular topic ... Specialised statutory appeal mechanisms may, in addition, be better suited to resolving complex issues of fact, and may possess expertise in the relevant area.'[33]

Consider *Harelkin v University of Regina*,[34] a case in which a student was denied procedural fairness by a university committee and sought judicial review instead of pursuing an appeal before the university senate. Beetz J held that to treat the initial decision as a nullity would 'produce undesirable practical effects' leading

[28] *EMI Records (Ireland) Ltd v The Data Protection Commissioner* [2013] IESC 34 [4.8] per Clarke J. See also *Forster v Jododex Australia Pty Ltd* (1972) 127 CLR 421, 427 per Walsh J:

> ... when a special tribunal is appointed by statute to deal with matters arising under its provisions and to determine disputes concerning the granting of rights or privileges which are dependent entirely upon the statute, then as a general rule and in the absence of some special reason for intervention, the special procedures laid down by the statute should be allowed to take their course and should not be displaced by the making of declaratory orders concerning the respective rights of the parties under the statute.

[29] *R (Great Yarmouth Port Company Ltd) v Marine Management Organisation* [2013] EWHC 3052 (Admin) [53] per Hickinbottom J.

[30] *R (G) v Immigration Appeal Tribunal* [2005] 2 All ER 165; [2005] 1 WLR 1445 [20] per Lord Phillips MR.

[31] See also *The State (Abenglen Properties) v Corporation of Dublin* [1984] IR 381, 405 per Henchy J:

> ... where Parliament has provided a self-contained administrative and quasi-judicial scheme, postulating only a limited use of the courts, *certiorari* should not issue when, as in the instant case, use of the statutory procedure for the correction of error was adequate (and, indeed, more suitable) to meet the complaints on which the application for *certiorari* is grounded.

[32] Clive Lewis, 'The Exhaustion of Alternative Remedies in Administrative Law' (1992) 51 *Cambridge Law Journal* 138, 140–141; *Norrie v Senate of the University of Auckland* [1984] 1 NZLR 129, 136, 141 and 148; *R v East Berkshire Health Authority, ex parte Walsh* [1985] QB 152, 168; *O'Donnell v Tipperary (South Riding) County Council* [2005] 2 IR 483, 489; *R (Great Yarmouth Port Company Ltd) v Marine Management Organisation* (n 29) [53].

[33] *Administrative Law*, 8th edn (Sweet and Maxwell, London, 2016), 872.

[34] [1979] 2 SCR 561. See also *Reid v Rowley* [1977] 2 NZLR 472.

to 'inconvenient and impractical results'.[35] Having considered the 'procedure on the appeal, the composition of the senate committee, its powers and the manner in which they were probably to be exercised' as well as 'the burden of a previous finding, expeditiousness and cost',[36] Beetz J concluded that the student's rights could be vindicated by an internal appeal: 'There is thus no jurisdictional lacuna in the senate committee which could have prevented it from giving full justice to appellant':[37] 'all of appellant's difficulties could have been resolved fairly, within a reasonable time and at little cost to himself and the university had he simply wanted to use all the remedies put at his disposal ... '[38] In addition, it was significant that an appeal had been provided for by 'the legislature in its wisdom': the applicant could not 'complain that his case be decided by the body whom the legislature has placed in the superior position'.[39] Concern for effective and efficient public administration and the vindication of legislative choice can be understood to have been influential in this analysis.[40]

Nonetheless, judicial concern to vindicate individual interests can be understood to be operative in this area. Faithful implementation of a statutory scheme does not inevitably trump individual interests: 'On discretion the question will be "how good is the alternative remedy?" '[41] For it is important to note that the principle relates to the exhaustion of remedies that are effective or adequate to address whatever errors were committed in the initial adjudication—one cannot reasonably insist that individuals seek statutory remedies which are not 'equally convenient and effective' to judicial review remedies;[42] the existence of an alternative remedy does not 'automatically exclude' judicial review.[43] Thus in *Leech v Deputy Governor of Parkhurst Prison*[44] the fact that two prisoners who wished to challenge a disciplinary finding made against them by the prison authorities could appeal against the punishment imposed but not against the underlying determination

[35] *Harelkin v University of Regina* (n 34) 585. See also *Volochay v College of Massage Therapists of Ontario* 2012 ONCA 541.

[36] *Harelkin v University of Regina* (n 34) 588.

[37] Ibid, 590.

[38] Ibid, 593.

[39] Ibid, 592.

[40] See also *R v Secretary of State for the Home Department, ex parte Swati* [1986] 1 WLR 477; *R v Birmingham City Council, ex parte Ferrero Ltd* [1993] 1 All ER 530; *R (Davies) v Financial Services Authority* (n 27); *R (C) v Financial Services Authority* (n 27). In dissent, at 613, Dickson J assigned different weight to the competing considerations: 'A defect in natural justice, on the part of the council, on the question of examinations is not, in my view, capable of being cured by the senate subsequently complying with the principles of natural justice. By statute, the appellant is entitled to fairness in both the scholarly forum of council, and in the lay forum of senate.'

[41] *Wislang v Medical Practitioners Disciplinary Committee* [1974] 1 NZLR 29, 44 per Speight J. See also *McGoldrick v An Bord Pleanála* [1997] 1 IR 497, 509.

[42] *R v Essex County Council, ex parte EB* [1997] ELR 327, 329 per McCullough J. See also *Ex parte Waldron* [1985] 3 WLR 1090, 1108; *P & F Sharpe Ltd v Dublin City and County Manager* [1989] IR 701, 721; *R v Falmouth and Truro Port Health Authority, ex parte South West Water* [2000] EWCA Civ 96; [2001] QB 445, 473; *Carr v Minister for Education and Science* [2001] 2 ILRM 272, 288.

[43] *Doherty v South Dublin County Council (No. 2)* [2007] IEHC 4; [2007] 2 IR 696, 724 per Charleton J.

[44] [1988] AC 533.

of their guilt mitigated in favour of permitting them to challenge the determination of guilt by way of judicial review. Lack of expedition in the appeal procedures was, meanwhile, the critical factor in granting the remedies sought in *R v Chief Constable of the Merseyside Police, ex parte Calveley*.[45] Put another way, effective and efficient public administration would not have been inhibited by permitting applications for judicial review to succeed in these circumstances. Similarly, in *Tomlinson v Criminal Injuries Compensation Tribunal*, the fact that the applicant could have appealed to a three-member panel of the Tribunal from an adverse decision of a single member did not bar her application for judicial review, in part because the single member had followed a settled internal policy and the outcome of the appeal (aside from the time and expense involved) would have been inevitable.[46] Moreover, it has been suggested that if requiring an applicant to exhaust alternative remedies would have deleterious effects on matters such as reputation and employment prospects, these effects on individual interests should also be taken into account in determining whether relief should be granted.[47] In these ways, individual self-realisation can be understood to exert a significant gravitational pull in respect of the exhaustion principle.

6.3 Collateral Attack

Administrative action is valid and binding until set aside by a competent court:[48] '[n]ullity does not automatically follow from jurisdictional error, and when it does follow, its effects can vary.'[49] As an Irish judge wisely said, '[i]t is usual to say that an ultra vires decision is void and a nullity but it is clear that it is wrong to conclude that such decisions are completely devoid of legal consequences.'[50] In dealing with the grant of remedies in respect of unlawful administrative action:

> ... though language like 'mandatory,' 'directory,' 'void, 'voidable,' 'nullity' and so forth may be helpful in argument, it may be misleading in effect if relied on to show that the courts, in deciding the consequences of a defect in the exercise of

45 [1986] QB 424.
46 [2005] IESC 1; [2005] 1 ILRM 394.
47 *Fraser v State Services Commission* [1984] 1 NZLR 116, 121.
48 *Chuck v Cremer* (1846) Cooper temp. Cottenham 205, 338; *Isaacs v Robertson* [1985] AC 97, 101.
49 Mark Aronson, Matthew Groves and Greg Weeks, *Judicial Review of Administrative Action and Governmental Liability* 6th edn (Thomson Reuters, Sydney, 2017) [10.90]. What will matter, Dixon J once observed, is (unless the administrative action in question is flagrantly invalid) the 'result of the construction placed upon a statute ...' *Posner v Collector for Inter-State Destitute Persons (Vict)* (1946) 74 CLR 461, 483.
50 *O'Keeffe v An Bord Pleanála* [1993] 1 IR 39 at 49 per Costello J. See also *Residual Assco Group Ltd v Spalvins* [2000] HCA 33; (2000) 202 CLR 629, 657 per Kirby J: 'illogicalities abound when courts are asked to take the doctrine of nullification to its extreme conclusion' and generally, *R (T) v Chief Constable of Greater Manchester Police* [2014] UKSC 35; [2015] AC 49 [156].

> power, are necessarily bound to fit the facts of a particular case and a developing chain of events into rigid legal categories or to stretch or cramp them on a bed of Procrustes invented by lawyers for the purposes of convenient exposition.[51]

Considerations of respect for legislative choice can be understood to support the principle that administrative action is lawful until declared otherwise: it is in the 'public interest' that laws need 'to be enforced'.[52] Generally, an individual cannot wait in the weeds until, say, prosecuted for breach of a regulatory requirement and then emerge to argue that the requirement is unenforceable because it was unlawful (and the individual thus innocent). This is a collateral attack on the decision, a challenge by indirect means; the courts do not look favourably on such maneouvres.

In cases where time limits or procedural restrictions have been imposed on access to judicial review, permitting collateral attacks would frustrate 'the legislature's decision not to confer the power to hear an appeal from the administrative order on the court responsible for hearing the charge'.[53] So in *R v Wicks*,[54] the existence of 'an elaborate statutory code, with detailed provisions regarding appeals' was fatal to an attempted collateral challenge.[55] Effective and efficient public administration can also be understood to be operative, in that the rules in this area can ensure that an expert decision-maker is not bypassed by means of a collateral challenge;[56] that courts or tribunals poorly equipped for the task are not required to entertain challenges to the legality, rationality or procedural propriety of the application of complex regulatory schemes[57] and that procedural requirements designed (sometimes by elected representatives) to protect administrative decision-makers are not circumvented.[58]

Nevertheless, concerns for the protection of individual interests can be understood to support the availability of collateral attack in some instances. In *Boddington*

[51] *London and Clydeside Estates Ltd v Aberdeen District Council* [1980] 1 WLR 182, 190 per Lord Hailsham. See similarly *Minister for Immigration and Multicultural Affairs v Bhardwaj* [2002] HCA 11; (2002) 209 CLR 597, 613 per Gaudron and Gummow JJ:

> To categorise decisions [as 'void', 'voidable', 'invalid', 'vitiated' or, even, as 'nullities'] tends to ignore the fact that the real issue is whether the rights and liabilities of the individual to whom the decision relates are as specified in that decision. And, perhaps more importantly, it overlooks the fact that an administrative decision has only such force and effect as is given to it by the law pursuant to which it was made.

See also *R (Privacy International) v Investigatory Powers Tribunal* [2019] UKSC 22; [2019] 2 WLR 1219 [129].

[52] *Percy v Hall* [1997] QB 924, 947 per Simon Brown LJ. See e.g. *R v Bird* 2019 SCC 7; [2019] 1 SCR 409 [38].

[53] *R v Consolidated Maybrun Mines Ltd* [1998] 1 SCR 706 [24].

[54] [1998] AC 92.

[55] Ibid, 109. See also *Krulow v Glamorgan Spring Bay Council* (2013) 306 ALR 315 [173], [175].

[56] See e.g. *R v Bird* (n 52).

[57] See e.g. *Jacobs v OneSteel Manufacturing Pty Ltd* (2006) 93 SASR 568.

[58] See Chapter 6.1.

v British Transport Police, a case involving a rail passenger who wished to contest the validity of a bye-law prohibiting smoking, the House of Lords permitted him to raise the invalidity of the bye-law as a defence to a criminal prosecution: 'It would be a fundamental departure from the rule of law if an individual were liable to conviction for contravention of some rule which is itself liable to be set aside by a court as unlawful.'[59] Where individual interests are at stake, a court considering whether to permit a collateral challenge may take into account whether *effective* alternative means of contesting the lawfulness of the underlying decision are available[60]—and in a case such as *Boddington* it would have been entirely unrealistic to expect Mr Boddington to bear himself, at considerable personal expense, the burden of challenging a bye-law that applied to the world at large. To hold otherwise would have been to significantly curb his autonomy and compromise the value of individual self-realisation.

Lastly, in some limited circumstances, effective and efficient public administration will not necessarily be undermined at all by permitting judicial review proceedings, because flagrant invalidity has been alleged:[61] the point here can be understood to be that it would be better for all concerned were manifest irregularities cured by some judicial process, if not judicial review.

6.4 Exclusion of Review

The extent to which legislatures can exclude judicial review of administrative action, typically by means of a privative clause—a statutory provision which seeks to oust the jurisdiction of the superior courts—can be understood in terms of administrative law values.

The classic case remains *Anisminic v Foreign Compensation Commission*.[62] Here, section 4(4) of the Foreign Compensation Act 1950 provided: 'The determination by the commission of any application made to them under this Act shall not be called into question in any court of law.' At issue was whether the Commission's interpretation of its governing statutory instrument could be challenged on judicial review (albeit that *Anisminic* began as an action for a declaration). On its face, the clause would appear to bar judicial oversight. But, as Lord Pearce explained, the consequences of accepting this interpretation would be to immunise

[59] [1999] 2 AC 143, 154 per Lord Irvine of Lairg, LC. See similarly *R v Bird* (n 52) (collateral attack of a residency requirement imposed as a condition on release by parole authorities). See also *Wandsworth London Borough Council v Winder* [1985] AC 461.

[60] See e.g. *R v Bird* (n 52).

[61] See e.g. *R v Ousley* (1997) 192 CLR 69; *Dún Laoghaire Rathdown County Council v West Wood Club* (n 21).

[62] [1969] 2 AC 147. The decision in *R (Privacy International) v Investigatory Powers Tribunal)* (n 51) is a pretender to *Anisminic's* throne but the analysis there largely tracks the analysis in *Anisminic*, albeit that the reasoning in the more recent case is not quite as formalistic.

determinations tainted by fraud or reached after egregious breaches of natural justice: 'A more reasonable and logical construction is that by "determination" Parliament meant a real determination, not a purported determination.'[63] A determination that was *ultra vires* would be a nullity, a 'determination', and no 'form of words limiting the jurisdiction of the court has been held to protect a nullity'.[64] A privative clause could protect only intra-jurisdictional errors arising from 'decisions given within the field of operation entrusted to the tribunal'.[65]

This formalistic reasoning—an *ultra vires* determination is, as a matter of logic, no determination at all and so not protected by the privative clause[66]—can be understood in terms of respect for legislative choice, judicial solicitude for individual interests and the preservation of the courts' distinct task of assessing the lawfulness of administrative action.[67] First, giving effect to the considered choice of the elected representatives is not straightforward, because privative clauses create internal contradictions in statutes.[68] On the one hand, a statute sets out the boundaries of a decision-maker's authority. On the other hand, a privative clause would seem to give the decision-maker unlimited authority to redraw these boundaries. Such an internal contradiction calls for 'a process of reconciliation' to give effect to the 'whole legislative instrument'.[69] Put another way, faithful implementation of the statutory scheme does not permit a judge to choose, exclusively, between either

[63] *Anisminic v Foreign Compensation Commission* (n 62).

[64] Ibid, 170 per Lord Reid.

[65] Ibid, 207 per Lord Wilberforce.

[66] See also *Plaintiff S157/2002 v Commonwealth of Australia* (2003) 211 CLR 531.

[67] A concern for effective and efficient public administration might be relevant too, but tends to be handily dismissed by judges. Lord Atkin's dictum is representative: 'Finality is a good thing, but justice is a better.' *Ras Behari Lal v King-Emperor* (1933) 60 IA 354, 361. See similarly *R (Privacy International) v Investigatory Powers Tribunal* (n 51) [167] per Lord Lloyd-Jones:

> [T]here is here a special allocation of judicial responsibility to the [Investigatory Powers Tribunal] in the national security context ... Similarly, the IPT's rules and procedures create a 'bespoke' system particularly well suited to the adjudication of controversial issues in the context of national security and directed to protecting the public interest. Furthermore, there can be no doubt as to the outstanding judicial quality of the members of the IPT. However, the exclusion of the review jurisdiction of the High Court in cases of error of law, if achievable at all, would require a provision of much greater clarity making abundantly clear that that was what it sought to achieve.

[68] David Dyzenhaus, 'Disobeying Parliament? Privative Clauses and the Rule of Law' in Richard Bauman and Tsvi Kahana eds, *The Least Examined Branch: The Role of Legislatures in the Constitutional State* (Cambridge University Press, Cambridge, 2006).

[69] *R v Hickman; ex parte Fox and Clinton* (1945) 70 CLR 598, 617 per Dixon J. See e.g. *Crevier v AG (Québec)* [1981] 2 SCR 220; *Kirk v Industrial Relations Commission (NSW)* [2010] HCA 1; (2010) 239 CLR 531. But see also the criticism of the 'tortuous path of statutory construction and reconciliation' followed by Dixon J in *Hickman* in *Federal Commissioner of Taxation v Futuris Corporation Ltd* [2008] HCA 32; (2008) 237 CLR 146, 167 per Gummow, Hayne, Heydon and Crennan JJ and the dissent of Lord Wilson in *R (Privacy International) v Investigatory Powers Tribunal* (n 51), a case in which the majority judges (Lord Carnwath and Lord Lloyd-Jones) can be said to have and one of the dissenting judges (Lord Sumption) in his own words followed the path of reconciliation (see e.g. [110] (Lord Carnwath), [166] (Lord Lloyd-Jones) and [211] (Lord Sumption)).

giving full effect to the privative clause or the other statutory provisions setting limits on the bounds of the decision-maker's authority.

Second, giving full effect to a privative clause would 'deprive the citizen of access to the courts'.[70] At the very least, '[b]ecause it is fundamental to the rule of law that persons affected by administrative decisions should have access to the courts to challenge those decisions, privative clauses are strictly construed'.[71] Furthermore, in Ireland, one reason for doubting the validity of such clauses is that they deprive individuals of their constitutionally protected right of access to the courts.[72]

Third, given that '[j]udicial review is the common law means by which the courts hold ... officials to account',[73] giving full effect to a privative clause would raise concerns about maintaining the distinct roles of courts and administrative decision-makers: 'if a tribunal goes wrong in law', it can in principle be corrected by the courts.[74] Such considerations are relevant in jurisdictions with constitutional provisions which have been interpreted as entrenching a guaranteed minimum of judicial review.[75] Constitutional concerns arise even in jurisdictions without a written, entrenched constitutional document, however. As McGrath J commented in *Tannadyce Investments Ltd v Commissioner of Inland Revenue*: 'Statutes limiting recourse to judicial review to challenge statutory decisions ... raise issues of constitutional concern. This concern is reflected in the presumption of the courts, when interpreting such legislation, that it was not Parliament's purpose to allow decision

[70] *Public Service Association (SA) v Federated Clerks' Union* (1991) 173 CLR 132, 160 per Dawson and Gaudron JJ.

[71] *Minister for Immigration and Multicultural Affairs v Bhardwaj* (n 51) 614 per Gaudron and Gummow JJ.

[72] *Macauley v Minister for Posts and Telegraphs* [1966] IR 345, 358 per Kenny J. See generally *Dunmanus Bay Mussels Ltd v Aquaculture Licences Appeals Board* [2014] 1 IR 403. On the other reason for doubt, see n 75.

[73] *Tannadyce Investments Ltd v Commissioner of Inland Revenue* [2011] NZSC 158; [2012] 2 NZLR 153, 160 per McGrath J. See further HRW Wade, *Constitutional Fundamentals* (Stevens & Sons, London, 1980), 82: 'The judges appreciate, much more than does Parliament, that to exempt any public authority from judicial control is to give it dictatorial power, and this is so fundamentally objectionable that Parliament cannot really intend it.'

[74] *Tehrani v Rostron* [1972] 1 QB 182, 187 per Lord Denning MR. On one view, the very effectiveness of statute depends on the availability of judicial review:

> If the meaning of statutory text is not controlled by such a judicial authority, it would at length be degraded to nothing more than a matter of opinion. Its scope and content would become muddied and unclear. Public bodies would not, by means of the judicial review jurisdiction, be kept within the confines of their powers prescribed by statute. The very effectiveness of statute law, Parliament's law, requires that none of these things happen. Accordingly, as it seems to me, the need for such an authoritative judicial source cannot be dispensed with by Parliament. This is not a denial of legislative sovereignty, but an affirmation of it: as is the old rule that Parliament cannot bind itself. The old rule means that successive Parliaments are always free to make what laws they choose; that is one condition of Parliament's sovereignty. The requirement of an authoritative judicial source for the interpretation of law means that Parliament's statutes are always effective; that is another.

R (Cart) v Upper Tribunal [2009] EWHC 3052 (Admin) [38] per Laws LJ.

[75] Cf *Crevier v AG (Québec)* (n 69); *Tormey v Attorney General* [1985] IR 289; *Kirk v Industrial Relations Commission (NSW)* (n 69).

makers power conclusively to determine any question of law'.[76] This can be understood as supported by a concern to ensure that courts maintain their decisional autonomy on issues of law: 'the rule of construction which protects ordinary rights to invoke the courts' jurisdiction for the determination of other legal rights and duties is an important adjunct of the separation of powers'.[77]

It has often been said that subject to constitutional limitations a legislature can, in principle, oust the jurisdiction of the courts.[78] But there is a 'strong' presumption against the ouster of judicial review.[79] As a result, '[i]t is a principle not by any means to be whittled down that the subject's recourse to Her Majesty's courts for the determination of his rights is not to be excluded except by clear words'.[80] Examples of successful legislative ouster of judicial review are far from abundant, which suggests that the threshold of 'express provision'[81] is, in reality, insurmountable.[82] In principle, a 'sufficiently clear and all-embracing ouster clause' might achieve this result, but 'it would be a strange thing for Parliament to intend, and although conceptually possible, it has never been done'.[83] This judicial 'hostility'[84] is unsurprising, when understood in terms of the values of individual self-realisation, good administration, electoral legitimacy and decisional autonomy, given the internal contradictions in statutes created by privative clauses and the impact that giving full effect to such a clause would have on individual interests and the courts' reviewing role.

Yet common law courts have tended to attempt to give some effect to privative clauses. For instance, legislation providing that an administrative decision shall be final and conclusive does not oust judicial review; such clauses are, rather, interpreted as excluding the possibility of an appeal.[85] In Canada, privative clauses have been treated as an indication that courts ought to defer to administrative

[76] *Tannadyce Investments Ltd v Commissioner of Inland Revenue* (n 73) 160–161.

[77] TRS Allan, *Law, Liberty and Justice* (Hart, Oxford, 1993), 65.

[78] See e.g. *Clancy v Butchers' Shop Employees Union* (1904) 1 CLR 181, 204.

[79] *Ramsay v Wellington District Court* [2006] NZAR 136, 142 per McGrath J.

[80] *Pyx Granite Estates Ltd v Ministry of Housing and Local Government* [1960] AC 260, 286 per Lord Simonds. See e.g. *R (Ignaoua) v Home Secretary* [2013] EWCA Civ 1498; [2014] 1 WLR 651.

[81] *R (Woolas) v Parliamentary Election Court* [2012] QB 1 [47].

[82] For example, the clause in *R v Cheltenham Comrs* (1841) 1 QB 467 was held to be ineffective to exclude judicial review even though it was said to be difficult 'to think of a statutory ouster clause in clearer terms'. *R (Privacy International) v Investigatory Powers Tribunal* (n 51) [35] per Lord Carnwath. The statute provided:

> That no order, verdict, rate, assessment, judgment, conviction, or other proceeding touching or concerning any of the matters aforesaid, or touching or concerning any offence against this Act, or any by-law or order to be made in pursuance thereof, shall be quashed or vacated for want of form only, or be removed or removable by certiorari, or any other writ or process whatsoever, into any of His Majesty's Courts of Record at Westminster; any law or statute to the contrary thereof in anywise notwithstanding.

[83] *R (Privacy International) v Investigatory Powers Tribunal* (n 51) [210] per Lord Sumption.

[84] Aronson, Groves and Weeks (n 49) [18.10].

[85] *R v Medical Appeal Tribunal, ex parte Gilmore* [1957] 1 QB 574, 583 per Denning LJ. See also *State (McCarthy) v O'Donnell* [1945] IR 126, 142; *Hockey v Yelland* (1984) 157 CLR 124, 130.

decision-makers,[86] whilst in Australia such clauses have been held to be capable of restricting judicial review of non-jurisdictional error, albeit that constitutional considerations relating to judicial review in Australia were central to that conclusion.[87] Such decisions can be understood as striking a balance between respecting legislative choice to limit judicial oversight and the considerations that militate against giving full effect to privative clauses—none of the values was treated as having absolute priority over the others but rather a 'détente'[88] is achieved.

Where the judicial review jurisdiction of the courts *has been* successfully ousted by statute, one finds more than a simple clause with privative language: the legislature has provided a particular channel for oversight of the legality, rationality and procedural fairness of administrative action. Ousting the jurisdiction of the courts is one thing, channeling it quite another; and the courts 'recognise the constitutional propriety' of measures which limit judicial review without excluding it altogether.[89] This phenomenon can, again, be understood in terms of administrative law values. A useful example is provided by the provisions considered in *Smith v East Elloe Rural District Council*.[90] These required individuals who wished to contest compulsory purchase orders to apply to the High Court within six weeks of receiving notice of the order, failing which the order 'shall not . . . be questioned in any legal proceedings whatsoever'.[91] This language was held to oust even an allegation that an order had been made in bad faith, though Viscount Simonds observed that the ouster could be justified on the basis of good administration, or 'administrative convenience' as Lord Reid put it in dissent[92] and partially on the ground that those affected could always sue the malicious officials personally for damages[93]—that is, an alternative mechanism existed for vindicating the individual interests at issue.[94] It was important however that there was, in Lord Radcliffe's words 'a complete statutory code for regulating the extent to which, and the conditions under which courts of law might be resorted to for the purpose of questioning, the validity of

[86] See especially, *Pushpanathan v Canada (Minister of Citizenship and Immigration)* [1998] 1 SCR 982 (but note that in *Canada (Citizenship and Immigration) v Vavilov* 2019 SCC 65 [24] privative clauses were not treated as relevant as any delegation of decision-making authority is sufficient to trigger a presumption of deferential review).

[87] *Kirk v Industrial Relations Commission (NSW)* (n 69).

[88] *Probuild Constructions (Aust) Pty Ltd v Shade Systems Pty Ltd* [2018] HCA 4 [84] per Edelman J.

[89] *Cooper v Attorney-General* [1996] 3 NZLR 480, 494 per Baragwanath J.

[90] [1956] AC 736. See also *R v Environment Secretary, ex parte Ostler* [1977] QB 122, 135.

[91] Acquisition of Land (Authorisation Procedure) Act 1946, Schedule I.

[92] *Smith v East Elloe Rural District Council* (n 90) 760, by ensuring that extant orders were not subject to the risk of legal action within the general limitation period.

[93] Ibid, 752.

[94] See e.g. the intermediate appellate decisions in *R (Privacy International) v Foreign and Commonwealth Secretary* [2018] 1 WLR 257; *H v Refugee and Protection Officer* [2018] NZCA 188 though note that on both occasions the apex courts took a different view: *R (Privacy International) v Investigatory Powers Tribunal* (n 51) and [2019] NZSC 13. See also *O'Toole v Charles David Pty Ltd* (1990) 96 ALR 1, 39–40 per Deane, Gaudron and McHugh JJ, though dealing primarily with an issue relating to the scope of the legislative power of the Commonwealth Parliament.

a compulsory purchase order within the protection of the Act'.[95] To put *Smith* in terms of administrative law values, neither the distinct role of the courts nor individual interests were obliterated by giving effect to the privative clause. Where judicial review is channelled rather than excluded, concerns about the privative effect of clauses ousting the jurisdiction of the superior courts can be assuaged.

The important decision of the United Kingdom Supreme Court in *R (Cart) v Upper Tribunal*[96] is to similar effect and can, again, be understood in terms of administrative law values. Under the regime created by the Tribunals, Courts and Enforcement Act 2007, an individual may appeal certain administrative decisions to a First-tier Tribunal and thence to the Upper Tribunal. Sometimes, however, the Upper Tribunal will refuse to grant permission to appeal. If the Upper Tribunal's refusal is challenged, what criteria should a reviewing court apply in determining whether or not to grant a judicial-review remedy? Baroness Hale of Richmond put the point bluntly: 'We all make mistakes . . . The question is, what machinery is necessary and proportionate to keep such mistakes to a minimum?'[97]

Several means of resolving this issue were proposed. First, the courts could carry on as before and review refusals for compliance with the general principles of administrative law. Yet this ran into a fundamental objection: the 'very fact' that Parliament had prescribed restrictive criteria for granting leave to appeal from the Upper Tribunal to the Court of Appeal 'destroys any possibility of an absolutist argument to the effect that the rule of law requires post-*Anisminic* unrestricted judicial review over all unappealable decisions of courts or tribunals of limited jurisdiction to ensure that they are not permitted, unsupervised by the higher courts, to commit errors of law'.[98] In short, the 'status, nature and role' accorded to the Upper Tribunal by Parliament had to be taken into account.[99] To this concern for the faithful implementation of the statutory design could be added one of effective and efficient public administration: the tribunal structure gave 'several occasions' to individuals to scrutinise an adverse decision, which reduced the need for vigorous judicial oversight;[100] and opening the judicial review sluice gates would not be wise: 'floodgates arguments . . . cannot be ignored'.[101] Second, the courts could limit the grounds of review by reviving the distinction between jurisdictional errors (which would be reviewable) and non-jurisdictional errors (which would not be reviewable even in egregious cases). Concerns for the protection of

95 *Smith v East Elloe Rural District Council* (n 90) 768. See also *Parker v Silver Fern Farms Ltd* [2011] NZCA 564; [2012] 1 NZLR 256, where an appeal was broad enough to encompass alleged breaches of procedural fairness.

96 [2011] UKSC 28; [2012] 1 AC 663.

97 Ibid, [38]. See generally Mark Elliott and Robert Thomas, 'Tribunal Justice, *Cart* and Proportionate Dispute Resolution' (2012) 71 *Cambridge Law Journal* 297.

98 *R (Cart) v Upper Tribunal* (n 96) [99] per Lord Brown of Eaton-under-Heywood.

99 Ibid, [123] per Lord Dyson.

100 Ibid, [123] per Lord Dyson.

101 Ibid, [126] per Lord Dyson.

individual interests and decisional accuracy can be understood to have counselled against this, however, because it left open the possibility 'that serious errors of law affecting large numbers of people will go uncorrected'.[102]

Third, the courts could adopt a set of limiting criteria, applying 'by analogy' the statutory criteria for permission to appeal from the Upper Tribunal to the Court of Appeal.[103] It was on this solution that the Supreme Court fastened, repeatedly invoking institutional considerations, most often in the guise of proportionality,[104] but in tandem with what can be understood as concerns for giving effect to the considered choice of elected representatives:

> Where statute provides a structure under which a superior court or tribunal reviews decisions of an inferior court or tribunal, common law judicial review should be restricted so as to ensure, in the interest of making the best use of judicial resources, that this does not result in a duplication of judicial process that cannot be justified by the demands of the rule of law.[105]

This approach could also be said to safeguard both effective and efficient public administration—by resolving 'important point[s] of principle affecting large numbers of similar claims'—and the protection of individual interests—by taking account of the 'compelling reasons presented by the extremity of the consequences for the individual'.[106]

In summary, although courts repeat the proposition that sufficiently clear statutory language is capable of ousting judicial review, the cases demonstrate that courts will either read down privative clauses (in a process of statutory construction which can be understood as striking a balance between administrative law values) or will only hold privative clauses to be effective if the relevant statutory scheme provides other means of individual redress and assessing the lawfulness of administrative action (ensuring, again, that respect for legislative choice does not obliterate the protection of individual interests and the preservation of the courts' distinct, reviewing role). Administrative law values—individual self-realisation, good administration, electoral legitimacy and decisional autonomy—can be understood to animate judicial analysis of privative clauses.

[102] Ibid, [44] (Baroness Hale of Richmond and [110] (Lord Dyson).

[103] Ibid, [129] (Lord Dyson). See Tribunals, Courts and Enforcement Act 2007, s 13(6), which provides that permission shall not be granted unless: '(a) the proposed appeal would raise some important point of principle or practice; or (b) there is some other compelling reasons for the relevant appellate court to hear the appeal'.

[104] See e.g. Ibid, [41] per Baroness Hale of Richmond: 'There must be a limit to the resources which the legal system can devote to the task of trying to get the decision right in any individual case' and also [104] (Lord Clarke of Stone-cum-Ebony).

[105] Ibid, [89].

[106] Ibid, [57] per Baroness Hale of Richmond. See further Joanna Bell, 'Rethinking the story of *Cart v Upper Tribunal* and its Implications for Administrative Law' (2019) 39 *Oxford Journal of Legal Studies* 74.

6.5 Ripeness and Prematurity

Article III of the US Constitution captures quite well the traditional nature of judicial power in common law systems: the authority to resolve 'cases and controversies'. Offering general opinions on the law, divorced from the context of a particular set of factual circumstances, is largely alien to common lawyers: 'the jurisdiction of the court is not to declare the law generally or to give advisory opinions; it is confined to declaring contested legal rights, subsisting or future, of the parties represented in the litigation before it and not those of anyone else.'[107] In the common law tradition, judicial decisions 'have the effect of resolving some controversy which affects or may affect the rights of the parties', such that if a given judicial decision 'will have no practical effect on such rights, the court will decline to decide the case'.[108] Judicial review is '*designed to remedy real and substantial injustice* rather than to give satisfaction, however legitimate';[109] a court is not 'a sort of debating society or deliberative assembly for the discussion of abstract issues'.[110] As Lord Atkin once put it, a court answering a hypothetical question 'would not be deciding an existing [issue] between the parties who are before it, but would merely be expressing its view on a legal conundrum which the appellants hope to get decided in their favour without in any way affecting the position between the parties'.[111] In short, common law courts do not exist to 'answer purely abstract questions in anticipation of an actual controversy'.[112]

Institutional considerations have been said to underlie this judicial reluctance: the diversion of scarce judicial resources[113] and the lack of an adversarial procedure (so central to the common law) to accurately identify the relevant facts.[114] But judicial reluctance to opine on hypothetical questions can also be understood in terms of administrative law values. For instance, the risk of trespassing in the political domain[115] evokes a need for judges to respect the decisional autonomy of other branches of government. In particular, it is interesting that there is judicial concern to address only concrete cases involving genuine individual interests. In this area, the courts can be understood to

[107] *Gouriet v Union of Post Office Workers* [1978] AC 435, 501 per Lord Diplock. Cf the constitutional and statutory mechanisms made available in various jurisdictions to provide for reference procedures. See the discussion of Canada and the states of the United States in Paul Daly ed, *Apex Courts and the Common Law* (University of Toronto Press, Toronto, 2019) and see also Carissima Mathen, *Courts without Cases: The Law and Politics of Advisory Opinions* (Hart, Oxford, 2019).

[108] *Borowski v Canada (Attorney General)* [1989] 1 SCR 342, 353.

[109] *R v Aston University Senate, ex parte Roffey* [1969] 2 QB 538, 551 per Donaldson J. Emphasis added.

[110] *Riordan v Government of Ireland* [2009] IESC 44; [2009] 3 IR 745, 764 per Murray CJ.

[111] *Sun Life Assurance Co of Canada v Jervis* [1944] AC 111, 113.

[112] *New Zealand Insurance Co Ltd v Prudential Assurance Co Ltd* [1976] 1 NZLR 84, 85 per McCarthy P.

[113] *R (Reilly) v Work and Pensions Secretary* [2013] UKSC 68; [2014] AC 4653.

[114] See e.g. *Attorney-General v Refugee Council of New Zealand Inc* [2003] 2 NZLR 577, 595; *R (Noor Khan) v Foreign Secretary* [2012] EWHC 3728 (Admin).

[115] *R (Burke) v General Medical Council* [2005] EWCA Civ 1003; [2006] QB 273.

have long followed an approach in which individual interests predominate. Contemporary courts have taken a more generous view of the class of individual interests that will justify recourse to judicial review, making a dispute a concrete case or controversy:[116] 'In a context where there is a statutory procedure involving preliminary decisions leading to a final decision affecting *legal rights*, judicial review may lie against a *preliminary* decision not affecting *legal rights*.'[117] This opening up of the availability of judicial review can be understood in terms of judicial desire to protect individual interests.[118]

Notwithstanding the preference—which can be understood in individual-centered terms—of common law courts for concrete cases and controversies, the courts have an undoubted residual discretion to opine on hypothetical questions.[119] Concerns for the accurate, effective and efficient public administration of statutory schemes can be understood as influencing judicial decisions to decide cases that have become moot[120] or cases involving an individual who seeks guidance on the lawfulness of future conduct:[121]

> The discretion to hear disputes, even in the area of public law, must, however, be exercised with caution and appeals which are academic between the parties should not be heard unless there is a good reason in the public interest for doing so, as for example (but only by way of example) when a discrete point of statutory construction arises which does not involve detailed consideration of facts

[116] See also the discussion in Chapter 3.3.1.

[117] *R v Hammersmith and Fulham London Borough Council, ex parte Burkett* [2002] UKHL 23; [2002] 1 WLR 1593 [38] per Lord Slynn of Hadley. Emphasis added. See also *Bradley v Attorney-General* [1988] 2 NZLR 454. Compare *Whale Watch Kaikoura Ltd v Transport Accident Investigation Commission* [1997] 3 NZLR 55, where mere 'opinions' contained in a report were not amenable to judicial review and see also *Australian Broadcasting Tribunal v Bond* (1990) 170 CLR 321, taking a restrictive approach to the meaning of 'decision' for the purposes of the Administrative Decisions (Judicial Review) Act 1977 (Cth), albeit that the High Court of Australia's decision left 'three significant escape hatches': Aronson, Groves and Weeks (n 49) [2.330]. See also the capacious lists in New Zealand's Judicature Amendment Act 1972, s 3.

[118] The general trend has been in favour of taking a broad view of the individual interests which would justify the exercise of the supervisory jurisdiction. See e.g. *Re Pergamon Press* [1971] Ch 388; *Martineau v Matsqui Institution Disciplinary Board (No. 2)* [1980] 1 SCR 602, 623; *MacPhartaláin v Commissioners of Public Works* [1994] 3 IR 353; *Hot Holdings Pty Ltd v Creasy* (1996) 185 CLR 149; *Royal Australasian College of Surgeons v Phipps* [1999] 3 NZLR 1; *de Burca v Wicklow County Manager* [2009] IEHC 54. See also the formulation in *Griffith University v Tang* (2005) 221 CLR 99, 130–131 per Gummow, Callinan and Heydon JJ: '[to be reviewable] the decision must itself confer, alter or otherwise affect legal rights or obligations.' But where a function is 'purely investigative' *Saraceni v Australian Securities and Investments Commission* 2013 FCAFC 42; (2013) 211 FCR 298, 313 per Jacobson and Gilmour JJ, procedural fairness obligations are much less likely to attach in the first place, pre-empting any issue as to ripeness.

[119] *R (Pretty) v Director of Public Prosecutions* [2002] 1 AC 800 [116] per Lord Hobhouse.

[120] *R (Reilly) v Work and Pensions Secretary* (n 113).

[121] See e.g. *R v Secretary of State for the Home Department, ex parte Rusbridger* [2003] UKHL 38; [2004] 1 AC 357; *R (Purdy) v Director of Public Prosecutions* [2009] UKHL 45; [2010] 1 AC 345.

and where a large number of similar cases exist or are anticipated so that the issue will most likely need to be resolved in the near future.[122]

In other words, the courts may proceed to hear a moot case where doing so will help to ensure that the relevant statutory provisions are respected by the administrative decision-maker and to settle the applicable principles for a large set of future cases. One goal here can be understood to be the accurate implementation of the statutory scheme designed by the legislature. In addition, when courts set out the law, in an authoritative judgment, this can be understood as facilitating effective and efficient public administration by removing lingering doubt about the scope of an administrative decision-maker's authority.

6.6 Standing

Standing to make a judicial review application was traditionally limited to those who could demonstrate a personal interest in the impugned decision. The rules varied depending on the remedy sought.[123] Where a mandatory order was sought, it was necessary to show 'a specific legal right to ask for the interference of the Court'.[124] Those seeking other remedies were subject to a slightly less restrictive test which nonetheless focused on the existence of a direct personal interest,[125] whilst certiorari—available to third parties[126]—had 'an element of the actio popularis'.[127]

This approach can be understood in terms of the protection of individual interests: it focuses on the existence of an individual right or interest in a decision

[122] *R v Secretary of State for the Home Department, ex parte Salem* [1999] 1 AC 450, 456–457 per Lord Slynn of Hadley. See e.g. *Pryce v Southwark London Borough Council* [2012] EWCA Civ 1572; [2013] 1 WLR 996 (a case which, though moot between the parties, was widely considered a test case involving a discrete point of law).

[123] They still do in Australia, though there has been a 'process of consolidation' in that jurisdiction. See generally Aronson, Groves and Weeks (n 49) [11.250].

[124] *R v Guardians of Lewisham* [1897] 1 QB 498, 500 per Wright J. In relation to the declaration and injunction, which had their origins in private law, a 'stricter approach' was taken. Gerard Hogan, David Gwynn Morgan and Paul Daly, *Administrative Law in Ireland* 5th edn (Roundhall, Dublin, 2019) [18–101]. See e.g. *Boyce v Paddington Borough Council* [1903] 1 Ch 109, 114.

[125] See e.g. *Australian Conservation Foundation Inc v Commonwealth of Australia* (1980) 28 ALR 257, 270 per Gibbs J.

> A person is not interested within the meaning of the rule, unless he is likely to gain some advantage, other than the satisfaction of righting a wrong, upholding a principle or winning a contest, if his action succeeds or to suffer some disadvantage, other than a sense of grievance or a debt for costs, if his action fails. A belief, however, strongly felt, that the law generally, or a particular law, should be observed, or that conduct of a particular kind should be prevented, does not suffice to give its possessor locus standi. If that were not so, the rule requiring special interest would be meaningless. Any plaintiff who felt strongly enough to bring an action could maintain it.

[126] *Australian Education Union v Fair Work Australia* (2012) 246 CLR 117, 148 per Gummow, Hayne and Bell JJ.

[127] HRW Wade, 'Unlawful Administrative Action: Void or Voidable? Part 1' (1967) 83 *Law Quarterly Review* 499, 503.

which, if made out, triggers the court's ability to intervene on behalf of the citizen who claims that he or she has been affected by unlawful administrative action. One might usefully contrast the position in the United States, where standing is restricted to those who can demonstrate a 'concrete and particularized interest' in the impugned decision,[128] such that in *Clapper v Amnesty International USA*,[129] individuals who feared they were under surveillance as part of a National Security Agency programme (the existence of which had been revealed by the media) did not have standing to challenge the legality of the programme because they could not point to any provable concrete harm they had suffered.

However, the personal interest test has for all practical purposes been supplanted by the capacious notion of public interest standing: 'All of the Commonwealth jurisdictions have relaxed the rules of standing under a uniform standing requirement.'[130] Although the different jurisdictions have varied in their enthusiasm for liberalising the standing requirement—from New Zealand at one end of the spectrum, where 'standing as a threshold issue is almost a dead letter'[131] to Australia and Ireland at the other, where the courts continue to insist on the existence of a cognisable individual interest in the decision at issue—there is general agreement across the common law world 'that a direct financial or legal interest is not now required, and that the requirement of a legal specific interest ... is no longer applicable.'[132] For many years, the courts were very wary of public-spirited litigants who professed an interest in matters of legality that affected the public in a broad way rather than identifiable individuals specifically. Litigation initiated by an individual who has no personal interest in the matter might, it was feared, lack 'the force and urgency of reality'.[133] Today, however, the legal landscape has shifted and the lie of the contemporary land was set out in evocative terms by Lord Diplock:

> It would, in my view, be a grave lacuna in our system of public law if a pressure group ... or even a single public-spirited taxpayer, were prevented by outdated technical rules of locus standi from bringing the matter to the attention of the court to vindicate the rule of law and get the unlawful conduct stopped ... It is not, in my view, a sufficient answer to say that judicial review of the actions of officers or departments of central government is unnecessary because they are accountable to Parliament for the way in which they carry out their functions. They are accountable to Parliament for what they do so far as regards efficiency and policy,

128 *Lujan v Defenders of Wildlife* 504 US 555 (1992), 560 per Scalia J.
129 568 US 398 (2013).
130 Joseph (n 2) 1225.
131 Jeffrey Jowell et al, *de Smith's Judicial Review* 8th edn (Sweet and Maxwell, London, 2016) [2–091].
132 *R v Inland Revenue Commissioners, ex parte National Federation of Self-Employed and Small Businesses Ltd* (n 3) 646 per Lord Fraser.
133 *Cahill v Sutton* [1980] IR 269, 282–283 per Henchy J.

> and of that Parliament is the only judge; they are responsible to a court of justice for the lawfulness of what they do, and of that the court is the only judge.[134]

There are a number of points to draw out of this famous passage, which can be understood in terms of administrative law values. First, there is a concern to ensure that 'unlawful conduct' can be 'stopped' by the courts—although this is expressed to be an aspect of the 'rule of law', it can be understood to be supported by a desire to ensure that the considered choices taken by elected representatives are respected by administrative decision-makers, engaging the value of electoral legitimacy. Second, there is a concern to ensure that courts and administrative decision-makers play distinct roles: it is for the courts to assess 'lawfulness' (a task much facilitated by a more liberal approach to standing), with political accountability mechanisms applying in the distinct domain of politics:[135] the value of decisional autonomy is thereby engaged. In sum, 'restrictive rules about standing are, in general, inimical to a healthy system of administrative law'.[136]

The liberal approach common law courts have taken in recent years is such that the idea can be floated 'that standing has been abolished as a restrictive principle of public law'.[137] Taking a restrictive approach to standing, which would mean 'the law regards it as preferable that an illegality should continue than that the person excluded should have access to the courts' has proved too bitter a pill to swallow.[138] The contemporary starting point is a presumption that an administrative decision should, in principle, be subject to the jurisdiction of the superior courts, at the

[134] *R v Inland Revenue Commissioners, ex parte National Federation of Self-Employed and Small Businesses Ltd* (n 3) 644. See similarly ibid, 660 per Lord Roskil: 'The appellants are, and must as a public body charged with the performance of a public duty of crucial importance be, amenable to the general law and liable to possible correction if their statutory powers are exceeded, or their statutory duties are not lawfully discharged.' See also *R v Greater London Council, ex parte Blackburn* [1976] 1 WLR 550, 559; *Finnigan v New Zealand Rugby Union Inc* [1985] 2 NZLR 159; *Canada (Attorney General) v Downtown Eastside Sex Workers United Against Violence Society* 2012 SCC 45; [2012] 2 SCR 524.

[135] See similarly *Peters v Davison* [1999] 2 NZLR 164, 188; *Finlay v Canada (Minister of Finance)* [1986] 2 SCR 607, 631.

[136] *State (Lynch) v Cooney* [1982] IR 337, 367 per Walsh J.

[137] Wade and Forsyth (n 23) 588. Cf the factors relevant to the court's decision to grant standing, as laid out in e.g. *R v Foreign Secretary, ex parte World Development Movement* [1995] 1 WLR 386, 395–396 per Rose LJ:

> [T]he importance of vindicating the rule of law . . . the importance of the issue raised . . . ; the likely absence of any other responsible challenger . . . ; the nature of the breach of duty against which relief is sought . . . ; and the prominent role of [the] applicants in giving advice, guidance and assistance with regard to [matters relevant to the statutory framework at issue].

See also *Finnigan v New Zealand Rugby Union Inc* (n 134) and, on the importance of a contextual approach, *Canada (Attorney General) v Downtown Eastside Sex Workers United Against Violence Society* (n 134) [37] per Cromwell J: 'In exercising the discretion to grant public interest standing, the court must consider three factors: (1) whether there is a serious justiciable issue raised; (2) whether the plaintiff has a real stake or a genuine interest in it; and (3) whether, in all the circumstances, the proposed suit is a reasonable and effective way to bring the issue before the courts.'

[138] Konrad Schiemann, 'Locus standi' [1990] *Public Law* 342, 342.

instance of any competent applicant.[139] As Keane CJ commented in *Mulcreevy v Minister for Environment*, it is 'not in the public interest that decisions by statutory bodies which are of at least questionable validity should wholly escape scrutiny because the person who seeks to invoke the jurisdiction of the court by way of judicial review cannot show that he is personally affected in some sense peculiar to him, by the decision'.[140]

This concern for giving effect to legislative choice by enabling courts to determine on judicial review whether an administrative decision-maker has exceeded the statutory limits set down by Parliament undoubtedly marks a shift away from an individual-centered approach to standing:

> Public law is not at base about rights, even though abuses of power may and often do invade private rights; it is about wrongs—that is to say misuses of public power; and the courts have always been alive to the fact that a person or organisation with no particular stake in the issue or the outcome may, without in any sense being a mere meddler, wish and be well placed to call the attention of the court to an apparent misuse of public power.[141]

Consistent with a concern for accurate implementation of legislative choices, the analysis will always be conducted with the contextual considerations raised by the statutory scheme in mind.[142] For instance, in *Walton v Scottish Ministers*, it was important, in determining whether an individual could litigate an environmental judicial review on behalf of an affected animal that 'the purpose of environmental law [is] that the quality of the natural environment is of legitimate concern to everyone. The osprey has no means of taking that step on its own behalf, any more than any other wild creature. If its interests are to be protected someone has to be allowed to speak up on its behalf'.[143] There, judicial solicitude for securing the

[139] On the concept of 'representational standing', see Peter Cane, 'Standing up for the Public' [1995] *Public Law* 276, 276. See e.g. *Lancefort Ltd v An Bord Pleanála (No 2)* [1997] 2 IR 270; *Great Christchurch Buildings Trust v Church Property Trustees* [2012] NZHC 3045; [2013] 2 NZLR 230, but cf *Construction Industry Federation v Dublin City Council* [2004] IEHC 37; [2005] 2 IR 496 (albeit a case where individual members of the Federation would clearly have had standing) and Michael Kirby, 'Deconstructing the Law's Hostility to Public Interest Litigation' (2011) 127 *Law Quarterly Review* 537; Matthew Groves, 'The Evolution and Reform of Standing in Australian Administrative Law' (2016) 44 *Federal Law Review* 167. See also *AXA General Insurance Ltd and others v HM Advocate and others* [2011] UKSC 46; [2012] 1 AC 868, 'A personal interest need not be shown if the individual is acting in the public interest and can genuinely say that the issue directly affects the section of the public that he seeks to represent' [63]; *Walton v Scottish Ministers* [2012] UKSC 44 [153].

[140] [2004] IESC 5; [2004] 1 IR 72, 78. See similarly *Environmental Defence Society Inc v South Pacific Aluminium Ltd (No 3)* [1981] 1 NZLR 216, 220 per Cooke J, who could 'see no reason why it must be left to individuals directly affected to undertake the burden' of challenging allegedly unlawful government action.

[141] *R v Somerset Council, ex parte Dixon* [1998] Env LR 111, 121 per Sedley J.

[142] *Access for All Alliance (Hervey Bay) Inc v Hervey Bay City Council* [2007] FCA 615; (2007) 162 FCR 313, 327–331.

[143] *Walton v Scottish Ministers* (n 139) [152] per Lord Hope.

accurate implementation of the statutory scheme can be understood to have influenced the relatively liberal approach of the court to the issue of standing.

Considerations of effective and efficient public administration may sometimes count against public interest standing, inasmuch as judicial review might be 'a distraction from the business of governing'.[144] That courts will not entertain any and all complaints about misgovernance can be understood as supported by a concern for the wise husbandry of scarce administrative resources (and judicial resources too[145]). In the context of tendering, standing—even public interest standing—is generally restricted to 'economic operators'.[146] In *Wylde v Waverley Borough Council*, a group of applicants interested in development in the respondent borough (for instance, a preservation organisation), were 'not remotely approximate to any economic operator, nor could they begin to demonstrate any interest in the procurement process which might be akin to or a proxy for status as an economic operator'.[147] The perceived danger is that allowing outsiders to challenge procurement decisions would inhibit the accurate, effective and efficient public administration of the statutory scheme; absent allegations of egregious misconduct.[148] Equally, the insistence that only those with direct interests have standing to challenge such decisions can be understood as sounding in an individual-centered approach, inasmuch as the judicial review jurisdiction is being made available to those whose autonomy interests (albeit commercial in nature) are undoubtedly engaged by the decision at issue.[149]

It has been argued[150] that the contemporary law of standing marks the displacement of an individual-centered, rights-based approach by one based on judicial vindication of the public interest. There is no doubt, as a matter of description, that the public interest features strongly in the contemporary law of standing and that there has been a significant shift away from an approach based on personal interest.[151] To suggest that standing is all about the public interest, however, goes too far. First, personal interest standing has not disappeared and continues to be applied, certainly in Australia and Ireland[152] (albeit, generally, 'generously interpreted'[153]). In Canada, one of the factors to take into account in considering

[144] Schiemann (n 138) 348–349.

[145] See generally Aronson, Groves and Weeks (n 49) chapter 11.2.

[146] *R (Chandler) v Secretary of State* [2009] EWCA Civ 1011 [77]–[78].

[147] [2017] EWHC 466 (Admin) [45].

[148] See also *Irving Shipbuilding Inc v Canada (Attorney General)* 2009 FCA 116; [2010] 2 FCR 488.

[149] A point made with great force in Joanna Bell, *The Anatomy of Administrative Law* (Hart, Oxford, 2020), chapter 6.

[150] Jason Varuhas, 'The Public Interest Conception of Public Law: Its Procedural Origins and Substantive Implications' in Bell et al eds, *Public Law Adjudication in Common Law Systems: Process and Substance* (Hart, Oxford, 2016).

[151] See especially *Finnigan v New Zealand Rugby Union Inc* (n 134).

[152] See e.g. *Onus v Alcoa of Australia Ltd* (1981) 149 CLR 27; *Finlay v Canada (Minister of Finance)* (n 135); *State (Sheehan) v Government of Ireland* [1987] IR 550; *ESB v Gormley* [1989] IR 734; *Annetts v McCann* (1990) 170 CLR 596; *Animals' Angels e V v Secretary, Department of Agriculture* [2014] FCAFC 173; (2014) 228 FCR 35; *Argos Pty Ltd v Corbell* [2014] HCA 50; (2014) 254 CLR 394.

[153] *State (Lynch) v Cooney* (n 136).

whether an individual has standing is whether the individual has a 'real stake in the proceedings or is engaged with the issues they raise'[154] and, as I have just noted, the limited standing accorded in the commercial context can be understood as being influenced by the 'rights' at issue. Second, private interest standing can, in addition, be parasitic upon the applicant's involvement in a decision-making process, even where the involvement is at the instance of the applicant: 'A person will now ordinarily be regarded as aggrieved [and entitled to standing] if they made objections or representations as part of the procedure which preceded the decision challenged and their complaint is that the decision was not properly made.'[155] It is difficult to view the concern to attach standing to an individual's participation—based, one might understand, on respect for her individual self-realisation—as sounding only in the public interest. Third, a judge considering questions of standing must have the purposes of judicial review in mind:

> What is to be regarded as sufficient interest to justify a particular applicant's bringing a particular application before the court, and thus as conferring standing, depends therefore upon the context, and in particular upon what will best serve the purposes of judicial review in that context.[156]

There is little reason to think that, in many cases, the importance of vindicating individual interests will not weigh heavily in the balance. Conversely, indeed, courts have taken a more restrictive approach to public interest standing where there are *other* potential litigants.[157] The point is that the individual interests of those intimately involved in an administrative decision will potentially be relevant to determining whether another person has standing to challenge the decision.[158] If so, the court's determination as to standing will not solely be a matter of identifying the effects on the 'public interest', but will also have to take account of individual interests. There is life yet in the allegedly obsolescent 'rights-based approach'.

[154] *Canada (Attorney General) v Downtown Eastside Sex Workers United Against Violence Society* (n 134) [43].

[155] Jowell et al (n 131) [2–069]. See also *Australian Conservation Foundation Inc v South Australia* (1989) 53 SASR 349 (though note, at 354, King CJ's emphasis on the 'threatened deprivation of . . . statutory rights' to participate in the administrative process); *Walton v Scottish Ministers* (n 139) [83]–[88].

[156] *AXA General Insurance Ltd and others v HM Advocate and others* (n 139) [170] per Lord Reed. See also *Walton v Scottish Ministers* (n 139) [152] per Lord Hope.

[157] See e.g. *Canada (Attorney General) v Downtown Eastside Sex Workers United Against Violence Society* (n 134); *Forest Ethics Association v Canada (National Energy Board)* 2014 FCA 245; *R (DSD) v Parole Board* [2018] EWHC 694 (Admin); [2019] QB 285; and, especially, *Iarnród Éireann v Ireland* [1996] 2 IR 321, 351 per Keane J: 'the nature of the constitutional challenge is such that a plaintiff will not emerge whose interests may be said to be either immediately or prospectively affected in a manner specific to him or her.'

[158] See e.g. *Canadian Council of Churches v Canada (Minister of Employment and Immigration)* [1992] 1 SCR 236. But cf. *Canada (Attorney General) v Downtown Eastside Sex Workers United Against Violence Society* (n 134) [50] per Cromwell J, specifying the need for a 'flexible, discretionary approach'.

6.7 Conclusion

This tour through the general principles relating to restrictions on remedies has been designed to demonstrate that the principles can be understood in terms of the values of individual self-realisation, good administration, electoral legitimacy and decisional autonomy. The promptness and permission requirements, the principle of exhaustion and the bar on collateral attack can be understood, straightforwardly, as sounding primarily in respect for the considered choices of elected representatives (electoral legitimacy) and the promotion of effective and efficient public administration (good administration), with their rougher edges smoothed out, however, by an appreciation of the importance of individual interests (individual self-realisation). Privative clauses are viewed with suspicion, because of their potential impact on individual interests and the decisional autonomy of the courts, but some effect is given to legislative choice, thereby striking a balance between the values. Meanwhile, the law on ripeness and prematurity and standing is marked by a variety of considerations, which operate in a complementary fashion: judicial solicitude for individual interests is important, as, however, are securing effective and efficient public administration and the accurate implementation of legislative choices. Despite the powerful suggestion that the principles in this area can and should be understood in terms of the 'public interest', individual self-realisation has significant traction in the domains traversed in this chapter. Even across a diverse range of topics, the influence of a plurality of values can be understood to be felt.

7

Scope of Judicial Review of Administrative Action

The focus of this chapter is slightly different from its predecessors. In respect of institutional structures, procedural fairness, substantive review and remedies, the law could be (relatively, albeit not always perfectly evenly) simply explained. The law relating to the scope of judicial review of administrative action, however, is somewhat unclear and has a particular tendency to be decided on a case-by-case basis.[1] Indeed, amenability to judicial review will often turn on the application of particular constitutional, statutory or regulatory provisions:[2] in Australia and Canada, for instance, there are multiple judicial review jurisdictions, at federal[3] and state/provincial/territorial level,[4] each with their own idiosyncrasies. Nonetheless, the apex courts in both Australia and Canada have striven to provide a measure of uniformity.[5]

[1] The position in Australia is particularly unclear. See Basten JA's discussion in *Chase Oyster Bar Pty Ltd v Hamo Industries Pty Ltd* [2010] NSWCA 190, (2010) 78 NSWLR 393. See also *Khuu & Lee Pty Ltd v Adelaide City Corporation* (2011) 110 SASR 235.

[2] See e.g. *University of Auckland v Tertiary Education Commission* [2004] 2 NZLR 668, discussing the Judicature Amendment Act 1972, s 4 and, in particular, the power to grant relief in respect of the 'exercise by any person of a *statutory power*'. Emphasis added. See also *Setia v Appleby College* 2013 ONCA 753; (2013) 118 OR (3d) 481, discussing a similar provision in the Canadian province of Ontario's Judicial Review Procedure Act 1990 RSO, c J 1 but also noting [21] how 'public law is to be contrasted with private law, which deals with private persons and bodies and their property and relationships. The challenge is to describe the respective domains of these two branches of law, and thus to determine whether public or private law principles and remedies govern in a particular case'. This highlights the importance of appreciating the general nature of the scope of judicial review, notwithstanding the need to focus, in any given case or jurisdiction, on the intricacies of the relevant local law.

[3] See, respectively, the Administrative Decisions (Judicial Review) Act 1977 (Cth) and the Federal Courts Act RSC 1985 c F-7.

[4] See e.g. Supreme Court Act 1970 (NSW); Judicial Review Procedure Act 1990 RSO, c J 1.

[5] See e.g. *Kirk v Industrial Court (NSW)* [2010] HCA 1; (2010) 239 CLR 531, 581:

> There is but one common law of Australia. The supervisory jurisdiction exercised by the State Supreme Courts by the grant of prerogative relief or orders in the nature of that relief is governed in fundamental respects by principles established as part of the common law of Australia. That is, the supervisory jurisdiction exercised by the State Supreme Courts is exercised according to principles that in the end are set by this Court.

See also *Highwood Congregation of Jehovah's Witnesses (Judicial Committee) v Wall* 2018 SCC 26 [13]–[23], an overview of the principles relating to the scope of judicial review with hardly a mention of provincial statutory or regulatory provisions; and, generally, on achieving coherence between the common law of judicial review and statutes providing for judicial review, *Canada (Citizenship and Immigration) v Khosa* 2009 SCC 12; [2009] 1 SCR 339.

Understanding Administrative Law in the Common Law World. Paul Daly, Oxford University Press. © Paul Daly 2021.
DOI: 10.1093/oso/9780192896919.003.0007

My argument will be that administrative law values are helpful in understanding the decided cases (although in this area, I am sure that other sets of considerations could perform equally well at that task). Again, the approach will be interpretive, rather than descriptive. As a historical or descriptive matter, it may be that the boundaries of judicial review depend upon 'changing perceptions of the judicial responsibility',[6] but my aim is to interpret, not to describe. My goal is, primarily, to provide further support for this book's central thesis—that contemporary administrative law can be understood as being structured by the values of individual self-realisation, good administration, electoral legitimacy and decisional autonomy. I will also, however, in the concluding section of this chapter, offer some suggestions as to how the law relating to scope of judicial review could be improved, further underscoring how useful it is to understand the law of judicial review of administrative action in terms of administrative law values. This concluding section will have more of a *prescriptive* then *interpretive* feel, and, as such, will link nicely to Chapter 8 (on legitimate expectation), where my focus will mostly be on prescription rather than interpretation.

As a preliminary matter, the issue of judicial review of prerogative powers ought to be addressed. This is best done at the outset, as the prerogative does not neatly fit into the framework for ascertaining the scope of judicial review. The prerogative is 'the residue of discretionary or arbitrary authority, which at any given time is left in the hands of the Crown'.[7] To what extent is it reviewable by the courts?[8] The case law on judicial review of the *existence* of prerogative power is instructive. The existence and scope of the prerogative are matters for the courts: 'the King hath no prerogative, but that which the law of the land allows him.'[9] This basic point can be understood in terms of administrative law values. First, it ensures that the courts have a distinct role to play, in determining the scope of the prerogative, which is not a matter committed to the absolute discretion of the executive.[10] Second, the importance of respecting legislative choice is also manifest. Where legislation and the prerogative overlap, the prerogative is placed in abeyance.[11] More generally, the prerogative cannot be used to frustrate the purpose of a statutory scheme.[12] It is also axiomatic that 'the King by his proclamation or other ways cannot change any

[6] Philip Joseph, *Constitutional and Administrative Law in New Zealand* 4th edn (Thomson Reuters, Wellington, 2014), 880.

[7] AV Dicey, *Introduction to the Study of the Law of the Constitution*, 10th edn (Macmillan, London, 1959), 424.

[8] Of course, the prerogative has much less traction in Australia and Ireland, where it has been superceded by those jurisdictions' written constitutions.

[9] *Case of Proclamations* (1611) 12 Co Rep 74.

[10] *R (Miller) v The Prime Minister* [2019] UKSC 41; [2020] AC 373.

[11] *Attorney General v de Keyser's Royal Hotel Ltd* [1920] AC 508, 539–540.

[12] *Laker Airways Ltd v Department of Trade* [1977] QB 643; *R v Secretary of State for the Home Department, ex parte Fire Brigades Union* [1995] 2 AC 513. See generally Robert Craig, 'Casting Aside Clanking Medieval Chains: Prerogative, Statute and Article 50 after the EU Referendum' (2016) 79 *Modern Law Review* 1041.

part of the common law, or statute law, or the customs of the realm'.[13] As the Privy Council has explained: 'The idea that the King in Council, or indeed any branch of the Executive, has power to prescribe or alter the law to be administered by Courts of law in this country is out of harmony with the principles of our Constitution.'[14] Third, the importance of protecting individual interests could be appreciated in the UK Supreme Court's conclusion in *Miller v Secretary of State for Exiting the European Union* that the prerogative in relation to foreign affairs could not be exercised so as to eliminate rights enjoyed in domestic law.[15] Put in terms of administrative law values, the point here is that prerogative power cannot be used to undo considered legislative choices; or eliminate individual interests, and the courts' role is to ensure that these things do not happen.[16]

7.1 Scoping the Scope of Judicial Review

Difficult issues arise in delimiting the scope of judicial review of administrative action. Whereas it is straightforward to justify judicial review of statutory powers, to make sure their holders stay within the limits set down by legislation,[17] the 'boundaries' of judicial review of non-statutory powers are 'uncertain'.[18] The same is true of judicial review of the exercise of contractual powers by statutory bodies, or of statutory functions that have been 'contracted out' to private entities.[19] It hardly helps that the distinction between public law and private law 'operates at different levels of discourse and serves as a medium for raising a considerable variety of issues'.[20]

It has been said that what must be identified to distinguish private matters from those public matters which are subject to judicial review 'is a feature or a

[13] *Case of Proclamations* (n 9).
[14] *The Zamora* [1916] 2 AC 77, 90.
[15] [2017] UKSC 5; [2018] AC 61.
[16] See e.g. *Hupacasath First Nation v Canada (Foreign Affairs and International Trade Canada)* 2015 FCA 4; 379 DLR (4th) 737. It is true that both the executive which exercises a prerogative power and the legislature which passed legislation blocking the exercise of a prerogative power in a particular way (or eliminating it altogether) can claim an electoral mandate, but in the case of any conflict the electoral legitimacy of the legislature trumps that of the executive in the Westminster system.
[17] See e.g. *Dunsmuir v New Brunswick* 2008 SCC 9, 211 per Bastarache and LeBel JJ: 'All decision-making powers have legal limits, derived from the enabling statute itself, the common or civil law or [constitutional principles]. Judicial review is the means by which the courts supervise those who exercise statutory powers, to ensure that they do not overstep their legal authority.'
See also *Ainsworth v Criminal Justice Commission* (1992) 175 CLR 564.
[18] William Wade and Christopher Forsyth, *Administrative Law*, 11th edn (Oxford University Press, Oxford, 2014), 532.
[19] See e.g. Paul Craig, *Administrative Law*, 8th edn (Sweet and Maxwell, London, 2016).
[20] Peter Cane, 'Public Law and Private Law: A Study of the Analysis and Use of a Legal Concept' in John Eekelaar and John Bell eds, *Oxford Essays in Jurisprudence, Third Series* (Clarendon, Oxford, 1987), 57, 78.

combination of features which impose a public character or stamp on the act'.[21] What is needed, however, is some guidance as to what 'public' might mean in this context, an urgent question given the complex intermingling of public duties and private rights in modern regulatory regimes.[22] As Dyson LJ has explained, 'the question whether the decision of a body is amenable to judicial review requires a careful consideration of the nature of the power and function that has been exercised to see whether the decision has a sufficient public element, flavour or character to bring it within the purview of public law', though he lamented 'that this criterion for amenability is very broad, not to say question-begging'.[23] Indeed the trend (observable around the common law world[24]) for relatively open-ended tests to determine a body's amenability to judicial review has been criticised: 'the reliance by the courts on so many and such disparate tests suggests that their approach to determining whether power is public for the purposes of judicial review is ad hoc and unprincipled.'[25]

The argument in this chapter will be to the contrary: that the law relating to the boundaries of judicial review of administrative action is neither ad hoc nor unprincipled—it is nourished from the same source as all the other areas of administrative law.[26] Far from being simply a 'matter of feel',[27] judicial determinations of the boundaries of judicial review can be understood as being structured by the

[21] *Poplar Housing and Regeneration Community Association Ltd v Donoghue* [2002] QB 48 [65] per Lord Woolf CJ.

[22] See e.g. *Cocks v Thanet District Council* [1983] 2 AC 286.

[23] *R (Beer t/a Hammer Trout Farm) v Hampshire Farmers' Markets Ltd* [2004] 1 WLR 233, 240–241.

[24] See e.g. *R v Panel on Takeovers and Mergers, ex parte Datafin plc* [1987] QB 815, 835–838 ; *Mercury Energy Ltd v Electricity Corporation of New Zealand* [1994] 1 WLR 521, 526; *Geoghegan v Institute of Chartered Accountants* [1995] 3 IR 86, 130–131; *O'Donnell v Tipperary (SR) County Council* [2005] 2 IR 483, 487; *NEAT Domestic Trading Pty Ltd v AWB Ltd* (2003) 216 CLR 277 [27]-[29]; *CECA Institute Pty Ltd & Anor v Australian Council for Private Education and Training* [2010] VSC 552 [101]-[113]; *Air Canada v Toronto Port Authority* 2011 FCA 347; [2013] 3 FCR 605 [60]; *Mita Michael Ririnui v Landcorp Farming Ltd* [2016] NZSC 62. The comment in Gerard Hogan, David Gwynn Morgan and Paul Daly, *Administrative Law in Ireland* 5th edn (Roundhall, Dublin, 2019) [19–120] is generalisable: 'the Irish courts have favoured a contextual approach, eschewing rigidity and conceptual neatness for flexibility designed to respond to the nuances of individual cases.'

[25] Colin Campbell, 'Monopoly Power as Public Power for the Purposes of Judicial Review' (2009) 125 *Law Quarterly Review* 491, 521. See also Murray Hunt, 'Constitutionalism and the Contractualisation of Government in the United Kingdom' in Michael Taggart ed, *The Province of Administrative Law* (Hart, Oxford, 1997), 21, 30, lamenting the 'unsatisfactory half-way house' the courts have constructed.

[26] There is a respectable argument that these boundaries ought to be obliterated altogether. See e.g. John Allison, *A Continental Distinction in the Common Law: A Historical and Comparative Perspective on English Public Law*, rev edn (Oxford University Press, Oxford, 2000); Carol Harlow, '"Public" and "Private" Law: Definition without Distinction" (1980) 43 *Modern Law Review* 241; Dawn Oliver, *Common Values and the Public-Private Divide* (Butterworths, London, 1999), critiquing the zealous approach of the English courts to procedural exclusivity (see also above Chapter 6.1). However, once one accepts that there are certain procedural eccentricities in administrative law (such as the restriction to the record that was before the decision-maker, a requirement to seek permission to pursue judicial review proceedings and time limits), it becomes necessary to delineate the boundaries of judicial review of administrative action. Even in systems, such as the Irish, which apply this public/private divide with much less zeal than the English courts did in the 1980s, the procedural eccentricities of the application for judicial review have been maintained and applied.

[27] *R (Tucker) v Director General of the National Crime Squad* [2003] ICR 599 [13] per Scott Baker LJ.

values of individual self-realisation, good administration, electoral legitimacy and decisional autonomy.

Given the open-ended nature of this area of the law, such that any lawyer worth their salt should be able to develop a novel theory to understand the decided cases, I think it prudent to justify my incursion—wielding 'administrative law values'—onto relatively crowded territory. Why, in short, I think my considerations have something to add beyond simply supporting the thesis of this book. Accordingly, I respectfully observe that the other approaches to determining the scope of judicial review that have been proposed from time to time are problematic for one reason or another. For instance, monopoly power, as a criterion for establishing the susceptibility of powers to judicial review,[28] suffers from an evident lack of fit with the decided cases. The argument for extending the scope of judicial review was relatively strong in *R v Football Association, ex parte Football League Ltd*, where the Association's powers were 'though in contractual form ... effectively a legislative code'[29] and it exercised a *de facto* monopoly over football. Nonetheless, Rose J held that the Association fell outside the purview of judicial review.[30] Moreover, theories based on ideas of monopoly or fiduciary duty[31] will inevitably face serious difficulties in defining the boundaries of judicial review because it is nigh-on impossible to confine the principle 'that it is strongly morally desirable for decisions that affect people to be made in accordance with the principles of good administration, at least if the people affected wish the decisions so to be made' to any readily definable group of actors.[32]

Reliance on a notion of 'governmental' functions seems doomed to fail, given the 'orthodox view ... that the British do not have a developed concept of the state',[33] and the wide variety of cases in which decidedly non-governmental bodies such as clubs and trades unions have been subjected to the constraints of natural justice.[34] Similarly, the idea that review should lie where, if the non-statutory

[28] Campbell (n 25) 521.

[29] [1993] 2 All ER 833, 841.

[30] As he explained: 'Despite its virtually monopolistic powers and the importance of its decisions to many members of the public who are not contractually bound to it, it is, in my judgment, a domestic body whose powers arise from and duties exist in private law only'. *Ibid*, 848–849.

[31] Evan Fox-Decent, *Sovereignty's Promise: the State as Fiduciary* (Oxford University Press, Oxford, 2011).

[32] Campbell (n 25) 507. Someone who doubts the utility of a divide between public and private spheres might not find this troublesome. But I do not seek to challenge the premise, on which the judges have proceeded, that public and private should be kept distinct, as far as the scope of public law is concerned. See also David Feldman, 'Equity in the Modern Administrative State' and Timothy Endicott, 'Equity and Administrative Behaviour' in Peter Turner ed, *Equity and Administration* (Cambridge University Press, Cambridge, 2016).

[33] Janet McLean, *Searching for the State in British Legal Thought: Competing Conceptions of the Public Sphere* (Cambridge University Press, Cambridge, 2012), 1. See especially Allison (n 26).

[34] See e.g. *Breen v Amalgamated Engineering Union* [1971] 2 QB 175; *Enderby Town Football Club v Football Association* [1971] Ch 591; *Glover v BLN Ltd* [1973] IR 388; *Forbes v New South Wales Trotting Club Ltd* (1979) 143 CLR 242; *Bolger v Osborne* [2000] 1 ILRM 250.

body did not exist, the legislature would have created it[35] has been thoroughly debunked.[36] Moreover, the scope of the prerogative writs does not provide a useful guide to this area. Although it has been said that 'the prerogative writs are available as a general remedy for *supervision of the machinery of government*',[37] this simply refers the reader back to the nebulous concept of 'governmental' functions: 'to concentrate on remedies would ... involve a degree of circularity or levitation by traction applied to shoestrings, since the remedy of certiorari might well be available if the ... authority is in breach of a "public law" obligation, but would not be if it is only in breach of a "private law" obligation'.[38] And the conclusion of Professor Beatson (as he then was) that the test is 'whether the issue involves challenging a power which has been committed to the jurisdiction of the authority in question'[39] is subject to avowed disadvantages, such that his test must be used in a 'flexible way'.[40]

Accordingly, I set out in this chapter to argue that the decided cases on the scope of judicial review of administrative action can be understood in terms of administrative law values: individual self-realisation, good administration, electoral legitimacy and decisional autonomy.

7.2 Electoral Legitimacy

The extent to which a decision-maker's functions are supported by statute or woven into a statutory and regulatory regime—what I will for the purposes of this chapter term the 'democratic nexus'—can be understood to have considerable influence over judges deciding whether to extend the boundaries of judicial review: 'The historic reliance by the courts upon the ultra vires doctrine as the justification for judicial intervention has led to a continuing search for statutory underpinning'.[41] This can be understood in terms of judicial respect for the considered choices of elected representatives.

[35] See e.g. *R v Imam of Bury Park James Masjid Luton, ex parte Sulaiman Ali* [1992] COD 132.

[36] See David Pannick, 'Who is Subject to Judicial Review and in Respect of What?' [1992] *Public Law* 1, 5–6, asking (rhetorically), 'why should the jurisdiction of the court depend on a hypothesis as to what Parliament would do but for the existence of the body in question?'

[37] *McDonald v Anishinabek Police Service* (2006) 83 OR (3d) 132 [70]. Emphasis added.

[38] *R v East Berkshire Health Authority, ex parte Walsh* [1985] QB 152 [162] per Sir John Donaldson MR.

[39] Jack Beatson, '"Public" and "Private" in English Administrative Law' (1987) 103 *Law Quarterly Review* 34, 53.

[40] Ibid, 61.

[41] *R v Servite Houses and Wandsworth London Borough Council, ex parte Goldsmith and Chatting* [2000] LGR 55, 72 per Moses J.

7.2.1 Democratic Nexus

In the seminal case of *R v Panel on Take-overs and Mergers, ex parte Datafin plc*,[42] judicial review remedies were held to be available, in principle, in respect of decisions of the Panel on Take-overs and Mergers. One of the reasons given to support the availability in principle of judicial review was that, '[a]s an *act of government it* was decided that, in relation to take-overs, there should be a central self-regulatory body which would be supported and sustained by a periphery of statutory powers and penalties wherever non-statutory powers and penalties were insufficient or non-existent or where [European Union] requirements called for statutory provisions.'[43] Relatedly, the Panel was 'without doubt performing a public duty', as evidenced by the '*expressed* willingness of the Secretary of State for Trade and Industry to limit legislation in the field of take-overs and mergers and to use the panel as the centrepiece of his regulation of that market'.[44] That Parliament and the executive had consciously woven the non-statutory body into a broader regulatory scheme was a justification for subjecting the body to judicial review.[45]

Consider also the decision of the Privy Council in *Mercury Energy Ltd v Electricity Corporation of New Zealand*.[46] Here, the plaintiff had applied for judicial review (and a variety of private law remedies) against a state-owned enterprise that had terminated contractual arrangements for the supply of electricity. Interestingly, the legislative basis for the enterprise's activities (the *State-Owned Enterprises Act 1986*) was an important consideration in making the defendant amenable to review:

> A state enterprise is a public body; its shares are held by ministers who are responsible to the House of Representatives and accountable to the electorate. The defendant carries on its business in the interests of the public. Decisions made in the public interest by the defendant, a body established by statute, may adversely affect the rights and liabilities of private individuals without affording them any redress. Their Lordships take the view that in these circumstances the decisions of the defendant are amenable in principle to judicial review . . . [47]

Plentiful further examples can be provided of cases in which a decision was so tied up in a regulatory system that judicial review was appropriate to ensure that legal

[42] *R v Panel on Takeovers and Mergers, ex parte Datafin plc* (n 24).
[43] Ibid, 835 per Sir John Donaldson MR. Emphasis added.
[44] Ibid, 838 per Sir John Donaldson MR. Emphasis added.
[45] See similarly *Masu Financial Management Pty Ltd v Financial Industry Complaints Service Ltd (No 2)* (2004) ACSR 554, 560.
[46] [1994] 1 WLR 521.
[47] Ibid, 526.

limits on decision-making power had been respected.[48] In *Volker Stevin NWT ('92) Ltd v Northwest Territories (Commissioner)*, a company's designation as an eligible business was revoked and although the policy under which the revocation had been ordered was non-statutory, it was mandatorily applied 'by all government departments in assessing tenders submitted to the Government' and thus came within the scope of judicial review.[49] Relationships that would ordinarily be private in nature can come within the scope of judicial review where they are 'closely controlled by statute'.[50]

This point is illustrated by *R (Beer t/a Hammer Trout Farm) v Hampshire Farmers' Markets Ltd*. The applicant participated in a farmers' market run by a local authority. After several successful pilot schemes the authority handed over responsibility for the operations to the stallholders.[51] When the applicant was subsequently refused permission to participate by the stallholders' company, he sought judicial review. Dyson LJ drew a distinction 'between (a) an unofficial market in respect of which there are no public rights of access and (b) a statutory market in respect of which public rights do exist'.[52] Dyson LJ concluded that the situation under review was much closer to the 'statutory market' end of the spectrum but this was not the sole basis for his conclusion that judicial review remedies were, in principle, available. First, the company owed 'its existence to the council';[53] second, the company 'stepped into the shoes of the council' in that it had run its affairs in the way the council had, in pursuit of the council's statutory objectives;[54] and third, the council had assisted the company 'in a number of respects'.[55] To the argument that there was no statutory underpinning for the company's refusal of permission to trade, Dyson LJ thus responded that the company had been 'established by a local authority to take over on a non-profit basis the running of the markets that the authority had previously been running in the exercise of its statutory powers in what it considered to be the public interest'.[56]

[48] See also *Webster v Auckland Harbour Board* [1987] 2 NZLR 129; *Air Nelson Ltd v Minister of Transport* [2008] NZAR 139; *Chase Oyster Bar Pty Ltd v Hamo Industries Pty Ltd* (n 1); *Treasury Holdings v National Asset Management Agency* [2012] IEHC 297.

[49] (1994) 113 DLR (4th) 639. See also *R v Advertising Standards Authority, ex parte Insurance Service plc* (1990) 2 Admin LR 77, where the Authority was non-statutory but was woven into a web of regulations; it shared jurisdiction with the Office of Fair Trading, the Director General of which would only intervene in situations where the Authority had failed to produce a satisfactory result; *Masters v Ontario* (1993) 16 OR (3d) 439, where investigators were operating as part of governmental machinery; and *Victoria v Master Builders' Association of Victoria* [1995] 2 VR 121, where a governmental taskforce drew up a blacklist of contractors who were excluded from government contracts, without according procedural fairness.

[50] *Canada (Attorney General) v Mavi* 2011 SCC 30; [2011] 2 SCR 504 [48].

[51] n 23.

[52] Ibid, [31]: 'A good example of the former is a car boot sale held on a person's private land. The paradigm example of the latter is a statutory or charter market held on land dedicated to public use and to which the public has a right of access'.

[53] Ibid, [36].

[54] Ibid, [37].

[55] Ibid, [38].

[56] Ibid, [40]. See also *Plaintiff M61/2010E v Commonwealth of Australia* [2010] HCA 41; (2010) 243 CLR 319, where the assessment of asylum claims had been outsourced to a private company: whilst the Australian courts could not quash these decisions, the High Court of Australia did issue a declaration to

Applying judicial review principles to non-statutory bodies might seem somewhat strained, on the basis that there is no statute on which they can bite. The point, however, is that *in principle* review ought to be available in situations where a non-statutory body has been interwoven into a statutory scheme: a considered choice to weave a non-statutory body into a regulatory web has the consequence that judicial review must be available in order to ensure that the non-statutory body does in fact respect the law; that the constraints thereby imposed upon a non-statutory body might be looser than those imposed upon a statutory body goes to the *application* of judicial review principles, not their availability *in principle*.[57] Indeed, a more relaxed attitude to judicial scrutiny may be justified, as we will see below, by considerations of effective and efficient public administration.

7.2.2 Commercial Activities

However, in cases where the body in question lacks a democratic nexus (and thus the value of electoral legitimacy is not engaged), judges have been reluctant to extend the scope of judicial review.[58] For instance, where 'an institution was created to be at arm's length from the government, the discretion [was] conferred on the institution to manage its business, and the government[] lack[ed] control over the finances of the institution', review did not lie.[59] A well-known example is *R v Disciplinary Committee of the Jockey Club, ex parte Aga Khan*, where judicial review was not available for a disciplinary decision made by the Jockey Club.[60] Hoffmann LJ focused on the absence of any statutory underpinning. There were incidental indicia of governmental approval (via a Royal Charter and the power to nominate members of the Horserace Betting Levy Board), but 'nothing to suggest that, if the Jockey Club had not voluntarily assumed the regulation of racing, the government would feel obliged or inclined to set up a statutory body for the purpose'.[61] For his part, Sir Thomas Bingham MR pointed out that the Jockey Club had 'not been woven into any system of governmental control of horseracing, perhaps because it has itself controlled horseracing so successfully that there has been no need for

the effect that the assessments were unlawful, a declaration to which the Minister was to have regard in deciding whether to act on the assessments.

57 See similarly Mark Elliott, *The Constitutional Foundations of Judicial Review* (Hart, Oxford, 2001), chapter 5.

58 For criticism of the view that the 'source' of a regulatory power should be taken into consideration, see Hunt (n 25) 21.

59 *Onuschak v Canadian Society of Immigration* 2009 FC 1135 [23], citing *Toronto Independent Dance Enterprise v Canada Council* [1989] 3 FC 516. See also *Allied Irish Bank v O'Brien* [2015] IEHC 260.

60 [1993] 1 WLR 909.

61 Ibid, 932. See similarly *R v Chief Rabbi of the United Hebrew Congregations of Great Britain and the Commonwealth, ex parte Wachmann* [1992] 1 WLR 1036, 1042.

any such governmental system and such does not therefore exist'.[62] A mere stamp of governmental approval does not cause a body to be subject to judicial review,[63] especially if the stamp specifically preserves or recognises the freedom of the body to develop 'private views about how it is best to proceed in all the circumstances'.[64]

Other examples can be found in cases where public bodies were involved in 'purely commercial' activities.[65] Even a general cloak of statutory authority has not been enough on its own to justify the exercise of the supervisory jurisdiction. As Stratas JA observed in *Air Canada v Toronto Port Authority* of a hypothetical situation in which a public body had terminated a contract for the provision of janitorial services:

> In doing so, it is not exercising a power central to the administrative mandate given to it by Parliament. Rather, it is acting like any other business. The tribunal's power in that case is best characterized as a private power, not a public power. Absent some exceptional circumstance, the janitorial company's recourse lies in an action for breach of contract, not an application for judicial review of the tribunal's decision to terminate the contract.[66]

A useful example is *R v National Coal Board, ex parte National Union of Mineworkers*, where a decision to close a coalmine was held to be unreviewable, because it was 'an executive, or business, or management decision in exactly the same category as a decision in similar circumstances made by a public company'—that the decision concerned 'a nationalised industry created by statute' did not transform it into a public law matter.[67] To similar effect is *R v Bolsover District Council, ex parte Pepper*, where the applicant alleged a legitimate expectation that the Council would sell land to him.[68] In Keene J's view, '[n]ormally a decision by a local authority to sell or not to sell land which it owns is to be seen as a private law matter unless a public law element is introduced into the decision making process by some additional factor'.[69] Hence, where a body refuses to grant a lease in the exercise of an 'inherent interest in its lands', review will not lie.[70]

[62] *R v Disciplinary Committee of the Jockey Club, ex parte Aga Khan* (n 60) 923.

[63] See e.g. *General Newspapers Pty Ltd v Telstra Corporation* (1993) 45 FCR 164; *Rajah v Royal College of Surgeons in Ireland* [1994] 1 IR 384; *Auckland Electric Power Board v Electricity Corporation of New Zealand* [1994] 1 NZLR 551; *NEAT Domestic Trading Pty Ltd v AWB Ltd* (n 24); *O'Connell v The Turf Club* [2015] IESC 57; [2017] 2 IR 43.

[64] *Air Canada v Toronto Port Authority* 2011 FCA 347 [78] per Stratas JA. See also *New Zealand Stock Exchange v Listed Companies Association Inc* [1984] 1 NZLR 699, 707.

[65] *Lawson v Housing New Zealand* [1997] 2 NZLR 474, 485 per Williams J.

[66] *Air Canada v Toronto Port Authority* (n 64) [52].

[67] [1986] ICR 791, 795 per Macpherson J.

[68] [2001] LGR 43.

[69] Ibid, [33].

[70] *Devil's Gap Cottagers (1982) Ltd v Rat Portage Band No 38B* 2008 FC 812; [2009] 2 FCR 27 [64] per ER Dawson J. See also *MBA Land Holdings Pty Ltd v Gungahlin Development Authority* [2000] ACTSC 89; (2000) 206 FLR 120 [214] per Higgins J: 'Clearly, if the function being exercised was merely that of selling vacant land for commercial development, it would be difficult to perceive any "public law factor"'.

7.2.3 Statutory Obligations

Notwithstanding the absence of a democratic nexus in the terms laid out in the previous section, all decision-making bodies must comply with relevant statutory provisions. Judicial review will be available in situations where a decision-making body has failed to comply with a relevant statutory provision. This is best observed by examining, first and *a contrario*, cases in which the relevant statutory provision *empowered* a decision-making body, before contrasting these with cases in which the statute *imposed* obligations to act in a particular way.

In *R v Servite Houses and Wandsworth London Borough Council, ex parte Goldsmith and Chatting*, the company, which had arranged with the Council to provide a residential home for the applicants, had promised them a home for life but subsequently reneged on the promise.[71] The Council had a statutory power to agree the placements with the company, pursuant to section 26 of the National Assistance Act 1948. As part of its contract with the Council, the company agreed to abide by certain statutory standards and the Council's code of practice for residential care homes. Here, Moses J held that there was an insufficient statutory underpinning to justify the extension of public law remedies:

> Servite is a private body which does not owe its existence to section 26. Its power to enter into a contract with Wandsworth does not depend upon section 26, but upon its own private rules ... It does not seem to me that the applicants can successfully contend that because legislation permits a public authority to enter into arrangements with a private body, the functions of the private body are, by dint of that legislation, to be regarded as public functions.[72]

It has been said that this reasoning is 'unconvincing', in part because 'this is a stronger instance of statutory underpinning than that in a *Datafin* type case' and, in addition, because other considerations (such as the absence of contractual protections and presence of a code of practice) militated in favour of access to public law remedies.[73] These points are well taken. It is significant to compare, however, *R v British Coal Corporation, ex parte Vardy*.[74] British Coal had decided, subject to consultation, to close ten coalmines. Significantly, the decision fell within the scope of a statutory duty to consult contained in section 46 of the Coal Industry Nationalisation Act 1946. That provision 'provided a regime for consultation on

[71] *R v Servite Houses and Wandsworth London Borough Council, ex parte Goldsmith and Chatting* (n 41).

[72] Ibid, 77. See also *R (Broadway Care Centre Ltd) v Caerphilly CBC* [2012] EWHC (Admin) 37 (the Council had contracted with the applicant to operate a care facility and its termination of the contract was entirely a matter of private law).

[73] Paul Craig, 'Contracting Out, the Human Rights Act and the Scope of Judicial Review' (2002) 118 *Law Quarterly Review* 551, 566–567.

[74] [1993] ICR 720.

the matters to which it refers, including colliery closures and resulting redundancies, which is unique to the coalmining industry. In other words, the statute places express duties on British Coal which are not placed on other employers.'[75] As such, British Coal was subject to judicial review for its failure to comply with this statutory duty, even though it was acting in a commercial capacity. Similarly, in *Mita Michael Ririnui v Landcorp Farming Ltd*, a decision of a state-owned enterprise relating to the sale of property in which a Maori community sought to claim an interest was held to be reviewable, on the basis that the enterprise was acting in accordance with its statutory obligations and, moreover, that its corporate statement of intent recognised its role in 'assisting the Crown to meet its Treaty obligations'.[76] In these last two cases, the democratic nexus was strong enough to justify the extension of the scope of judicial review to activities that would ordinarily have been considered commercial in character (though, plainly, this is not to suggest that *all* commercial decisions of such bodies would be reviewable: a distinct sphere of commercial activity could be preserved free from judicial review, beyond relevant statutory constraints). This conclusion can be understood to sound in the value of electoral legitimacy, as the concept of a democratic nexus plays on respecting the considered choices of elected representatives to impose statutory or regulatory requirements on a given decision-making body.

7.3 Good Administration

A concern for effective and efficient public administration can be understood to be operative in cases relating to the scope of judicial review in two ways.

7.3.1 Codes of Practice

First, the courts have been more willing to intervene to review the decisions of non-statutory bodies where such bodies are regulated by comprehensive codes of conduct. In general, the courts will require administrative decision-makers to abide by their published policies.[77] The underlying reason can be understood in terms of the value of good administration: if the policy was adopted, it ought presumably to be followed (absent good reasons for abandoning or adapting it). A similar feature can

75 Ibid, 751 per Glidewell LJ.

76 (n 24) [66] per Elias CJ and Arnold J. See further *Moncrieff-Spittle v Regional Facilities Auckland Limited* [2021] NZCA 142 [51-70]. See also *Mass Energy Ltd v Birmingham City Council* [1994] Env LR 298. Although the dispute (relating to waste disposal) was primarily commercial in nature and thus did not attract the courts' judicial review jurisdiction, part of the case turned on compliance with statutory requirements, in respect of which judicial oversight was held to be exercisable.

77 *Mandalia v Home Secretary* [2015] UKSC 59; [2015] 1 WLR 4546. See similarly *Keogh v Criminal Assets Bureau* [2004] IESC 32; [2004] 2 IR 159.

be observed in the scope of review cases. Where a non-statutory decision-maker has adopted a regulatory code, the courts have been less hesitant about imposing judicial review remedies for failures to follow the code. One can understand this tendency in terms of effective and efficient public administration. For all courts are doing is enforcing policies the decision-makers have themselves adopted in order to achieve their objectives more efficiently and effectively; furthermore, this can also be understood by reference to concerns for certainty and predictability, inasmuch as published policies permit individuals to plan their affairs.[78]

For example, in *R v Advertising Standards Authority, ex parte Insurance Service plc*,[79] the Authority had adopted an advertising standards code which required advertisements to be legal, decent, honest and truthful. Advertisements found to be in breach of the code would not, in practice, be carried by newspapers and other media. Pursuant to the code, final decisions were to be made by the council of the Authority. There was no right of appeal. Here, however, it had delegated important functions to its secretariat, such that the necessary information was not before the council when it took its decision, a straightforward application of the rule against sub-delegation.[80] On judicial review, the decision was quashed.[81] Similarly, in *R v Press Complaints Commission, ex parte Stewart-Brady*,[82] there was no difficulty in subjecting the Commission to judicial review (though Lord Woolf MR expressly reserved judgement on this point), because it had made an adjudication on the compatibility of an article published in *The Sun* about one of the Moors Murderers (Ian Brady) with the terms of the Commission's Code of Practice.[83]

Major deviations from settled expectations (even if these are not memorialised in a policy) will also justify judicial review. For example, in *Irving Shipbuilding Inc v Canada (Attorney General)*, Evans JA identified 'powerful reasons for leaving procurement disputes to the law of contract', but would have permitted judicial review in 'extraordinary situations' involving 'fraud, bribery, corruption or other kinds of grave misconduct which, if proved, would undermine public confidence in the essential integrity of the process'.[84] In such circumstances, understood in light of administrative law values, the presence of concerns for effective and efficient public administration makes judicial intervention easier to justify.

[78] See Chapter 2.3.3.

[79] (1990) 2 Admin LR 77.

[80] See Chapter 2.3.1.

[81] See similarly *Volker Stevin NWT ('92) Ltd v Northwest Territories (Commissioner)* (n 49). See also *R v General Council of the Bar, ex parte Percival* [1991] 1 QB 212.

[82] [1997] EMLR 185.

[83] See also *Scheerer v Waldbillig* (2006) 208 OAC 29; 265 DLR (4th) 749 [20]–[21]; *Coulter v Independent Press Standards Organisation* [2018] EWHC 1017 (Admin) [28]–[37].

[84] 2009 FCA 116; [2010] 2 FCR 488 [61]–[62]. See, to similar effect, *Lawson v Housing New Zealand* (n 65) 485J; *Lab Tests Auckland Ltd v Auckland District Health Board* [2008] NZCA 385; [2009] 1 NZLR 776 [91], but compare the observations of William Young J, in *Mita Michael Ririnui* (n 24) [214].

7.3.2 Deference

Second:

> Decisions of unincorporated bodies exercising public regulatory functions may not easily fall for examination on conventional grounds of illegality, irrationality and procedural impropriety. In appropriate cases a more flexible approach may be called for.[85]

As Popplewell J put it in *R v Code of Practice Committee of the British Pharmaceutical Industry, ex parte Professional Counselling Aids Ltd*, '[w]here there is a committee dealing with a matter which is not immediately familiar to the court and laying down standards which are peculiar to that organisation or profession, a court should not be too ready to criticise that body for reaching a decision which the court itself might not have reached'.[86] This echoes an Irish judge's comment, in the context of a potential challenge to an application of the rules of racing by the Turf Club or Irish National Hunt Steeplechase Committee, that 'the more the disputed matters relate *purely* to questions of sporting judgement, the less likely it will be that there will be any judicial involvement in the resolution of the dispute'.[87]

In *Datafin*, for instance, Sir John Donaldson MR insisted that in any judicial review proceedings the courts would have to give the panel 'considerable latitude', such that judicial review of the panel would be attenuated.[88] Similarly, giving the advice of the Privy Council in *Mercury Energy Ltd v Electricity Corporation of New Zealand*[89] Lord Templeman held that no case for judicial review had been made out. His speech was somewhat ambiguous. He was quite clear that a court can intervene where the decision of a body such as the defendant 'was not made according to law'.[90] But it would be very difficult to establish *Wednesbury* unreasonableness: 'It does not seem likely that a decision by a state enterprise to enter into or determine a commercial contract to supply goods or services will ever be the subject of judicial review in the absence of fraud, corruption or bad faith.'[91] Instead,

[85] *Electoral Commission v Cameron* [1997] 2 NZLR 421, 430 per Gault J. See also Dawn Oliver, 'Towards the Horizontal Effect of Administrative Justice Principles' in Michael Adler ed, *Administrative Justice in Context* (Hart, Oxford, 2010), 229, 233: 'In public decision making, issues may arise as to the need for the courts to defer to the decisions of public bodies on the grounds of their democratic accountability. In private decision making, there will be no case for deference to decision makers on that ground. There may, however, be a need for a version of deference based on the decision maker's expertise, managerial prerogatives and so on.'

[86] (1990) 10 BMLR 21, 30.

[87] *Hyland v Dundalk Racing (1999) Limited* [2014] IEHC 60 [41] per Hogan J. See also *Typing Centre of New South Wales v Toose* ((SC(NSW), 15 December 1988, unreported); *Fassi v Dublin City University* [2015] IEHC 38 [30].

[88] *R v Panel on Takeovers and Mergers, ex parte Datafin plc* (n 24) 841.

[89] (n 24).

[90] Ibid, 528. See e.g. *Electoral Commission v Cameron* (n 85).

[91] *Mercury Energy Ltd v Electricity Corporation of New Zealand* (n 24) 529.

'[r]etribution for excessive prices is liable to be exacted on the directors of the state enterprises at the hands of the ministers' and on them in turn by their follow politicians and members of the public.[92] These justifications for relatively less intrusive judicial review can be understood (just as in the area of substantive review) in terms of a desire to safeguard effective and efficient public administration, by preventing courts from interfering with the substance of decisions made by bodies with relatively more subject-matter expertise than judges.[93]

This sort of reasoning might be criticised on the basis that it provides a semblance of judicial review without the substance,[94] but reductions in the intensity of review to take account of the relative institutional competence of decision-makers and courts are well known to the common law.[95] Moreover, good reasons for restraint 'do not mean that we should decline jurisdiction altogether';[96] it is possible to understand limited judicial oversight as the result of a balance having been struck between effective and efficient public administration on the one hand and the preservation of a distinct oversight role for the courts in assessing the lawfulness of administrative action on the other (albeit at a lower level of intensity in these circumstances). This will be particularly so in cases where the other principles would point in favour of extending the scope of judicial review. Moreover, where breaches of procedural fairness, or a failure to adhere to procedures laid down in a published policy, are at issue—rather than the substance of a regulatory decision—the courts will be more willing to intervene.[97]

7.4 Decisional Autonomy

A concern for maintaining distinct roles for distinct bodies can also be understood to be operative in the area of the scope of judicial review of administrative action: 'Like public figures, at least in theory, public bodies are entitled to have a private life'.[98] In this section, the concern is not with the preservation of decisional autonomy for administrative decision-makers empowered by statute but rather for the decisional autonomy of public and private bodies in respect of certain matters. We have already had a glimpse of how the law relating to the scope of judicial review ensures that *some* commercial activity can be carried out by statutory bodies without judicial review (although private law remedies are, of course, available).

[92] Ibid.
[93] See also Chapter 4.1.
[94] See e.g. Michael Taggart, 'Corporatisation, Contracting and the Courts' [1994] *Public Law* 351.
[95] Sir John Laws, '*Wednesbury*', in Christopher Forsyth and Ivan Hare eds, *The Golden Metwand and the Crooked Cord* (Oxford University Press, Oxford, 1998), 185, 187. See Chapter 4.2.
[96] *R v Panel on Takeovers and Mergers, ex parte Datafin plc* (n 24) 846 per Lloyd LJ.
[97] See e.g. *Masu Financial Management Pty Ltd v Financial Industry Complaints Service Ltd (No 2)* (n 45).
[98] Harry Woolf, 'Public Law—Private Law: Why the Divide?' (1986) *Public Law* 220, 223.

The focus in this section is on how the same concern—to preserve decisional autonomy—in respect of at least some matters—can be understood to be operative in the cases dealing with the amenability to judicial review of private bodies.

7.4.1 An Exclusionary Rule

A well-established basic principle is that judicial review does not lie against private bodies: 'Private or domestic tribunals have always been outside the scope of certiorari since their authority is derived solely from contract, that is, from the agreement of the parties concerned.'[99] Such private bodies can be seen as a site for human flourishing on the basis of consent, a site that ought to be preserved:

> Where purely private power is concerned, three factors argue against extensive judicial supervision. Respect for the individual liberty of the parties, certainty in the law, and the needs of the market, would indicate that the courts ought not, in the name of good administration, to impose too many restraints on personal liberty, or introduce a general duty to subordinate private interests to the public interest unless a statute so requires.[100]

There is thus a difference 'between a domestic or private tribunal on the one hand and a body of persons who are under some public duty on the other.'[101] Accordingly, no review lay in *R v Lloyds of London, ex parte Briggs*,[102] where the powers exercised over the complainants were exercised solely by virtue of contractual arrangements that they had freely entered into.

The subject of the application for judicial review in *R v Chief Rabbi of the United Hebrew Congregations of Great Britain and the Commonwealth, ex parte Wachmann*[103] was a decision by the Chief Rabbi, after an inquiry, to declare that Wachmann was no longer fit to hold rabbinical office. Simon Brown J held that the decision was unreviewable. In general, he said, 'where non-governmental bodies

[99] *R v Criminal Injuries Compensation Board, ex parte Lain* [1967] 2 QB 864, 882 per Lord Parker CJ. See also *New Zealand Stock Exchange v Listed Companies Association Inc* (n 64) 707; *Beirne v Garda Commissioner* [1993] ILRM 328, 334; *Auckland Electric Power Board v Electricity Corporation of New Zealand* (n 63) 560; *D'Souza v Royal Australian and New Zealand College of Psychiatrists* (2005) 12 VR 42, 57; *Bloxham (In Liquidation) v Irish Stock Exchange* [2013] IEHC 301; [2014] 4 IR 91 [15]; *Highwood Congregation of Jehovah's Witnesses (Judicial Committee) v Wall* 2018 SCC 26; [2018] 1 SCR 750 [13].

[100] Dawn Oliver, 'Is the *Ultra Vires* Rule the Basis of Judicial Review?' [1987] *Public Law* 543, 566. It is interesting to note the equivocation with which Professor Oliver puts her point. The argument is against 'extensive' judicial oversight, not judicial oversight *tout court*; and against 'too many restraints' on individual freedom, not any restraints at all. That such equivocation marks the literature in this area suggests that an approach that relies on a plurality of values may prove to be fruitful.

[101] *R v Panel on Takeovers and Mergers, ex parte Datafin plc* (n 24) 847 per Lloyd LJ.

[102] [1993] 1 Lloyd's Rep 176.

[103] *R v Chief Rabbi of the United Hebrew Congregations of Great Britain and the Commonwealth, ex parte Wachmann* (n 61). See also *State (Colquhoun) v D'Arcy* [1936] IR 641.

have hitherto been held reviewable, they have generally been operating as an integral part of a regulatory system which, although itself non-statutory, is nevertheless supported by statutory powers and penalties clearly indicative of government concern'.[104] The functions of the Chief Rabbi, however, were 'essentially intimate, spiritual, and religious—functions which the government could not and would not seek to discharge in his place were he to abdicate his regulatory responsibility'.[105] It is notable that Simon Brown J expressed some reluctance about extending the judicial review jurisdiction to such matters because 'if judicial review lies here, then one way or another this secular court must inevitably be drawn into adjudicating upon matters intimate to a religious community'.[106] This point can be understood in terms of ensuring that distinct bodies play distinct roles: the value of decisional autonomy.

In a more earthly field, the suspension under the Rules of Racing of a greyhound trainer who had a doped dog in his charge was said to be unreviewable in *Law v National Greyhound Racing Club Ltd*, because the powers at issue 'were derived from a contract' between the plaintiff and defendants: 'A stewards' inquiry under the defendants' Rules of Racing concerned only those who voluntarily submitted themselves to the stewards' jurisdiction.'[107] Here, however, the challenge was to the substance of the suspension, not to a failure to abide by the principles of procedural fairness or to any misinterpretation of the Rules of Racing. There was no attempt to hold the Club to its own published policies (which would have sounded in a concern for effective and efficient public administration) or to rely upon a democratic nexus (which would have sounded in a concern to respect the considered choices of elected representatives). Accordingly, judicial review could not plausibly have been said to be available.

7.4.2 Contractual Powers and Public Purposes

Where contractual powers are used by a public body with a view to achieving political purposes, however, judicial review is available. At issue in *R v Lewisham London Borough Council, ex parte Shell UK Ltd*[108] was the Council's participation in an anti-apartheid campaign, pursuant to which it boycotted Shell due to the latter's business activities in Namibia and (especially) South Africa. But Shell's activities overseas did not breach any provision of domestic law. As a result, Neill LJ found it 'impossible in the light of the authorities to escape from the conclusion that by seeking to bring

[104] *R v Chief Rabbi of the United Hebrew Congregations of Great Britain and the Commonwealth, ex parte Wachmann* (n 61) 1041.
[105] Ibid, 1042.
[106] Ibid, 1043.
[107] [1983] 1 WLR 1302, 1307 per Lawton LJ; see similarly ibid, 1309 per Fox LJ.
[108] [1988] 1 All ER 938.

pressure on Shell UK to change the Shell policy towards South Africa the council was acting unfairly and in a manner which requires the court to intervene': 'the statutory powers of a local authority cannot be employed in order to persuade other authorities to bring pressure to bear on trading companies in circumstances such as the present'.[109] This conclusion can be understood in terms of administrative law values: the Council was undermining the statutory scheme and, inasmuch as it was acting in a public capacity, it could hardly suggest that judicial review would in some way impinge upon its activities in the commercial sphere.[110] Similarly, in *R (Molinaro) v Kensington and Chelsea Royal London Borough Council*, the Council's decision to use a contractual power (under a lease) to frustrate the applicant's desire to operate a restaurant 'was taken for the purpose of giving effect to its planning objectives' and, accordingly, was reviewable:[111] 'Public law bodies should not be free to abuse their power by invoking the principle that private individuals can act unfairly or abusively without legal redress.'[112] That there may be 'an undertaking or a contractual consequence of the application of the [legislation] ... does not mean that the [legislation] is left behind once the undertaking or contract is made'.[113] Pleas for decisional autonomy in the private sphere fall on deaf ears when the action in question cannot plausibly be said to be commercial.

7.4.3 Accountability Gaps and Individual Interests

There are two sides to the coin of ensuring distinct bodies play distinct roles and benefit thereby from a measure of decisional autonomy in some areas. Sometimes, the implications of permitting a powerful body to exercise power over an individual will militate in favour of judicial review being made available. As Lloyd LJ explained in *Datafin*, some self-regulating bodies, such as the committee of a club, are 'wholly inappropriate for judicial review' but a body like the Panel 'wields enormous power' and has 'a giant's strength', such that: 'The fact that it is self-regulating, which means, presumably, that it is not subject to regulation by others, and in particular the Department of Trade and Industry, makes it not less but more

[109] Ibid, 952.
[110] See similarly *Browne v Dundalk UDC* [1993] ILRM 328; *MBA Land Holdings Pty Ltd v Gungahlin Development Authority* (2000) 206 FLR 120 [217]–[218]. By contrast, in *R v Lord Chancellor's Department, ex parte Hibbit and Saunders* [1993] COD 326, no public law remedy was available even though the applicants had been treated unfairly in a tendering process for court reporting services. As Rose LJ put it, 'it is not appropriate to equate tendering conditions attendant on a common law right to contract with a statement of policy or practice or policy decisions in the spheres of Inland Revenue, immigration and the like, control of which is the especial province of the State and where, in consequence, a sufficient public law element is apparent'. However, where private law protections are inadequate, the case for extending the boundaries of judicial review will be stronger. See further Chapter 7.5.
[111] [2001] EWHC 896 (Admin) [63].
[112] Ibid, [69].
[113] *Rhine v The Queen* [1980] 2 SCR 442, 447.

appropriate that it should be subject to judicial review by the courts.'[114] The courts have a role to play as well and, by making judicial review remedies available, can plug accountability gaps that would otherwise exist.

In this regard, it is worth emphasising that some non-statutory bodies have 'near monopolistic powers in an area in which the public generally have an interest and in which many persons earn their livelihoods'.[115] *Datafin* is a modest example. Because private law controls were insufficient, public law remedies would have to be made available. It was unacceptable that 'the panel should go on its way cocooned from the attention of the courts in defence of the citizenry',[116] because 'rights of citizens are indirectly affected' by decisions of the Panel; 'some, but by no means all of whom, may in a technical sense be said to have assented to this situation'.[117] As Lloyd LJ put it: 'So long as there is a possibility, however remote, of the panel abusing its great powers, then it would be wrong for the courts to abdicate responsibility. The courts must remain ready, willing and able to hear a legitimate complaint in this as in any other field of our national life.'[118] In Hardiman J's characteristically pungent phrase: 'Non-statutory bodies are as capable of abusing their powers as is government',[119] especially, one might add, where there is an 'imbalance in authority' between the parties.[120] One might also mention the fact that Denham J (as she then was) in the Irish Supreme Court found it important in *Geoghegan v Institute of Chartered Accountants in Ireland* that the applicant had 'no choice but must contract out of their right of access to the courts' in order to become a member of the Institute.[121] Finally, albeit *a contrario*, consistent with a concern for individual interests, the absence of coercive powers has also been a relevant consideration in determining the scope of judicial review, as in *R (Holmcroft Properties Ltd) v KPMG LLP*, where one reason for refusing to extend the judicial review jurisdiction was that at issue was an 'essentially voluntary scheme of redress'.[122]

[114] *R v Panel on Takeovers and Mergers, ex parte Datafin plc* (n 24) 845.

[115] *R v Disciplinary Committee of the Jockey Club, ex parte Massingberd-Mundy* [1993] 2 All ER 207, 223 per Roch J.

[116] *R v Panel on Takeovers and Mergers, ex parte Datafin plc* (n 24) 839 per Sir John Donaldson MR. Though see *New Zealand Stock Exchange v Listed Companies Association Inc* (n 64); *R v Code of Practice Committee of the British Pharmaceutical Industry, ex parte Professional Counselling Aids Ltd* (n 86) 32. The argument will be even stronger in the case of coercive powers, employed 'without the need for consent from those affected and [that] can seriously affect the rights of citizens and [officials] alike' (*McDonald v Anishinabek Police Service* (n 37) [75]).

[117] *R v Panel on Takeovers and Mergers, ex parte Datafin plc* (n 24) 838.

[118] Ibid, 846.

[119] *O'Connell v The Turf Club* (n 63) [15].

[120] *University of Auckland v Tertiary Education Commission* (n 2) 685 per Williams J, coming to the conclusion that universities were at a disadvantage relative to the Commission.

[121] *Geoghegan v Institute of Chartered Accountants* (n 24) 129. There was, however, no majority on the availability of judicial review in the circumstances. Egan J agreed with Denham J, Blayney and O'Flaherty JJ took the opposite view, and Hamilton CJ expressly reserved judgment.

[122] *R (Holmcroft Properties Ltd) v KPMG LLP* [2016] EWHC 323 [42] per Elias LJ and Mitting J. See e.g. *Murtagh v Board of Governors of St Emer's School* [1991] 1 IR 482; *O'Donoghue v South Eastern Health Board* [2001] IEHC 165; *R v General Council of the Bar, ex parte Percival* (n 81) 1 QB 212; *Lakeside Colony of Hutterian Brethren v Hofer* [1992] 3 SCR 165; *R v Visitors to the Inns of Court, ex parte Calder* [1994] QB 1; *CECA Institute Pty Ltd v Australian Council for Private Education and Training*

These observations can be understood in terms of judicial concern for the protection of individual interests—of course, individuals who enter into contractual relationships do so in the furtherment of their self-realisation, but where a consensual contractual relationship does not exist, the courts may play a more active role. And, and as I will explain in the next section, different considerations apply when contractual remedies are unavailable or ineffective.

7.5 Individual Self-realisation

In general, the rights of parties bound by consent are protected by contract law: 'Members of trade unions, business associations and social clubs and also students in universities and colleges have ... contractual rights based on their contracts of membership, with implied terms which protect them from unfair expulsion.'[123] Their contracts are 'held to include a duty to act fairly; by accepting them as members and receiving their subscriptions the trade union or club impliedly undertakes to treat them fairly and in accordance with the rules.'[124] It been said that 'Where private law remedies are available in contract, there is no necessity, *in order that justice may be done,* for a public law remedy to be available.'[125] Where this is not, so, however, review may lie.[126]

Accordingly, the robust protection that Canadian public employees enjoy as a matter of contract (pursuant, usually, to collective agreements) can be understood as having contributed to the Supreme Court of Canada's conclusion in *Dunsmuir v New Brunswick* that '[w]here a public employee is employed under a contract of employment, regardless of his or her status as a public office holder, the applicable

(n 24) VSC 552; (2010) 245 FLR 86; *Zhang v Athlone Institute of Technology* [2013] IEHC 390; *O'Connell v The Turf Club* (n 63) [16]–[17], [28].

[123] Wade and Forsyth, *Administrative Law* (n 18) 535.

[124] Ibid, 377. See e.g. *McClelland v Burning Palms Surf Life Saving Club* [2002] NSWC 470; (2002) 191 ALR 759; *Aga v Ethiopian Orthodox Tewahedo Church of Canada*, 2020 ONCA 10 [43]; *Miller v Soroptimist International of the South West Pacific* [2020] QSC 242. Contractual powers, moreover, may now be subject to the same constraints as public law discretionary powers: see e.g. *Braganza v BP Shipping* [2015] UKSC 17; [2015] 1 WLR 1661 [28]–[30] (Lady Hale), [53] (Lord Hodge) and [103] (Lord Neuberger); *Patersons Securities Ltd v Financial Ombudsman Service Ltd* [2015] WASC 321. Although there has been strong criticism of this point (see e.g. Chris Himsworth, 'Transplanting Irrationality from Public to Private Law: *Braganza v BP Shipping Ltd*' (2019) 23 *Edinburgh Law Review* 1) there is also a relatively robust common law tradition of using the rules of private law to constrain the powers of monopolists (see e.g. *McCord v ESB* [1980] ILRM 153; *Vector Ltd v Transpower NZ Ltd* [1999] 3 NZLR 646; *Sky City Auckland Ltd v Wu* [2002] 3 NZLR 621) and of imposing stringent standards on the process of tendering for government contracts (see e.g. *Hughes Aircraft Systems International v Airservices Australia* (1997) 76 FCR 151; *Mellco Developments Ltd v Portage La Prairie (City)* 2002 MBCA 125; 222 DLR (4th) 67; *Tercon Contractors Ltd v British Columbia (Transportation and Highways)* 2010 SCC 4; [2010] 1 SCR 69). See generally Sir Stephen Sedley, 'The Lion Beneath the Throne: Law as History' [2016] *Judicial Review* 289.

[125] *Becker v Duggan* [2005] IEHC 376; [2009] 4 IR 1, 15 per Ó Néill J. Emphasis added.

[126] See e.g. *O'Leary v Health Funding Authority* [2001] NZAR 717.

law governing his or her dismissal is the law of contract, not general principles arising out of public law'.[127] Where, however, the protections provided by contract law are illusory or defective, concerns for the protection of individual interests can be understood to have weighed heavily in the balance. Claims for a zone of decisional autonomy from public law are less likely to meet with judicial approval where private law remedies are inadequate;[128] this can also be understood in terms of ensuring that the *courts* play their distinct role of ensuring lawfulness, a point of especial importance in situations where private law remedies would be inadequate. Indeed, blanket refusal to extend the judicial review jurisdiction on the basis that contractual protections exist would be 'to restrict judicial review in a way that is both arbitrary and which pays inadequate regard to the normative factors that justify and require judicial review in the first place'.[129]

Support, albeit *a contrario*, for the view that judicial review remedies will be made available where contractual remedies are inadequate can be found in *R v Disciplinary Committee of the Jockey Club, ex parte Aga Khan*.[130] Here there was no statutory underpinning for the Club's regulation of horse-racing. It was important to the decision not to extend the boundaries of judicial review 'that the powers which the Jockey Club exercises over those who (like the applicant) agree to be bound by the Rules of Racing derive from the agreement of the parties and give rise to private rights on which effective action for a declaration, an injunction and damages can be based without resort to judicial review'.[131] The alleged breach of natural justice would, it follows, have given rise to contractual remedies. As Hoffmann LJ explained, 'The club has an implied obligation under the contract to conduct its disciplinary proceedings fairly. If it has not done so, the Aga Khan can obtain a declaration that the decision was ineffective (I avoid the slippery word void) and, if necessary, an injunction to restrain the club from doing anything to implement it.'[132] Indeed, '[c]ases where the applicant or plaintiff has no contract on which to rely may raise different considerations and the existence or non-existence of alternative remedies may then be material'.[133] Farquharson LJ agreed on this point, but went further: 'I do not discount the possibility that in some special circumstances the remedy might lie. If for example the Jockey Club failed to fulfil its obligations under the charter by making discriminatory rules, it may be that those affected

127 2008 SCC 9; [2008] 1 SCR 190 [81] and, especially [102]–[111] per Bastarache and LeBel JJ.

128 See e.g. *R v Governors of Haberdasher's Aske's Hatcham College Trust, ex parte Tyrell* [1995] COD 399. Though see *R v Lord Chancellor's Department, ex parte Hibbit and Saunders* (n 110) per Rose LJ: 'The absence of any alternative remedy, like the presence of an alternative remedy in private law, is immaterial to the question of whether a public law remedy exists.'

129 Mark Elliott, 'Judicial Review's Scope, Foundations and Purposes: Joining the Dots' [2012] *New Zealand Law Review* 75, 105.

130 (n 60). See also *Setia v Appleby College* (n 2).

131 *R v Disciplinary Committee of the Jockey Club, ex parte Aga Khan* (n 60) 924 per Sir Thomas Bingham MR.

132 Ibid, 933.

133 Ibid, 924 per Sir Thomas Bingham MR.

would have a remedy in public law'.[134] Egregious maladministration might be too much to ignore. As it happens, this was how Hoffmann LJ explained the decision in *Nagle v Feilden* to leave open the possibility of declaratory relief in favour of a woman who had been refused a trainer's licence for (allegedly) sexist and discriminatory reasons.[135]

7.6 Conclusion

It follows then, that the same concerns that can be understood to structure the law in relation to institutional structures, procedural fairness, substantive review, remedies and restrictions on remedies can also be understood as providing the structure within which judges determine the width or narrowness of the scope of judicial review. Respect for the considered choices of elected representatives exerts a powerful pull in this area, drawing within the ambit of judicial review those nominally private powers that form part of a regulatory regime. Effective and efficient public administration will often provide a justification for the availability of judicial review remedies. In particular, where a body has adopted its own policy, the courts can comfortably assume that enforcing the policy will help the body to achieve its objectives, not hinder it. A concern to create distinct spheres of activity—including spheres in which individuals can flourish free from oversight by outside bodies—can exert a pull in the opposite direction. Finally, judicial concern for the protection of individual interests promotes the availability of judicial review in some circumstances, especially where contractual protections are inadequate and/or where the holder of a contractual power has coercive authority over an individual. Together, the values of individual self-realisation, good administration, electoral legitimacy and decisional autonomy can be understood to provide structure to the law in this area.

On occasion, one value might not be present at all: for instance, in run-of-the-mill tendering cases, concerns for effective and efficient public administration will generally not be pressing. On other occasions, the relevant values might point in the same direction, where, for instance, an individual seeks to hold a body woven into a statutory scheme to a policy that it has created. On still other occasions, the values can be understood to play a complementary role: in *Datafin*, respect for the decisions of elected representatives and a concern to protect individual interests militated in favour of extending the scope of review whilst a concern for effective and efficient public administration can be seen as having been accommodated by decreasing the intensity with which the judges would exercise their reviewing function. The courts might be said to be engaged in a process of reconciliation of

[134] Ibid, 930.
[135] [1966] 2 QB 633.

values which seem to conflict, a process in which no one value has priority and all are accommodated to the extent possible. The result is that the striking of a balance between potentially conflicting values can be understood to play a role in the resolution of difficult cases.

In situations of potential conflict between the values, it is now possible to argue that judges *should reconcile* the values in order to guide their development of doctrine and decision of individual cases.[136] By adjudicating based on values immanent in the decided cases, they would be relying on legal sources of unimpeachable validity, and developing the law in a principled manner. At first glance, it might not seem especially helpful to observe that a 'number of relevant factors' will have to be considered in any given case to determine 'whether a matter is coloured with a public element, flavour or character sufficient to bring it within the purview of public law', which will depend 'on the facts of the case and the overall impression registered upon the Court'.[137] Yet, as Beatson has observed, 'at the level of generality at which the question is posed one should not be surprised that what emerges is a statement of principle rather than a litmus test with which to decide concrete cases'.[138] This anticipates the argument to be developed in the next chapter, on legitimate expectation.

Those who seek comfort in rules rather than standards and in fine-grained conceptualism rather than free-wheeling contextualism need not recoil. There is no reason that the values must be weighed on a case-by-case basis.[139] Relatively hard-edged rules could be justified. At the very least, the values can be employed to justify the creation of paradigm cases for reviewability and for non-reviewability. On the one hand, decisions taken by bodies that are statutory or otherwise woven into a scheme of regulation, pursuant to existing policies, that have an impact on individual interests which cannot be addressed by other means, should always be reviewable. On the other hand, where a statutory basis for decision is lacking, where the decision-maker is not subject to or implementing a policy, where alternative means of redress exist and where judicial intervention might compromise the decision-maker's autonomy, judicial review should not be available. Similarly,

[136] See e.g. Paul Daly, 'A Pluralist Account of Deference and Legitimate Expectations' in Matthew Groves and Greg Weeks eds, *Legitimate Expectations in the Common Law World* (Hart, Oxford, 2017).

[137] *Air Canada v Toronto Port Authority* (n 64) [60] per Stratas JA.

[138] Beatson (n 39) 64.

[139] Cf the analysis of Charleton J in *Mac Uaid v Bus Éireann* [2013] IEHC 551; [2013] 3 IR 378, an exemplar of an avowedly contextual approach. Police vetting of the applicant school bus-driver revealed that he had two criminal convictions, one involving possession of explosives, for which he had spent three years in prison, and his employment was terminated pursuant to an inflexible policy. Relying on a variety of considerations, Charleton J held, at [8], that the decision was amenable to judicial review:

> This court is most influenced by the factors that the national school system consists of the public provision of primary education, that transport to and from school in appropriate instances has been an entitlement over at least two generations, that these services are publicly funded, that interference with contractual relations between the contractor and subcontractor is likely to give rise to serious consequences and that the functions of Bus Éireann come from a statutory origin.

presumptive rules could be developed in reliance on the values. For instance, that it is presumptively the case that a body that has been woven into the fabric of the administrative state will be subject to judicial review; the presumption could be rebutted if extension of the scope of judicial review would undermine effective and efficient public administration or compromise decisional autonomy. On this approach, it would also be presumptively the case that a contractual relationship does not come within the purview of a reviewing court, a presumption that could be rebutted where contractual remedies would be demonstrably deficient or there has been egregious misconduct, especially (in either case), where coercive authority has been exercised.[140]

Even if paradigm cases and presumptive rules can be identified, difficult cases will, no doubt, still arise. My point is not 'to suggest that easy answers would thereby be supplied' by reference to the considerations I have derived from the cases, but rather to make clear 'that hard questions are best confronted within a clearly articulated framework of principle',[141] constructed by reference to the decided cases.

140 See generally Craig (n 73).
141 Elliott (n 129) 110.

8
Legitimate Expectation

In Chapters 2 to 7, I laid out my argument that contemporary administrative law can be understood in terms of the values of individual self-realisation, good administration, electoral legitimacy and decisional autonomy (grouped under the headings of institutional structures, procedural fairness, substantive review, remedies, restrictions on remedies and the scope of judicial review of administrative action). These values can be understood to operate in a complementary fashion, giving an intelligible structure to the core features of contemporary administrative law. Inasmuch as they might come into conflict, judges can be understood to have struck a balance between them. In this chapter, I am less concerned with *interpreting* the decided cases than I am with *prescribing* how judges ought to deal with potential conflict between the values. My analysis in the concluding sections of Chapter 7 gives a large hint about the argument contained in the present chapter. My extended case study of legitimate expectation will allow me to demonstrate how the values might *guide* the resolution of difficult administrative law questions. I begin this chapter by explaining why it is necessary to broach this issue and then outline how the values can be deployed to guide the development of administrative law, where the law is uncertain or where counsel urge a judge to change it.

On occasion, the values might all point in the same direction. Consider procedural legitimate expectations, whereby an individual who has been promised a procedure pursuant to which their substantive interests will be determined is entitled to insist that a public body abide by its promise.[1] Individual interests are protected by enforcing a promise which an individual could reasonably have relied upon; effective and efficient public administration is most unlikely to be compromised by providing a procedural right which the administrative decision-maker already decided to promise to the individual concerned; the participation in the decision-making process by the affected individual is, all things considered, likely to enhance the probability that an accurate decision will be reached, thus facilitating the faithful implementation of the statutory scheme; and distinct bodies play distinct roles, because the court need not trespass outside the bounds of the judicial domain (of providing oversight of the administrative process) and venture any opinion on the forbidden merits of the matter under review.[2]

[1] See e.g. *Attorney-General of Hong Kong v Ng Yuen Shiu* [1983] 2 AC 629; *Tara Prospecting v Minister for Energy* [1993] ILRM 771, 778; *University of Auckland v Tertiary Education Commission* [2004] 2 NZLR 668, 690.

[2] See e.g. *Morrissey v Minister for Defence* [2018] IEHC 672.

Understanding Administrative Law in the Common Law World. Paul Daly, Oxford University Press. © Paul Daly 2021.
DOI: 10.1093/oso/9780192896919.003.0008

On other occasions, however, the values might need to be reconciled. I argue that the best approach in such circumstances is for judges to accommodate each of the values as much as possible, reconciling them where necessary. I call this a pluralist approach.[3] It can already be understood to be present in the decided cases.[4] Of course, if the values prove to be genuinely irreconcilable, one of them would have to yield and the attraction of the pluralist approach would be diminished.[5] However, what seems on first glance to be an irreconcilable difference may disappear on closer inspection, perhaps due to consideration of empirical evidence, or due to reconsideration of values which, once applied to a concrete problem, turn out to have been too broadly conceived in the abstract. Indeed, the reflective approach I have adopted to the writing of this book has involved following this process.[6] Declarations of irreconcilability should be a last resort.

The approach in this chapter is different in a subtle but important way from the approach taken in Chapters 2 to 7. Whereas in the previous chapters I have sought to construct a values-based framework for administrative law, in this chapter I address what judges *ought* to do in situations where the values appear to come into conflict. This chapter is normative or prescriptive rather than interpretive; whereas an interpretive approach focuses on 'what the judge should have said', a prescriptive approach advises on 'what the judge should do'. In the absence of my pluralist account, judges and jurists might reasonably ask what guidance the values-based approach is capable of providing in difficult cases. My goal in this chapter is to illustrate the guidance it can provide, by reference to contested areas of legitimate expectation.

Legitimate expectation, Lord Fraser of Tullybelton said in the early 1980s, is an 'apt' term to 'express the underlying principle', but 'it is somewhat lacking in precision'.[7] Decades later it was described as 'a relatively young doctrine'[8] that is 'still developing'.[9] Authors have questioned the status of the doctrine of legitimate expectation. Courts are said to have 'experienced some difficulty in producing a coherent body of law',[10] because '[i]t has never been precisely clear what

[3] See Paul Daly, 'A Pluralist Account of Deference and Legitimate Expectations' in Matthew Groves and Greg Weeks eds, *Legitimate Expectations in the Common Law World* (Hart, Oxford, 2017). This approach relies heavily on Stephen R Munzer, *A Theory of Property* (Cambridge University Press, Cambridge, 1990).

[4] See Chapter 1.2.5.

[5] Developing priority rules would be one way of ensuring coherence even if the values were to prove irreconcilable in some circumstances. However, I do not propose to develop priority rules. See Chapter 8.3.

[6] See Chapter 9.1. One can compare the definition of the values of the rule of law, good administration, democracy and separation of powers found in Paul Daly, 'Administrative Law: A Values-Based Approach' in Bell et al eds, *Public Law Adjudication in Common Law Systems: Process and Substance* (Hart, Oxford, 2016) and the values defined in Chapter 1.2 of this book.

[7] *Attorney-General of Hong Kong v Ng Yuen Shiu* (n 1) 636.

[8] Mark Elliott, 'Legitimate Expectations and the Search for Principle' [2006] *Judicial Review* 281, 282.

[9] *R (Niazi) v Secretary of State for the Home Department* [2008] EWCA Civ 755 [3].

[10] Iain Steele, 'Substantive Legitimate Expectations: Striking the Right Balance?' (2005) 121 *Law Quarterly Review* 300, 303.

jurisprudential basis has been adopted' for the development of legitimate expectations.[11] A period of 'rapid growth' has occurred 'without proper exploration as to why legitimate expectations ought to be protected'.[12] As a result, the doctrine is 'highly uncertain'.[13] In short, 'many questions about it remain unanswered'.[14]

Such a crescendo of criticism may cause one to doubt the existence of any coherent doctrine of legitimate expectation. In my view, however, a measure of coherence can be attained. That the doctrine may not map clearly onto the various justifications offered for it from time to time is not a great surprise. As with other areas of administrative law and as is the case with the common law more generally, its development has not followed inexorably from an agreed set of first principles. Searches for a meta-value meta-principle or meta-concept of legitimate expectation have so far proved unavailing,[15] as they have in other areas.[16] In the pages that follow, I will set out a pluralist account of legitimate expectation, building on the values present in the decided cases. I begin with an overview of the different values provided in the case law—individual self-realisation, good administration, electoral legitimacy and decisional autonomy—some which support judicial enforcement of legitimate expectations, some which seem to counsel against it. I then proceed to outline how these values should be reconciled so as to guide the resolution of difficult questions, focusing on the contentious areas of knowledge and reliance, substantive legitimate expectations and enforcement of *ultra vires* legitimate expectations.

8.1 The Plurality of Legitimate Expectation

Legitimate expectation may 'take many forms'.[17] A distinction is typically drawn between procedural and substantive legitimate expectations.[18] An individual with a procedural legitimate expectation will benefit from procedural protection—such as notice and an opportunity to comment—before a decision

[11] Christopher Knight, 'Expectations in Transition: Recent Developments in Legitimate Expectations' [2009] *Public Law* 15, 17.

[12] Paul Reynolds, 'Legitimate Expectations and the Protection of Trust in Public Officials' [2011] *Public Law* 330, 330.

[13] Jack Watson, 'Clarity and Ambiguity: A New Approach to the Test of Legitimacy in the Law of Legitimate Expectations' (2010) 30 *Legal Studies* 633, 633. See e.g. *R (Gallaher Group Ltd) v Competition and Markets Authority* [2018] UKSC 25; [2019] AC 96.

[14] Farrah Ahmed and Adam Perry, 'The Coherence of the Doctrine of Legitimate Expectations' (2014) 73 *Cambridge Law Journal* 61, 61. See further Joanna Bell, *The Anatomy of Administrative Law* (Hart, Oxford, 2020), chapter 5.

[15] Joe Tomlinson, 'Do We Need a Theory of Legitimate Expectations?' (2020) 40 *Legal Studies* 286.

[16] See e.g. Chapter 3 on instrumental and dignitarian approaches to procedural fairness, Chapter 6 on the public interest conception of public law and Chapter 7 on the various attempts to provide a theory relating to the scope of judicial review of administrative action.

[17] *Council of Civil Service Unions v Minister for Civil Service* [1985] AC 374, 415 per Lord Roskill.

[18] Elliott (n 8) 285.

can lawfully be made against her. A substantive legitimate expectation prevents an administrative decision-maker from resiling from a promise or changing a policy without good reasons for doing so. Accordingly, a substantive legitimate expectation represents a much greater interference by the courts with the administrative decision-maker in question, for it reduces the range of options available to it, whereas a procedural legitimate expectation simply imposes a procedural barrier without reducing the range of decision-making options. But this dichotomy should not be over-emphasised. The line between procedure and substance is a notoriously slippery one.[19] Moreover, '[i]t is difficult to see why it is any less unfair to frustrate a legitimate expectation that something will or will not be done by the decision-maker than it is to frustrate a legitimate expectation that the applicant will be listened to before the decision-maker decides whether to take a particular step'.[20]

Drilling further down into this distinction, Paul Craig has suggested that there are four very different ways in which a legitimate expectation might arise:

i. A general norm or policy choice, which an individual has relied on, has been replaced by a different policy choice.
ii. A general norm or policy choice has been departed from in the circumstances of a particular case.
iii. There has been an individual representation relied on by a person, which the administration seeks to resile from in the light of a shift in general policy.
iv. There has been an individualised representation that has been relied on. The administrative body then changes its mind and makes an individualised decision that is inconsistent with the original representation.[21]

Synthesising the learning on legitimate expectation is challenging, because relevant materials may be found in many different places, layered by many different concerns.[22] Indeed, at times the language of legitimate expectation may seem inapposite. For instance, where an individual holds a protected interest[23] accorded

[19] See generally David Dyzenhaus and Evan Fox-Decent, 'Rethinking the Process/Substance Distinction: *Baker v Canada*' (2001) 51 *University of Toronto Law Journal* 193; *Canada (Citizenship and Immigration) v Vavilov* 2019 SCC 65 [76]–[81].

[20] *R v Minister for Agriculture, Fisheries and Food, ex parte Hamble (Offshore) Fisheries Ltd* [1995] 2 All ER 714, 724 per Sedley LJ. See also Geneviève Cartier, 'A "Mullanian" Approach to the Doctrine of Legitimate Expectations: Real Questions and Promising Answers' in Grant Huscroft and Michael Taggart eds, *Inside and Outside Canadian Administrative Law: Essays for David Mullan* (University of Toronto Press, Toronto, 2006).

[21] Paul Craig, *Administrative Law* 8th edn (Sweet and Maxwell, London, 2016), 671–672. See also Bell (n 14) 163.

[22] See also Claudine Roy, *La théorie de l'expectative légitime en droit administratif* (Yvon Blais, Cowansville, 1992), 99: 'Il en résulte un mélange de concepts différents en jurisprudence'.

[23] Interest here is shorthand for a longer list of triggers for judicial review, for example, 'the rights, privileges or interests of an individual': *Cardinal v Director of Kent Institution* [1985] 2 SCR 643 [14].

by an administrative decision-maker, courts will impose procedural protections should the administrative decision-maker seek to withdraw the interest; but this is part of the general administrative law requirement of fairness,[24] to which legitimate expectation seems not to add a great deal.[25] Similarly, where an administrative decision-maker seeks to change a policy, constraints of rationality or reasonableness[26] will be imposed independent of the existence of any legitimate expectation.[27] In short, '[l]egitimate expectation may play different parts in different aspects of public law'.[28] Nonetheless, each of the situations Craig enumerates has an important common feature: an expectation[29] engendered by sufficiently clear and unambiguous official action at Time X which is defeated by official action at Time Y.[30] Anxious to resist the 'lure of over-classification',[31] I will concentrate on this common feature.

[24] For example, Denning LJ employed the terminology of 'legitimate expectation' in a sense related purely to the overall fairness of the administrative process in *Schmidt v Secretary of State for Home Affairs* [1969] 2 Ch 149, 170. See also *Fowler & Roderique v Attorney-General* [1987] 2 NZLR 56, 74; *Gutrani v Minister for Justice* [1993] 2 IR 427, 436; *Minister for Immigration and Multicultural Affairs, ex parte Lam* (2003) 195 ALR 502, 510; *Minister for Immigration and Ethnic Affairs v Teoh* (1995) 183 CLR 273, 305-306. More interestingly, he distinguished between a 'right' and a 'legitimate expectation' (ibid, 171), thereby suggesting that a legitimate expectation could be understood as grounding a judicial review application even in the absence of a concrete right. See similarly *Council of Civil Service Unions v Minister for Civil Service* (n 17) 401. Compare *Minister for Immigration and Multicultural Affairs, ex parte Lam* [2003] HCA 6; (2003) 195 ALR 502, 537.

[25] See e.g. *Minister for Immigration and Border Protection v WZARH* [2015] HCA 40; (2015) 326 ALR 1 [30].

[26] *Attorney General of New South Wales v Quin* (1990) 93 ALR 1, 10–11 per Mason CJ.

[27] See e.g. *Altus Group Limited v Calgary (City)* 2015 ABCA 86, where a municipality's change of position in respect of a taxing bye-law was quashed as unreasonable, a notable decision given that Canada does not officially protect substantive legitimate expectations (*Canada (Attorney General) v Mavi* 2011 SCC 30; [2011] 2 SCR 504) and also *R (Gallaher Group Ltd) v Competition and Markets Authority* (n 13); *Canada (Citizenship and Immigration) v Vavilov* (n 19) [129]–[132].

[28] *R v North and East Devon Health Authority, ex parte Coughlan* [1999] EWCA Civ 1871; [2001] QB 213 [71].

[29] It is difficult to improve upon Lord Diplock's suggestion that the term 'legitimate expectation' simply means 'consequences to which effect will be given in public law…' *Council of Civil Service Unions v Minister for Civil Service* (n 17) 408.

[30] See e.g. the formulation of the Privy Council in *New Zealand Maori Council v Attorney-General* [1994] 1 NZLR 513, 525: 'The assurance once given creates the expectation, or to use the current parlance the 'legitimate expectation', that the Crown would act in accordance with the assurance, and if, for no satisfactory reason, the Crown should fail to comply with it, the failure could give rise to a successful challenge on an application for judicial review'; and Laws LJ's formulation in *R (Nadarajah) v Secretary of State for the Home Department* [2005] EWCA Civ 1363 [68]: 'Where a public authority has issued a promise or adopted a practice which represents how it proposes to act in a given area, the law will require the promise or practice to be honoured unless there is good reason not to do so.' Of course, whether a given official action is sufficiently clear and unambiguous will often be a matter of dispute: see e.g. *R (Bancoult) v Secretary of State for Foreign and Commonwealth Affairs (No 2)* [2008] UKHL 61; [2009] 1 AC 453.

[31] *R (Nadarajah) v Secretary of State for the Home Department* (n 30) [49] per Laws LJ. Compare *Mount Sinai Hospital Center v Quebec (Minister of Health and Social Services)* 2001 SCC 41; [2001] 2 SCR 281 [27] per Binnie J: 'it is inevitable that sub-classifications must be made to differentiate the situations which warrant highly intrusive relief from those which do not.'

8.2 Administrative Law Values in the Decided Cases

'Perhaps unhelpfully', many different conceptual bases for legitimate expectations can be found in the case law.[32] Abuse of power figures prominently, as do concerns for the protection of individual interests and effective and efficient public administration. These are often tempered, however, by reference to the legislative choice to vest power in a non-judicial body and judicial solicitude for the decisional autonomy of administrative decision-makers.

8.2.1 Abuse of Power

Abuse of power is a term found in some foundational cases on legitimate expectations.[33] However, abuse of power is probably better understood as an overarching principle of judicial review of administrative action in general, a 'rationale' rather than a rule,[34] which does not provide much in the way of concrete guidance to judges charged with determining whether an individual has a legally cognisable interest which can be overridden by a subsequent administrative decision.[35]

8.2.2 Good Administration

A concern for effective and efficient public administration features regularly in the jurisprudence, often bearing the label of good administration.[36] Professor Forsyth suggests that the term is as vague as abuse of power.[37] Properly understood as a concern with the efficient attainment of statutory objectives, however, good administration is neither a hopelessly general term nor beyond the ken of judges. While judges are not generally well-equipped, by reason of evidentiary limitations

[32] Knight (n 11) 17.

[33] See e.g. *In re Preston* [1985] 1 AC 835, 851, (Lord Scarman), 864 (Lord Templeman); *R v North and East Devon Health Authority, ex parte Coughlan* (n 28) 246–247. See also *Apotex Inc v Canada (Attorney General)* [2000] 4 FC 264; [2000] 4 FCR 264 [123].

[34] *R v Department of Education and Employment, ex parte Begbie* [1999] EWCA Civ 2100; [2000] 1 WLR 1115 [76].

[35] See e.g. *New Zealand Assoc for Migration and Investments Inc v Attorney-General* [2006] NZAR 45 [52] per Randerson J: 'Some English authorities have recently described legitimate expectation as falling within the concept of abuse or process but, with respect, the use of further expressions of this kind only adds to complexity without advancing clarity'; *R (Gallaher Group Ltd) v Competition and Markets Authority* (n 13) [41] per Lord Carnwath: 'Substantive unfairness ... is not a distinct legal criterion. Nor is it made so by the addition of terms such as "conspicuous" or "abuse of power". Such language adds nothing to the ordinary principles of judicial review, notably in the present context irrationality and legitimate expectation.'

[36] See e.g. *Apotex Inc v Canada (Attorney General)* (n 33) [123]; *R v North and East Devon Health Authority, ex parte Coughlan* (n 28) 246–247; *R (Bibi) v London Borough of Newham* [2001] EWCA Civ 607 [24]; *R (Nadarajah) v Secretary of State for the Home Department* (n 30) [68].

[37] Christopher Forsyth, 'Legitimate Expectations Revisited' [2011] *Judicial Review* 429.

and a relative lack of institutional competence, 'to impose upon the executive branch [their] ideas of good administration',[38] they may properly take some account of the effect of judicial review doctrine on the administrative process. For instance, it is surely reasonable for judges to presume that participation by affected individuals prior to an administrative decision being taken is likely to increase the accuracy of outcomes.[39] And in the context of legitimate expectation, judges may reasonably take the view in the absence of empirical evidence to the contrary that holding officials to policies, published or unpublished,[40] would further the ends of effective administration: 'there is a public interest in holding a public authority to promises made in the interests of proper public administration and allowing people to plan with some assurance',[41] whereas '[l]oss of trust in public bodies and their ability to be fair can lead to more, and more complex and time-consuming challenges to decisions, putting additional burdens on initial decision-makers'.[42] It is true that reference to 'good administration' alone will not resolve all of the difficult questions that arise in administrative law cases. Nevertheless, reminding judges to focus on the efficient and effective achievement of statutory goals by administrative decision-makers can assist in resolving these questions.

8.2.3 Individual Self-realisation

Reference is often also made to unfairness operating against an individual or group of individuals. The formulation in *Attorney-General of Hong Kong v Ng Yuen Shiu*, that 'expectations may be based upon ... [action] that would make it unfair *or* inconsistent with good administration ...', is instructive.[43] A concern for effective and efficient public administration can be understood not to have been the only driver of the judicial imagination on this subject. In its evident concern with fairness *to* individuals—that 'holding government to a procedural undertaking that was solemnly given on its behalf to an individual is more a matter of individual

[38] *Minister for Immigration and Multicultural Affairs, ex parte Lam* (n 24) 512 per Gleeson CJ. See similarly *R (S) v Secretary of State for the Home Department* [2007] EWCA Civ 546 [41].

[39] See e.g. Paul Craig, 'Legitimate Expectations: A Conceptual Analysis' (1992) 108 *Law Quarterly Review* 79, 85: 'Giving a person a hearing of some kind can help to ensure that the desired end is attained; the procedural rights perform an instrumental role in the sense of rendering it more likely that there will be an accurate decision on the substance of the case.'

[40] See generally *Lumba (WL) v Secretary of State for the Home Department* [2011] UKSC 12; [2012] 1 AC 245.

[41] *New Zealand Assoc for Migration and Investments Inc v Attorney-General* (n 35) 51 per Randerson J. Though equally, '[t]o hold that ... pre-election promises bound a newly elected Government could well be inimical to good government' (*R v Department of Education and Employment, ex parte Begbie* (n 34) [56] per Peter Gibson LJ).

[42] UK Administrative Justice Institution, *A Research Roadmap for Administrative Justice* (Nuffield Foundation, 2018), 19.

[43] (n 1) 637. Emphasis added. See also ibid, 638 where good administration is said to be 'primarily' the justification for enforcing legitimate expectations.

justice'[44]—unfairness in this context plays a role distinct from the general common law guarantee of fair procedures. Courts intervene to provide fair outcomes rather than fair procedures alone.[45]

Examples can be found in *Ex parte Unilever plc*, where Simon Brown LJ (as he then was) commented that a legitimate expectation will be enforced where 'it is illogical or *immoral* or both for a public authority to act with conspicuous unfairness and in that sense abuse its power';[46] in *R (Bibi) v London Borough of Newham*, where Schiemann LJ for the Court of Appeal invoked the 'moral detriment' suffered by a refugee family that sought enforcement of a legitimate expectation to secure housing;[47] and in *Webb v Ireland*, where Finlay CJ noted that it would be 'inequitable and unjust' for the state to 'repudiate' an assurance that individuals who had handed over valuable treasure to the state would be honourably treated.[48] Similarly, in explaining the foundations of legitimate expectation, Bingham LJ invoked the inter-personal relationship created by the law of contract: 'If in private law a body would be in breach of contract in so acting or estopped from so acting [contrary to a legitimate expectation] a public authority should generally be in no better position.'[49] When a public body makes a representation to an individual, it finds itself in a domain where promises may be enforced: 'The regime of contract law, which respects the dispositions individuals make of their rights, carries to its natural conclusion the liberal premise that individuals have rights.'[50]

Judicial concern to protect those individual interests which may be at stake in individuals' dealings with administrative decision-makers can be understood to be operative here. In legitimate expectation cases where individual interests are invoked, courts are typically concerned by the effect on individuals of promises being broken or settled expectations disrupted. As Schiemann LJ put it, for the Court of Appeal in *R (Bibi) v London Borough of Newham*, 'there is value in holding authorities to promises which they have made, thus upholding responsible public administration *and allowing people to plan their lives sensibly*'.[51] Where individuals rely upon official action to plan their affairs, their individual self-realisation is very much in play. Similarly, they are not treated with respect when officials go back on

[44] *Apotex Inc v Canada (Attorney General)* (n 33) [121] per Evans JA.

[45] Cf *SZBEL v Minister for Immigration and Multicultural and Indigenous Affairs* (2006) 228 CLR 152, 160.

[46] [1996] STC 681, 695. Emphasis added.

[47] *R (Bibi) v London Borough of Newham* (n 36) [55].

[48] [1988] IR 353, 379.

[49] *R v Inland Revenue Commissioners, ex parte MRK Underwriting Agents Ltd* [1990] 1 WLR 1545, 1569–1570.

[50] Charles Fried, *Contract as Promise: A Theory of Contractual Obligation* 2nd edn (Oxford University Press, Oxford, 2015), 2.

[51] *R (Bibi) v London Borough of Newham* (n 36) [24]. Emphasis added. See similarly *Glenkerrin Homes Ltd v Dún Laoghaire-Rathdown Corporation* [2007] IEHC 298 per Clarke J: 'where third parties reasonably arrange their affairs by reference to … a practice … [they] are entitled to rely upon an expectation that the practice will not be changed without reasonable notice being given.'

their word or change a policy. The human dimension of a case like *R v North and East Devon Health Authority, ex parte Coughlan*[52] cannot be overstated: promising a home for life was an important engagement by the state towards the severely disabled applicant; departing from the promise was a significant blow to individual interests of the highest possible importance.

The cautious reader might object that the concerns for effective and efficient public administration and protecting individual interests are simply two sides of the same coin: is it not always effective and efficient public administration to respect individual self-realisation and, in particular, enforce promises made to individuals; indeed, does not holding decision-makers to their promises increase trust in government thereby enhancing administrative effectiveness?[53] In many cases, no doubt, these concerns will point to the same outcome. But not always.[54] A representation might have been mistaken, in which case, 'the court should be slow to fix the public authority permanently with the consequences of that mistake'.[55] Or giving effect to a representation made to an individual or group of individuals might have negative wider consequences:

> Seen from the point of view of administrators focusing on the problem immediately before their eyes a promise seems reasonable ... [b]ut when they, or their superiors, focus on a wider background it appears that the making of the promise was unwise or that, in any event, its fulfilment seems too difficult.[56]

Administrative law values are distinct and should be treated as such.

8.2.4 Electoral Legitimacy and Decisional Autonomy

Concern for good administration and individual self-realisation serves primarily to support the legitimacy of expectations. But establishing a legitimate expectation is not the end of the analysis. As courts repeatedly emphasise, invoking concerns for legislative choice and the decisional autonomy of administrative decision-makers, a decision can be made contrary to a legitimate expectation in appropriate circumstances.

52 *R v North and East Devon Health Authority, ex parte Coughlan* (n 28).
53 See e.g. Christopher Forsyth, 'The Provenance and Protection of Legitimate Expectations' (1988) 47 *Cambridge Law Journal* 238, 239; Søren J Schønberg, *Legitimate Expectations in Administrative Law* (Oxford University Press, Oxford, 2000), 25.
54 Steele (n 10) 301.
55 *R v Department of Education and Employment, ex parte Begbie* (n 34) [61]. See similarly *Cromane Seafoods Ltd v Minister for Agriculture, Fisheries and Food* [2016] IESC 6; [2017] 1 IR 119, 144 per Clarke J: 'the fact that there may have been an error in the past cannot create a legitimate expectation that that error will be continued into the future.'
56 *R (Bibi) v London Borough of Newham* (n 36) [36].

Where decision-making authority has been granted by the legislature to an administrative decision-maker, it would be inappropriate for a court to step into the other body's shoes and take the decision it ought to have taken: 'to do so would be to assume the powers of the executive.'[57] On occasion, indeed, a statutory provision may seem to shut the door to the recognition of a legitimate expectation.[58] Moreover, the administrative decision-maker cannot, by adopting a decision or policy at Time X bind itself; it must remain free at Time Y to depart from the earlier decision or policy:[59] 'To regard a legitimate expectation as requiring the decision-maker to act in a particular way is tantamount to treating it as a rule of law'.[60] Performance of an undertaking must be 'compatible with [a decision-maker's] public duty':[61]

> Public authorities typically, and central government *par excellence*, enjoy wide discretions which it is their duty to exercise in the public interest. They have to decide the content and the pace of change. Often they must balance different, indeed opposing, interests across a wide spectrum. Generally they must be the masters of procedure as well as substance; and as such are generally entitled to keep their own counsel.[62]

As Lord Templeman explained in *In re Preston*, a case in which a taxpayer complained of a change of policy by the Inland Revenue Commissioners:

> [A] taxpayer cannot complain of unfairness, merely because the commissioners decide to perform their statutory duties ... to make an assessment and enforce a liability to tax. The commissioners may decide to abstain from exercising their powers and performing their duties on grounds of unfairness, but the commissioners themselves must bear in mind that their primary duty is to collect, not

[57] Ibid, 41. See also *Thames Valley Electric Power Board v NZFP Pulp & Paper Limited* [1994] 2 NZLR 641, 653..

[58] See e.g. *Mount Sinai Hospital Center v Quebec (Minister of Health and Social Services)* (n 31) [30] per Binnie J: 'The expectations must not conflict with the public authority's statutory remit'. But see Chapter 8.4.3.

[59] See e.g. Gerard Hogan, David Gwynn Morgan and Paul Daly, *Administrative Law in Ireland*, 4th edn (Roundhall, Dublin, 2010), 1033: 'This bar on the fettering of future executive action is part of a wider principle that statutory powers must be freely exercised.'

[60] Minister for Immigration and Ethnic Affairs v Teoh (1995) 183 CLR 273, 291, Mason CJ and Deane J.

[61] *R v Liverpool Corporation, ex parte Liverpool Taxi Fleet Operators' Association* [1972] 2 QB 299, 308 per Lord Denning MR. See also *Laker Airways v Department of Trade* [1977] 1 QB 643, 707, where Lord Denning MR explained that:

> The underlying principle is that the Crown cannot be estopped from exercising its powers, whether given in a statute or by common law, when it is doing so in the proper exercise of its duty to act for the public good, even though this may work some injustice or unfairness to a private individual ...

See similarly *Tara Prospecting v Minister for Energy* (n 1) 789.

[62] *R (Niazi) v Secretary of State for the Home Department* (n 9) [41].

> to forgive, taxes. And if the commissioners decide to proceed, the court cannot in the absence of exceptional circumstances decide to be unfair that which the commissioner by taking action against the taxpayer have determined to be fair.[63]

I quote this passage from Lord Templeman's speech at length because it can be understood as illustrating two related ideas. First, an administrative decision-maker must act pursuant to the mandate given to it by the legislature. A democratic choice made by a parliamentary majority ought to be respected. Second, judges should not second-guess the merits or wisdom of courses of action taken by administrative decision-makers. Accordingly, respect for, first, electoral legitimacy and, second, decisional autonomy as between legislative, executive and judicial power can be understood to be present in arguments for judicial restraint in the enforcement of legitimate expectations.[64]

8.3 A Pluralist Approach to Legitimate Expectation and Administrative Law Values

These competing values might seem to give rise to difficulties. Even individual self-realisation and good administration might be unruly bedfellows, for a breach of a promise may sometimes be very good administration indeed, even if it undermines the interests of the individual concerned. Of course, as with administrative law (and the common law) generally, it may be that the judges have been lurching wildly from case to case with no guiding principle in mind, that these values are 'little more than a smokescreen for an erratic and subjective assortment of judicial ideas',[65] in which case the better approach may simply be to concentrate on the individual strands of case law in isolation, allowing judges to refine them case by case with the incrementalism for which the common law is famous, perhaps using them to develop detailed taxonomies of legitimate expectation.[66]

This, however, is an unattractive approach, given the common thread running through the legitimate expectation cases: an expectation engendered by official action at Time X which is defeated by official action at Time Y. Moreover, jurists have spent decades searching for 'more precise principles'[67] behind this common thread. As a branch of the law, legitimate expectation is relatively new; as a result,

[63] (n 33)864.
[64] See similarly *Mount Sinai Hospital Center v Quebec (Minister of Health and Social Services)* (n 31) [47]–[51].
[65] Matthew Groves, 'Substantive Legitimate Expectations in Australian Administrative Law' (2008) 32 *Melbourne University Law Review* 470, 487.
[66] Jason Varuhas, 'In Search of a Doctrine: Mapping the Law of Legitimate Expectations' in Matthew Groves and Greg Weeks eds, *Legitimate Expectations in the Common Law World* (Hart, Oxford, 2017).
[67] Reynolds (n 12) 335.

some confusion is surely unavoidable,[68] but surely not ineradicable: 'it is all too easy to make separate compartments of the law where, in truth, different applications represent a single principle or at least interlocking principles'.[69] And what is true of legitimate expectation may also be true of judicial review of administrative action generally, which in its modern guise is of relatively recent provenance.

Faced with values found in the cases which are individually appealing but which may come into conflict with one another, one response is to adopt a pluralist approach. Rather than assigning priority to any one value—or casting about for an alternative meta-value that is not easily found in the cases—I set out to accommodate them all, reconciling them where necessary.[70] The utility of this approach is best appreciated in the treatment of concrete problems, where the limits of the competing values can be better understood, but some preliminary comments are in order.

First, a pluralist approach is explicitly normative. It speaks to how jurists *ought* to think about legitimate expectations. It is descriptive and interpretive only to the extent that it draws its values from sources of positive law. As a result, only values that are attractive on their own terms may be accommodated: hence the time I spent above in describing the values found in the case law and mounting a defence of each of them.

Second, if values are genuinely irreconcilable, one of them must yield. Should irreconcilability prove to be the case, there would be reason to doubt the attraction of the pluralist approach based on the values found in the cases. Often, however, what seems to be an irreconcilable difference could be resolved by further study, especially by consideration of empirical evidence, for instance as to whether enforcement of legitimate expectations really increases trust in officialdom or the efficiency of public administration. Moreover, it may be possible to resolve any conflict by revising the values which, when applied to concrete problems, may prove to have been drawn too broadly in the abstract.

Third, although it would be possible in theory to formulate priority rules to address conflicts these are unlikely to be appropriate. The rules would only operate in situations where one or more values come into conflict. If all values point to the same result, there is no conflict to resolve: indeed, that common law courts have 'had little difficulty in recognising the existence of procedural legitimate expectations',[71] which vindicate individual self-realisation and good administration concerns without impinging on decision-makers' autonomy on matters of substance, reflects the absence of any conflict. The difficulty with priority rules is that they

[68] See *Abrahamson v Law Society of Ireland* [1996] 1 IR 403, 422 per McCracken J: 'it is only to be expected that in an evolving concept there will be contradictory judgments.'

[69] *R (Nadarajah) v Secretary of State for the Home Department* (n 30) [49] per Laws LJ.

[70] What follows owes a significant debt to Munzer (n 3).

[71] Paul Craig, 'Substantive Legitimate Expectations in Domestic and Community Law' (1996) 55 *Cambridge Law Journal* 289, 290.

might not take account of the strength of the competing values in more difficult areas. For instance, a plausible priority rule would be majoritarian. But even in a situation where three values are ranged against one, the one value may nonetheless be extremely weighty. As a rule of thumb, a majoritarian preference might be useful, but it would be a dangerously facile priority rule if cast in absolute terms.

8.4 Protecting Legitimate Expectations: Pluralism in Action

Three controversial questions form a crucible within which the appropriate interaction of the individual self-realisation, good administration, electoral legitimacy and individual autonomy can be observed. These are, first, the role of knowledge and reliance, second, the enforceability of substantive legitimate expectations and third, the enforceability of expectations based on *ultra vires* representations. I argue that neither knowledge nor reliance should be a pre-requisite to the enforcement of a legitimate expectation. On substantive legitimate expectations, I take the side of the Court of Appeal in *Coughlan*, arguing in the teeth of strong criticism of that decision that there are indeed good reasons for courts to enforce substantive legitimate expectations, though I also observe that the Court of Appeal probably went too far in one important respect. And as to *ultra vires* representations, I advocate an approach that would permit courts to enforce them in some circumstances.

8.4.1 Knowledge and Reliance

Does an individual need to know of and rely on the official action said to give rise to a legitimate expectation? In respect of knowledge it has been suggested, for instance, that '[a] person cannot lose an expectation that he or she does not hold'.[72] And as to reliance, Binnie J would have refused to protect substantive legitimate expectations in the absence of a need to demonstrate detriment: 'One would normally expect *more* intrusive forms of relief to be accompanied by *more* demanding evidentiary requirements.'[73] The objection here seems to be that in the absence of knowledge and reliance there is little or no imperative for judicial intervention because the individual's interests have not been compromised by a broken promise. I suggest, however, that neither knowledge nor reliance should be required.

To begin with, a concern for effective and efficient public administration supports a requirement that policies and decisions be public and that they should be

[72] *Minister for Immigration and Ethnic Affairs v Teoh* (n 24) 314 per McHugh J.

[73] *Mount Sinai Hospital Center v Quebec (Minister of Health and Social Services)* (n 31) [31]. Emphasis original.

departed from only where there is a 'reasoned justification'[74] to do so. Personal knowledge of and reliance on a policy or decision is not a pre-requisite:[75] 'When a legitimate expectation arises from an agency's past practice, or non-statutory procedural guidelines, it serves to preclude procedural arbitrariness, not the actual expectation of the individual who may have been unaware of its existence.'[76] Although concerns about the non-performance of personalised promises to individuals are absent, effective and efficient public administration supports the desirability of judicial enforcement even where there has been no knowledge or reliance.

Judges, to be sure, cannot be certain that holding administrative decision-makers to their policies will, in fact, promote effective and efficient public administration. Common sense, however, teaches that once set in place, '*every* policy of a public authority, not subject to a stated terminal date or terminating event, may no doubt be expected to continue until rational grounds for its cessation arise'.[77] The point that knowledge and reliance need not be pre-requisites can be understood as sounding in good administration, without requiring a detailed theory of the concept, as Lord Kerr explained in *Re Finucane's Application for Judicial Review*: 'It cannot conduce to good standards of administration to permit public authorities to resile at whim from undertakings which they give simply because the person or group to whom such promises were made are unable to demonstrate a tangible disadvantage.'[78]

But, of course, the force of knowledge and reliance in a particular case may vary.[79] On the one hand, knowledge and reliance can 'reinforce' a legitimate

[74] *R (Nadarajah) v Secretary of State for the Home Department* (n 30) [38] per Laws LJ. See also Fennelly J's equivocal formulation in *Glencar Exploration v Mayo County Council* [2002] 1 IR 84, 162–163:

> ... the representation must be addressed or conveyed either directly or indirectly to an identifiable person or group of persons, affected annually or potentially in such a way that it forms part of a transaction definitively entered into or a relationship between that person or group and the public authority or that the person or group has acted on the faith of the representation.

[75] See *R v Department of Education and Employment, ex parte Begbie* (n 34) [101] per Sedley LJ: 'in cases where the government has made known how it intends to exercise powers which affect the public at large it may be held to its word irrespective of whether the applicant had been relying specifically upon it.' See also *R (Bancoult) v Secretary of State for Foreign and Commonwealth Affairs (No 2)* (n 30) [60]; *Re Finucane's Application for Judicial Review* [2019] UKSC 7 [62]. Indeed, in the foundational case of *Attorney-General of Hong Kong v Ng Yuen Shiu* (n 1), the individual concerned had no personal knowledge of the announcement that gave rise to his enforceable legitimate expectation of a procedural protection: see 635. See also *Heatley v Tasmanian Racing and Gaming Commission* (1977) 14 ALR 519; *Minister for Immigration and Ethnic Affairs v Teoh* (n 24); *Keogh v Criminal Assets Bureau* [2004] IESC 32; [2004] 2 IR 159.

[76] *Apotex Inc v Canada (Attorney General)* (n 33) [122] per Evans JA. See similarly, *Haoucher v Minister for Immigration, Local Government and Ethnic Affairs* (1990) 19 ALR 577, 590.

[77] *R (Niazi) v Secretary of State for the Home Department* (n 9) [34]. Emphasis original. Compare *O'Donoghue v South Kerry Development Partnership* [2018] IECA 10, discussed in GerardHogan, David Gwyn Morgan and Paul Daly *Administrative Law in Ireland* 5th edn (Roundhall, Dublin, 2019) (n 59) [21.53]–[21.57].

[78] *Re Finucane's Application for Judicial Review* (n 75) [72].

[79] As is observed in Hogan, Morgan and Daly (n 77) [21–58], commenting on Fennelly J's analysis in *Glencar Exploration v Mayo County Council* (n 74) 1 IR 84:

expectation,[80] calling for a 'much more rigorous standard' of judicial scrutiny.[81] On the other hand, however, an individual whose legitimate expectation is based on 'a policy which itself is liable to change' cannot expect the expectation 'to survive a policy change'.[82] That a policy may be changed at some point in the future is inherent in the policy's very existence:[83] it follows inexorably from the decision-maker's appointed role as the regulator of the portion of the administrative state assigned to it by the legislature that it should be able to change policy to suit changed circumstances. Knowledge of and reliance on a policy does not generate expectations as forceful as those engendered by personalised representations, for the concerns for individual interests will be less weighty.[84] Indeed, a concern for effective and efficient public administration counsels against imposing a high threshold for policy changes, for fear of 'ossify[ing] administrative policy'.[85]

A better way of capturing the greater moral force of knowledge and reliance—supported by a concern for individual self-realisation—is to place more exacting requirements on the decision-maker who goes back on their word than on the decision-maker who changes a generally applicable policy. Once this point is appreciated, the force of Binnie J's reason for rejecting substantive legitimate expectations is greatly reduced: although the evidentiary requirements are lower, the burden on the decision-maker who wishes to change a policy will be lighter than

> ... the point is that a general statement made to the world at large will rarely if ever be capable of giving rise to a legitimate expectation. Indeed, as Fennelly J. rightly observed, the essence of legitimate expectations is found in the creation of a *relationship* between an identifiable individual or group of individuals and a public body. It would be unduly formalistic to insist on the identification of a specific individual or group of individuals for the purposes of establishing a legitimate expectations claim (for the point is to hold public bodies to their word, in the interests of good administration), but it is perfectly proper to note that situations where it would be unfair, unreasonable or disproportionate for a public body to resile from a promise or a previous policy or practice are much more likely to arise where there is an identifiable group whose relationship with the public body has been affected or altered by a promise or a previous policy or practice. In such circumstances, the case for holding the public body to its promise or previous policy or practice will be much stronger.

See also Yoav Dotan, 'Why Administrators Should be Bound by Their Policies' (1997) 17 *Oxford Journal of Legal Studies* 23, 27.

[80] *Paponette v Attorney General of Trinidad and Tobago* [2010] UKPC 32; [2012] 1 AC 1 [37] per Lord Dyson.

[81] *R (Niazi) v Secretary of State for the Home Department* (n 9) [35] per Laws LJ.

[82] *R v Minister for Agriculture, Fisheries and Food, ex parte Hamble (Offshore) Fisheries Ltd* (n 20) 729 per Sedley LJ. See e.g. *McCarthy v Minister for Education and Skills* [2012] IEHC 200.

[83] See e.g. *Thamotharem v Canada (Minister of Citizenship and Immigration)* 2007 FCA 198; [2008] 1 FCR 385.

[84] See also Schønberg (n 53) 17: 'Reliance is only relevant in so far as it strengthens the Rule of Law justification for protection of legitimate expectations.' See e.g. *Lawson v Housing New Zealand* [1997] 2 NZLR 474, 489–491.

[85] Craig (n 39) 90. See also *New Zealand Assoc for Migration and Investments Inc v Attorney-General* (n 35) 51–52 per Randerson J: 'there is also a public interest in allowing governments and other public authorities to change policy from time to time when it is perceived to be appropriate to do so. Indeed, the adoption of new policy to meet changing circumstances may be viewed as the duty of any government in furthering the public interest.'

the burden on the decision-maker who wishes to resile from a personalised representation. Less exacting requirements for policy changes protect the efficient use of scarce resources by holding administrative decision-makers to their published policies until such time as they are revised, reflect the relative lack of imperatives for heightened protection to protect individual interests and preserve a higher degree of decisional autonomy for the legislature's chosen regulator. Conversely, where a personalised promise places a heavier justificatory burden on a decision-maker, this is offset by the more demanding evidentiary requirements placed on the applicant and, in any event, does not fatally compromise the decision-maker's authority to resile from a promise in appropriate circumstances, as the decision to do so can, in principle, be justified. Another way of putting the point is to say that the range of reasonable responses to a legitimate expectation (or tightness of the factual and legal constraints) may vary, in accordance with the force administrative law values exert in a given content.

In summary, the absence of individual interests should not mean legitimate expectations can never be enforced without proof of knowledge and reliance, because the value of good administration may also be engaged and respect for electoral legitimacy and decisional autonomy ensures that administrative decision-makers' freedom to change policy in appropriate circumstances is preserved. A balance can be struck between potentially conflicting values.

8.4.2 Substantive Legitimate Expectations

Enforcement of procedural legitimate expectations does not compromise decisional autonomy: 'Judges feel far more comfortable telling public bodies what procedures they should follow rather than what outcomes they should procure.'[86] As Laws LJ explained in *R (Niazi) v Secretary of State for the Home Department*, in this sort of case 'the unfairness or abuse of power which the court will check is not merely to do with how harshly the decision bears upon any individual'.[87]

When it comes to substantive legitimate expectations, however, enforcement by courts is more controversial. At times, courts and commentators have claimed that concerns about the undermining of considered legislative choices and encroaching on administrative decision-makers' autonomy have such force as to defeat substantive legitimate expectations outright:

> A significant weakness in the analysis of ... academic supporters of substantive legitimate expectations is the failure to acknowledge that the doctrine clearly narrows the freedom of the executive government and, more importantly, the effect

[86] Steele (n 10) 300. See similarly, Elliott (n 8) 288.
[87] *R (Niazi) v Secretary of State for the Home Department* (n 9) [30].

that this may have on the relationship between the judicial and executive arms of government.[88]

As an Australian judge put it, if legitimate expectations could be given substantive force, 'the notion would become a stalking horse for excesses of judicial power', liable to set courts 'adrift on a featureless sea of pragmatism'.[89]

But this represents a drastic denial of the agency of individuals who respond to and rely on promises made by officials. It would give individualised representations designed to induce action or expectation no effect whatsoever. It would permit governments to make cynical promises. Officials could instrumentalise the citizenry, treating individuals as means rather than ends. Treating reliance by individuals on official representations as entirely irrelevant to the lawful exercise of state power does great violence to the interests of those affected by making it more difficult for individuals to plan their affairs: 'to break a promise is to directly interfere with the liberty of the person or persons who have relied on that promise.'[90]

In addition, permitting concerns for legislative choice and decisional autonomy to predominate would prevent courts from drawing distinctions between different types of expectation. On this approach, all engagements would be equally unenforceable: the engagement made in a general policy document is treated no differently from the solemn promise with 'the character of a contract'[91] offered to an individual. Ruling out substantive legitimate expectations altogether would deprive jurists of the opportunity to hone legal principles so as to make appropriate distinctions between different types of expectation. It discounts completely the 'greater moral force' of individualised representations relative to general policies.[92] To treat policies as 'a type of promise ... distorts the nature of policies and promises'; only the latter 'creates a duty or obligation to someone to act in some way'.[93]

There is a means of striking a balance between the values in such a way that the decision-maker's primacy in policy matters is respected and courts respect the limits of the judicial role. The concerns expressed above need not necessarily exclude the possibility of judicial protection of substantive legitimate expectations. The goal of protecting substantive legitimate expectations 'is not to impede executive activity but to *reconcile* its continuing need to initiate or respond to change with the legitimate interests or expectations of citizens or strangers who have relied, and have been justified in relying, on a current policy or an extant promise'.[94] Indeed, procedural protection will often not be enough: 'a hearing will be of no

[88] Groves (n 65) 492.
[89] *Attorney General of New South Wales v Quin* (n 26) 27 per Brennan J.
[90] Watson (n 13) 641.
[91] *R v North and East Devon Health Authority, ex parte Coughlan* (n 28) [59].
[92] Steele (n 10) 302–303.
[93] Ahmed and Perry (n 14) 66.
[94] *R v North and East Devon Health Authority, ex parte Coughlan* (n 28) [65]. Emphasis added.

value to the applicant if the authority in making its decision is free to ignore the legitimate expectations it has previously aroused.'[95]

Recognising substantive legitimate expectations does not place an insurmountable barrier before an administrative decision-maker who wishes to resile from a promise or change a policy; it simply imposes an additional constraint in the form of a reason for the final decision that takes adequate account of the initial promise or policy: 'It recognises the primacy of the public authority both in administration and in policy development but it insists, where these functions come into tension, upon the adjudicative role of the court to ensure fairness to the individual.'[96] It reduces, in other words, the range of reasonable responses to the legitimate expectation.

Moreover, this additional constraint can be tailored to the strength of the expectation created by official action: 'The facts of the case, viewed always in their statutory context, will steer the court to a more or less intrusive quality of review.'[97] Where there has been an individualised representation on which there has been detrimental reliance, the burden on a decision-maker who refuses to give effect to the representation is greater than where an individual seeks to rely on the continuance in force of an official policy which the decision-maker wishes to adapt to new circumstances: 'the incurrence of expenditure on foot of a representation may form part of the court's assessment in determining whether it would be appropriate to allow a public authority to resile from a representation made.'[98] So, in *Coughlan*, where residents of a home for severely disabled patients were promised a 'home for life' which the public authority subsequently sought to close, it was appropriate to require '[s]trong reasons ... to justify resiling from [the] promise.'[99] Or, to put this in the argot of substantive review, the range of reasonable outcomes in a case like *Coughlan* will be relatively constrained.[100]

In at least one respect, however, the Court of Appeal in *Coughlan* went too far by asserting 'that it is for the *court* to decide in an arguable case whether such a judgement, albeit properly arrived at, strikes a proper balance between the public and the private interest';[101] it adjudged the authority at fault for having 'failed to weigh the conflicting interests *correctly*'.[102] This is to substitute judicial judgement on the merits for the considered wisdom of the administrative decision-maker identified by the legislature.[103] It is not for courts to determine 'fairness of outcome' or the

95 Forsyth (n 53) 253.
96 *R v North and East Devon Health Authority, ex parte Coughlan* (n 28) [70].
97 *R v Department of Education and Employment, ex parte Begbie* (n 34) [80] per Laws LJ.
98 *Cromane Seafoods Ltd v Minister for Agriculture, Fisheries and Food* (n 55) 144 per Clarke J.
99 *R v North and East Devon Health Authority, ex parte Coughlan* (n 28) [86].
100 See similarly *Philips v Medical Council* [1991] 2 IR 115; *R (Patel) v General Medical Council* [2013] EWCA Civ 327; [2013] 1 WLR 2801.
101 *R v North and East Devon Health Authority, ex parte Coughlan* (n 28) [52]. Emphasis added.
102 Ibid, [89]. Emphasis added. See similarly *R (Niazi) v Secretary of State for the Home Department* (n 9) [35].
103 Philip Sales and Karen Steyn, 'Legitimate Expectations in English Public Law: An Analysis' [2004] *Public Law* 564, 590–591; Groves (n 65) 480.

'propriety' of the balancing exercise undertaken by the decision-maker.[104] On a pluralist approach, some effect must be given to the concerns about undermining legislative choice and decisional autonomy. Yet maintaining distinct roles for distinct bodies implies that the reviewing court has a distinct role, that of checking the legality of administrative action, rather than assessing its correctness.

A substantive legitimate expectation should not be treated as sacrosanct; rather, the strength of the expectation would require more by way of explanation from the decision-maker seeking to resile from its previous representation.[105] So, 'where the representation relied on amounts to an unambiguous promise; where there is detrimental reliance; where the promise is made to an individual or specific group; these are instances where denial of the expectation is likely to be harder to justify . . .'[106] Conversely, an applicant will face a 'steeper climb' in cases where a policy change adopted in the public interest has a general effect on a diffuse group of individuals.[107] In any event, what matters is whether the justification provided by the decision-maker can survive substantive review, not whether the court would prefer to have struck the balance differently.

Courts should generally be less willing to constrain administrative decision-making in the 'macro-political' realm.[108] Generalist judges are poorly placed to pull on the spider web of carefully balanced interests woven by an expert decision-maker as the web might unravel in an unfortunate way.[109] Respect for relative expertise has its place—especially in the macro-political realm—and will enlarge the range of reasonable outcomes in some circumstances but it cannot permit administrative decision-makers to ride roughshod over legitimate expectations they themselves created. It is difficult to improve upon the analysis of Randerson J:

> Where very specific promises are made to an individual or a small class with serious consequences for them if the promises are not kept, the Court's approach is likely to be one of particularly close examination of the decision to ensure that the legitimate expectations of individuals are not unfairly or unreasonably thwarted. The Court will be astute to ensure the decision maker has conscientiously considered the position of those affected, has sound and logical reasons for reneging on the promises made, and has otherwise acted lawfully, fairly, and reasonably in the administrative law sense. In other cases, such as where the policy choices are very much in the macro-political field and there are strong countervailing

[104] *R v North and East Devon Health Authority, ex parte Coughlan* (n 28) [71]. See also the formulation, ibid, [82].

[105] *R (Bibi) v London Borough of Newham* (n 36) [39].

[106] *R (Nadarajah) v Secretary of State for the Home Department* (n 30) [69] per Laws LJ.

[107] Ibid per Laws LJ. See also Dotan (n 79) 31–33.

[108] *R (Nadarajah) v Secretary of State for the Home Department* (n 30) [69]. See also *Attorney General of New South Wales v Quin* (n 26) 12.

[109] See generally Paul Daly, *A Theory of Deference in Administrative Law: Basis, Application and Scope* (Cambridge University Press, Cambridge, 2012), chapter 3.

grounds to support the course adopted, the Court may give greater recognition to the wider public interest in enabling governments to adjust policy, including when change is required, and how, in their judgment, it is to be achieved. Even so, the Court will not in those situations, forego its proper constitutional role on judicial review of ensuring that the decision maker has acted in accordance with law, fairly and reasonably.[110]

8.4.3 *Ultra Vires* Representations

The conventional view is that *ultra vires* representations can never give rise to legitimate expectations: 'there can only be a legitimate expectation founded on a lawful representation or practice.'[111] Unlawful representations cannot create enforceable rights, interests or obligations, as the Supreme Court of Canada explained in respect of a local authority that had long permitted a company to operate a commercial parking lot in violation of a zoning provision: 'The authorization by a municipal employee or elected official of a use that violates a provision of a by-law cannot create rights or oust the applicable standards set out in the by-law.'[112]

Here, a concern to give effect to the considered choices of elected representatives as memorialised in statutory language dominates. In particular, courts have concluded, administrative bodies should not be able to expand the limits of their statutory mandates by making representations that are beyond their powers:[113] 'Any doctrine of estoppel in that context would threaten to undermine the doctrine of ultra vires by enabling public authorities to extend their powers both de facto and de jure by making representations beyond power, which they would then be estopped from denying.'[114] It has even been suggested that the system of government could be threatened by the enforcement of ultra vires representations: 'When the Government is unable to enforce the law because the conduct of its agents has given rise to an estoppel, the interest of the citizenry as a whole in obedience to the rule of law is undermined.'[115]

Nonetheless, there are examples of judicial concern about unfairness created by non-enforcement of *ultra vires* representations. In *Stretch v West Dorset District Council*, Peter Gibson LJ had 'considerable sympathy' with the individual defeated by a local authority's ability to assert the illegality of its own stance (an 'unattractive'

[110] *New Zealand Assoc for Migration and Investments Inc v Attorney-General* (n 35) 56.

[111] *Rowland v Environment Agency* [2005] Ch 1 [81] per Peter Gibson LJ.

[112] *Immeubles Jacques Robitaille Inc v Québec (City)* 2014 SCC 3; [2014] 1 SCR 784 [25] per Wagner J. See also *Wiley v Revenue Commissioners* [1994] 2 IR 160; *Bates v Minister for Agriculture, Fisheries and Food* [2011] IEHC 429; [2012] 1 IR 247.

[113] See e.g. *Re Green Dale Building Co* [1977] IR 256.

[114] *Minister for Immigration, Local Government and Ethnic Affairs v Kurtovic* (1990) 92 ALR 93, 108 per Gummow J.

[115] *Heckler v Community Health Services* 467 US 51 (1984), 60 per Stevens J.

proposition),[116] and in *Rowland v Environment Agency*, May LJ concluded that there was no legitimate expectation with 'undisguised reluctance' at the 'unjust' outcome.[117]

Indeed, a blanket rule of non-enforcement of *ultra vires* representations clashes with the concerns for individual interests and effective and efficient public administration which support the protection of legitimate expectations. Great unfairness may be done to an individual who relied on an official representation whose validity they had no reason to doubt. They may have ordered their affairs accordingly; and they certainly will have relied upon the word of a fellow person. As such, it is doubtful that the legal system is better protected by requiring losses caused by *ultra vires* representations to fall on individuals than by blanket refusal to entertain the enforceability of an *ultra vires* representation, given the effect on individual self-realisation.

Furthermore, requiring individuals to interrogate administrative officials at length about the scope of the latter's authority, or engaging a legal representative to do so, is not a recipe for the efficient use of scarce resources. Indeed, individuals may be dissuaded from dealing honestly—or at all—with administrative decision-makers if they cannot trust the words of officials. And even though one might want to guard against the deliberate expansion of powers accorded by the legislature, causing the loss to fall on an individual is 'misdirected': 'In the rare cases of intentional expansion of power it strikes at the wrong person, the innocent representee, rather than the public officials.'[118]

Moreover, respect for legislative choice is not necessarily compromised by the enforcement of all types of *ultra vires* representations. An Irish judge has suggested that there might be some cases where there may be 'greater scope' to enforce an *ultra vires* representation which involves 'something more marginal than the essence of the [administrative] action which is impugned—for example, its scope of extent rather than its nature . . .'[119] Sometimes a breach of a statutory provision will be technical or *de minimis*, such that enforcement by the courts would hardly drive a stake through the heart of the statutory scheme. One might add that the fact that an official would have made the representation in the first place surely indicates—absent proof of malice or bad faith—that the official believed the representation furthered the administrative decision-maker's statutory mandate. Indeed, in jurisdictions that use a holistic reasonableness test for invalidity rather than the 'all-or-nothing' *ultra vires* principle, a blanket rule against the enforcement of *ultra vires* representations is particularly inapt, for there is a good chance that a statutory

116 [1998] 3 EGLR 62, 67.
117 [2005] Ch 1 [100].
118 Paul Craig, 'Representations by Public Bodies' (1977) 93 *Law Quarterly Review* 398, 420.
119 *Ashbourne Holdings v An Bord Pleanála* [2003] 2 IR 114, 137 per Hardiman J.

provision will ultimately be interpreted in conformity with the stated views of the administrative decision-maker.[120]

Professor Craig has advocated for a balancing test: 'Where the harm to the public would be minimal compared to that of the individual, there is good reason to consider allowing the representation to bind',[121] by focusing on 'more sensitive ways of reconciling the needs of ... innocent individuals and the requirements of the public body'.[122] A pluralist approach leads to a similar conclusion. Enforcement of *ultra vires* representations should not be barred outright. Rather, courts should examine the interplay of a plurality of values to determine whether, on the facts, an *ultra vires* representation should be enforced, aware that in some cases '[t]he public interest may be better served by honouring [the] undertaking than by breaking it'.[123] That is, by acknowledging 'that legality is not absolute, but rather an important *aspect of* the legal system, the consequences of which are subject to important countervailing considerations'.[124] Of course, courts should not engage in an independent balancing exercise that pays no heed to the decisional autonomy of the administrative decision-maker under review, but, as in the area of substantive legitimate expectations, should assess whether any failure to give effect to an official representation can survive appropriately rigorous substantive review, unencumbered by a dogmatic refusal to countenance the enforcement of *ultra vires* representations.

8.5 Conclusion

In response to the crescendo of criticism of the incoherence of the common law doctrine of legitimate expectations, I have applied my pluralist approach to this difficult area of contemporary administrative law. My starting point was to recognise that diverse values have been identified in the cases. On the one hand, good administration and individual self-realisation have been invoked to support judicial enforcement of legitimate expectations. On the other hand, electoral legitimacy and decisional autonomy have been relied upon by judges fearful that enforcement of legitimate expectations will cause them to trespass in the political domain.

Each of these values is important, but evidently there is tension between them. Nevertheless, by following a pluralist approach the values can be reconciled. Through my analysis of three difficult questions relating to legitimate expectation—knowledge and reliance, substantive legitimate expectations and

[120] See e.g. *McLean v British Columbia (Securities Commission)* 2013 SCC 67; [2013] 3 SCR 895 [38].

[121] Craig (n 21) 703.

[122] Craig (n 39) 89.

[123] *R v Liverpool Corporation, ex parte Liverpool Taxi Fleet Operators' Association* (n 61) 308 per Lord Denning MR.

[124] Schønberg (n 53) 104.

ultra vires representations—I was able to demonstrate the utility of a pluralist approach in reconciling the four values found in the decided cases, so as to guide the development of administrative law.

The argument made in the preceding pages transcends the topic of legitimate expectation. It is potentially a guide to judicial action in *every* area of administrative law. I have demonstrated in Chapters 2 to 7 that the values of individual self-realisation, good administration, electoral legitimacy and decisional autonomy permeate contemporary administrative law and, moreover, that judges can be understood to have deployed them in a *complementary* way. There is ample evidence, moreover, that judges *can* balance these four values where they would potentially come into conflict. It is then a small step to the position that judges *should* seek a balance between competing values. Hence why the argument in this chapter is transcendent: whenever a judge seeks, or is asked by counsel, to change the law of institutional structures, procedural fairness, substantive review, remedies, restrictions on remedies or scope of judicial review of administrative action, the values provide relevant guidance, and a balance between them an appropriate destination.

9
Defending Administrative Law

In this book, I set out to do three things. First, to provide a *fresh framework for understanding administrative law*: this was the subject of Chapters 1 to 7. Second, to explain how this framework can be used to *guide the future development of the law*: this was the subject of Chapter 8, building on the analysis contained in the preceding chapters. Third, to *justify today's law of judicial review of administrative action*: this is the subject of much of this chapter.

This chapter is primarily concerned with legitimacy. In it, I aim to achieve two objectives. First, to underline the robustness of my interpretation of contemporary administrative law. Second, to defend the legitimacy of the core features of judicial review of administrative action, as these have been developed over the years by judges. Understandably, my defence will be cast in terms of my pluralist approach, but in setting out my defence, I should not be taken as denying that robust defences may be mounted on other grounds, be they normative,[1] historical,[2] or interpretive.[3] In achieving these two objectives, I rely on the criteria for testing the robustness of legal theories set out by Professor Stephen Smith in *Contract Theory*: fit, transparency, coherence and morality.[4] My interpretation of contemporary administrative law fits the decided cases, it is reasonably transparent, it is coherent and it rests on recognisably moral foundations.

9.1 Fit

A typical difficulty for interpretive theories is that the core features of the area of law being theorised will not perfectly 'fit' the theory developed. Tort theorists, for example, often struggle with strict liability and the economic torts: it is difficult to develop a theory which 'fits' both the law of negligence (with its various sub-fields relating to economic loss, public authority liability and psychiatric harm) and

[1] See e.g. Evan Fox-Decent, *Sovereignty's Promise: the State as Fiduciary* (Oxford University Press, Oxford, 2011).

[2] See e.g. Paul Craig, 'English Administrative Law History: Perception and Reality' in Michael Ramsden and Swati Jhaveri eds, *Judicial Review Across the Common Law World: Origins and Adaptations* (Cambridge University Press, Cambridge, 2021).

[3] See e.g. TRS Allan, *The Sovereignty of Law: Freedom, Constitution and Common Law* (Oxford University Press, Oxford, 2013).

[4] (Oxford University Press, Oxford, 2004), chapter 1.

Understanding Administrative Law in the Common Law World. Paul Daly, Oxford University Press. © Paul Daly 2021.
DOI: 10.1093/oso/9780192896919.003.0009

other areas where the basis of liability is quite different.[5] Economic analysts of law, meanwhile, must confront many areas of legal doctrine and features of legal practice which do not 'fit' a model of economic efficiency.

My pluralist approach has been designed, however, to 'fit' the core features of administrative law as best as possible. I have been concerned to design an intelligible structure which contains the contemporary law of judicial review of administrative action. My approach has been reflective, perhaps something akin to the approach of an explorer, who 'must map what he sees from the ground, feeling his way where he must as well as taking the bird's eye view where he can', thereby bringing 'order to chaos, but not by turning away from the chaos, and not by refusing to bear the responsibility of imposing order'.[6] Throughout the preparation of this book, I have followed an iterative approach, beginning with the identification in the abstract of a value capable of explaining the decided cases but then modifying the abstract definition of the value to ensure it better fits the particularities of the decided cases. As my work continued, and the cases piled up and details accumulated, I further modified the values, as in a Rawlsian 'reflective equilibrium':[7]

> [W]e might ... borrow from Rawls and say that fully to understand law we have first to take a crude statement of all the rules in the statute book and all the precedents in the case books; then inquire into the motivating principles and values of those whose rules they are; then in the light of that modify our initial crude grasp of the verbally replicated rules; then consider again the principles and values, and so until we reach a stage of 'reflective equilibrium'.[8]

I am somewhat less ambitious, of course, interested only in 'fully ... understand[ing]' administrative law, in particular the common law of judicial review of administrative action. Professor McCormick identifies an additional problem for the application of a Rawlsian approach to legal reasoning generally: 'by the time we have got [to a reflective equilibrium] the law will have moved on.'[9] Given that I am interested in the core features of administrative law as they exist at the present point in time, this problem does not arise for me.

5 See e.g. James Goudkamp and John Murphy, 'The Failure of Universal Theories of Tort Law' (2015) 21 *Legal Theory* 47.

6 Elise Bant and Matthew Harding, 'Introduction' in Elise Bant and Matthew Harding eds, *Exploring Private Law* (Cambridge University Press, Cambridge, 2010), 1, 3. Of course, any '"map" metaphor is misleading insofar as it suggests that it is possible to draw a picture unrelated to any point of view'. Michele Graziadei, 'The Functionalist Heritage' in Roderick Munday and Pierre Legrand eds, *Comparative Legal Studies: Traditions and Transitions* (Cambridge University Press, Cambridge, 2003), 100, 118. See also Stephen Gageler, 'The Underpinnings of Judicial Review of Administrative Action: Common Law or Constitution?' (2000) 28 *Federal Law Review* 303, 303.

7 John Rawls, *A Theory of Justice* rev edn (Belknap, Cambridge, 1999).

8 Neil McCormick, *Legal Reasoning and Legal Theory* rev edn (Clarendon, Oxford, 2003), 245.

9 Ibid.

Building an intelligible structure to 'fit' the facts is a delicate task. It is possible that in order to accommodate all of the relevant core features, the theory—the four values of individual self-realisation, good administration, electoral legitimacy and decisional autonomy—will have to be drawn at such a high level of abstraction as to be deprived of all explanatory, descriptive or interpretive force. In my case, however, although the values have capacious labels, their content is well-defined: each contains several core considerations which can be seen to operate in various areas of administrative law.

As discussed in Chapters 2 to 7, the four values can be understood to structure the core features of the contemporary law of judicial review of administrative action: they 'fit' the facts *and* help the reader to understand them. I demonstrated how the law of institutional structures, procedural fairness, substantive review, remedies, restrictions on remedies and scope of judicial review can be understood to be structured by the four values I have identified, sometimes operating in a complementary fashion, sometimes arranged in balance, but always present in some form.

Institutional structures (Chapter 2) is the group of principles relating to how administrative decision-making processes can be structured: the no-bias principle, with its various applications including to elected officials and those contemporary agencies where the functions of investigation, enforcement and policy development are often intermingled, and the retention of discretion principle, which covers delegation (and the *Carltona* exception) and fettering of discretion. In this area, the value of individual self-realisation can be understood to be prominent in the structure of the no-bias principle, the application of the no-delegation principle, the scope of the *Carltona* exception and in ensuring that individuals are almost always entitled to a say as to whether an administrative guideline should be applied to their unique situation. Good administration can be understood to support the *de minimis* exception to the no-bias principle, a contextual approach to determining whether a particular administrative decision-maker is sufficiently impartial and the lee-way given to administrative decision-makers to rely on third parties in exercising their powers (without delegating the powers per se) and to develop policies to guide their exercises of discretion. Electoral legitimacy can be understood to underpin the special principles applied to elected officials, the principle of necessity and the starting point in the area of retention of discretion that an administrative decision-maker identified by statute should exercise the discretionary power granted by the legislature. Lastly, decisional autonomy can be understood to ensure that the no-bias principle applies with less stringency to administrative decision-makers than to courts, a point evident in the general structure of the no-bias principle and determinations as to the impartiality of a given administrative decision-maker.

Procedural fairness (Chapter 3) regulates the fairness of administrative decision-making procedures, which covers the general structure of the duty of fairness, several exceptions to the duty and individual procedural rights, such as notice and comment and the provision of oral hearings. Individual self-realisation can be understood to be prominent in supporting a broad scope for procedural fairness—which now applies to a wide range of interests which might be affected by administrative action—and in increasing the stringency of procedural fairness obligations to match the seriousness of the impact an adverse decision would have on the individual concerned, both in general terms and in terms of the individual procedural rights to which individuals may claim they are entitled. Good administration can be understood as supporting expansive procedural fairness obligations, inasmuch as these might produce relevant information and thereby facilitate effective and efficient public administration, both in general and in specific cases. But it can be understood as more prominent in supporting limits on what can reasonably be expected by way of provision of procedural rights, because there will invariably come a point at which increased procedures would impose intolerable burdens on the administrative decision-making process. Electoral legitimacy can also be understood as supporting procedural protections, as the involvement of an affected individual will, all things being equal, enhance decisional accuracy and lead to a more accurate implementation of the legislative design—but it can sometimes be understood to militate against more intensive procedural obligations, where the legislature has given the administrative decision-maker in question discretion to determine the appropriate decision-making processes or where the administrative decision-maker is an elected official. Electoral legitimacy can also be understood to support the concept of 'legislative' decisions to which no (or greatly reduced) procedural protections attach and the related concept of legislative ouster of procedural fairness (albeit that successful ousters are very rare). Overhanging the discussion of procedural fairness is the overbearing presence of decisional autonomy, as it is fundamental in the area of procedural fairness that administrative decision-making procedures need not and should not be modelled on the procedures used by courts.

Substantive review (Chapter 4) covers the territory of 'jurisdiction', deference, abuse of discretion and relevancy and propriety. Across this territory, where decisions will affect individuals' ability to plan their affairs or their treatment with concern and respect by officials, the courts are more willing to increase the intensity of review and require exacting justifications from administrative decision-makers, which can be understood to be supported by individual self-realisation. Good administration sometimes also supports judicial willingness to closely scrutinise administrative decisions, where the decisions at issue relate to matters within the ken of judges; but it sometimes supports judicial deference, as where decision-makers must make difficult decisions about the allocation of scarce resources in areas where judicial oversight might be more of a hindrance than a help. Electoral legitimacy can be understood to increase the intensity of judicial review where statutory language is relatively clear, but counsels in favour of judicial restraint where decisions are taken by elected officials on matters of broad cultural, economic, foreign-affairs and social policy. Decisional autonomy can be understood to support judicial insistence on court scrutiny—of appropriate intensity—of all or almost all administrative decisions and to explain the complicated principles relating to judicial treatment of issues of relevancy and propriety.

If a breach of the principles relating to institutional structures, procedural fairness or substantive review is established, attention then shifts to remedies (Chapter 5). The general structure of the principles regulating the grant of remedies in administrative law cases can be understood to be influenced by decisional autonomy: the default remedy is typically certiorari or declaratory relief, as these involve minimal interference with the decisional autonomy of the decision-maker in question, who is free to take a fresh decision in accordance with the judgment of the reviewing court. As the remedies become more intrusive, as with prohibition (which prevents administrative decision-makers from embarking on certain courses of action) and mandamus (which operates to compel administrative action), judicial reluctance to grant them increases, a point which can be understood in terms of decisional autonomy. Individual self-realisation can nonetheless be understood to be of importance, in supporting the remedy of prohibition or mandamus in some circumstances and also in acting as a brake on judicial discretion not to grant a remedy. Good administration can be understood to loom large in judges' ability to choose between more and less intrusive remedies, with certiorari and declaratory relief leaving it to administrative decision-makers to discharge their policy-making mandates as effectively and efficiently as possible, but also in discretion to withhold relief, for instance where a remedy would precipitate administrative chaos. Electoral legitimacy, lastly, can be understood to have traction in situations where it is proposed to sever the unlawful part of a decision from the lawful.

There are some general restrictions on judicial ability to grant remedies in respect of breaches of the principles of institutional structures, procedural fairness and substantive review (Chapter 6). These can be understood to support good administration: procedural requirements give administrative decision-makers some shelter from frivolous and poorly timed legal challenges which might disrupt the effective and efficient discharge of their policy mandates; requiring individuals to exhaust alternative remedies before seeking judicial review allows disputes to be handled by internal administrative machinery, in a cost-effective manner which relies on administrative expertise rather than generalist judges; the jurisprudence on collateral attack and exclusion of review channels challenges to administrative decisions into appropriate fora; the usual judicial suspicion of issues unripe for consideration by the courts can be set aside if a decision would clarify areas of uncertainty; and the principles of standing are shaped in part by concern for effective and efficient public administration. Electoral legitimacy further supports the basic structure of these restrictions on judicial review, as they tend to ensure that the administrative decision-maker identified by the legislature has the primary responsibility for taking decisions in a particular area of regulation. Individual self-realisation can be understood, however, to underpin the various exceptions to these restrictions on remedies: where individuals have interests at stake, they will be permitted to vindicate them to some degree, in appropriate circumstances. Moreover, individual self-realisation continues to play a role in the contemporary principles relating to standing. Decisional autonomy can also be understood to exert influence in this area, especially in relation to judicial desire to preserve the supervisory jurisdiction even in the face of legislative efforts to exclude it by way of privative clauses and to the expansive approach taken in the contemporary jurisprudence to the issue of public interest standing, enabling public-spirited litigants to bring important matters relating to legal values before the courts for resolution.

The scope of judicial review (Chapter 7) relates to the range of decision-making bodies, statutory and non-statutory (and sometimes private) subject to the judicial review jurisdiction and, hence, to the principles of institutional structures, procedural fairness and substantive review. Here, electoral legitimacy can be understood to exert significant influence, as where a democratic nexus exists, binding a non-statutory or private body into a web of official regulation, judicial review will be available. Good administration can be understood to further support the expansion of judicial review to non-statutory bodies, at least where they have adopted their own codes of practice, but also to counsel judicial restraint in the application of judicial review principles to these bodies. Decisional autonomy can be understood to militate in favour of limits on the supervisory jurisdiction of the common law courts, inasmuch as sites for private flourishing should, all things being equal, be permitted to exist without judicial oversight or interference. However, claims of decisional autonomy ring hollow when the individuals in such sites have no avenues of redress in private law and thus no means of vindicating their interests—where this is so, the value of individual self-realisation can be understood to support the availability of judicial review remedies.

9.2 Transparency

Professor Smith distinguishes between strong, weak and moderate forms of the transparency criterion, which relates to the extent to which any proposed theory is consistent with the reasons legal officials offer for their decisions.

In its strongest form, transparency requires a perfect match between theory and reasons (albeit that here theory must surely lapse into mere description). In its weakest form, transparency is satisfied by any plausible explanation of why judges say one thing but really mean to say another. I do not suggest that my four values satisfy the strongest form of the transparency criterion: as I have repeated throughout, my argument is that contemporary administrative law 'can be understood' as being structured by the values of individual self-realisation, good administration, electoral legitimacy and decisional autonomy. But my approach certainly goes further than the weak form of transparency; it meets Professor Smith's moderate form of transparency, by showing 'how judges could sincerely, even if perhaps erroneously, believe that the reasons they give for deciding as they do are the real reasons'.[10]

Mine is a 'theoretical account of the institution and its constitutive practices' which 'makes *explicit* what is *implicit,* articulating the commitments participants incur by virtue of what they do and say'.[11] Professor Smith suggests a 'test' for meeting the moderate form of the transparency criterion: 'whether the theorist's explanation is of the sort that, once translated into concrete concepts, could be accepted by a court, even if no court has yet done so'.[12] I think a court certainly could accept the explanation I have offered in this book, of administrative law as a whole and of its different components. Indeed, in the case of my pluralist approach, there is evidence that it satisfies the transparency criterion because it has already been accepted by a court, namely the Federal Court of Appeal of Canada.[13]

In Chapter 8 I argued, furthermore, that the pluralist approach can be used to resolve difficult doctrinal questions: striking a balance between the values of individual self-realisation, good administration, electoral legitimacy and decisional autonomy is a means of changing administrative law. The pluralist approach, in other words, provides not only an intelligible structure for the present, but also a template for the future.

9.3 Coherence

While it is true that interpretive theorists typically set out to offer 'a unified explanation of the law',[14] my use of the term 'values' should not be taken as a claim to conceptual unity, for I am mindful of the 'heterogeneity' of administrative law. In a recent article on tort law, Professor John Murphy doubts several interpretive theories of tort law which advance a unifying explanatory principle, on the basis that these fail to account for *juridical* (the variety of torts), *structural* (the different structure of different torts) and *remedial* heterogeneity (the variety of remedies available in tort claims).[15] In administrative law, remedial heterogeneity has mostly been removed by procedural reform and juridical heterogeneity has been reduced by the rationalisation of judicial review of administrative action as having three

[10] (n 4) 28.

[11] William Lucy, 'Method and Fit: Two Problems for Contemporary Philosophies of Tort Law' (2007) 52 *McGill Law Journal* 605, 620.

[12] Smith (n 10) 30.

[13] *Paradis Honey Ltd v Canada* 2015 FCA 89; [2016] 1 FCR 446 [138].

[14] Allan Beever, *Rediscovering the Law of Negligence* (Hart, Oxford, 2007), 24.

[15] 'The Heterogeneity of Tort Law' (2019) 39 *Oxford Journal of Legal Studies* 455.

main heads (legality, rationality and procedural propriety) and an overarching purpose (controlling abuse of power).[16]

But there is a significant degree of structural heterogeneity. Judicial review of administrative action is a 'gallimaufry' of rules and standards,[17] varying between relatively well-defined 'grounds' of review (such as the no-delegation principle and each of the procedural rights), variable 'intensity' of review (such as the context-sensitive duty of fairness and review for abuse of discretion) and open-ended 'contextual' analysis (such as remedial discretion and the scope of judicial review).[18] Quite what the values of individual self-realisation, good administration, electoral legitimacy and decisional autonomy are capable of illuminating in any given area, and at what level of generality, depends on whether the area is one dominated by grounds, intensity or context. Hence, for example, why Chapter 7, on the scope of judicial review—an area of law dominated by a contextual approach—is structured around the four values whereas Chapter 3.3 on procedural fairness rights is structured around the rights, as befits an area where the grounds of review approach is dominant.

This reservation should not be overstated, however: even if conceptual unity is just out of reach, 'a requirement of perfect unity seems not only unattainable in practice, but also inappropriate in theory';[19] and my analysis in this book has nonetheless revealed a significant degree of unity. Contemporary administrative law is, in Professor Murphy's terms, homogeneous, not heterogeneous.

My pluralist approach aims at as high a degree of coherence as possible. Following a pluralist approach to administrative law ensures that judges strike an appropriate balance when the values seem to come into conflict. As a result, neither individual right nor good administration reigns supreme. As has been said of judicial review, 'the distinctively judicial public-law task ... is the protection of individual rights and interests against undue encroachment in the name of social interests'.[20] Of course, 'abstract values might be incommensurable in the abstract'.[21] But they are not weighed against each other in the abstract: 'the *facts* matter crucially when balancing.'[22] For instance, even though the importance of robustly protecting interests that are important for an individual's autonomy and dignity

[16] See Chapter 1.1.3.

[17] Peter Cane, 'Review' (2019) 82 *Modern Law Review* 202, 204.

[18] The terms are drawn from Dean Knight, *Vigilance and Restraint in the Common Law of Judicial Review* (Cambridge University Press, Cambridge, 2018). Knight's other analytical term, 'scope', does not have as much force in contemporary administrative law.

[19] Smith (n 4) 13.

[20] Peter Cane, 'Theory and Values in Public Law' in Paul Craig and Richard Rawlings eds, *Law and Administration in Europe: Essays for Carol Harlow* (Oxford University Press, Oxford, 2003), 3, 15.

[21] Steven J Burton, 'Normative Legal Theories: The Case for Pluralism and Balancing' (2013) 98 *Iowa Law Review* 535, 551.

[22] Ibid, 552. Emphasis added. See also Chief Justice James Allsop, 'Values in Public Law' (2017) 91 *Australian Law Journal* 118, 130, describing values as 'influential, but not necessarily dispositive, in each case'.

has been recognised by judicial development of a general duty of procedural fairness, this duty is tempered by the need to permit administrative decision-makers to render decisions in an efficient and effective way; the procedures that courts may impose vary based on the context of the regulatory regime under review. This is just one example of the courts striking a balance—achieving coherence—between potentially conflicting values. This book is littered with others.

Sometimes the values operate in a complementary fashion: in the law relating to institutional structures, the structure of the no-bias principle[23] and the scope of the *Carltona* exception;[24] in the law relating to procedural fairness, the exceptions to the duty of fairness,[25] evidence in administrative proceedings,[26] the right to reasons;[27] in the law relating to substantive review, the construction of ranges of reasonable outcomes in the context of judicial review of alleged abuses of discretion[28] and the general principles of relevancy and propriety;[29] in the law relating to remedies, the general structure of the different remedies available in administrative law cases[30] and the tailoring of declaratory relief in a given case;[31] in the law relating to restrictions on remedies, the principle that an applicant should exhaust alternative remedies,[32] the bar against collateral attack,[33] judicial discretion to entertain moot claims[34] and the principles of standing.[35]

Sometimes the values are found in balance: in the law relating to institutional structures, the principle that an individual may waive the right to an impartial decision-maker,[36] the cases on the extent to which an administrative decision-maker might have prior knowledge of a regulatory area or individual regulatee[37] and the scope of the no-delegation[38] and fettering principles;[39] in the law relating to procedural fairness, the general structure of the duty of fairness,[40] the ability of the legislature to oust procedural protections by statute,[41] the scope of the right to notice, disclosure and comment,[42] the availability as a matter of law of an oral

[23] See Chapter 2.1.
[24] See Chapter 2.3.2.
[25] See Chapter 3.2.1 and 3.2.2.
[26] See Chapter 3.3.5.
[27] See Chapter 3.3.7.
[28] See Chapter 4.3.
[29] See Chapter 4.4.
[30] See Chapter 5.1 and 5.2.
[31] See Chapter 5.4.
[32] See Chapter 6.2.
[33] See Chapter 6.3.
[34] See Chapter 6.5.
[35] See Chapter 6.6.
[36] See Chapter 2.1.
[37] See Chapter 2.2.
[38] See Chapter 2.3.1.
[39] See Chapter 2.3.3.
[40] See Chapter 3.1.
[41] See Chapter 3.2.3.
[42] See Chapter 3.3.2.

hearing,[43] the right to cross-examine witnesses in an administrative setting[44] and the right to legal representation before an administrative decision-maker;[45] in the law relating to substantive review, the identification of 'jurisdictional' errors;[46] in the law relating to remedies, the decision to grant or refuse the remedy of mandamus,[47] to refuse a remedy in a given case[48] or to sever a partially unlawful component of a decision;[49] in the law relating to restrictions on remedies, the treatment of privative clauses[50] and in the law relating to the scope of judicial review, the determination of whether a given decision by a given decision-maker is amenable to the supervisory jurisdiction of the courts.[51]

9.4 Morality

The values of individual self-realisation, good administration, electoral legitimacy and decisional autonomy have structured administrative law in a normatively attractive way, a way which supports the legitimacy of the core features of the contemporary law of judicial review of administrative action. Administrative law is, in short, 'supported by recognizably moral principles'.[52]

These values reflect the basic commitments of modern liberal democracy to the protection of individual dignity and autonomy,[53] the existence of an administrative state which is effective in ensuring the welfare and safety of its citizens,[54] the importance of paying due regard to the outcomes of the electoral process[55] and the desirability of ensuring that no one governmental organ has a monopoly on decision-making authority.[56] For instance, the importance accorded to decisional autonomy maintains distinct roles for courts and administrative decision-makers. While administrators remain responsible for the merits of the decisions they render, courts provide oversight to ensure that primary decision-makers respect

43 See Chapter 3.3.3.
44 See Chapter 3.3.4.
45 See Chapter 3.3.6.
46 See Chapter 4.1.
47 See Chapter 5.3.
48 See Chapter 5.6.
49 See Chapter 5.7.
50 See Chapter 6.4.
51 See Chapter 7.
52 Smith (n 4) 22.
53 See e.g. Allan (n 3).
54 See e.g. Nick Barber, *Principles of Constitutionalism* (Oxford University Press, Oxford, 2018); Gillian Metzger, 'Foreword: 1930s Redux: The Administrative State Under Siege' (2017) 131(1) *Harvard Law Review* 1; Jacob Weinrib, 'Maitland's Challenge to Administrative Law Theory' (2021) 84 *Modern Law Review* 207.
55 See e.g. Richard Bellamy, *Political Constitutionalism* (Cambridge University Press, Cambridge, 2007); Jeremy Waldron, *Law and Disagreement* (Clarendon Press, Oxford, 1999).
56 See e.g. Eoin Carolan, *The New Separation of Powers* (Oxford University Press, Oxford, 2009); Nick Barber, *The Constitutional State* (Oxford University Press, Oxford, 2012).

legal principles in their decision-making processes and decisions. Similarly, the value of electoral legitimacy is respected because administrative law gives appropriate importance to legislative pronouncements and to the democratic process, by enforcing statutory limits and by honing administrative law principles to take account of the need to promote open debate in the public sphere. In short, the values that can be understood to give judicial review of administrative action its structure are normatively attractive and, taken together, provide a defensible basis for judicial development of administrative law.

9.4.1 Legitimacy

It has, nonetheless, been suggested that administrative law is in or on the cusp of a 'legitimacy crisis'.[57] Felix Frankfurter once remarked that jurisdiction is 'a verbal coat of too many colors'[58] and the same could surely be said of legitimacy. At the very least, the legitimacy of an activity can be assessed in a number of different ways: sociologically (whether an activity is accepted as a matter of social fact), democratically (whether there is popular input that shapes the activity), procedurally (whether the procedures that generate the activity are appropriate) or morally/normatively (whether the activity is morally or normatively attractive in view of the substantive interests it protects); and these assessments may, indeed, be interlinked.[59]

Some can nonetheless be discarded quite easily for the purposes of the assessment of the legitimacy of administrative law. In the absence of barricades outside the Royal Courts of Justice and its equivalents elsewhere in the common law world, it is doubtful that an inquiry into the sociological legitimacy of judicial review of administrative action would be especially fruitful. In addition, given that common law judges develop the law incrementally and only after hearing argument, the procedural legitimacy of administrative law seems secure (at least, that is, in the absence of a more general attack on common law adjudication).

Excluding sociological and procedural legitimacy leaves us with democratic and normative legitimacy. Sure enough, it is some combination of these two that makes administrative law vulnerable to accusations of illegitimacy. Here is how Professor Jason Varuhas concludes his critique of the legitimacy of judicial review:

> As the courts increasingly and more readily encroach upon the executive sphere, determining what are substantively good or bad reasons for executive action, the

[57] See Jason Varuhas, *Judicial Capture of Political Accountability* (Policy Exchange, London, 2016), 50–51; Richard Ekins, 'A Legitimacy Crisis in Judicial Review', *ConservativeHome* (June 8, 2016).

[58] *United States v LA Tucker Truck Lines* 344 US 33 (1952).

[59] See generally Jack Balkin, *Living Originalism* (Harvard University Press, Cambridge, 2011).

> traditional conception of judicial review as a secondary, supervisory jurisdiction begins to break down, as do the dividing lines between the responsibilities of courts and government, and the provinces of law and politics. This is highly problematic because the ideas that judges were only exercising a long-stop, supervisory jurisdiction on review, and that the judicial role is one distinct from the functions of government and removed from ordinary politics have long served to legitimise judicial review. If those struts are removed, judicial review shall be plunged into a legitimacy crisis. Arguably we are already there.[60]

It will immediately be seen that Professor Varuhas is quite measured in his critique (which is appropriate given the focus of his report on a small but important area of administrative law concerning the review of political responses to Ombudsman decisions). Indeed, he stops short of declaring a 'legitimacy crisis'; his view seems to be that judges are in danger of crossing the dividing line between appropriate and inappropriate judicial intervention. The Rubicon has not yet been crossed—but it is nonetheless wise to consider Professor Varuhas's reasons for believing the judges have come too close to doing so, because these reasons form the basis of the claim about an imminent 'legitimacy crisis'.[61]

Implicit in the passage quoted above is an understanding of the appropriate role of judges. They are there to provide a sober second look at administrative action, ensuring that administrative decision-makers remain within the boundaries laid down by statute, but never venturing an opinion on the merits of the decision under review. Indeed, the administrative decision-maker has a democratic pedigree, having been assigned by the legislature primary responsibility for making the decision in question. Accordingly, one could characterise Professor Varuhas's critique as an attack on the normative legitimacy of administrative law, underpinned perhaps by a concern for electoral legitimacy, in the sense that judges have not adequately respected the input of the elected representatives who chose to vest decision-making authority in bodies other than courts. But the core of the critique is that judges have moved beyond the judicial domain and are trespassing in the executive and legislative spheres.[62]

As I have argued, however, the contemporary law of judicial review of administrative action is heavily influenced by the value of electoral legitimacy: in a wide variety of areas of administrative law, courts can be understood to have respected the considered choices of elected officials sitting in legislative chambers and exercising discretionary powers in shaping legal principles. Similarly, courts can be

[60] Varuhas (n 57) 50–51.

[61] And have perhaps contributed to the impetus in the United Kingdom for reform of judicial review: see Chapter 1.1.2.

[62] The converse of this critique has recently been made in the United States: Philip Hamburger, *Is Administrative Law Unlawful?* (University of Chicago Press, Chicago, 2014). Hamburger argues that the executive branch is illegitimately trespassing in the judicial and legislative spheres.

understood to have manifested concern for good administration—there is nothing undemocratic about facilitating the effective and efficient implementation of their statutory mandates by administrative decision-makers. In addition, judicial respect for the value of decisional autonomy can be understood to be designed precisely to prevent courts from trespassing into territory occupied by administrative decision-makers working to reach the best possible decisions on the merits of the matters that come before them.[63] Complaints about the lack of democratic legitimacy of contemporary administrative law are, in my view, unfounded.

9.4.2 The Moral Character of Contemporary Administrative Law

In this book, I have offered an interpretation of administrative law, arguing that the values of individual self-realisation, good administration, electoral legitimacy and decisional autonomy form an intelligible structure around the core features of the contemporary law of judicial review of administrative action. I have called this a 'pluralist' approach, because it relies, in developing an understanding of the subject of administrative law, on a plurality of values rather than one single meta-value, meta-concept or meta-principle. This approach, moreover, rests on 'recognizably moral foundations'.[64]

Individual self-realisation is concerned with how individuals are treated by administrative decision-makers, in particular, their ability to plan their affairs and their interest in being dealt with humanely as autonomous, dignified and rational beings. Administrative law protects individual interests, thus allowing individuals to plan their affairs. To take a selection of the examples covered in this book, the no-fettering principle is designed to allow individuals to anticipate how decision-makers are likely to use their powers and to prepare accordingly; the law of procedural fairness ensures that individuals have a say in matters which affect them; in substantive review, the greater the interference with individual interests, the greater the judicial oversight; judicial review is a backstop where individuals' contractual protections are unavailing; and the possibility of waiver allows individuals to shape the procedures by which they are treated. In these ways, the contemporary law of judicial review of administrative action facilitates individual autonomy. Moreover, through administrative law individuals are treated with concern and respect, enhancing their dignity: the ability to delegate decision-making functions is constrained by respect for individual interests, tending to ensure face-to-face interactions between individuals and administrative decision-makers in important

[63] These points are only sharpened if one thinks that democratic legitimacy is enhanced by the protection of individual rights, to which judicial solicitude for individual self-realisation can certainly be understood to contribute.

[64] Smith (n 4) 24.

matters; procedural fairness is conceived of as a free-standing construct which applies whenever important matters are addressed by administrative decision-makers, with individuals able to participate in decision-making proceedings and benefit from reasoned decisions in many cases; individuals are presumptively entitled to a remedy for administrative action which fails to satisfy the principles of institutional structures, procedural fairness and substantive review; and restricted review of private bodies protects a site for individual and group activity free from outside interference. From a detailed study of contemporary administrative law, the individual emerges as an autonomous agent, entitled to dignified treatment by the state: judicial review of administrative action evidences a sustained commitment to individual self-realisation.

Good administration involves judicial solicitude for effective and efficient public administration, permitting administrative decision-makers to develop and implement policies without running down their scarce resources. In one sense, the courts assist administrative decision-makers in the achievement of their missions: in terms of institutional structures, for example, administrative decision-makers are held to their policies and they are permitted to delegate routine functions down the decision-making chain to free up top-level decision-makers to focus on significant issues of general policy; in the area of substantive review and in giving declaratory relief, courts provide guidance to administrative decision-makers in setting the range or jurisdiction in which the decision-maker may operate; and courts also ensure, when determining restrictions on remedies, respect for procedural requirements designed to permit administrative decision-makers to focus on achieving their statutory goals. In another sense, the courts take care to stay out of the way of administrative decision-makers, consciously shaping the law of procedural fairness so as not to gum up the works of public administration, deferring to their expertise when reviewing the substance of their decisions and refusing remedies where they would cause administrative chaos. In sum, good administration is a consistent concern for contemporary courts, who aim to facilitate effective and efficient public administration.

Electoral legitimacy involves respect for the mandates won by elected politicians who sit in legislative assemblies and exercise decision-making authority. This value is taken into account directly in a number of areas, by ensuring the accurate implementation of legislative choices, a feature across the law of institutional structures, procedural fairness, substantive review and restrictions on remedies; and it is visible too in extending the scope of judicial review where there is a sufficient democratic nexus and where statutory constraints have not been respected by a body claiming to exercise private power. The value of electoral legitimacy is also taken into account indirectly, in shaping the no-bias principle, procedural fairness and the application of jurisdiction and ranges of reasonable outcomes to take account of the electoral mandates held by some ministerial and municipal administrative decision-makers. In sum, those who have run an electoral gauntlet and won the support of the voters benefit from judicial recognition of their status; this solicitude on the part of courts for electoral mandates supports the foundations of liberal democracy.

Finally, decisional autonomy respects the distinctive roles played by distinctive bodies—the judiciary, administrative decision-makers and private actors—in the contemporary legal system. Contemporary administrative law ensures distinctiveness in a number of ways: in developing the no-bias principle and procedural fairness courts recognise that administrative decision-makers need not model themselves after courts; in the area of substantive review, reviewing courts do not substitute their judgment on the merits of matters decided by administrative decision-makers; certiorari and declarations are the favoured remedies in administrative law cases, as they preserve the primacy of the administrative decision-maker; and in articulating legal principles about restrictions on remedies, the courts ensure that they play their proper role in elaborating and enforcing legal principles. Furthermore, the contemporary law of judicial review of administrative action carves out space for decision-makers to fulfil their functions, allowing them to decide whether to develop policies to guide exercises of discretion, permitting them to go over and above the basic requirements of procedural fairness, allowing them to operate freely within a range of reasonable outcomes and, in the area of consensual relationships, shielding contractual arrangements from judicial review (to the extent individual interests are adequately protected). This preservation of limited spheres of exclusive competence allows different decision-makers the space to perform their functions on their own terms.

Notably, the coherence and normative attractiveness I have described are provided by values that are found *in the decided cases*. They are drawn from what any lawyer or layperson would recognise as sources that judges can legitimately rely upon. They are *legal* values. While they may be congruent with understandings of values found in political theory or discourse, they are not *political*; they do not represent judges' personal preferences as to how the law ought to evolve. Administrative law values thus provide a structure that is cohesive and legal in nature. It is perfectly democratically legitimate, as its basis is legal sources of unimpeachable validity: decades and centuries of carefully crafted jurisprudence, which can be arranged into an intelligible structure provided by the values of individual self-realisation, good administration, electoral legitimacy and decisional autonomy.

9.5 Conclusion

My interpretation of contemporary administrative law—the intelligible structure provided by the four values—is robust and, moreover, sufficiently normatively attractive to provide a strong defence of the legitimacy of the law of judicial review of administrative action as developed by common law courts. Judges have not been guilty of overstepping the mark, of trespassing in the domain of politics. Rather, they should be understood as having used a plurality of values—individual self-realisation, good administration, electoral legitimacy and decisional autonomy—to provide an intelligible structure to contemporary administrative law.

This intelligible structure is, moreover, normatively defensible. Individual self-realisation ensures that individuals are treated with concern and respect by governmental decision-makers and are permitted to flourish; good administration facilitates governmental decision-makers' achievement of their objectives and thus allows them to serve the public; electoral legitimacy empowers representatives who have been chosen by voters; and decisional autonomy preserves distinct areas in which different decision-makers can do what they do best. In short, contemporary administrative law facilitates the flourishing of individuals, of public administration and of the liberal democratic system.

Index

For the benefit of digital users, indexed terms that span two pages (e.g., 52–53) may, on occasion, appear on only one of those pages.